Jebbie

Vamp

to

Victim

Judith Thompson Witmer, EdD

Author's Note

This narrative biography, *Jebbie: Vamp to Victim*, tells the poignant true story of a victim of elder abuse. However, it is not an account of physical abuse, but rather, the tale of a slow, insidious road of dishonesty which stripped a once vibrant woman of her money, her dignity, and, most precious, her selfhood. It is in many ways a tragedy of betrayal—of trust, of promises, and of family.

Jessie is a real person, as real as the reader, and as complicated as most human beings. My Aunt Jessie, like your great aunt, or perhaps your grandmother, was a full human being who lived, learned, and loved. She grew up in a small town and went from being the **stylish girl with all the gentlemen callers** to becoming a town legend as a very popular elementary school teacher who, as one of her students remembers, "greeted us every morning as if we were the joy of her life."

Viewed in her youth as a coquette, Jessie was lively and witty, and always an independent person who asked help from no one. Through her own savings, she had made financial plans "for a rainy day," as she quaintly termed "growing old." What she had not planned for, however, was deception by a member of her family. By the time other family members realized that all of them had been duped by lies and treachery, the situation with Jessie was irresolvable.

I wrote this book as a tribute to my Aunt Jessie, providing a keen and personal perspective of growing up in a small town, a community that nurtured many of us—author and reader alike. The reader is drawn into this family as they not only become products of the era, but also are caught in a web of deceit. Laughing with Jessie and living with her family makes the tragedy, when it occurs, all the more real and unforgiving.

It is my intent that, through the example of Jessie, we are reminded that we must honor and protect the personhood of older citizens who are trying to maintain autonomy and personal dignity in the face of those who may prey upon them.

About the Author

Judith Thompson Witmer is a graduate of Curwensville High School and holds a B.A. in English Literature from Penn State, an M.S. in Humanities, a Doctorate in Educational Administration from Temple, and both graduate and post-doctoral credits from Harvard University.

A former high school English teacher, principal, central office administrator at Lower Dauphin School District, adjunct professor for Temple University's Graduate School, and currently Director of the Capital Area Institute for Mathematics and Science at Penn State, Judith T. Witmer has managed various projects for the Pennsylvania Department of Education (PDE), including the Keystone Integrated Framework, Service Learning, and the Coalition of Essential Schools. She also has been an evaluator and researcher for the Penn State College of Medicine, Johns Hopkins Medical Center, Milton Hershey School, PDE, and numerous private institutions.

Dr. Witmer served two terms as President for the Advisory Board of the Pennsylvania Governor's Schools of Excellence and was a long-standing member of the Ethics Committee for Penn State's Milton S. Hershey Medical Center. She co-chaired the local fund-raising committee for building a new town library, which exceeded goal; chaired the 50th Anniversary celebration of Lower Dauphin High School, a year-long program culminating in four major events in a final 30-hour grand finale; and currently is serving as committee chair and editor of the commemorative publication for the Bicenquinquagennial Celebration of Hummelstown.

Judith Witmer's passion is historical research as evidenced by her publications. In addition to the number of books she has written, she has published numerous articles in professional journals, a cover feature in *Penn State Medicine*, newspaper columns, monographs, national speeches, and book reviews. She also has a long record of initiating innovative academic programs, directing high school musicals and Commencement programs, and advising high school yearbooks.

With the heart of a small town girl, she embraces her classmates and her former students as her inspiration and her family heritage as her lodestar.

Dedication

Jebbie is dedicated

To the memory of my aunts, the Pifer Sisters: **Josephine** Smith Pifer Hamilton, **Ruby** Idora Pifer Wayne, **Jessie** Beverly Pifer Mohney, **Katherine** Shields Pifer Thompson, and Margaret **Jean** Pifer Bloom, as well as my paternal aunt, **Mary Alice** Thompson Jackson Crunk;

To the strong matriarchal lineage of my grandmother, **Matilda** Adeline Smith Pifer and her four sisters: Evelena (aka **Lena** or Lennie), **Rosanna**, **Jessie**, and **Ella** (aka Nell);

To the unconditional support and affection of my sisters **JoEllen Lorenz** and **E. Nan Edmunds**; and

To the gratitude and love we three sisters share for our Mother, **Kate**.

Acknowledgements

The devotion and contribution of my sister, **Elizabeth Nan Edmunds** cannot be measured, for she has donated endless hours of collaboration, advice, and creative talent to the design, formatting, layout, and editing of *Jebbie* since its inception a decade ago. She deserves co-credit for any success this memoir enjoys.

Those who read and critiqued early sections or versions of the book:

Marjorie Cassel
Margaret DeAngelis
Peggy Decker
Dr. Peter & Mrs. Mary Houts
Dr. Jean Jones
Heide Melnick
Carol Weiss Rubel

Those who provided research sources:

Catherine Shields
William Young

Special photography

Joel K. Edmunds

ISBN 978-0-9837768-0-2

Published in the United States by Yesteryear Publishing.

Books are available at www.amazon.com as well as through the publisher:

Yesteryear Publishing

P.O. Box 311

Hummelstown, PA 17036

www.yesteryearpublishing.com

yesteryearpublishing@gmail.com

(717) 566-8655

Jebbie: Vamp to Victim is the biography of Miss Jessie Beverly Pifer, belle of her class, beloved elementary teacher, doyenne of the community, and victim of elder abuse. Everything within the pages of this book is verifiable. Fifteen years in the research and writing, it has been edited from a manuscript nearly twice the current length. The book was written to let the world know by this account that even the most public members of a community can be robbed by unscrupulous persons of their resources, independence, and dignity.

There is documentation for all that is mentioned in the book, including legal documents, bank records, historical publications, social cards, valentines, homework, notebooks, many personal letters, Field Day programs, mementoes from Clarion—such as "Songs of Clarion," bluebooks, letters from beaux, receipts for music lessons, favorite sheet music, photos, news clippings, various Alumni Banquet programs, and samples of Jebbie's exquisite handwriting.

Also by Judith T. Witmer, EdD

All the Gentlemen Callers:
Letters Found in a 1920s Steamer Trunk (in press)

Growing Up Silent in the 1950s:
Not All Tailfins and Rock 'n' Roll (2012)

Loyal Hearts Proclaim: A Historical Compendium
of Lower Dauphin High School, 1960 – 2010 (2012)

Hummelstown Celebrates 250 Years (Editor) (2012)

I Am From Haiti: The Story of Rodrigue Mortel, MD

Je Suis D' Haiti: Par Rodrigue Mortel, MD

Moving Up! A Guide for Women in Educational Administration

Team-Based Professional Development:
A Process for School Reform

The Keystone Integrated Framework: A Compendium

A Style Manual for Publications

How to Establish a Service-Learning Program

Cast of Characters

The Pifers

Matilda, Dillie, Mama	Matilda Adeline Smith Pifer; Mother of Jessie, Josephine, Ruby, Katherine, and Jean
John, Papa	Father of Jessie, Josephine, Ruby, Katherine, and Jean
Josephine, Josie	Josephine Smith Pifer Hamilton; Sister to Jessie; Eldest of the Pifer Sisters
Ruby	Ruby Idora Pifer Wayne; Sister to Jessie; Second of the Pifer Sisters
Jessie	Jessie Beverly Pifer Mohney; Third of the Pifer Sisters
Katherine, Kate	Katherine Shields Pifer Thompson; Sister to Jessie; Fourth of the Pifer Sisters; Mother to Kay, Judith, Jo Ellen, and Nan
Margaret Jean	Margaret Jean Pifer Bloom; Sister to Jessie; Youngest of the Pifer Sisters

The Hamiltons

Josephine	Identified above
Droz	Droz Hamilton; Husband of Josephine
Noel	Noel Franklin Hamilton; Only Child of Josephine

The Waynes

Ruby	Identified above
Tom	Thomas J. Wayne; Husband of Ruby
John, Johnny	John Pifer Wayne; Older Son of Ruby
Tom, Tommy	Thomas J. Wayne, Jr.; Younger Son of Ruby

The Thompsons

Kate	Identified above
Howard, Jr., Howd, Bubby	Howard Vincent Thompson; Former husband of Kate; Father of Kay, Judith, Jo Ellen, and Nan; Brother of Mary Alice
Mary Alice	Mary Alice Thompson Jackson Crunk; Sister of Howard V. Thompson; Aunt of Kay, Judith, Jo Ellen, and Nan
Kay	Matilda (Mavis) Kay Thompson Brunetti Walker; Niece of Jessie; Eldest Daughter of Kate
Bob	Robert Allen Walker; Husband of Kay
Kim	Mavis Kim Brunetti Richards; Daughter of Kay and first husband Albert R. Brunetti
Judith	Judith Evelyn Thompson Ball Witmer; Niece of Jessie, Sister of Kay; Second Daughter of Kate
Wally	Walter C. Witmer; Husband of Judith
Jeanie	Jean Rochelle Ball Jacobs; Daughter of Judith and first husband Thomas E. Ball

Cast of Characters

Thomas	Thomas Ross Ball; Son of Judith and first husband Thomas E. Ball
Jo Ellen	Jo Ellen Thompson Lorenz; Niece of Jessie; Sister of Kay; Third Daughter of Kate
Ken	E. Kendall Lorenz; Husband of Jo Ellen
Janelle	Janelle Corinne Lorenz Wright; Daughter of JoEllen
Kendall	E. Kendall Lorenz, Jr.; Son of Jo Ellen
Nan	Elizabeth Nan Thompson Edmunds; Niece of Jessie; Sister of Kay; Youngest Daughter of Kate
Joel	Joel Keith Edmunds; Husband of Nan
Shayne	Shayne Scott Edmunds; Son of Nan
Jesse	Jesse Joel Edmunds; Son of Nan
Elizabeth Bailey Spencer Thompson	Mother of Howard V. and Mary Alice
Howard Jefferson Thompson	Father of Howard V. and Mary Alice

The Spencers

Vincent Uriah Spencer	Grandfather of Howard V. and Mary Alice Thompson
Lavinia Spencer	Sister of Vincent Spencer, Diarist

The Blooms

Margaret Jean	Identified above
Chester	Husband of Jean
Gene	Chester Eugene Bloom; Oldest Son of Margaret Jean
Mabel	Mabel Riddle Bloom; Wife of Gene
Don	Donald Dwight Bloom; Second Son of Jean
Lorraine	Kathryn Lorraine Valimont Bloom; Wife of Don
Janet Lynn	Janet Lynn Bloom Carter; Youngest Child of Margaret Jean
Jim	Jim Carter, Husband of Janet Lynn

Others in the Tale

Joanne	Joanne Yacabucci; Kay's Best Friend in California, a classmate from Curwensville
Marie	Marie Tiracord Sturniolo; Kay's Best Friend in Curwensville, a classmate
Evelyn and Alvin	Evelyn and Alvin Milligan; Next door neighbors to the Thompson sisters, 1935-1946
Laura and John	Laura and John Bressler; Next door neighbors to the Thompson sisters, 1935-1946
Peg	Margaret Hamilton; Neighbor of Jessie
Jean	Jean Boyce; Long time friend of Jessie
Joe	Joseph Errigo; Lifelong friend of Jessie and Kate

Smith Sisters

Jebbie and Kate

Matilda Smith Pifer

Pifer Sisters

Thompson Sisters

Kate and Jebbie

Contents

Introduction: Identities

If you do all your growing up in the same small place, you don't shed identities. You accumulate them.

— *Tracy Kidder*[1]

Jessie Beverly Pifer accumulated many identities in the century that was her lifespan, yet she was completely the product of Curwensville, Pennsylvania, where she was born, grew up with her parents and four sisters, attended the local schools, became a legendary teacher in the community, served her church as a deacon, became active in the DAR, and then spent her final days. She lived, laughed, and loved in Curwensville, remaining true to herself through every phase of her life. She was dashing, independent, and ever fashionable. Jessie revealed many personas, but all reflected the identity for which she is best remembered—as the beautiful, stylish, and vibrant "Jebbie," belle of the Class of 1924. She viewed herself as urbane, yet remained a small town girl whose beginnings are traced to the 18th Century, when her forebears arrived in the new country, and are rooted in the 19th Century, particularly the period immediately following the Civil War.

Identities

In 1862, six years prior to the birth of Jessie's father, President Abraham Lincoln crafted the Emancipation Proclamation, a document that confirmed the dignity and sanctity of an individual human being and placed worth on each person to determine his own destiny by making his own choices. This basic and founding principle has been tested countless times both on national and personal issues and has been the keystone of all executive, legislative, and judicial decisions since that time. As it has for millions of people throughout our history, the theme of "the dignity and sanctity of an individual human being" was to reverberate one hundred and twenty years later in the life of Jessie, pitting sister against sister on the issue of the dignity and sanctity of each person to determine one's own destiny by making one's own choices.

Following the Civil War in 1868 when Ulysses S. Grant was elected President, reconstructed governments had been set up in eight of the eleven southern states. This same year is the birth date of John Pifer, noted in no history books, but with whose lineage the story of Jessie begins. The lineage of John's father Jonas is German-Irish, his own father John having been one of the first two settlers in Jefferson County.[2] Jonas Pifer (Jessie's grandfather whom she would never know) and his wife Rachel lived in Brookville where they reared a family of four boys and two girls. It is likely that John Francis Pifer (father of Jessie) and his twin sister Katherine (also sometimes spelled Catherine), born on July 25, 1868, were the second and third children and that they were baptized by either Rev. J. J. Marks, a charge minister, or a Rev. Samuel who had led his congregation in building a new Presbyterian Church which still stands at the corner of Main and Valley Streets in Brookville.

The town of Brookville, 165 miles northwest of the state capital of Harrisburg, dates from 1796, eight years prior to the establishment of Jefferson County of which it is a part. Brookville's early growth can be attributed to its strategic location along the Susquehanna River and the Waterford Turnpike. Farms surrounding the town were self-contained and self-sufficient by necessity. Many of the newcomers to the town of Brookville were attracted by a prosperous lumber industry. Area raftsmen constructed large rafts of timber or sawn boards, and in the spring and fall were busy plying the waters between the small town of Brookville and the large lumber markets in Pittsburgh. A low grade division of the Allegheny Valley Railroad opened in 1853 and trains began running regularly to Brookville, thus increasing business opportunities to send and receive goods.

The first school in Jefferson County, constructed of rough logs, opened in 1803. Classes were offered for only three months and patrons of the school paid the teacher's salary. The first school in Brookville opened in 1830 and by 1854 there were nine schools with a total enrollment of 500 pupils: four primary, three intermediate, and two grammar schools. The Pifer twins, John and Katherine, presumably attended a lower school in the town and spent some time in the high school built in 1878.

Brookville was home to several newspapers, the earliest being the *Jeffersonian Democrat,* the first newspaper in Jefferson County, established in 1832. This was followed by many others of similar names. Richard (Dick) Pifer, brother of John Pifer, served a time as editor. Another of several newspapers in this small city was *The Morning Herald,* published by Charles J. Bangert and V. King Pifer, a cousin to John Pifer.

Matilda Adeline Smith, later to be the wife of John Pifer and mother of Jessie, was the daughter of Robert and Mary McElheney Smith of Beech Woods, a hamlet in Washington Township near Brookville. There were five daughters in the Robert and Mary Smith family: Lena (Lennie), Jessie, Matilda (born June 2, 1872 and called "Dillie" by her four sisters), Rosanna (Rosie) E., and Ella (Nell), the youngest, as well as one son, Robert. Matilda was likely baptized by the Rev. W. H. Filson, pastor of the Presbyterian Church in Brookville from 1871 to 1875. These six children were orphaned when their mother died shortly following the birth of her youngest child. The task of caring for the household and rearing the younger siblings thus fell to the older two girls, particularly Lena.

Despite hardships, all five girls attended and completed common school. Girls as a rule did not go beyond this common school (6th, 7th, or 8th grade, depending on the town). As noted above, in the early years public school was held for only a three-month term beginning in December; this was later extended to four and then to five months. If a young man (rarely woman) wanted additional education he had to attend one of the academies scattered throughout the state. This lack of opportunity for education is the main reason for Matilda's firm determination that her own daughters would not only finish high school, but also attend Normal School.

Perhaps because of their early difficulties, the five Smith sisters as adults remained in close contact with one another despite the geographic distance between them. Several of them lived only twenty or thirty miles from one another, but because not all had personal transportation, visits were rare. Instead they relied on letters as their primary means of communication.

The Smith sisters very seldom spoke about the untimely loss of their mother. In fact, they related very few stories of early life to their own children, other than the poverty and the implausible similarity of Matilda's being one of five daughters and later having five daughters of her own, and one of those five producing four daughters. When Matilda Smith was entering ninth grade, the same year as the formal unveiling in New York Harbor of the Statue of Liberty, she was not aware that a few miles away John Pifer, five years older and the man she would marry, was busy trying to establish himself in a business.

It is almost certain that John cut his education short to join his brother Joe as an employee of the Keystone Drilling Company in Beaver Falls. A year later brother Dick joined Joe and John when they left the Keystone Company to become the Pifer Brothers Company of Brockwayville and DuBois.

The three brothers remained in business together for another year. Transporting their drilling rig by train, they traveled around the nation to wherever their services were needed. Joe in particular enjoyed the travel and seeing the country firsthand. More adventuresome than his younger brothers, Joe decided he would like to try his luck further West. In 1886 he packed up and left for what was called "Oregon country" (later to be divided into three states Washington, Oregon, and Idaho), attracted by the advertisements of the great transcontinental railroads that followed the line of the old Oregon Trail. This was a perfect opportunity for a young well driller, and Joe joined the fortune hunters and would-be western settlers as they traveled by uncomfortable trains, packed in on narrow wooden benches.

Portland remained Joe's home base, although his well drilling took him throughout the entire country and occasionally he would meet John, along with Dick or Hugh (their other brother), for a collective well-drilling job in the country's heartland of Indiana and Ohio. Occasionally the brothers found themselves traveling into Canada.

Identities

Immediately following Joe's leaving Pennsylvania, John and his brothers remained a team until many years later when Dick also decided to leave the area and move to Ohio. John then became an independent jobber, complete with business cards identifying him as a Drilling Contractor, specializing in "water wells, pump holes, and wire holes for mines."[3] Like most equipment of this time, John's well-drilling machine, half the size of a railroad boxcar, was fired by coal. For local jobs, the machine was guided up planks onto a low wagon that was hauled by horses. When it was necessary to travel any greater distance, the rig was transported by railroad.

The history of the town of Curwensville somewhat parallels that of Brookville, forty miles distant, and is a part of Clearfield County. Founded three years later than Brookville, Curwensville is situated on the West Branch of the Susquehanna River and was named for John Curwen, Sr., of Montgomery County, Pennsylvania. This John Curwen never lived in the town that bears his name. In December of 1797 he had obtained from the state of Pennsylvania letters patent "for land and allowances that included the mouth of Anderson Creek."[4] He deeded the land to his son, John Curwen, Jr. who predeceased his father; John's Will conveyed the acreage back to his father. In turn, the land was deeded to the next son, George Fisher Curwen.

The area of Curwensville, like most early settlements, was appealing because of its waterways as a means of transportation and an early source of potable water. By 1811 Curwensville was the largest upriver village on the West Branch of the Susquehanna River and was known as the gateway to the wilderness beyond. Within a decade, following the completion of the Erie Turnpike, the village saw a rapid influx of newcomers.[5]

White pine lumber found along the West Branch of the Susquehanna River was said to be superior in quality. Straight and clean, it could be cut into 90 and 100 foot lengths. It was strong and easy to manufacture as well as durable against weather elements or warp. The river provided a natural highway across the county, then traveled southward to Sunbury and Northumberland where it joined its North Branch, then flowed on through Harrisburg and to Baltimore and Philadelphia. By 1818 a local lumber industry had begun with several small mills springing up along the river, and by 1889 there were a number of sawmills in the area so that much of the lumber could be "finished" locally rather than the logs being shipped to other points.

In 1889 the Irvin family began building what would become known as "The Big Mill," the largest mill of its kind in the state. Soon mill workers from nearby settlements began arriving with their families, building homes in the "White Settlement" or "South Side" of town. This large mill was Curwensville's leading industry until the end of the 19th Century when the building was converted into a tannery.

Curwensville with 372 persons was incorporated as a borough on February 3, 1851, becoming the second borough in the county. It was predicted that electricity and automatic machinery would so transform life and relieve drudgery that "within a half century machinery would perform all work and automatons would direct the machinery."[6] The telegraph had been invented a few years earlier, industrial development expanded, railroads reached toward the West, and immigration from Europe reached a new high level. However, in 1853 the only daily mail in the area was from the East to Clarion, 80 miles from Curwensville.[7]

While the question of slavery had little personal relevance to most central Pennsylvanians, their patriotism was notable by the number of young men from Pike Township who served in the Civil War. Curwensville produced one of the first volunteer companies of the North. Initially identifying themselves as the Raftmen's Rangers, these men later became part of the regiment known as the "Bucktails," later to become one of the most famous regiments in the Army of the Potomac, particularly "for their proficiency with the rifle."[8]

Following the Civil War, most citizens resumed their quiet normalcy, their roots developed from those who would assure a solid foundation and later become part of the history of the town. A drugstore opened in 1865, owned by Joseph M. Irwin.

The first schoolhouse in Clearfield County was built in 1803, a year before the County was formally organized by an Act of Legislature. Originally constructed in Pike Township which surrounds Curwensville, it was open only a few months each year. Eventually the term lengthened so that by the 1880s school began in mid-September and ran until April. In the village of Curwensville itself, the first school was opened in 1812. To accommodate a growing population, in 1813-1814 "the people of Curwensville and vicinity gathered together, and by their united and voluntary effort put up a log house for school purposes," located on what is now Filbert Street.[9] In 1833 a school house was built through subscription on land contributed by John Irvin. Known as the Curwensville Academy, the school was located on upper Filbert Street. Its first teacher was John Patton (father of the Honorable John Patton who figures prominently in the history of the town).

Sometime between 1852 and 1856[10] William H. Irvin, at his own expense, built what was known as the Brick Schoolhouse, which he later rented to the borough.[11] In 1860 the old Methodist Episcopal Church was purchased and used as a school. The first completely public borough school was built in 1867 after the school directors were authorized to borrow money and build new schools as needed; this building, costing $2,750, was used for the next twenty years.

A Normal and Select School was opened on April 10, 1882.[12] These normal schools were established for the purpose of teacher training and by the end of the century there were a number of small

Normal Schools in the region, including Mahaffey (a town even smaller than Curwensville) and West Clearfield. They operated independently and in addition to the State Normal Schools which were established in 1886 by the Pennsylvania legislature.

The citizens of Curwensville then began to talk of the possibility of providing a high school education, and on September 2, 1884 the cornerstone for a new school was laid complete with Masonic ceremonies. The Honorable John Patton, known as "General John Patton" (the honorary title derived from his commission as Brigadier General of the Pennsylvania Militia and his later service as a U.S. Congressman), donated $20,000 for this school constructed of native sandstone, 62 by 71 feet, with eight classrooms, four on each floor connected by halls and two stairways. Dedicated and opened on October 1, 1885, the monolithic stone building was the pride of the town. Later photos, such as the Columbus Day Celebration in 1892, show the building laden with bunting and many of the attendees carrying American flags. Townspeople came out in full force for both events and the new building became the focal point of the town and the place for many community activities. The first class was graduated at the First Commencement on April 8, 1886 with General Patton, the school's benefactor, conferring the diplomas.

In the last decade of the 19th Century the growing population of Curwensville needed more school rooms, and in 1892 an addition was built on the back of the Patton Building, disturbing its proportions, but providing the needed space for science labs (a narrow chemistry room and a physics classroom with elevated arena seating) and four additional classrooms.

This building was heavily used for the next sixty years, sending off its last class in 1955, although the building continued to be used for a short time as elementary classrooms.

Teachers were expected to improve themselves by attending annual institutes such as the 29th Clearfield County Teachers Institute held December 19-23, 1892 in Clearfield. The cost to teachers was high at $1 (equivalent to a day's earnings); however, the fee entitled the registrants to attend all lectures. By 1894 Clearfield County published an annual broadside listing the name of every teacher employed by the Public Schools of the county for the school year. Listed this year was the name of Vincent Uriah Spencer whose grandson would marry a daughter of John Pifer. A program note for the 1895 session indicated that four hundred and five teachers were employed in the county.[13] The proceedings of the 1897 Institute, published in the spring of 1898, included a tribute to Hon. John Patton who had died December 23, 1897.

For the general population, lecturing was one of the most popular methods of education. Traveling circuit speakers stopped periodically to lecture in town halls and churches, usually to a good turnout that was eager for information and a live presentation. Brick Pomeroy is one such example. According to Lavinia Spencer's 1871 Diary, Mr. Pomeroy passed through Bridgeport from Luthersburg to Clearfield where he gave a lecture "taking in $500" with an individual admission charge of fifty cents.[14]

Not all children of the community, however, were fortunate enough to attend lectures or enjoy a formal education. Some began work at the age of ten, if their families were in need of the wages they could earn. Photographs of the Big Mill reflect the sad young faces in the group pictures. Other children who had to earn wages were sent out to work with tradesmen as part of the apprenticeship system originating in Pennsylvania at a very early date as a way to help the poor. Under this system children could be ordered by either the parents or surviving relatives or by the

Overseers of the Poor who could bind the children in servitude for years.

Winters could be harsh in the mountains of central Pennsylvania and temperatures often were near zero. Travel by horseback, carriage, or in winter, by sleigh, was not easy, but travelers could find lodging at nearly every crossroads.

Most illnesses in the mid-century were treated by home remedies and general medicine that addressed no particular disease. Doctors could do little more than give advice and make patients more comfortable. Not even the aspirin had yet been developed and no one knew how to manage or cure tuberculosis, diphtheria, and other such diseases. A typical case is that of Lavinia Spencer who, in a word, simply faded away, never able to give her "not feeling well" a name, despite daily entries in her 1871 Diary.

> *Feeling very badly.*
>
> *I do not think that I am any better than yesterday.*
>
> *...feeling poorly, weak and nervous.*
>
> *Have been weaker for several days but think it is the medicine.*
>
> *Went to the mill and got weighed; have lost 16 ¼ lb. since last autumn." (Her weight: 83 ¾ lb.)*
>
> *My cough is very troublesome and side (is) sore today*
>
> *Got three more boxes of the Anti-Canker Pills.*[15]

Her last entry was June 20, 1871, followed by a notation by her brother Vincent, indicating that Lavinia had died of consumption in August at 20 years of age, with her weight that week only 77 lbs.

Transportation in central Pennsylvania was limited to horses until the later 19th Century. Even though the Susquehanna River passed through the town, it was not navigable except by barge. Speculators had begun to build canals as a series of waterways to connect cities, and a canal craze resulted in a complex network of waterways. Canals were to be the new rivers with promises to make the towns on their banks the new world ports. The Erie Canal in northwestern Pennsylvania opened up the hitherto neglected northern regions of Ohio, and of Indiana and Illinois and made New York City the principal gateway to the Northwest, leading to a forced rivalry among Boston, Philadelphia, and Baltimore when Philadelphia realized that its cheapest route to Pittsburgh was by way of New York City, Albany, Buffalo, and by wagon road or canal from Lake Erie.

Encouraged by this potential of high travel volume and its resulting revenue, Pennsylvania put through a portage system of canals surmounting the Alleghenies at an elevation of 2,300 feet by a series of inclined planes, up which canal boats, and later railroad cars, were hauled by stationary steam engines, near Hollidaysburg. Barges, passengers, freight—everything was hauled up one side and let down the other with hemp ropes thick as a man's leg. "It was a thrilling experience for travelers, a goodly number of whom chose to go by way of the Pennsylvania Canal, rather than the Erie Canal, for that very reason."[16]

Yet the canals soon were to be doomed as the major means of transportation because of a little horse-drawn rail line, the first railroad in the United States, built in Quincy, Massachusetts. With the completion of the Hudson River Railroad from New York to Albany, where it connected with the New York Central for Buffalo, and of the Pennsylvania Railroad from Philadelphia to Pittsburgh, there was an almost universal transfer of freight from canals to railroads, particularly in the winter season when access to the canals could be difficult. The superiority of rail for long-distance hauls was clear, and the locomotive proved itself as the best investment for providing transcontinental travel.

The new focus on railroads had a positive impact on central Pennsylvania which previously had relied on river barges for haulage. In 1863 the Pennsylvania Railroad was the first line into Clearfield County, marking the beginning of the disappearance of the old stage lines.[17] By February 1869 the railroad had been completed and passenger service began from Philipsburg to Clearfield. In 1871 a mail route was established between Penfield and Clearfield, by 1873 railroads were in DuBois, [18] and in 1874, the Pennsylvania Railroad extended from Clearfield to Curwensville, made possible by a $60,000 subscription of the townspeople, led by Hon. John Patton. Known as the Tyrone and Clearfield R.R. and later as the Tyrone Division, the rail service was later extended to Grampian, a few miles west of Curwensville.

Also by 1874 more businesses had been started in Curwensville, including A. M. Kirk & Son, Jewelers and Optometrists, a company and service that remained active in the community for nearly a century. Despite being destroyed by fire in 1882, the store was rebuilt in 1883, and Kirk Jewelers became one of the longest standing enterprises in the history of the town, second only to Murphy's Drugstore (first owned by Joseph M. Irvin). Running close in business longevity is Way's Stationery Store, established by R. K. Way in 1896. Gates Hardware holds a claim of being the "oldest family operated business in town" based on the establishment of a blacksmith shop by Solomon Jefferson Gates in 1850.

The first newspaper in Curwensville is said to be *The Clearfield County Times*, started in the summer of 1872, the first issue urging its readers to re-elect General Ulysses S. Grant as president[19] although the lead article in the first edition was a thesis on whether a broken heart could cause a woman's death. In 1903, *The Curwensville Mountaineer*, a four-page weekly—later to become recognized as one of the foremost county newspapers in the Commonwealth, was established and became the leading Republican newspaper of Clearfield County. In 1905 V. King Pifer (remembered as the editor of the short-lived *The Morning Herald* in Jefferson County and also a cousin to John Pifer) purchased a newspaper called the *Review*, which he operated for several years.

The first telephone line in the county was built from Curwensville to Cherry Tree in 1881,[20] and by January 1882 a line was constructed from Curwensville to Clearfield. This small exchange probably did not exceed 10 to 15 telephones. In 1885 a telephone (toll) line was built from Curwensville to DuBois by the Central Pennsylvania Telephone Company, but it was not until late in the century that a toll line was built through to Curwensville to connect with the Clearfield and Huntingdon Company. One telephone served the entire town of Curwensville, as was the case in DuBois. When a person wished to use the telephone he went into the pay station to have a number dialed for him; he would then wait until a messenger (in the town he was calling) was sent to inform the person with whom the caller wished to converse. The caller could only hope that this person was able to come in good time to the pay station to receive the call.

In 1882 the Pennsylvania Railroad placed Curwensville on its list of summer resorts and the town was billed as "one of the most picturesque in the county with abundant natural resources, two banks, a building and loan association, two newspapers, seven churches, and six hotels."[21] By 1893, the railroad offered direct passenger service, not available on either the early barges or the freight trains.

The year 1889 is considered a landmark in American history because, while its military position was nearly insignificant, the United States was the strongest industrial power in the world. "The country seemed hell-bent for a glorious new age,"[22] and everyone wanted to be a part of that ride. There seemed to be a strong spirit of national unity everywhere and, while life in most of America meant a great deal of hard work for just about everybody, people held the belief they were getting somewhere.

Also in 1889, the Constitutional government (defended by the Grand Army of the Republic to whom Curwensville had contributed its men) was celebrating its one hundredth birthday.

David McCullough notes that there is little doubt that the nation was *certain* that the next hundred years would be even better, bringing wondrous advantages and rewards to millions of people.[23] In reality America was enjoying one of four relatively good years in the middle of a long-wave depression that had begun in 1873 and would run in fits and starts to 1897. During that time somewhat more than 900,000 (4% of the labor force) were out of work, even though the six million persons employed in manufacturing, construction, and mining were somewhat better off than those in Britain and far better off than in mainland Europe.

Despite the unemployment, newspapers of the time told of the World Exhibition opening in Paris with its 1,056 foot high Eiffel tower; the opening of the Oklahoma Territory; and the statehood of North Dakota, South Dakota, Montana, and Washington. In 1889 America's first skeletal skyscraper was built, L. H. Sullivan's ten-story Auditorium Building of Chicago was completed, and Joseph Pulitzer's 375-foot high, 26-story, World Tower Building in New York City was started.

The year 1889 also marked the first Oklahoma land rush. On buckboards, hacks, drays, and covered wagons, would-be settlers rushed to stake a claim, denoting the beginning of what was to be called "The Last Frontier."

Of greater interest to central Pennsylvanians in 1889, however, was something far more seemingly mundane but always of concern. The snow and high water that winter and spring was the major topic of conversation among residents, as there had been more than a hundred days of rain since mid-fall and the rivers were running high. Rafting enjoyed the higher water, but running the water had to be halted numerous times because of the danger of the currents. The first sign of really serious trouble, though, was a heavy snow in April, which melted almost as soon as it came down. Then in May came eleven days of rain.

Identities

The storm that would bring tragedy to much of western Pennsylvania had started out of Kansas and Nebraska on May 28. The following day there had been hard rains in seven states where trains had been delayed and roads washed out. Warnings had been telegraphed east, and on the night of the 29th the U.S. Signal Service issued notices that the Middle Atlantic States should expect severe local storms. On the morning of May 30 all stations in the area reported threatening weather. By the time the storm struck western Pennsylvania it was the worst downpour ever recorded and the most extensive rainfall of the century for so large an area.

Unaware of the siege under which its western neighbors had fallen, Curwensville residents arose on Memorial Day anticipating holiday picnics and festivities. The weather cleared long enough on Thursday, May 30 to hold the annual Memorial Day parade just as it had been held for more than 40 years. Stores closed for the holiday and the men were off from the lumber mills, tanneries, and sandstone quarries. As usual, most of the town turned out for the parade with plans to pack a picnic lunch to join family or neighbors in the outdoors.

Late that evening the rain came, first fine and gentle, just a bit more than a fine mist. During the night the rain was heavier and steady and by dawn of the next morning (Friday, May 31) Anderson Creek, which divided the main section of town from South Side and Windy Hill, was bank full. During the next few hours the Susquehanna River, which also bordered the town and into which Anderson Creek emptied, rose rapidly and in a short time the bottom land from Bridgeport, less than a mile to the west of Curwensville, to the Big Mill began to look like a lake, with what appeared to be several small islands scattered about. These islands were houses which had been surrounded by the flood.

Lost were the saw mill at Bridgeport, the Walnut Street Bridge (over Anderson Creek), the Filbert Street Bridge (connecting the main part of town with its South Side), and the new railroad bridge. Spared were both the main span of the Covered Bridge (whose approaches were destroyed) and the $10,000 Iron Bridge which connected the town to Irvin Hill. Lumber, logs, and drift were driven into the flat area around Filbert Street, moving the railroad tracks. Trains could go no farther than the Susquehanna House and it was weeks before rail service was restored. Fortunately no human lives were lost and the approximate loss between Arnold's dam and the iron bridge which held was given at $75,000. By October both bridges had been replaced by iron structures.[24]

Yet the townspeople counted themselves fortunate, especially when news of the disaster at Johnstown reached them by telegraph, newspapers, and then through travelers from Pittsburgh. Sixty-five miles southwest of Curwensville, 2,209 souls were lost in the Johnstown flood when an earthen dam broke with the weight and force of water it had never been designed to contain. Nothing could stop the wall of water that thundered down the mountain, smashing everything in its path. Because of the topography of Johnstown, the 30,000 residents of the city never saw the water coming. They only heard it, a deep, steady rumble, growing louder and louder until it had become an avalanche of sound, charging through the valley. Called one of the worst natural disasters America had ever known, it would be five years before Johnstown was rebuilt. The destroyed bridges along the line of the Pennsylvania Railroad from South Fork to Johnstown were rebuilt from sandstone taken from Curwensville's Roaring Run Quarries.

By 1890 the railroad, the telegraph, the sewing machine, and oil or gas lighting were common. Most towns the size of Curwensville had a bank (in Curwensville it was the First National Bank, organized in 1865), high school, and theatre. General stores provided much of household needs. There were typewriters in most offices—at least in the county seat of Clearfield, and several people had purchased one of the new Kodak "detective" cameras.

In 1890 Tolbert J. Robison, a Civil War veteran, founded a printing company which continued to bear his name for more than 100 years, and the nascent Anderson Creek Electric Company was purchased by F. I. (Ignatius) "Nace" Thompson. It was here that Nace's sons, Walter, Howard J. (whose family later would be related to the Pifers by marriage), Fred, and Francis learned the electric business. With the invention of the incandescent lamp, Nace sold the direct current plant to Wm. F. Patton who built a new alternating current plant; in turn the company was again sold and became known as the Curwensville Electric Light Company.[25]

This same year the Raftsman's Water Company was given a 20-year contract with the village to provide fire protection after the devastating 1879 fire that had occurred in the town. At the same time the first water system—for 32 fire plugs throughout the village—was established.

The year 1890 was also significant to John Pifer as it marked the decade during which he met and began courting Matilda ("Dillie") Smith. In the summer of 1894 (June 28) John and Matilda were married in a small ceremony with Matilda's sisters and two of John's brothers the only persons in attendance. Matilda wore a white dress of fine muslin and lawn with leg-of-mutton sleeves and a tucked bodice. She had designed it herself and had sewn it by hand. Her hair was dressed in a plainer version of the fashion of the day, pulled off the face and secured in a roll at the crown of the head. John stood young and handsome with a full handlebar mustache and hair parted slightly to the left of center. He wore a black wool suit, white shirt, and black silk cravat tied in a flat bow, sometimes called a gambler's tie. The ceremony was held early on a Friday evening after which the wedding party took the train to Clarion for dinner. With the exception of the bride and groom, everyone returned home after dinner. John and Matilda continued by train to Johnstown (a distance of 85 miles). The city had started to be rebuilt following the flood, and neither John nor Matilda had ever seen this area that had suffered such great devastation.

Two days later the newlyweds returned to Brookville (75 miles from Johnstown) on Sunday afternoon to accommodations they had taken in a small rooming house. Here they lived for nearly a year until the birth of their first child in 1895. They named their firstborn Josephine Smith Pifer, in honor of John's brother Joe and in recognition of Matilda's family name.

John had been considering moving out of the immediate area and the young couple found a small house to rent until he decided where to relocate. Matilda liked Brookville and would have been content remaining there. She had personal calling cards identifying her as "Mrs. John Pifer" and she was beginning to feel very settled and quite happy. Her sisters lived nearby and she enjoyed their company. She told John she would prefer to stay in Brookville or nearby DuBois where Rosie had moved or even Brockway where Ella lived with her new husband, a Mr. Jordan. John, of course, would have to make the final decision, based on business.

By the spring of 1897, shortly after the birth of their second daughter, whom they named Ruby Idora, it had been decided. They would relocate. With two children, John needed to find an area that was growing and could support a well driller who wanted at least half his business to be local. In preparation for choosing a location, with each job he spent time asking questions and calculating if the area looked promising for well-drilling. He considered DuBois until he learned that it was filled with underground springs and many residents had only to tap into these natural sources of water without having to drill wells. He also rather liked the idea of locating a bit further east into Clearfield County, preferably somewhere along the Susquehanna River.

The timing was right. There was a new toll road between Curwensville and the Jefferson County line and with travel made easier there would be increased interest in Clearfield County for settlement. This would lead to new industries and that meant opportunities for John Pifer. Further, among the larger businesses in Curwensville were a mine car company, a machine shop and a small foundry which John saw as being useful for the maintenance of his well-drilling machine.

Even though the population of Curwensville was just under 800 persons, homes and businesses still relied on wells for their water supply. As John told Dillie, "They need us to make an even 800 residents." Indeed, Curwensville held promise for a young man in the well business, and the young Pifer family made the 40 mile journey to a place farther east than Matilda had ever been. The family arrived in Curwensville in time to enjoy the annual Fourth of July celebration.

John Pifer was able to support his growing family, although not in any extra comfort. It fell to Matilda to use her ingenuity and skill to stretch the earnings of her husband. She made most of her daughters' clothing, at first by hand and later with the aid of a treadle Singer sewing machine, her first luxury (and one of the few in her life). Her only social life was associated with church activities, and the rare visits to her sisters. She did a little embroidery and tatting and also took up quilting, both as a pastime and as a practical measure.

On Christmas 1898 when John Pifer was thirty and Matilda was twenty-five and the parents of two baby girls, John's fondness for his wife revealed itself in a book he gave her as a Christmas gift. It was not a historically important book; in fact, one might even term it frivolous. However, taken in context, it perhaps shows that John still saw his bride of several years and the mother of his children as young and pretty and, like the title of the book, a true "Miss America."

Written by Alexander Black, noted author and credited as creator of the "picture play" that became the movies, *Miss America, Pen and Camera Sketches of the American Girl,* is a tribute to what the author thought was flattering to women of that time. It is unlikely that John Pifer selected this book by reading through it, but rather by its title and presumed content. That he chose this for his wife is touching and loving despite the fact that Black's cloying views provide the stereotypical view of women of the 1800s:

> " . . . it is pleasantly easy to detect many interesting changes in the situation of the American girl within the span of the century . . . . We have seen her bidding good-bye to the school ma'am at a time when any education was good enough for a girl . . . and we have seen her at a later time when no education is too good for her, bidding good-bye to an army of instructors at commencement time, radiant in her cap and gown, the class song ringing pleasantly in her ears, the breath of June in her life, with a crisp diploma to symbolize her triumphs . . . .

The author also takes the opportunity to comment on the growing interest of women to join clubs, a topic of general interest because numerous clubs and societies for men were forming in the late 1800s and an informal debate was occurring in the nation as to "woman's place," especially by those husbands who were not pleased at their wives' sudden passion for joining literary and other societies of serious discussion:

> "It has been said that a man often goes to his club to be alone . . . a woman goes to a club *not* to be alone . . . . . That independence

which is so characteristic of the American girl, which . . . somewhat disconcerting to men, is, undoubtedly, largely the result of the American girl's improved relations with her sister women."[26]

While many of the examples Black uses are condescending, they are indicative of the prevailing attitude of a society wrestling with a developing, evolving national persona, including spinsterhood and the changing mores toward marriage between people who first share friendship rather than an arranged marriage of whatever style.

In Curwensville the Women's Christian Temperance Union was organized in 1885 after the County organization was formed in 1884. In 1897 the Susquehanna Chapter, Daughters of the American Revolution, was organized at Clearfield with eleven of its charter members descended from Col. John Patton of the 16th Colonial Regiment of Pennsylvania and grandfather of the Hon. John Patton who had financed the Patton Graded School. On the national scene, in 1892 the National Federation of Women's Clubs was formed, although Curwensville did not have a Woman's Club until 1936. The trend toward societies was reflected in many smaller clubs and societies in many American towns, such as the Ladies Aid Societies, Chautauqua Society, and literary study groups.

Black believed these clubs assisted in "the American girl's achieving true individuality, a positive and admirable trait."[27] While few women of Matilda's generation enjoyed Black's ideal, profiles such as this set the stage for the next generation, a prototype of whom was the third child of Matilda and John, the yet-to-be-born Jessie Beverly Pifer.

WHEN I HEAR A DREAMY WALTZ MELODY
WORDS BY GRANT CLARKE
MUSIC BY JIMMIE MONACO
SLOW AND EASY
WORDS BY HARRY WILLIAMS
MUSIC BY NORMAN SPENCER
ALL BY MYSELF
By Irving Berlin
Some Sunny Day
By Irving Berli
Good Gracious ANNABELLE
INSPIRED BY THE PARAMOUNT PICTURE
Starring BILLIE BURKE in 'Good Gracious Annabelle'
by ED. ROSE GEO. WHITING & LEW POLLACK
BY ARRANGEMENT WITH THE FAMOUS PLAYERS LASKY CORPORATION
LOVE SENDS A LITTLE GIFT OF ROSES
A BALLAD
WORDS BY LESLIE COOKE
MUSIC BY JOHN OPENSHAW
HARMS, Incorporated

Chapter 1

The Young Jessie

The real voyage of discovery consists not in seeking new landscapes but in having new eyes.

—*Marcel Proust*

The Twentieth Century arrived with the World Exhibition in Paris and the first trial flight of the Zeppelin, barely noticed in small-town USA where most families were struggling to live on average "real wages" of $10.73 per week,[1] a rate that had remained constant for years. The basic cause of this standstill in wages paid to laborers was the unrestricted immigration begun in the early years of the 1900s when more than a million people a year immigrated to the United States. The sheer number of workers kept wages low and hampered the unions' attempt to organize them. However, even these low wages were high enough to attract the poor and ambitious from Europe and more than 12 million people came to America between 1890 and 1910.

It was an exciting time for those graduating from high school or college poised on the edge of a new century. The Class of 1900 of Curwensville High School that spring was more concerned with graduation and their own futures than they were with immigration. They barely noticed that they were the largest class to have graduated to date with 12 members that included Elizabeth B. Spencer, soon to marry Howard J. Thompson and in 1904 bear a son who would marry a daughter of John and Matilda Pifer.

In 1900 Sigmund Freud, a name not yet widely known by the average American, had just published *The Interpretation of Dreams* and John Sargent was completing a portrait of the Sitwell family that would assure his place as one of the finest portrait painters of his time. At the end of the year the American scientist R. A. Fessenden successfully transmitted human speech via radio waves, setting the stage for Marconi to transmit telegraphic radio messages the following year.

Across America young people enjoyed riding bicycles and helping to make the Cake Walk a fashionable dance, although it was nothing compared to the music by which the era would be identified and which held far more fascination for the young. At the turn of the century, Ragtime Jazz was in its infancy, but was in position to dominate the first half of the 20th Century.

Merchandise was still somewhat limited in the dry goods stores of small towns, but individual buyers had two other options: buy from traveling salesmen and/or purchase from the mail order catalogue. Traveling salesmen, or peddlers as some called them, either carried their merchandise with them in valises or used horse-drawn wagons. Other salesmen carried only samples of merchandise which they showed to their customers who would then place an order to be delivered at a later date.

Mail order companies, though in their infancy, were a boon to rural America, thanks to the entrepreneurial foresight of companies such as Montgomery Ward and Sears, Roebuck and Co. A glimpse into the 1902 Sears catalog gives an idea of the variety of merchandise available, ranging from small items such as buttons, hymnals, and hosiery to major purchases such as pianos, house furnaces, and commercial scales. Later, entire houses could be ordered to be built on site. Mail ordering in a small town was limited only by what the peddlers—or railroads—could handle.

By the early 1900s Curwensville had its own post office. However, because parcel post service was not available until the

1940s, mail order items were shipped by rail, the closest terminal for Sears, Roebuck and Company being Blairsville (Jefferson County) or Driftwood (Cambria County).

To a great extent unaffected by much of the larger world, John and Matilda Pifer, with their two young daughters, had settled into family life in Curwensville. Matilda was pleased with the Presbyterian Church in town, attending Sunday School with the children. She read her Bible daily, using it as a reference for the Sunday School lessons and as a guide to her personal life.

Like many women of the time, Matilda's long days were filled with the tasks of running a household and rearing her family. She had artistic skill and found an interest in what in later years would be termed a hobby. Matilda enjoyed painting on pieces of porcelain china—cups and saucers, dinner and dessert plates, and such decorative accessories as bedroom dresser trays, a pastime that had become "fashionable" in the latter part of the 19th Century.[2] Examination of this china suggests that the painting had been glazed, as it has not chipped or rubbed off from the time it was originally painted. Most of the pieces are dated and signed.

In the fall of 1902, Matilda's daughter Josephine enrolled in first grade at the Patton Graded Public School, shortly after a two-room annex increased the number of classrooms. From the day she sent her firstborn to school, Matilda vowed that her children would complete their education, and she carefully studied the school's Course of Study that required at least eleven years for completion and graduation.[3] The school day began at 8:45 a.m. and recessed at 11:35 a.m.; it reconvened at 1:00 p.m. and dismissed at 3:35 p.m. As a public school, only those students who were not residents of Curwensville were required to pay tuition of $1.00 per month for grades 1–6 and $1.25 for all upper grades.[4]

A wedding of some social note occurred on June 17, 1903, when Elizabeth Bailey Spencer (daughter of Vincent Uriah Spencer and his wife, the former Alice Bailey) married Howard J. Thompson. Elizabeth's sister gave her a book, *Bridal Greetings,* that contained not only the wedding service and pages on which to write the names of the bridal party and guests, but also contained in its 148 gilt-edged pages much advice for the newlyweds, ranging from handling domestic servants to the dangers of quarreling. Its language formal, its tone instructive, the book is properly positive in tone, as befitting the times.[5] In the florid style of the day, the newspaper account of the marriage of Elizabeth Spencer and Howard Thompson reads thus:

> A very pretty home wedding took place at 7 o'clock Wednesday morning, at the home of Mr. and Mrs. Vincent U. Spencer, Walnut Street, when their daughter, Elizabeth Bailey, was united in marriage to Howard Jefferson Thompson, of Clearfield.
>
> The beautiful ring service of the Methodist Church was performed . . . in the parlor where the bride and groom stood under an arch made of fern and laurel. . . . The bride wore a beautiful gown of chiffonette trimmed with silk medallions. . . . The groom and best man wore conventional black.

> After a wedding trip to Philadelphia, Atlantic City, New York, and Washington, Mr. and Mrs. Thompson will make their home in Clearfield. The groom is superintendent of the Central Penn's Light and Power Co. He is an energetic, thorough, up-to-date businessman and all who know him are his friends as his disposition demands it.
>
> The bride is one of Curwensville's fairest young ladies, having lived here nearly all her life, and is endowed with many traits of heart and mind which have endeared her to many friends. The bride received a large number of valuable presents of cut glass, China, silverware, and other useful articles, tokens of the esteem in which she is held.[6]

The following year on April 10, 1904 Elizabeth gave birth to her first child, a son, Howard Vincent Thompson, named for both his father and maternal grandfather. This son would later become good friends with the daughters of John and Matilda Pifer, particularly so with Jessie and her next younger sister, and would marry this younger sister Katherine (Kate). Fewer than two years later, on November 21, 1905, a daughter, Mary Alice, was born, completing the family until the surprise arrival of Philip Bell fourteen years later on October 20, 1919.

The year 1903 also saw the beginning of industries that would change life forever, including the manufacturing of automobiles. The first Model T Ford at $850 had no direct impact on the lives of most citizens (except to have a picture taken standing beside the car in the showroom).[7] However, by the end of the following year, two or three of the wealthier businessmen in the county were among the nearly 20,000 men in the country who ordered automobiles. By the early 1920s the price of the Model T, then produced by a more efficient assembly line, dropped to $310 making it more affordable.[8]

The attitude of the general public toward cars was ambivalent, with automobiles being held in the same status as playing tennis and golf, smoking cigarettes, or wearing wrist watches, none of which savvy politicians would dare be seen doing. In 1907

Woodrow Wilson, then President of Princeton College, cautioned the students there against indulging in the snobbery of motoring. "Nothing," he said, "has spread socialistic feelings in this country more [than this] picture of the arrogance of wealth."[9] The more accurate reason for the slow sales of automobiles, however, was American roads. Maintained locally, they were full of ruts and pot-holes because landowners were not eager to be taxed to keep the roads in good shape for automobiles that only a few men owned.

John Pifer, who traveled near and far drilling wells, saw the potential in automobiles, realizing that it would be only a matter of time before the horse-drawn wagon for his rig would be obsolete. On the other hand, Matilda viewed the advent of motorized vehicles as a future opportunity to increase the number of visits to her sisters, although realistically she knew that it would be very unlikely that she and John would ever have money enough to purchase a car. There was little money for anything viewed as a luxury.

That summer (1903) Matilda took time to visit some of her neighbors and was fascinated with the stereoscope belonging to one of them. She thought of the pleasure these "magic lantern" sets would provide for her girls. While the initial cost would not have been entirely prohibitive, she knew the cost would not have ended with the viewer but would continue in the purchase of stereoscopic views, something their financial circumstance could not support.

At this time none of Matilda's neighbors had yet heard a graphophone, or "talking machine," as they were commonly called, yet these "contraptions," as John called them, were very appealing—one even advertised itself as having an amplifying horn large enough to be used in a concert hall. Making "records" at home was intriguing to think about, but surely out of their reach. Rather than dwelling on what could not be, however,

Matilda regarded the visits to homes of those who could afford "new-fangled things" as a treat for Josephine and Ruby.

It wasn't long before Curwensville's Opera House featured traveling public speakers who enhanced their lectures with stereopticons, providing the audiences with sets of pictures ranging from travelogues to the assassination of President McKinley. One of the most popular subjects shown on these viewers was "the method of conducting the wonderful packing houses at the Chicago Stock Yards . . . showing the entire workings and method of a modern packing house from the time of the shipping of the animals, their reception at the stock yards, the slaughtering, curing, saving and inspecting . . ."[10] By 1906 the shocking stock yard conditions were exposed by Upton Sinclair in his novel *The Jungle* in which eight of the 308 pages so vividly described the filth in the meat packing industry that it gave rise to the U.S. Pure Food and Drug Act.

Matilda had little time to attend lectures, but a few years later she did go to a showing of "The Great Train Robbery" which, when produced in 1903, was the longest moving picture film to date at 12 minutes. Regular showings of what are now called "the movies" were not common until after 1908 or so, as the first neighborhood movie theatre in America was not established until 1905 (in McKeesport, Pennsylvania by two men from nearby Pittsburgh),[11] and it took some time for small towns to follow this new trend for public entertainment.

By 1904 the first radio transmission of music was successfully completed in Gratz, Austria, opening vast possibilities for all to enjoy concerts. Two years later the first radio program of voice and music was broadcast in the United States. The first telegraphic transmission of photographs, also in 1904, allowed for faster publication of "live photos" in newspapers and magazines which theretofore had relied on illustrations. This same year New York City opened its Broadway subway and the first railroad tunnel under the Hudson River was completed. America was gaining even more confidence in its ability to harness machinery and, before the year was out, work began on the Panama Canal which would, upon completion, provide a direct route from the Atlantic to the Pacific Ocean.

With so much construction occurring, more foreign (and cheaper) labor was needed and announcements were sent out to European countries, telling of work opportunities in the United States. Between 1900 and 1910 nine million immigrants had arrived,[12] some bringing their families, others hoping to return to Europe with money enough to buy a farm, and still others planning to send for their families at a later time.

In late 1904, Matilda suspected she was pregnant. With two children ages eight and nine, she had not expected to increase her family, and, after all these years, a pregnancy at the age of 31 was a surprise. She had packed away infant items, not expecting to need them again. With the infant mortality rate still high, Dillie had been thankful that her two little girls were healthy and had not pressed her good fortune. She shared the grief of her sister Jessie who had lost a baby son during the winter of 1901 and felt guilty that she was to bear another child when her sister had been so misfortunate. She considered what to name the expected baby and wondered if her sister would be pleased or hurt if she had a boy and named him Clark, in remembrance of Jessie's child.

The winter of 1905 was cold, but Matilda didn't mind. It was easier being pregnant in the winter than in the hot summer. As she anticipated the birth of her third child, she thought it would please Josephine if the baby would be born near her birthday in late June. At age ten, Josephine would be a great help with an infant. As it turned out, the baby missed her oldest sister's birthday by about two weeks, but Josephine and Ruby were to be so delighted with a real baby to play with that the suggestion of its being a birthday present would soon be forgotten.

The Young Jessie

Like most babies of that time, this one was born at home in her mother's bed, attended by a midwife. Dillie felt fortunate to have even that assistance, as many of her acquaintances gave birth assisted only by an untrained female relative. As she had neither a mother nor a sister nearby, she had made arrangements with a woman known in the town for her skill in deliveries. Dillie knew the signs of pending birth, and when she felt it was time, she sent Josephine to fetch the midwife. Josephine knew that something very important was happening to be sent alone on an errand to the home of an almost stranger. She had heard her friends talking about this woman she had been sent to fetch and she also knew that this had something to do with babies, but she just wasn't quite sure what this was. Even at age ten Josephine had not been told that a baby was expected. She remembered that the last time Aunt Rosanna had visited there had been whispering and sudden halting of conversation the minute the children came into the room, but she had not known why.

By the time John came home from drilling a well near Bilger's Rocks, the new baby had been born. Josephine and Ruby could hardly contain their excitement as they rushed to greet their father, "Papa, Papa, did you know we have a new baby? It came this afternoon and Mama sent Josephine clear down to Filbert Street, all by herself. Come see the baby! She is so sweet, but Mama hasn't named her yet." John smiled to himself, "So, another girl." He hurried up the stairs to greet his new daughter and to see how Dillie had come through the ordeal. The new baby had dark hair and was smaller than he had remembered the first two being. "How are you, my girl?" he asked of Matilda. "It's another girl, John," she said in response to his question. "I hope you don't mind." He walked over to the bed and sat on its edge, looking at his wife and baby daughter. "She's pretty as a picture," he said reassuringly. "And you know I love all my girls."

This third daughter born to Matilda and John Pifer was as welcome as the first. John never expressed disappointment about not having produced a son and namesake and Matilda certainly was pleased with another daughter, as she would be able to use most of the baby clothing she had saved from Josephine and Ruby. John and Matilda were happy with their new infant, but were having a minor dilemma in naming her. John wanted to name this baby for his two sisters, his twin Katherine and his younger sister Margaret. Dillie wanted to name her for her sister Jessie, especially since she had been thinking about using the name Clark, had the child been a boy. She was also quite fond of Jessie and had always liked her name. She initially deferred to John and told her sisters and aunts that the baby probably would be named Margaret Katherine. She may have indicated a bit of disappointment at having a girl, or at least her Aunt Agnes assumed it from Dillie's letter to her. A month following the baby's birth Matilda received a letter from Aunt Agnes, her own mother's sister in Warren, Ohio:

> *Dear Dillie, . . . I sent you a little sack for the little girl that has come to your home and may she be a great joy and comfort to you. Don't feel bad at all that she is not a boy for there is just as much need and room in the world for girls as boys and the One who gave her to you knows best. I don't think you will feel bad, but you know what I mean. Everyone seems to think people want boys and while it is nice to have both we take what is sent . . . .*
>
> *Kiss Margret Katherine for me.*[13]

Because her name was not definite until she was six months old, baby Jessie was not baptized until the following spring. She was one of the first group of babies to be baptized in the recently refurbished Curwensville Presbyterian Church which had installed a dark oak interior finish and stained glass windows. Matilda dressed her three daughters in white dresses for the occasion, Josephine and Ruby in full skirts with hand-tucked bodices, white stockings, and white shoes with large hair bows and baby Jessie in the white christening dress Matilda had first made by hand for Josephine. John, not typically a church-going man, accompanied his little family to Sunday service where Jessie Beverly Pifer was christened.

No "educated" home at that time was complete without a dictionary and a general reference book. *The Universal Manual of Ready Reference,* first published in 1904, was one of the most popular. Its 750 pages claimed to contain knowledge of antiquities, history, geography, government, law, politics, industry, invention, science, religion, literature, art, education and miscellany. One of the areas not covered in much depth in the reference manual, however, is medicine. For that information, families turned to *The People's Common Sense Medical Adviser* by R. V. Pierce, MD. *The Adviser,* in its fifty-fifth printing by 1895,[14] was inclusive for its time, explaining common treatments that could be followed in most households.

Most people "doctored" themselves with home remedies, using homeopathic approaches. Vapor bath cabinets were especially popular because advertisers claimed these treatments could cure more than fifty ailments including the common cold. While there was no bath cabinet in the Pifer household, Matilda did have a vapor chamber which she placed on a chair beside the bed of whoever needed treatment; a blanket would then be draped from the headboard of the bed to the back of the chair, forming a tent to contain the vapors for the person in bed to inhale.

Baby Jessie thrived under the care of her mother and two older sisters. Josephine and Ruby practiced their school lessons by reading to the baby, beginning when Josephine was in fourth grade and Ruby in third. Matilda also read to all three children, particularly enjoying holding the baby with Josephine seated on one side of her and Ruby on the other, the two little girls occasionally anticipating the words in the story and supplying them as the tale unfolded. Snug in their little world, the family faced only two problems: (1) the house they were renting was too small for their growing family and (2) John's income was not substantial enough to buy a larger house. Matilda began to plan how they could resolve the first dilemma, as she had no control over the second.

Because John's work often took him far from home, Dillie learned to take complete charge of the household in his absence. She was a capable young woman who, like many others of her station in life, coped with whatever circumstances faced her. Money was a constant worry, as John, being self-employed, did not draw a regular salary. There were many lean days and months (even years) when only Matilda's resourcefulness kept the family going. She made much of their clothing, this task becoming easier after she had saved money for several years to purchase a sewing machine. By her own admission she was not a skilled seamstress, but she taught herself well enough to produce garments as well-made as those of her daughters' friends. She also canned in the summer, buying vegetables and fruit by the bushel. Each of the girls in turn learned how to cut vegetables and peel fruit for the canning process, as it took all available hands to prepare for this growing family. Matilda knew that particularly in the winter months well-drilling work was scarce once the ground froze and the snow fell, and so the canning was essential for survival.

A coal stove kept the kitchen warm and a small parlor stove heated the front room, the term used by those living in smaller houses that did not have both a parlor and a sitting room. (Only later did Jessie, in the presence of guests or her friends, refer to this room as the parlor, believing this description sounded more grand.) Open grates in the floors of the two bedrooms allowed the heat from the stoves to lessen the chill upstairs. The family generally gathered in the kitchen, cozy and warm, using the large oak table for most activities. In addition to the four chairs at the table, there were two "sitting" chairs, one a rocking chair. Mama usually sat in the rocker, mending, while the children gathered around the table. When John was home, he preferred the larger chair where he would read the local newspaper, sometimes aloud to his wife and, occasionally, the children.

On wintry nights John would recite Emerson's "The Snow Storm," the poem he had memorized when he was a schoolboy. The girls loved this, and never tired of hearing his recitation. They enjoyed teasing their father about his being born the same year as Louisa May Alcott's *Little Women* was published. "Look, Papa," each would say, as she discovered the novel and its date of 1868, "you were born the same year as this book, and you have become the papa of little women!" He had not read the book, but enjoyed being compared to a character in one of the most popular books of its own and later times.

When he traveled, John wrote letters to the family, keeping his wife informed of his whereabouts and the progress of the drilling work. He was faithful in his writing, addressing comments to both Dillie and the children. He was sorely aware of the meager income upon which the family subsisted. It was difficult for him, too, that there was no money for luxuries for his family. In a letter of March 3, 1906, he wrote from Richmond, Virginia:

> *Dear Mama and Children, Today finds me in Richmond where I had a breakdown. I had to come here to get repairs. Came here last night and will be ready to go back in the morning. We did not get much done last week. It stormed a couple of days and was bad weather in general. We are down 240 feet; nothing yet that looks like coal. We expect to try and get two holes completed this month, if possible, before we go home but we will have to hustle.*
>
> *Dillie, how is your cash holding out? If you think you will need any before I get home you had better let me know and I will write Dick to send you $5.00. I don't think he has collected much [money owed for drilling services], if any, since I left but probably can raise that amount—or you could write him yourself and ask him if he has collected any and could send you that much till I come home. Well, the time is going along and will not be long till April 1st when you can begin to look for me. Ed is beginning to feel homeward bound, too. Hoping this will find you all well as ever. Good bye, Pop.*

The summer Jessie was a year old, Matilda and the three girls could be seen taking walks throughout the streets of Curwensville. To any observer, this looked only like a mother and her children on an outing. What Matilda was doing, however, in addition to enjoying the fresh air with the girls, was looking for a house to rent. She believed that if she would only look long and hard enough she would find something larger—yet within their means—for her family. The four of them walked up and down Pine Street, then the same on Walnut, crossing over State, and up Thompson Street. One day they would travel down North Alley to Filbert Street and another down Thompson Street to Meadow Street to Filbert Street. Other trips to the Presbyterian Church took them to Locust Street after which they would return by way of George Street, past the Snyder home where there also were two daughters younger than Ruby and older than Jessie. Occasionally Marian and her younger sister Cora would be playing on the porch under the watchful eye of their own mother, and Mrs. Snyder would invite the Pifers to stop and "rest a spell."

One day, late in the summer, Matilda found what she had been seeking. Turning right from State Street, she became aware of something posted on a house. She had noticed this property on other days and had not thought much about it because it was a double house and she was seeking a single. As she approached 411 West Thompson Street, there it was, a sign announcing "For Rent. 3 bedrooms." Her mind was racing. "What shall I tell John? What will he think? He doesn't even know I have been looking all summer for a larger house." She decided she would wait a couple of days before saying anything to her husband. The next day was raining, so the following day she went again to what she was starting to think of as "her house." She then noted the shed, and knew she had a case to make to John. A shed would provide protection for his well-drilling rig.

That same day, after supper and with the children in bed, Dillie sat down with John in their kitchen. "John," she began. "I think I have found a house we might be able to rent." He said nothing. She began again, "You know we have been very crowded ever since the baby came and I just don't know where she will sleep once she outgrows the crib. She is already trying to climb out of it. Do you think we might at least look at a house I found this week?" "Where is it?" he asked. "On West Thompson Street," she replied. "It is half a double—with three bedrooms. And, John, there is a shed for your rig!" "I'll take a look at it tomorrow, if you like," he said. "Oh, John, thank you!" she replied, her hopes soaring.

In October they signed the lease to rent the house. Dillie was delighted with the additional bedroom. The baby could have the small room as a nursery, Josephine and Ruby would have a very large bedroom to share, and the front bedroom she and John would have was larger than any other bedroom they had ever had. The front room was also a good size and there was a dining room. A dining room! She was excited, even though she had no dining room furniture to speak of. She was sure their round, oak kitchen table would do very nicely. She also had a plan she kept to herself. She would save whatever money she could, even a dollar a month would help, and in several years perhaps they might someday purchase this or another house. There was a large front porch and a back porch on which the children could play. A small backyard provided the finishing touch.

During the summer of 1907, much to her astonishment, Dillie realized she was expecting again. Her first thought was that she was so glad they had moved to this larger house, yet her mind was already racing as to the bedroom situation. She had two options, although the decision would not have to be made for another five years. By that time Josephine would be graduating from high school and Jessie could share a room with Ruby if the baby were a boy. If the new baby turned out to be yet another girl, then Ruby could take the smaller room and the two younger children would share the larger bedroom. It would all work out, she was sure. Her excitement of welcoming another baby far outweighed the reality of the cost of rearing a fourth child.

By August, once she was positive of her pregnancy, she shared her news with John. "Surely this time it will be a boy," is how Dillie announced the pending birth. "Are you really with child?" John asked incredulously, yet he already knew the answer. He had suspected her condition, but was reluctant to ask until she was ready to tell him herself. "Don't worry," he added. "We'll manage." Those words were reassuring, but Dillie knew better than John what a drain this would be on their limited resources.

That fall in the small nursery Jessie was moved from her crib to a bed. She didn't like it at all when Mama told her that she was growing up and that the crib was needed for a new baby brother or sister. Even though she was only two, she had a mind of her own. She was used to being the baby and a bit spoiled by her mother and sisters, and she liked to be in the center of whatever was happening. She didn't understand the import of a new baby, but what she did understand was that someone else would be sleeping in her crib.

That someone else arrived on Monday, February 11, 1908. It was another girl. "Well, my dear, you really are trying to create another family of girls like you and your sisters, aren't you?" He smiled, and his wife knew that this fourth daughter would be loved as much as the first, the second, and the third. Katherine Shields[15] was named for John's twin sister to assure that his sister's married name also was honored. Josephine was in seventh grade and Ruby was in sixth at this time and these two older girls again eagerly accepted their role as older sisters.

Life centered around the family and church, so being at home most of the time to help was not at all unusual for girls this age. A family of six provided enough work for everyone in the household. Laundry alone took a full day. First, water had to be heated on the stove and poured into a large tub. The clothes were placed into this tub and washed by hand by rubbing each garment over a washboard. The clothes were then wrung out by hand, rinsed in a separate tub, again wrung out, then hung outside on a rope line to dry in the summer and hung in the cellar or attic in the winter. Ironing also took a full day, as everything needed to be ironed because of the wrinkles in the fabric caused by the twisting of the wringing. The iron had to be heated on the kitchen stove and did not retain a consistent heat; as a result, items ironed first were likely to be scorched unless a cloth for that purpose was first placed on top of the item to be pressed. The electric iron was invented around this time (1908), but no one in Curwensville would have one for several years.

Except for a midwife for births and the occasional nurse for the first few days following the arrival of a new baby, many of the families in Curwensville did not have hired help. The Pifers were no exception. There was no extra money to ease anyone's daily burden of rearing a family at 411 West Thompson Street.

Jessie paid little attention to her baby sister Katherine unless there was someone present to impress. Being used to having most of the attention focused on herself as the youngest child, she innately understood that "playing with the baby" would assure her of a continuing spot in the limelight. Baby Katherine, as this new child was called, did not create nearly the stir that Jessie's arrival had. In fact, neither Matilda nor John was as astonished at this birth as they had been with Jessie's having occurred after a gap of ten years.

The baby's crib was set up in her parents' room, but all the necessaries for the infant were kept in the small nursery where Jessie slept. Josephine and Ruby enjoyed the summer of 1908, dressing the babies (Katherine an infant and Jessie age three) and playing with them. They were also permitted to take the little ones for a stroll, but not out of the sight of Mama, who kept a watchful eye from the front porch. Most of the time the children's world was the back porch and its yard where they could play within earshot of the kitchen.

Early the following summer, in 1909 when Baby Katherine was a year old and Matilda turned 37, she began to wonder if she was having an early "change of life." She had been feeling a bit poorly, but had attributed it to the lingering effects of an early spring catarrh. By the end of June, the realization that she was yet again expecting a child struck her almost to silence. John was out of town on a job and for nearly a week she barely spoke to anyone, but went about her chores in a state of preoccupation. John returned Saturday afternoon, and that evening, once the children were asleep, he asked her what was wrong. "You're so pale and quiet," he said, speaking softly, "Are you not well?" "Oh, John," she began, then started to cry. Fearing the worse, he took her hand. "No, John, I am fine," she said. "It's just that there is going to be another baby and I worry about money." John intuitively knew what she was fearing. Her own mother had died shortly after giving birth to a fifth daughter. "Another baby is a gift to us, Dillie," was all he needed to say.

On Katherine's second birthday, two special events occurred. The first was an illustrated birthday card, the first piece of mail ever sent to her. This came from the Sunday School Superintendent because Katherine was a member of the Cradle Roll of the Presbyterian Church.[16] The second special event was the birth of Margaret Jean on February 11, 1910, exactly two years from the date of Katherine's birth. Now the names (Margaret Katherine) that Dillie's aunt had tried to apply to Jessie would be duly used. Katherine Shields and Margaret Jean were to become each other's best friends as well as sisters.

The five Pifer sisters were reared by their loving, though not demonstrative, mother who may have been a bit overly concerned with appearances and propriety. With their father's frequent traveling to do well-drilling, the girls' mother was the strongest influence on their young lives. Their father was stern, typical for the time. There was, in fact, little outward expression of affection in the family. One reason was that the days of working class families were so filled with chores that there was little time for personal interaction. Another reason was that Matilda Smith had been orphaned at an early age and had not had expressions of maternal affection available to her, and perhaps a third was because of John's stoic German heritage. Matilda did the best she could, bringing up her children to expect more from life than she had had. She almost never spoke of her own childhood, except in times of exasperation when one of the girls would complain about some chore they all found to be unpleasant. There were no stories about "when Mama was a girl," even about the poverty.

Mama never commented on the unusualness of being one of five daughters and then having five daughters of her own, although she most identified with Jessie, as each was the middle child of a family. On the other hand, the two older girls were so many years older that Jessie was more like the oldest child of three, and, indeed, those who knew the family referred to Matilda Pifer's two families.

Once the children were old enough to understand the reality of family economics, they realized that their father was not a good breadwinner. Notwithstanding this, Mama instilled in the girls a filial respect for him. Fortunately since Mama sewed, the girls were always neatly, if not well, dressed. "Poor, but proud" is how the girls as adults described their upbringing.

The three younger Pifer daughters were very cognizant of a wealthier family in the neighborhood, a father and mother with only one child on whom they doted. The sisters later described this little girl as "a beautiful child who had many toys and wore fine clothing." She, like they, was "overprotected" by her mother, but the three sisters believed that was more than compensated for by the girl's family wealth. After all, they thought, this desirable playmate – although neither family allowed their respective offspring to play at the home of the other—had everything! The girl's mother repeatedly rationalized indulging her daughter by saying, "But I only have one little girl." The envy of the Pifer girls abruptly turned to sympathy and guilt when this child died in the deadly influenza epidemic of 1918. That was a lesson in humility they never forgot.

Matilda Smith Pifer very much enjoyed her own bevy of five girls. As children, the girls addressed their mother as "Mama," but later Ruby and sometimes Josephine addressed her as "Momsie." Their father was known as "Papa" and, later, "Dad." The girls' clearest recollections of their father is of reading the newspaper and his ritual of checking his gold pocket watch and then winding the shelf clock—termed a shelf clock because in the Pifer house this clock sat on a shelf in the dining room between two matching windows which overlooked the backyard. Had that same clock been placed above a fireplace it would have been known as the mantle clock.

None of the five girls had naturally curly hair, although their hair was thick and had a lot of body. It took to curling with a bit of help. When they were young girls, Mama created rag curls by wrapping the damp hair in strips of cloth. Starting at the top of the head with the child's own hand holding the edge of the strip against the head, Mama wrapped the hair around the cloth until she came to hair ends when she then would reverse the direction, wrapping the cloth around the hair until the cloth strip met its beginning at the top of the head. The result was what some called "sausage curls," and the thicker the hank of hair, the heavier and looser the curl. The girls did not have their hair cut until their last years of high school. By that time permanent waves were available, although the three younger Pifer girls preferred to use a curling iron to crimp or curl the ends of their hair in a modified "bob,"

leaving the top smooth, sometimes held back with a barrette.

Traveling photographers were a mainstay in small towns such as Curwensville, and Matilda somehow found the money to have formal portraits taken of her children, although this did not occur with great frequency. In a group photograph taken when Jessie, Katherine, and Margaret Jean (known as Jean) were respectively six or seven, four, and two, Jessie is wearing an enormous bow in her hair, at least half the size of her head, and a large, round locket, perhaps borrowed for the occasion. In contrast, Katherine is dressed plainly, with no ornamentation. She always confessed to acting "contrary" that day, hiding her wrist encircled by a gold bracelet and deliberately extending the unadorned arm. Jean, barely a toddler, wore no finery. Individual formal portraits remain of Josephine when she was about age 12 and of Ruby at age ten. Each is dressed in a white dress with deep eyelet ruffles, wide short sleeves, and tucking. Both girls also wore white leather shoes and white stockings—Ruby's fine gauge and Josephine's of thicker wool-like thread, with very large bows in their hair.

A three-bedroom house, one of which was a small nursery, was not very commodious for a family of seven, so Mama, always resourceful, carved out sleeping space in the attic. Not insulated, except where Mama had tacked cardboard between the rafters, the attic room was hot in the summer and very cold in winter. Opening the windows helped in the summer, and in the winter Mama heated bricks and placed them in the attic beds to warm them. When all five children still lived at home, two of the girls, usually Katherine and Jean, slept in the attic. Jessie managed to claim the tiny single room, while the second bedroom continued to be shared by the two older girls, Josie and Ruby. Early on winter mornings the girls would scurry down the stairs to dress in the warmer part of the house. During the hottest part of the summer, they begged to sleep on the back porch, but their mother did not think that was appropriate for families who lived in town. She considered sleeping outside an indication of lacking refinement.

Bedtime for everyone was 9:00 p.m. both winter and summer. Baths were taken once a week, on Saturday nights. The washtub was used for this activity until after the Great War when plumbing was installed upstairs. Just as in the clothes-washing process, water was heated on the stove and poured into the washtub. Hair was washed only every two weeks because it was generally believed that more frequent shampooing would harm the hair by washing away the natural oil. Drying hair in the winter was difficult, as it required standing by the kitchen stove and rubbing the hair with a towel. In the summer the girls dried their hair by sitting in the sunny part of the backyard and either brushing their hair or running their fingers through it, spreading the hair out as much as possible.

During the winter, the girls all wore long underwear, covered with black stockings, a petticoat, and a dress. In the summer the long underwear was shed, but the stockings and other garments remained. The Pifer girls were not allowed ever to go barefoot.

While the family lived only a half block from State Street, which was the primary thoroughfare of the town and its two-block shopping district, the girls were not permitted to go downtown, not even to the corner. Their boundary was the back porch for play and the front porch for company and for sitting quietly on Sunday afternoons or summer evenings. While Katherine and Jean were content to play on the back porch, Jessie often would find a reason to deliver something to a friend in the next block or even farther away if her story were plausible enough. The younger girls liked to play house under the back porch, large enough for the little ones to stand in. They used cardboard boxes and old cushions for pretend furniture and a few old pans contributed by Mama. Occasionally when their father was out of town for several weeks, they would set up a play house in the shed, which had been rebuilt and was now referred to as the garage. They preferred under the back porch to the garage, however, as the ground floor of the garage was oily, even though Mama placed cardboard on the ground to make a clean floor to play on. On rare occasions or when it rained, Mama allowed them to shape a play room on the back porch using the adult furniture there.

Christmas was an exciting time because of the decorated tree and small gifts. There was no extra money to purchase special gifts, and years later Katherine would recall for her own children that there were many Christmases when there were no gifts except needed items; further, she would have them believe that one Christmas the Pifer girls received only a lump of coal. That may have been an exaggeration or perhaps Katherine was remembering a joke of some sort, for it is not very likely that Mama would not have prepared something. The girls surely received newly made clothing, yet as adults they did not have memories of many gifts. An orange was the major treat they received. Since citrus fruit was not usually available during the winter, the oranges shipped in to grocery stores during December were a rarity and very expensive.

John provided a tree a day or two before Christmas because Mama did not follow the German tradition of the parents decorating the tree the night before Christmas while the children slept. She believed the girls should have the fun of helping to decorate and enjoying the tree in advance, a practice followed by her daughters later in their own families. The tree was placed in the front room in the coolest corner away from the heat register so that the pine needles would not dry too quickly and drop. The family spent Christmas Eve together, perhaps popping corn, then stringing it to place on the tree.

Despite a shortage of cash in the family, Mama managed to purchase a piano on credit, paying for it in time payments, although formalized installment buying was not popularized throughout the country until 1915. The price of home pianos at that time ranged from $100 to $300 and the payment plan was typically one-third down and relatively large payments thereafter. The piano purchased by Matilda was likely in the upper mid-range. She wanted her girls to have lessons, although she was their first teacher, training each one in the fundamentals. It was important to Mama that her girls be refined, and being able to play the piano was one indicator of social class.

In addition, there was an unspoken rivalry between Matilda and her sister Rosanna. Aunt Rosie was described by Mama as "having married well" (at least to someone financially more secure than John Pifer) and she had the habit of subtly bragging about her possessions, sometimes by reporting what she had and sometimes by bemoaning what she lacked. The following excerpt from a letter sent to Matilda (circa 1912) supports the passing comments Mama would occasionally make concerning Rosanna's higher station in life,

> *How are the girls? I suppose Josephine can play nicely on the piano and Ruby the mandolin. I will be delighted to have them play for me when they come over. We had our piano exchanged. We like this one better [as] it has a larger case and is mahogany. Is John working these days? Ed said he would like to go over to John's some of these days and promised we will go when he is not working. With love to all. Your sister Rosa.*

The Young Jessie

Jessie entered school the fall of 1911 accompanied by her high school age sisters. All three girls attended the Patton Graded School, only a block from their home. Several months past her sixth birthday, Jessie was more than ready to take on the school. Even at this young age, she was full of spunk and confident in her ability to read. Ragtime music, which reached its apex that year in the United States with Irving Berlin's "Alexander's Ragtime Band" seemed to have been written with Jessie in mind. Legend has it that Berlin wrote the song in only eighteen minutes;[17] that, too, was the kind of speed by which Jessie moved.

According to her second grade report card, Jessie was a good student, and her confidence never lagged, unlike that of her next younger sister. Only five years old when she entered first grade, Katherine was a shy child with a strong sense of fairness. She later believed that she had not been ready to go to school at such a young age, and she described her young self as a "scaredy cat" who cried every morning.[18]

Finishing her junior year in high school the spring of 1913, Josephine might have been permitted on occasion to attend a movie or perhaps a live performance at the Opera House. Among the movie offerings in 1913 were "Mabel's Hero" and "Pecos Pete in Search of a Wife." However, of greater local interest in the spring of that year was the Junior Class Play, "Lost—A Chaperon."[19] The tickets were priced relatively high at 25 and 35 cents, but the profit helped defray graduation expenses and most families did not complain. Josephine had a small part in the play and her mother and sisters were all in attendance.

The younger Pifer girls and their classmates were among the first to be taught by the newer Palmer method of writing which had recently replaced the more ornate Spencer style of penmanship. Along with learning to write, the children were occasionally permitted to "color," although in the early days of this century crayons were expensive and very frugally doled out in the schoolroom. Few children had crayons at home.

Later that year, the school was closed for several days when the Blizzard of 1914 struck on the first and second of March as a nor'easter moved up the Atlantic Coast with intense winds that blew roofs off buildings in Baltimore and knocked down telephone and telegraph wires, signs, and awnings. Sustained winds of 44 mph were recorded there, with stronger winds as the storm traveled north.[20]

Spring was most welcome after a harsh winter, and the focus of the Pifer family was the graduation of the eldest daughter, Josephine Smith Pifer, one of 24 graduates in the Class of 1914. The Faculty's Farewell Reception was held on April 14, in the Park House, the words on the program both prescient and wistful: "Those joyous days are gone. I little dreamed till they had flown, how fleeting were the hours." The signature of each classmate can still be seen on Josephine's printed program, carefully saved with other school mementos.[21]

Two weeks later, Josephine received a letter from Aunt Rosie,

> *My dear Josephine, I am glad and pleased to receive your announcement and send you all our congratulations and I would like to go over but I can't very well go now. I am just in the middle of cleaning and am really too tired. [Rosa was only 34 years of age at this time.] I will be thinking of you, though, and I am sending you a little present which I hope you will like. I just thought what I would like if I was a girl and had a notion to get you silk stockings, but thought the gloves would suit best. . . Affectionately, Your Aunt Rosie.*

Mama was determined that all five Pifer girls be graduated from high school, and made it very clear to the three younger girls that they would be expected to follow in their older sisters' path. This was ambitious for the times, but Mama knew the importance of an education. She also wanted all of her daughters to be prepared as teachers, just in case they would not marry and would have to support themselves.

Josephine attended Normal School that summer and was assigned to teach at a country school near DuBois for the fall term. She boarded during the week, coming home on week-ends, continuing to share a room with Ruby. The family routine was not much different, even with the oldest daughter now an adult. Josephine paid board from her salary and that relieved the family finances a bit.

John continued to travel to wherever work took him and in August 1914 he wrote from Ridgway, a community 30 miles from home,

> *Dillie, I got the beadle machine and am going to load it while I am here at St. Mary's ordering a [railroad] car this morning. Tell Jim if he can to get a helper to go to work, as it will take me a day or so here.*
>
> *John.*

In September (1914) Ruby began her senior year. Her exotic appearance made heads turn and those meeting her for the first time were intrigued by both her features and her name. Kate, as she was by then called by her family, entered second grade, continuing her good academic performance as well as greatly improving her grades in deportment. First encountering the confusion she would meet throughout her life, Kate saw the first of many variants on the spelling of her name. It is also interesting that in every instance, the parent who signed the report cards for the Pifer family was Mama. This is probably a result of John's often not being home, but still indicates the matriarchal structure of this family.

While the date of Ruby's graduation from the Patton Graded Public Schools, Curwensville High School, is listed on her sheepskin diploma as June 15, 1915, mid-June was unusually late into the summer for the closing of school. The annual Alumni Banquet, the town's largest social event, also bears the date of June 15, 1915, as it was customary for the Alumni Banquet to follow Commencement, sometimes the same evening. One must, therefore, wonder why the events were scheduled so late.

Ten days following graduation Ruby, her trunk packed and shipped in advance, left by train for Grove City College, happy to be off on a great adventure, but grumbling that she would miss being in Curwensville on July 27 when the "Women's Liberty Bell," accompanied by suffragettes, would be stopping to garner support for voting rights for women. Ruby was to discover that the bell, a replica of the original Liberty Bell in Philadelphia, would be displayed—at least for a short time—in every county in Pennsylvania and that, if she paid attention, she might be able to see it when it made a stop in the Grove City area.

After completing her course work that first summer, Ruby was certified to teach, with the provision that she, like all other beginning teachers, continue taking summer courses toward permanent certification. The following summer she was again granted a provisional certificate stating she was "of good moral character and had passed an examination in ... 13 various subjects."[22] The next two summers Ruby returned to Grove City, evidenced by a post card sent to her mother from Grove City College on June 29, 1918.

Ruby had begun teaching in the fall of 1915. Her school, while only fifteen miles from Curwensville, might well have been two hundred, because there was no way for her to live at home and commute. Teachers lived in the community or township in which they taught with a family or families on a rotating basis, and with room and board usually part of their contracted payment. It was in this town where Ruby first taught that she met her husband-to-be. Tom Wayne's family had a farm near the schoolhouse, and he was immediately smitten by the new teacher, so much so that he tried very hard to convince his mother to offer room and board to the young woman. When his mother did not agree, Tom made it his business to become friendly with most of the host homes where Ruby would be staying that year. He found various reasons to visit these homes in the late afternoon around the expected arrival time of the school teacher. After several weeks,

Tom tried to arrange his work schedule in order to walk Ruby home. Josephine, too, had met a young man, Droz Hamilton, whose family lived in an area west of Curwensville.

There were not many incidents to mark one day from the next in the usually quiet town of Curwensville, and, if asked, most residents would have answered that nothing had happened there since William Jennings Bryan passed through Curwensville in March 1909. However, in June 1916 the unthinkable occurred with a bank robbery at the Curwensville National Bank. A masked man entered the bank with guns drawn. He fired, wounding a clerk. The cashier ran out of his office, foiling any further action. The gunman then ran from the bank toward Anderson Creek where he was apprehended by the deputy county sheriff who, according to the newspaper account, happened to be in town on business.

As word of the assault spread, mothers within five miles of the town called their children indoors. Matilda, whose house was less than half a block from the bank, heard the shouting and ordered the three younger girls "not to even go near the windows." On the pretense of going to her room, Jessie, almost eleven, ran up the stairs to the landing to try to watch from the small windows on either side of the outside chimney that faced State Street where the bank was located. Kate and Margaret Jean were more inclined to obey their mother and remained in the dining room at the point of the house farthest from the bank.

Rumblings from Europe increased and by March 1917 it was becoming evident that America would be pulled into the War. However, with only 110,000 men in the regular Army, the country was not ready for battle and volunteers were not easily found to increase the ready fighting force. Everyone everywhere was talking about President Wilson's April 2 address to Congress where he pronounced, "The world must be made safe for democracy." Four days later Congress declared war on Germany.

"I Didn't Raise My Boy to be a Soldier" quickly became one of the most popular songs of the time.[23] Once conscription was initiated and 516,000 draftees had been sent to camp, Irving Berlin's tune, "Oh, How I Hate to Get Up in the Morning,"[24] was on the lips of every soldier. The same year George M. Cohan wrote the song "Over There," with its thunderous, "for the Yanks are coming, the Yanks are coming, the drums rum-tumming everywhere," and this song became the rallying cry for the war.[25] Other songs that became favorites in households, memorized, and years later resurrected for the Second World War included "Till We Meet Again," "Smiles," and "There's a Long, Long Trail."

The movingly beautiful "Sometime" by Rudolf Friml was also released in 1918 and remained a favorite solo number for decades. Mama purchased this sheet music, along with "A Perfect Day" and "Mighty Lak' A Rose" as Jessie's young voice was already showing an extraordinary range and timbre. Jessie enjoyed the attention her singing brought, especially from the neighbors who often would comment that they enjoyed the music on summer evenings when the windows and doors of the neighborhood were open. Jessie could be counted on to have a solo on Children's Day at the Presbyterian Church the family attended, and Mama basked in the reflected attention after services when many of the church members complimented her on Jessie's performance.

The girls all learned quickly that practicing the piano or simply gathering around the piano to sing relieved them of the cleaning up after supper. Mama expected them to help wash the dishes, but if they were at the piano she never requested their assistance. Instead, she would listen and quietly enjoy the music provided by her girls. When Ruby came to visit she could be counted upon to arrive loaded with new sheet music, everything from ragtime to songs she knew Mama would like, such as "Love Sends a Little Gift of Roses." Ruby's own favorite was "Ah! Sweet Mystery of Life," which she memorized at age sixteen and continued to play at family visits for the remainder of her life.

The Young Jessie

In 1917 Memorial Day and the Fourth of July received more attention than in previous years with more flags being flown and the national anthem[26] being played more often than anyone could remember from earlier years.[27] The local Crescent Band played on Memorial Day, standing at the corner of State and Thompson Streets. The band then marched up Thompson Street to Oak Hill Cemetery, playing Chopin's "Funeral March,"[28] processing by drum cadence to the band shell where citizens gathered for the annual Memorial Day program.

In the midst of a country gathering for war, Matilda Pifer took the biggest step of her life when she purchased the house she and John had been renting for the past ten years. It was John's decision that the house should be in Matilda's name because he thought it would be best to separate the purchase of the house from his business account. By a deed dated November 23, 1917, a double house at 411-413 Thompson Street was conveyed to Matilda Smith Pifer. The younger children did not notice any difference in their lives with this momentous passage, but Ruby and Josephine sensed a palpable distinction in their mother's posture in being a homeowner. Matilda was sure she could manage the mortgage payments with the assistance of rent from the other side. She did not even raise the rent of $9 per month that the occupants of 413 had been paying. Matilda, also now a landlord, felt more secure than she had in years. Even sitting on the swing on the front porch was sweeter. And with the country in the midst of war, she also thanked the Lord that her children were daughters, not sons.

Once the United States entered the war, men from every walk of life were enlisted in the war campaign, and the country was inundated by a flood of printed material (as yet there were very few private radio sets), while some 75,000 Four Minute Men, including Curwensville's own Roland D. Swoope,[29] delivered patriotic speeches throughout the country.[30] In schools, contests were held to make posters in support of American troops. Children played games in which the villain was always Kaiser Wilhelm; many persons with German names were suspected of being spies; and the New York Philharmonic banned compositions by living German composers. Bond rallies were popular and even John Pifer with his meager earnings did his part by buying Liberty Bonds.[31]

Planting victory gardens was another popular way in which all citizens were able to help the war effort, as were attempts to conserve food, energy, and clothing, and to increase production in every line of work. As a result, in 1918 the United States was able to export approximately thrice her normal amounts of breadstuff, meats, and sugar.[32] Even with that assistance from the United States, however, the food shortage in Britain led to the establishment of national food kitchens.

As unprepared as the American soldiers were, their very presence in Europe infused the war effort with a spirit of enthusiasm and confidence. Harold Evans thus describes, ". . . the psychological impact of the glowing young Americans singing, 'Hail, Hail, the Gang's All Here!' at the top of their voices as they marched east to battle, was quite prodigious." "We all had the impression," wrote Jean de Pierrefeu, an officer on the staff of General Henri Pétain, "that we were about to see a wonderful transfusion of blood. Life was coming in floods to reanimate the dying body of France."[33]

The ranks of the in-pouring American troops joined in the general forward movement that ended with the gigantic Meuse-Argonne offensive, and the Germans laid down their arms on Armistice Day—at eleven o'clock on the eleventh day of the eleventh month of 1918. Total casualties of the war were 8.5 million killed, 21 million wounded, and 7.5 million reported as either prisoners of war or missing.

In the fall of 1918 the Spanish influenza epidemic struck America and claimed more victims (22 million worldwide by

1920) than did the war in Europe. Late in October, unusually warm that year, people started to become ill and soon many of them died. The Pifer girls later remembered the many deaths and the quarantine signs, marked with a black wreath signifying a household's loss, including the little girl they once had envied. Each week, the newspapers published a column of deaths, and a pall hung over Curwensville and almost every other town in the country. To make matters worse, the winter of 1918-1919 was also unforgettable with its record-breaking cold, snow, and ice. Schools were closed and even the mail delivery was halted for a time, although not before Aunt Agnes (Matilda's sister) and her husband Uncle Will sent Jessie a Christmas post card.[34]

On May 17, 1919, the anniversary of the attack upon the *Lusitania,* an assembly program was arranged for the students to hear an "eye-witness" account of the sinking of the British liner. As the Pifer girls recall, a "survivor" of the disaster at sea came to speak to the students. As there had been only a total of 726 survivors, it is unlikely that an actual survivor would find herself (the girls always referred to the speaker as a woman) in Curwensville. Likely the speaker had some experience either as a lecturer or as a relative of a passenger on that fated ship, for the children recall being spellbound by her account of the *Lusitania.* This only added to the horror with which they regarded Germans, and Jessie, at nearly 13 years of age, began to deny that their family name and heritage was German.

During the days in which the two older girls (Josephine and Ruby) were being courted, young men would arrive at Thompson Street with flowers or candy. One ardent pursuer in particular often brought boxed candy, a rarity in the Pifer household. Jessie, with great largess and the recipient sister's permission, liked to open the candy box and offer one piece per person to whichever family members were present. She then would firmly place the lid back on the box. On one such occasion, the box of candy, after being ceremoniously passed around, was placed on the arm of the settee (by accident or design was forever after debated). Jessie bumped into the settee, sending the candy box flying, its contents spewing on the floor. Outwardly looking mortified but remaining cool-headed, she hastened to pick up the candy, ostensibly to return the pieces to their assigned positions in the sectioned box. Shielding her actions, for every two chocolates she replaced in the container, she pushed one piece under the settee for later retrieval.

As unassuming as her younger sisters were, Jessie lived to be noticed and strove to be regarded as "having style." She had plenty of moxie, and was the center of her small universe, confident, full of spunk, and without fear. She was outwardly obedient, but knew how to get her own way. Fun-loving as she was, friends gravitated to her and her teachers enjoyed having her in class. At home she did what was expected of her, seeming to know innately that by responding as required, she could earn trust and a bit of freedom not necessarily granted to her sisters. Just as she had found a reason to deliver something to a friend in the next block while her younger sisters were confined to the back porch, she later learned that she would be permitted during the summers to visit her married older sisters, one of whom lived in Altoona and one in Canton, Ohio. Adventuresome, she would pack a bag and travel by train to a household that would be more lenient than her own.

Chapter 2

The Early, Not-So-Roaring Twenties

"All the wars are over and there will never be another one. . .
At last, at last, everything's ahead."

—*Toni Morrison*[1]

On the cusp of the 1920s, the year following the end of the World War saw turmoil in Europe, widespread strikes, an unprecedented number of riots, and the fear of anarchy in the United States. Yet even with these major political concerns, there was great optimism that this war really had made the world safe for democracy. In the John Pifer family the year 1919 would be remembered as the summer Josephine's engagement was announced.

"Mama," Josephine had approached her mother in late June, "Droz would like to speak to Papa." Mama, with a blend of excitement and reluctance at what she thought would be her first-born's next words, found herself saying, "Are you sure?" That was not at all what she knew Josephine wanted to hear, but the words were out.

Mama was painfully aware that even though her daughter had had admirers, by age twenty-three Josephine still had not had any "serious prospects." She had met Droz Hamilton four years earlier at the home of friends and their courtship had been slow even by standards of the day. On the one hand, Mama thought Droz would never get around to proposing as he seemed to take forever to do anything; on the other hand, she was glad for the slowness of the courtship, thinking this would give Josephine time to see for herself Droz's seeming lack of ambition. Certainly he was a nice-looking man who had served in the Great War, but upon his return he was not quick to seek employment. He eventually took a position in the plumbing business as a traveling salesman, which his parents immediately aggrandized into "going into business." Droz had a younger brother Karl and a younger sister Elizabeth, as well as his parents who, according to Mama, "put on airs." The Hamiltons were nice enough folk, but Mama sensed they were no more pleased with their son's choice than she was, though for very different reasons.

Josephine answered her mother's question with a bit of defensiveness in her voice. "Yes, Mama. I am sure. Droz is really very kind and it is time that I am married. May he come next Saturday to ask Papa?" Mama responded, "Of course, if that is what you want." No one in the family mentioned that Josephine was of age and would not need their consent. However, John gave his permission for the marriage and plans were made for a simple ceremony in Butler where Droz was working for Frank T. Hastings Plumbing Supplies. Mama was concerned that Josephine would not finish her teaching contract in Hyde City that year, but Josephine assured her that she would honor the commitment for the first half of the year as she and Droz would not marry until December.

Although Josephine did not share her thoughts with anyone except Ruby, she sensed the slightly superior attitude of Droz's family and knew comparisons would be drawn between the wedding of Elizabeth and any that the Pifers could provide. Josephine knew well that her family could not afford to pay for a wedding, and she never voiced her wish for one. At fifteen Jessie would have been delighted to participate in a fancy wedding; nonetheless, she was content to bask in the attention of her friends who did not have so much as a marriage occurring in their families. The fact of a sister being married provided speculation for many conversations among Jessie and her pals, most of whom had little else to occupy their thoughts either about Josephine's marriage or the prospects of their own futures.

On December 19, 1919 Josephine and Droz traveled with Ruby Pifer and Karl Hamilton, who would serve as their witnesses, by train to Butler where Josephine and Ruby shared a room in the Nixon Hotel while Droz and his brother went to the boarding house where Droz was a frequent guest. The young couple were married the next morning in a brief ceremony in the parsonage of the First Presbyterian Church. For her marriage Josephine wore a silk crepe, cream-colored two-piece dress which flattered her solid figure. Droz was beaming and even made it to the ceremony on time, not a slight consideration.

The newlyweds took a short wedding trip to Erie, Pennsylvania— a distance never before ventured by anyone in the Pifer household except John on a drilling job several years earlier. Traveling to Erie was an adventure for Josephine, even though it was not a destination she personally would have chosen for a wedding trip. She knew Droz wanted to take her to see the city where the company he represented was based, and while there was not much to see in Erie except the lake, Josephine was satisfied to have the excursion and beamed when Droz introduced her as "my sweet bride."

Following their marriage, the Hamiltons took residence at 303 W. Mercer Road in New Brighton, Pennsylvania, a hundred miles from Erie, but only 42 miles southwest of Butler which was to be Droz's territory. Their first purchase as a couple was a mahogany bedroom suite, with a bed, chest of drawers, and vanity dresser with a mirror and matching bench; this became Josie's prized possession and remains in the family in the care of Josephine's great-niece.

Christmas 1919 was the first holiday that not all of the Pifer daughters awoke under Mama's roof. While she was not one to openly sentimentalize or to speak of her own childhood, Christmas always had been difficult for her as she could not help but remember the first Christmas after her own mother had died. It was that holiday when she first realized her life and that of her sisters had forever changed. They had cried most of the day, even though for the first time ever their own Aunt Jessie had sent each of them a small gift. While Mama often thought of her sisters, it was the Christmas season that brought back the specific memories of her own childhood.

She liked to think that life for her daughters was better than what she and her sisters had experienced, but she sometimes had her doubts. John, like most men she knew (although her understanding was quite limited), was not very sentimental and thought she made too much of Christmas. She and John did not make a habit of sending Christmas cards nor did they receive many. However, she did save the first Christmas card she received from her oldest daughter as a reminder of how life was changing for her family as Josephine and Ruby began their own lives.

The country was also embracing the future, as new art modes were being developed in the form of movies and jazz, musical plays, and skyscrapers. American artists were enhancing musical appreciation for the masses through the phonograph and the radio and by the launching of new journalism, notably with *The New Yorker* and *The American Mercury.* Westinghouse opened the first American broadcasting station in Pittsburgh in 1922, transmitting regular radio programs the following year. By 1924 coast-to-coast radio was available; however, choices for those in Curwensville who had radios were confined to KDKA as it was the strongest—and usually the only—station accessible by those in Clearfield County, deep in the central mountains of Pennsylvania.

With the world's attention increasingly drawn to the United

States following the Great War, by the 1920s American literature was gaining more notice as the voice of contemporary issues and youth. During this same time H. G. Wells published his *Outline of History*, the superficial but easy reference generations of college students followed, and on the suggested reading list by the time Jessie applied to Clarion State Normal School in 1924.

Across the country "flaming youth" was having its fling and by mid-decade skirts were becoming shorter and women were striving for the first time to create a "boyish figure" by dropping the waistline of their dresses to the hips. This, together with a loose and flopping coat and unbuttoned galoshes, suggested the description "flapper."[2] Self-styled flappers also displayed rolled down stockings, leading some state legislatures to add new regulations to the existing sumptuary laws prohibiting knee-length skirts and bobbed hair.[3] With cigarettes dangling from reddened lips, some of these flappers further enjoyed shocking their elders by dancing the Charleston, the Black Bottom, and other so-called inventions of the devil. In Curwensville, however, Jessie and her pals could only dream of and yearn for such sophistication, doing their best to appear to be "savvy," a favorite word of the high school juniors who had begun to connect English words with the Latin they were struggling to learn in their classes.

Notwithstanding the attention given to the "golden twenties," some adults longed for the past, although few could define what that might mean; politicians called it "normalcy" and Spaulding Grey termed it "nostalgia."[4] Many of the young people of Curwensville High School wanted neither normalcy nor nostalgia, instead hungering for a bit of the modern decadence described by Fitzgerald, wishing it to add some "pep" (another new slang word just making its way into the popular culture) to their mundane existence.

Even though the concept of social classes was losing favor during this period of history, it was also possible to improve one's social station. Thus, Matilda Pifer was determined that all of her daughters would learn to play the piano, one of the defining skills that in her own generation separated the classes. Therefore, all of the Pifer girls took piano lessons locally and later, when they were of high school age, they took the train to the next town (six miles distance). Once a week, each daughter, in turn, traveled to Clearfield to attend classes at the Susquehanna College of Music. Jessie loved these trips to Clearfield and, by the summer of 1920 when she turned fifteen, she enjoyed meeting people on the train and running into the stores in town before taking the train home.

Kate, on the other hand, dreaded the travel. She would scurry from the train station to the studio, paying her fifteen cents for a half-hour's lesson, then with lowered head, she would hurry back to the relative safety of the train station where she would wait for the seven o'clock train to return to Curwensville, never once walking the one block even to window shop. Jean was a junior in high school before she became more confident traveling by herself.

Niceties such as playing the piano and other cultivated activities were intensely important to Mama and she was very aware of being the mother of girls whose every move, she believed, would be scrutinized by the general public. The Pifer sisters were expected to behave in a ladylike manner at all times, not wear rouge or lipstick, not be boisterous or call attention to themselves, not to be seen eating in public or talking to boys, and *never* to be *chewing gum.*

Jessie welcomed 1920 because she entered high school as the now oldest Pifer girl. While she had been too young when her older sisters were in high school to have paid attention to their excitement, by the time Jessie finished eighth grade she had become enamored with the idea of being a high school student, particularly after the family received an announcement of the graduation of Catherine P. Shields, the daughter of Papa's twin sister and the Pifer girls' cousin, from Brookville High School. Jessie liked the feel of the heavy stock paper used in the announcement and the importance it conveyed. The enclosed calling card, of course, was even more appealing. Jessie began writing in a notebook how she wanted her name to appear on her own cards when the time came: *Jessie B. Pifer, Jessie Beverly Pifer,* or, perhaps, *Miss Jessie Pifer.*

Even though she was intimately familiar with the Patton School, Jessie felt a sense of momentousness in moving to high school as one of 36 members of the Freshman Class, a number that, by graduation, would be reduced by one-fourth.

The second week of school a class meeting was held, at which time Supervising Principal Grant Norris explained to the freshmen that they were to select class colors and a motto, and to elect class officers. Some of the class meetings that were held "resembled miniature battle fields, but when the smoke of battle had cleared away, we found that purple and gold were to be our class colors...."[5] At the third class meeting, they predictably elected by acclimation one of the boys as class president who then

convened the Class of 1924 to choose the class motto by which their class members were to be guided. Charles Murray offered for their consideration his personal motto, "Seek and you will find in this world as well as the next." He paused while his classmates waited for him to finish. "What is the rest of it?" asked Kay Wrigley. "That's all there is," said Charles, his face reddening. To cover the awkwardness, Mildred ("Babe") Leib, whose older sister was majoring in Latin at Grove City College, quietly said, "Why don't we pick some Latin phrase everyone knows?" "What about *Te amo*?" Ray La Porte asked, stifling a laugh. "Or *extempore,* since we aren't prepared," added Kay. President Orville Hipps called for order following a warning look from Professor Norris. Babe, with as much solemnity as she could maintain, suggested *Veni! Vidi! Vici!*, adding its translation for those who might need it.[6] Jessie called for the vote, and all agreed to Babe's suggestion.

Their class colors were much easier to decide since the boys cared even less about the colors than they did the motto. Margaret Rhodes said, "Let's have gold for one." Jessie, whose personal favorite color was purple, quickly added, "Purple and gold would be smart." That settled the matter. Yellow roses won out over purple iris on the point that irises weren't elegant. The Class of 1924 had made its choices, later to be duly noted in their yearbook and graduation program.

Jessie already knew some of the fight songs sung at the football games, and when in 1922-23 Curwensville's "Alma Mater"[7] was composed with lyrics attributed to biology teacher Lois Vashti Gregory, Jessie was among the first to memorize it and entertain her chums by singing it on their way to and from school, with no idea that two years later the Senior Girls Quartette, with Jessie as soprano lead, would sing this in many programs. "Where the Susquehanna's silvery waters glide, Where gleams nature's beauty from the mountain side, Our Alma Mater stands in grandeur fair, Claiming the love of all who enter there" began their melodious Alma Mater.[8]

Outgoing and gregarious, by high school Jessie had honed a style that would remain with her into her ninth decade. She and her friend Helen Martin had purchased and actually used Tangee lipstick, nearly a decade before *The Ladies Home Journal* agreed to advertisements for the product. Tangee was an early popular make-up with a waxy texture and odd orange shade that turned closer to red once on the lips. Jessie, tired of biting her lips to make them redder, saw nothing wrong with using the lipstick, despite warnings from her father that explicitly forbade the use of make-up for any of his daughters. She and Helen applied the outlawed cosmetic on their way to the high school, using a tiny sliver of mirror attached to a comb Helen's sister had given to her after teasing her about her unruly, naturally curly hair. Kate and Jean noticed their older sister's brighter lips, but said nothing, protecting her from having to face their father's wrath on this particular transgression.

On a more serious note, however, was the resurgence at this time of the Ku Klux Klan which had nearly disappeared after 1870. Revived in Georgia in 1915, the Klan had gained considerable political clout by 1920. Most prevalent in the Midwest, the Klan with its secrecy, exaggerated forms of address, and concealing robes appealed to enough men that the organization quickly gained significant political strength.

By September 1921, rumors were circulating in Curwensville that a recruitment campaign for membership in the Klan had begun in Clearfield County. Matilda first heard about it at church and John had heard the rumor while on a drilling operation in a neighboring county, but neither of them was concerned that anything serious would happen in Curwensville. It surprised everyone when one late Sunday evening as the family was sitting on the front porch Mama saw flames in a clearing across Anderson Creek, high on the hill above the opposite bank of the creek about a quarter of a mile distance from the porch. Neighbors began to gather in the street and the girls watched in awe and terror as it became clear that a cross-burning was occurring on the hillside.

Despite Jessie's protests, the girls were sent into the house and not permitted to remain outside to watch from the porch. Their mother, still remembering the bank robbery of five years earlier, feared the clan members might cross Anderson Creek and head toward the center of town several yards from their house. Her fears were unfounded, however, as the men, reportedly in white robes, remained on the hill. Despite Mama's admonitions to the contrary, all three girls had run to the attic where they had a clear view of the fire from two small windows facing the hillside. Kate and Jean were terrified and watched in silence, while Jessie boldly opened one of the attic windows, hoping to get a clearer view of whatever it was the Ku Klux Klan might be doing in addition to burning a cross. This unusual event was, of course, the major topic of conversation at school the following day and Jessie enjoyed giving her first-hand account of the incident, for she had had one of the best vantage points in town from the attic window.

As is true with most young people, this small, personal incident of the Klan loomed in their minds as being more important than what was then occurring in Europe, and they talked about the incident for months, oblivious to the brewing war on foreign shores. While Mussolini was forming his Fascist government, Jessie and her classmates were plotting ways to obtain permission to see "Orphans of the Storm" and "The Last of the Mohicans" at the Strand Theatre, which Fred and Francis Thompson had recently built on State Street. The impressionable high schoolers were enthralled with "the pictures" and the exciting times therein portrayed. Despite what their teachers might have told them, the friends could better imagine themselves as heroines in "the picture shows" than characters in their classroom reading of "The Garden Party."

Even though Jessie and her friends may not have been able to be heroines in the movies, they did have the next best thing a small town could offer. On the heels of organizations like the highly successful Chautauqua Institution and subsequent "little chautauquas" with more than 400 local assemblies of lecturers and musicians traveling from one community to another, many traveling theatre companies frequently were booked in small towns that had facilities for performances. In addition, every year professional touring companies went from town to town, and produced an annual musical, using all local talent. The John P. Rogers Company scheduled Curwensville on its tour, sending out, over the years, a series of producers/directors with important-sounding names. Each was in charge of the local production, casting the stage show with nearly everyone who auditioned. Following two intense weeks of rehearsals, the production culminated in two nights of performance with packed houses.

The earliest available evidence of Jessie's participation in these productions was "Miss Bob White," performed at the Curwensville Opera House, a theatre on the second floor of the Opera House Building whose major architectural feature was a round rose window on the second floor facing State Street. A double stairway, easily wide enough for a piano, led to the second floor hallway where the Opera House and the W. F. Patton Academy of Music were located. According to the playbill, December 15 and 17, 1920, "This is the original 'Miss Bob White,' which ran for several years in New York and on tour."[9] The chorus of Milkmaids and Farmers included Jessie Pifer and several of her friends.

The following year the same production company presented "Oh! Oh! Cindy!" based on a popular story line resulting from the enormous publicity generated by the Ziegfeld Follies. Jessie, at that time sixteen and a sophomore, was part of the Dance Harlequinade, leaving the roles of the Show and Chorus Girls to the young women age seventeen and above. Kate and those of her age group, most of them barely thirteen, made up an ensemble known as the Drum Corps.

Sophomore year was also the time students could purchase class rings and Jessie was on the committee to select the style for her class. Curwensville High did not have a class ring style distinctive only to its own institution. Rather, each class designed its ring from the samples provided by the salesman who worked through the local jeweler. Rings styles, therefore, might change yearly, and it was an important honor to be on the selection committee. Jessie certainly was determined to have the ring for the class of 1924 be quite uncommon.

The first meeting with the salesman was exciting, as he addressed the students as young adults about to make a decision "impacting the rest of their lives." At their easily influenced age, they believed him, not able to understand that while some graduates would keep their rings for a lifetime, few would wear them much beyond high school. A sophomore sees only the glamour, the symbolism, and the prominence of sporting a high school ring, and none on the committee could be expected to see beyond the immediate high school experience. Jessie's eyes lit upon a magnificent, large ring, with a stone, similar to Masonic and other fraternal rings. Holding it in her hand, she could imagine impressing all who would notice the ring on the ring finger of her right hand. When she heard the price, however, her heart sank, as she realized if she pushed for the selection of a ring beyond the financial means of her family, she would not have a class ring at all.

The committee recognized that if they continued with a style similar to the one used the previous year, the cost could be within the reach of more students. With practicality overriding their desire to be unique, the other members turned to Jessie, "What do you think?" "Well," she said with authority, "I, of course, prefer this one," holding up the ring with the ruby center. "But, thinking of my classmates, I suggest we continue with the style chosen by last year's class." She then hastily added, with a tone of magnanimity, "This will also make it easier for anyone in our class who decides to graduate early with the Class of '23." Following her lead with measured relief, the committee voted to retain the design. The salesman also assured them that by continuing with that style, their rings would be guaranteed for Christmas delivery. That suited Jessie perfectly.

The Sophomore Class also had the distinction of being a part of the first high school yearbook at Curwensville High to be printed and bound. Prior to 1922, the high school publication, *The Echo,* had first been printed twice a month as a news sheet, then in booklet form. To have an entire book commemorating a full year of high school was a challenge to the editorial staff, particularly as they had no precedent to follow. Fortunately, some of the students were able to borrow copies of yearbooks for Clearfield and Dubois, and the staff set to work, determined that their first edition would be worthy of CHS. When The *1922 Echo* was published, Jessie and her pals pored over the book, soft-bound with a leatherette cover, looking for photos and references to themselves. They very likely did not even read senior Elizabeth King's editorial, a plea to the community to take an interest in the schools.

The yearbook reports these events of Jessie's class: "During our sophomore year we entertained the seniors at a banquet in the Presbyterian Church, and then at a dance at the Park House, where everyone stayed until the wee small hours of the morning. Monty's Orchestra of DuBois furnished the music. We also enjoyed a sleighing party during this year with Miss Laura Burkett as chaperone."[10]

Like the thousands of rising juniors who followed, that summer Jessie and her friends were filled with their own self-importance. Jessie had already bobbed her hair, much to the dismay of her mother, and her parents were concerned that she was becoming far too outspoken and independent. Mama did not like this attitude of Jessie, and, like most parents, believed her daughter was being negatively influenced by her friends. She told her daughter that some of her friends were loud and silly and that she preferred Jessie not to spend time with them. While Jessie protested, it did no good as far as Mama was concerned.

Jessie, of course, had no intention of giving up her friends; she would just have to figure out a way to appear to be obeying. That avenue presented itself with the new family who moved into the neighborhood. Mr. Howard J. (H. J.) Thompson, a Curwensville native, who owned the water company and electric company in Bellefonte and had recently purchased the local water company, had moved his family to Clearfield several years earlier. After his son, also named Howard (V.), but called Howard Junior by his family, was graduated from Clearfield High School in the spring of 1922, Mr. Thompson moved his family to a brick duplex in Curwensville where they took residence on Thompson Street across from the Pifer family. Mrs. Thompson, the former Elizabeth Spencer, was pleased to return to the hometown where she had been graduated with the Class of 1900.

Howard Junior was scheduled to attend Williamsport Business School, daughter Mary Alice enrolled in the junior class of Curwensville High School, and Philip, fourteen years younger than his sister, was home with his mother. Jessie welcomed Mary Alice into her circle of friends, sensing from Mary Alice's fine clothing, the large brick house, and Mr. Thompson's success as a businessman that Mama would approve of their friendship. This provided Jessie credibility in leading her mother to believe she had found a new set of friends with "quality." She was counting on this also to give her the latitude to do what she wanted.

Jessie usually enjoyed herself immensely and from an early age never let work get in the way of having a good time. She was very popular with both girls and boys and "palled around" in pairs and groups. Wherever the fun was, one could be certain that Jessie was in the center of it. She was indifferent to school, but, like many young people, enjoyed it for the socializing it provided. Her friends believed she typified the flapper, but on a much lesser scale, of course, because only by personality could she remotely be thought of as a modern miss. Nothing was more important to

Jessie and her crowd than to be thought "smart," a word that in the 1920s took on the connotation of fashionable.

For all their dashing spirit, young people in small towns did not have the same problems faced by following generations. The high school students heard tales of speakeasies—or pretended they did—and assumed people frequented them, but they did not personally know anyone who actually did. Jessie would experience more of the speakeasy scene later in Clarion where good-looking college men, sporting raccoon coats, were noticeably the "young men about town," flashing bootleg hooch in silver hip flasks and dancing the night away. Of course, no one saw anything of this revelry in Curwensville or most other small towns. Nonetheless, families who wished to purchase liquor or wine could always find a local bootlegger. Those who did not wish to patronize bootleggers made their own "bathtub gin" at home or got along with home-brewed beer and hard cider.

The kind of skullduggery that led to disobeying the new Prohibition laws also encouraged hypocrisy in politics and set the stage for youth to demonstrate a defiance of adult authority across social classes. Until this time, resistance of the status quo was usually limited to the upper, educated classes. Prohibition leveled this class distinction and created a major problem for the legal system. By 1922 the problems and litigation surrounding the Eighteenth Amendment engaged 44% of the work of United States District Attorneys.[11]

The growth of leisure time led to a vast increase in sports, especially in spectator sports. Smaller colleges began to expand interscholastic competition, college football became more popular with the general public, and a wider use of personal automobiles created a burgeoning cult of Saturday afternoon college football fans who began to dress in the easy style and panache of the carefree collegiate. This trend increased Jessie's longing for a raccoon coat, almost counting the days until she might earn her own money, enough to buy a possum coat and hope that no one would notice the difference.

While horses continued to be used on farms, they took on new importance as an upper class vehicle for hunting and racing. Jessie's interest in horses began with her first visit to the harness races at the Clearfield County Fair in the early 1920s, launching her lifelong fascination with the sport. While it was only in her later adult life that she would travel to other states to watch the races, she was a faithful spectator at both the Clearfield County and nearby Cambria County Fairs.

"Bubby" and Kate

Golf and tennis also became more popular in the 1920s. Curwensville had been surprisingly quick to respond to the building of public tennis courts, and the young people found playing tennis an acceptable form of recreation—as well as a way to spend time with friends. Because it was a relatively safe activity and one that attracted the youth in groups, parents were generally willing to agree to their growing children's requests to go to the tennis courts.

Jessie pretended to be more interested in observing than playing since there was no money for tennis racquets and balls. She joined her friends at the tennis court, laughing while she convincingly explained that she wasn't very good at hitting a tennis ball. The fellows scoffed at this excuse because in backyard badminton Jessie was considered a formidable competitor. She would never, however, admit that the family could not afford the equipment needed for tennis. Better, she thought, to simply say, "I'd rather just watch," and smile fetchingly.

Occasionally Howard V. Thompson would coax Jessie into borrowing a tennis racquet and playing tennis with him. While not romantically interested in Bubby (a nickname bestowed upon him by his sister), Jessie was flattered to be asked, since he was an acknowledged stellar player who was to win the Clearfield

Tennis Association trophy in both 1923 and 1924 and recognition in the county paper, "Howard Thompson, Jr. continues to lead the Curwensville Tennis Association standings with nine victories and no defeats."[12] Oddly, Bubby's father had discouraged his interest in sports or any other activity and had forbidden him to play tennis. This situation piqued Jessie's interest.

When she first met him in the summer of 1922 Jessie had found Howd—as she liked to call him—somewhat fascinating for three reasons: (1) he was new in town, (2) his younger sister would be entering the junior class in the fall and would be a classmate of Jessie's, and (3) his own father seemed to be so disapproving of him. Jessie was curious as to whether he had a bad reputation. She knew he was working for his father's electric and water companies and while he told Jessie he would be going to Williamsport Business School that fall, he did not seem to be particularly pleased.

He later confided that he had wanted to attend Pennsylvania State College. Many of his friends were commuting from Bellefonte (where his family had lived until 1920) and he had his heart set on joining them. For some reason his father would not send him to a four-year college, a decision Bubby never would understand since he had been a strong student, had worked for his father since the age of 10, and had never been in any trouble. His father, however, was adamant. Howard Junior, as his mother called him, would attend Williamsport Business, where he would board during the week and come home weekends to work.

Josephine and Droz Hamilton had recently relocated in Altoona. However, while Altoona was only fifty miles from Curwensville, it might well have been 500 because often Droz was on the road all week and did not want to spend time traveling to Curwensville on week-ends. Thus, while Josephine kept in touch with her mother through letters, particularly expressing interest in her younger sisters and their school activities, she was not able to visit her family very often. Mama sensed a longing in her daughter's letters and missed talking to her eldest.

Not unexpectedly, Jessie was the first to visit her oldest sister. She had convinced her mother the summer between her sophomore and junior years that it would be "nice to keep Josephine company" while Droz was traveling. Jessie was well aware that she would have more freedom under the supervision of her sister than her parents. Mama agreed, hoping that Jessie would somehow cheer Josephine. Because Josephine had expressed disappointment to her mother that she had not yet started a family, Mama thought Jessie might be able to take Josephine's mind away from fretting. Her married daughter reminded Mama of own sister who had been childless, and Mama worried that Josie was fearing the same.

Jessie, who turned seventeen that summer, loved Altoona, the largest city she had ever seen. As the center city had been laid out in a perfect grid except for the angle following the rail tracks, it was easy to find the shops on 10th and 11th Streets, not far from the railway station. Although she had no money, Jessie quickly made friends with other young people in the neighborhood and found willing company to join her in exploring the shops and theatres. Bretts, a fine dress shop, was her favorite store for browsing the window displays. In later adulthood, Jessie returned many times to Altoona just to shop at Bretts.

After her month-long visit with Josephine, Jessie was ready to return to school as an upperclassman and to audition for the lead in Curwensville's production of the musical comedy "Kathleen."

Although only a junior, she won the lead role and later carefully placed in her memory book the promotional green cardboard cloverleaf which advertised the show. Kate, even though she had a pleasant singing voice, preferred the chorus, leaving the larger roles to her sister Jessie who had a voice townspeople spoke of even years later when there were few persons left to remember her singing. "A beautiful, crystal clear soprano, a strong voice that commanded listeners to silence," is what they said. A newspaper review of the performance confirms this,

It would take much searching, far and wide, before an equal of Kathleen, the heroine of the play, as rendered by Jessie Pifer could be found. This was really Miss Pifer's stage debut and she certainly gathered in a large share of the honors. Folks were delightfully surprised at her beautiful voice, and her song "Don't Forget that I Still Love You", will linger with its hearers for a long time to come. Her acting appealed to all.

It would take much searching, far and wide, before an equal of Kathleen, the heroine of the play, as rendered by Jessie Pifer could be found. This was Miss Pifer's stage debut and she certainly gathered in a large share of the honors. Folks were delightfully surprised at her beautiful voice, and her song, "Don't Forget That I Still Love You," will linger with its hearers for a long time to come…

SCENES

ACT I—Exterior of Hans Swinder's Grocery, Flynnville, Mass.
ACT II—Veranda of the Flynn Residence—One week later.

CAST OF CHARACTERS

(In Order of Appearance)

...Byron McDowell
Lem Underduck, Flynnville's Police Force ...Clarence Ammerman
Teckley Bramble, Champion Checker Player ...Lucinda Clark
Arabella Wilkins, the Village Postmistress... Frederick Mullen
Jimmie Stanton, the Grocery Clerk ...Helen Clark
Flossie Neverset, who vamps and dances... Jessie Pifer
Kathleen, the town's Sweetheart... Harold V. Smith
Michael Flynn, Flynnville's wealthiest citizen... George L. Benner
Hans Swindler, proprietor of the General Store ...Saul Robinson
Ned Rollingston, with a college education... Guerry Brunetti
Higgins, the Butler...

Furni... ...ngs in Second Act loaned by McLaughlin Furniture Co.
Floor L... ...Electric Supply Co.

MUSICAL NUMBERS—ACT I.

1. Opening Chorus introducing "In the Advocate" ...
... Mr. McDowell, Mr. Ammerman, Lassies and Villagers
2. "Tennis" ...Miss Helen Clark and Tennis Girls
3. "Every Road is the Right Road" ... Miss Pifer and Mr. Mullen
4. "Kathleen" ...Mr. Mullen
5. "Shy Maids" ...Mr. Robinson and Shy Maids
6. "Arabella" ...Miss Lucinda Clark, Mr McDowell and By Heck Girls
7. "Deduction" ... Miss Lucinda Clark, Mr. Benner and Mr. McDowell
8. "Don't Forget" ... Miss Pifer

MUSICAL NUMBERS—ACT II.

9. Opening Chorus, introducing "Dance My Lady" ...
...Mr. Robinson, Guest Girls, Party Guests and Dance My Lady Couples
10. Dance Rural ...Mr. McDowell and Mr. Ammerman
11. "Childhood Dreams" ... Miss Pifer and Miss Helen Clark
12. "Dance O'Mania" ... Mr. Robinson and Dance O'Mania Girls
13. Grand Finale ...Ensemble

In her scrapbook notes Jessie wrote only that "Terry came to see me perform Kathleen" and that she had "just started to go with [Wynfield] Sykes."[13]

Later, in the fall of 1924, following Jessie's freshman summer in college, a voice teacher moved into town. All were sure that Jessie would become the star pupil, and they waited in eager anticipation to hear how such a voice could be further enhanced by formal singing lessons. Something terrible happened, however, and, presumably as a result of the lessons, Jessie lost her beautiful singing voice.

One can only speculate what might have occurred and while no one can verify it, rumor had it that the vocal teacher, jealous of this golden-voiced student, "ruined" her voice. Jessie never sang again and, curiously, never spoke of this personal tragedy. The story has remained a mystery with no explanation. Subsequent productions, such as "Spanish Moon" in 1929, show Jessie in a featured speaking, but not singing, role. This production also lists Kate and Evelyn Williams, later to be influential in the lives of Kate's children, as one of several "Collegians."

The *1923 Echo* relates that from the viewpoint of the class, Jessie's junior year was a very eventful one. "The Seniors were entertained by us at Viewpoint and everyone enjoyed that trip. A trip to Clearfield was enjoyed in our junior year, too. This proved quite an exciting time for all. Next a social was held at the Grange Hall and one at the Moose Hall."[14] A milestone for Jessie was permission by her parents to occasionally stop after school at Jimmy's Sweet Shoppe. The Sweet Shoppe was the place where the young people gathered to talk and pool their resources if only to share an ice cream soda.

Jessie's new friend Mary Alice Thompson, officially a junior, had earned enough credits to join the graduating class of 1923, but decided to remain at home for a year and take two additional courses with the class of which she had been a member. Jessie, Mary Alice, Marjorie Wall (Jessie's long-standing pal as well as Mary Alice's cousin) became fast friends. All living on Thompson Street, it was easy for Jessie to ask permission to visit friends whose front porches could be kept in sight of Mama, even though Mama was reluctant to have Jessie—even at age 18—cross State Street and travel a full block to reach the Wall residence. When Papa was home, he often told Jessie she could go only to Mary Alice's home, almost directly across from the Pifer house. Because Mary Alice's father didn't like the young people gathering on his front porch, Jessie had an acceptable explanation for her father to be permitted to join the young people who congregated on the back porch, blessedly obscured from Papa's sight line.

Here on warm summer nights could be heard talking, laughing, and, when Harold Smith brought his ukulele, occasionally singing. Jessie's voice often could be heard above the others, and neighborhood families sitting on their porches would stop their conversation to listen. Bubby would sometimes join his sister's friends, providing an opportunity for Jessie to know him better.

The highlight of the summers for the three younger Pifer sisters was the Annual Clearfield County Sunday School Field Day, an event planned to promote friendship among the Sunday Schools of the County and so popular that one year a record crowd of 15,000 people attended. The Field Day had begun operation in 1921 and continued for nearly 20 years until World War II intervened. All programs were broadcast throughout the park. Prominent speakers were brought in for the programs, including the Attorney General of Pennsylvania.[15]

The planned festivities were enhanced through the efforts of another organization known as the Yellow Dogs, a fraternal organization devoted solely to promoting "friendship, frivolity and fun." The organization built a Community Building (K-9 Kennel) at Irvin Park and constructed a dam on the river at the Park so that the river could be used for swimming and water sports. They also sponsored a Labor Day Program with many competitive events, dances, a moving picture show, live performances, a parade, and meals, although families were welcome to bring a basket lunch or supper. Reflected of the frivolity of the Yellow Dogs, one of the most popular songs of 1923 was "Yes, We Have No Bananas," with lyrics purportedly written by the husband of a Curwensville native.

Curwensville underwent a number of changes and a period of growth during the 1920s, including H. J. Thompson's purchase of the Raftsman Water Company. He made repairs and improvements to the company which encouraged customers to forego wells for city water, an advertisement not particularly pleasing to John Pifer, well-driller.

In general it was a profitable time to be in business. In 1922 Isaac Kantar expanded his retail establishment and formed a partnership with his three sons to form "Kantar's" with "nothing over one dollar." Dotts Motor Company built a new yellow brick building on Filbert Street. In 1924 the Sanitary Milk Company opened, offering the first pasteurized milk available in the area, with milk deliveries being made by horse and buggy, and H. J. Thompson established the Mid-State Theatres, Inc. a chain of eventually sixteen movie theatres.

In 1924 there were 25 million radios in use in the U.S. and three years later 40 percent of homes in the United States had telephones, every third home had a radio, and two-thirds had electricity.[16] The typical employed factory worker had a third more real purchasing power than in 1914 and the newly devised installment plan allowed the worker to buy what he wanted. Soon after, many merchants in Curwensville began to offer an easy payment plan.

Also in this year, John Pifer purchased an Atwater Kent radio after finalizing his decision the previous year. The radio was placed in the front room beside the front window, which was really the window on the side of the house, everyone's favorite vantage point for viewing events occurring in the center of town.

Mama, who had said she did not think they needed a radio when there was a newspaper available, surprised herself by discovering that she enjoyed listening to the programs as she did her mending.

Papa preferred to listen to the news or the monologues of Will Rogers. One of the more serious highlights for him, however, was listening to the live broadcast of the Democratic Convention of 1924. He also listened to parts of the Scopes Trial, more to hear the orations of William Jennings Bryan than to follow the points of the trial, as its outcome was considered to be a foregone conclusion.

After an initial trial period of taking turns wearing the required headset, the girls didn't spend a great deal of time with the radio at home. They were just glad Papa had finally bought a radio, since they were among the last of their friends to have one in their homes. They preferred to listen to broadcasts with friends in homes where they occasionally congregated—houses of a size where the young people could gather in the parlor while the parents kept close watch from an adjoining sitting room. However, the only way all of them could hear the music was to place the radio headset in a wash tub so that the sound reverberated enough for more than one person to hear. While the sound was a bit tinny, Jessie loved to dance and, when there were orchestras "broadcast live from New York," she was the first on her feet. (The phonograph, they all agreed, still was better for musical listening, but the novelty of live music was the attraction.) Jessie had a knack for learning the latest dances, usually from observation of the college crowd (a handful at best) who infrequently joined the high school group.

Except for listening to music while socializing, Jessie did not pay much attention to radio broadcasts. She preferred the picture shows even though she was rarely permitted to attend. As rising seniors in high school, Jessie and her friends giggled among themselves the evening they all had convinced their parents that it would be good for them to see Cecil B. DeMille's "The Ten

Commandments." They had heard the film's attraction was not its Biblical accuracy but rather its spectacular staging. In addition, the boys were talking about the revealing costumes, and the girls wanted to see for themselves. Leaving the Opera House at the conclusion of the performance, the young people agreed that the movie was well worth the bit of deception it had taken to get them there. Only Jessie demurred, even though it had been her planning that allowed for them to attend. "I would rather have seen Douglas Fairbanks in 'The Thief of Bagdad' " she announced dramatically. That would have to wait until she got to Clarion Normal School the following summer.

On the first Tuesday in September 1923, the new seniors were the first to enter the school, a privilege afforded the graduating class. Jessie and Stell Bulkley climbed the front stairs and entered the "sacred senior homeroom," a large room on the second floor. For as long as the Patton Building was in use, every high school student looked forward to senior homeroom, a double room that also served as an assembly hall with a piano and a raised platform. The room next to it was separated by a folding wall and when the wall was opened, the entire high school population could squeeze in for special assemblies. This was also the room used for the literary societies who met in the evenings for public readings to which parents and other interested townspeople were invited.

By itself, the larger room could easily accommodate 120 students sitting at double desks (more with three in a seat), although no actual classes needed 60 seats. When it wasn't being used for large study halls in later years, the English teacher was usually assigned this room, because of the platform which lent itself to readings and public speaking. The partitioned room was generally used for science, even though there was no laboratory for any of the sciences until a tiny chemistry lab was installed in the 1930s.

Entering the sacred homeroom, Jessie continued her conversation with Stell, "I'm determined to enjoy every minute of this year and, after that I want to have a good time and meet lots of people." Stell replied, "I haven't thought that much about it." Then she laughed, "Mama is just hoping I finish high school. She knows I want to get married." "Not me," said Jessie. "There are too many things I want to do. Once I graduate, it's 'Good-bye, Curwensville.'"

At eighteen, "Jebbie" (a variation of "J.B.," for Jessie Beverly), as she was called by her friends, was what both boys and girls called "a looker." Slender and tall, she also boasted a long waist, a figure trait not shared by her four sisters, although all were shapely. True to the style of the time, Jessie's high school graduation portrait shows a properly pouting beauty with a styled bob, double-dropped pearl earrings, a fine wool dress trimmed with marabou and, as a finishing touch, a long strand of pearls.

Jessie liked nice things, especially clothing and accessories. Because there was no way to acquire these, she quickly learned to talk a good game so that friends would never suspect the Pifers were not too far from gentile poverty. Mama always held her head high and her sewing needle steady so that the girls could at least dress the part of a middle-class family. There was no money, however, for any extras, be it candy or accessories. On one particular occasion, a visiting friend of Jessie's—Jessie seemed to have an endless stream of friends, both male and female—found herself ready to leave as a rain shower began. The Pifer family owned only one large umbrella (Mama's prized possession used only in great emergency), and certainly it was not available to be loaned to a guest. Not to be deterred by fact, Jessie, with great poise, asked of the household, "Where is the pearl-handled one?" Fortunately, the rain abated, and there was no need for embarrassment at not being able to offer the use of an umbrella, a non-existent pearl-handled one notwithstanding.

The Senior Class of 1924 had twice the number of girls (18) as boys (9) for a total of 27, reduced from 36 members when they had entered as freshmen. Class colors (purple and gold), class flowers (yellow roses) and class motto (*Veni! Vidi! Vici!*) had been debated and decided upon during their freshman year. As it had been the past three years, the class was headed by a male president and vice-president.

One of the first things they did as a class was to hang the class banner in the Senior Homeroom. Years later, one of them mused, "You would have thought we were the French who had conquered England." This hanging of the colors signaled an esprit de corps that had been missing in their class to date. The members had squabbled among themselves over everything from the class colors and motto to who would be photographed in the yearbook with the class pennants, the triangular shaped flags used to wave at football games and to decorate bedrooms. In fact, it was in exasperation that Victor Grande and Orville Hipps tied the pennants around their necks, wearing them like giant table napkins, stuck the class banner on two vertical poles, and posed for the official yearbook photograph.

As for social calling cards, each class member could choose his or her own style. Jessie repeated the exercise she had first attempted as a freshman and tried out every version of her name, wishing her middle name were more reminiscent of grander heritage, something like the name of her cousin: Catherine Princetta Shields. Without that, the best she could do, she decided, was to use the Gothic font style which at least looked significantly important. Throughout her lifetime Jessie kept the metal engraving plate in its original envelope ready to mail to Quayle & Son, Inc. should she ever choose to order additional cards. And she kept until her death cards bearing the names of her classmates.

While the game of football had became a national athletic sport in most colleges and high schools by the 1920s, Curwensville stood forefront among high schools by having formed a varsity team in 1912. Well-established by 1920, football as a varsity sport had been embraced by students, alumni, and the town citizens by the 1923 fall season. Twenty-six boys (from a total high school student population of 163 boys and girls), joined the team in September and twenty-one finished the season that had begun with only three lettermen. The season was the best year in the history of the game,[17] both financially and by attendance, and the team of 1923 found themselves champions of Clearfield County with 4 wins, 3 ties, and 3 losses.[18] Jessie and her pals attended all home games and Jessie was permitted to travel by train to two or three games played in nearby towns. This initiated her lifelong interest in the sport and, for many years, her attendance at football games, both high school and college.

Even in a small town with a senior class of only 27 members, Jessie and her friends found ways to have fun. On October 31 the seniors held a Halloween Social in the American Legion rooms. The Ladies Auxiliary served as chaperones, and all members of the class arrived masked and in costume, with dancing, fortune telling, and refreshments as features of the evening. The class agreed that each senior could bring a guest to increase the number attending and to help even the number of boys in the class. According to the school yearbook, "Everyone who attended declared that it was the best held yet."[19]

The Senior Girls Quartette (designed around Jessie's exceptional voice) was popular in the town and surrounding areas, and the girls sang at many functions, including several times at the Opera House. The final evening of performances there was noted in the local paper: "Tonight at the Opera House will be the last evening ... the Susquehanna Glee Club and the Senior Class Girls' Quartet are on the program."[20] Between Thanksgiving and Christmas, the girls performed at every local civic organization, frequently being invited to the dinners associated with the events. The quartette always closed with the school's "Alma Mater."

Literaries made up a great part of what would later be called extra-curricular activities. By the fall of 1923, the high student enrollment led to formation of five literary societies. Each society met and performed every other week, usually in the large assembly hall, which during the day was senior homeroom.

The charge for each program was ten cents, the money going into each class treasury to help defray graduation expenses. The programs gave the students an opportunity to recite or read in front of an audience and the parents a chance to see their offspring in a different context. The new Senior Class presented their first program November 23, 1923 and, in hyperbole typical of youth, one of them wrote, "The seniors are endeavoring to make their class the best that has ever been graduated from the Curwensville High School."[21]

By January, the yearbook process had begun. Every member of the class was involved and had an assigned position, if only in name. None of inexperienced staff had any idea of how to publish a yearbook. While the students had more fun planning than working, they did produce a credible book. Every editorial position had its own assistant editor, and deadlines were met. Jessie, not particularly interested in the structure a publication required, was satisfied to be one of two "Wise and Otherwise Editors." They were responsible for only two pages, one of jokes and the other titled "A Personal Table" which was a listing of all seniors' names, what they were fond of, future occupation, and nickname. Jessie's listing shows her "fond of dateology," and her nickname as "Jebbie."

In late January Jessie obtained a college catalogue from Clarion State Normal School. This she frequently carried with her, as if to announce that she soon would be headed off to college. She wasn't really serious about becoming a full-time student because first, there was no money to send her full-time, scholarships were relatively unknown, and working one's way through college was not an option for females; and second, she wasn't convinced that she wanted to spend four years studying. What did attract her, however, was the *idea* of college. She could picture herself participating in the social life, and, truth told, she would like the prestige of a college degree. Since that was not feasible, she simply pored over the catalogue, dreaming of dormitories and socials, fraternities and football games. She retained a longing to be in the midst of youthful activity, with books and pennants, friends and suitors, and she tried to anticipate life on a college campus by questioning her older friends about what life there was *really* like.

Clarion State Normal School appealed to Jessie because it was far enough from home without being too far, a common determinant for women in those days. The State Normal Schools had been established specifically as professional institutes for young men and women to be trained as teachers for the common schools of the state. Both Josephine and Ruby had attended colleges offering teacher training, a path Mama had insisted be taken, as she wanted all her daughters to be able to support themselves in a respectable occupation. At their mother's urging, Josephine and Ruby had attended Grove City College, a small Presbyterian liberal arts school, which Mama thought appropriate to their Christian values. Each attended during the two summers following graduation from high school.

Jessie, however, had other ideas. She wanted a school with a bit more social life and a lot less religious attitude. Headstrong, she would not be satisfied with anything except a school like Clarion. Even with that decision, Jessie decided to put her final plans on hold until May when it would be time enough to decide her future. Right now, in the winter of 1924, she was enjoying herself.

On Monday, February 12, 1924, the seniors embarked on a class sleigh ride. They left from the high school at nine-fifteen in the morning, full of energy and ready for adventure. Waving to the underclassmen who were readying for their first class period, the Class of 1924 attached their class banner to the rear of the large sleigh, and vied for the best seats, preferably near a member of the opposite sex. Jessie, in her usual manner, had promised at least half a dozen classmates (both girls and boys) that she would sit with them, and when she arrived all were clamoring for her favor. "Here, Jebbie, I saved you a seat." "Jess, I brought a warm sleigh blanket for us." "Jessie Beverly, remember, you promised you would sit with me." Acknowledging none of their pleas, Jessie instead turned to Joe Errigo, who had moved from the Junior Class at the beginning of the second semester, and asked, "Can someone help me climb in?" In a flash she was surrounded by many male arms very willing to oblige.

Jessie wore a "smart" pair of boots, impractically trimmed with ruching sewn to resemble fur. These were a Christmas present from Mama, who knew such boots were not a sensible choice for long wear, but that Jessie had her heart set on something fashionable. Jessie's coat was wool, rather than the raccoon she longed for, but she had begged Ruby to borrow her brightly colored muffler, promising to return it by mail immediately after the excursion.

Jessie was as noticeably chic as anyone in Curwensville in 1924 could be. "Very Vo-goo," said Clifford Kelly, complimenting Jessie and laughing at the way the entire class liked to mispronounce the few French words they knew such as "vogue." "And chic, chic, chick!" added Kay Wrigley.[22] By now all were merry and full of themselves, anticipating the scene they would make as they traveled down the highway to Clearfield, seven miles distance, to their destination, near the center of town where the high school was located. Twenty-four of them were crowded in the sleigh intended for sixteen, but no one complained. They sang and shouted cheers for most of the way, drawing attention to themselves, which was, of course, their intention.

The entourage arrived at Clearfield High School around eleven o'clock, creating, as they had planned and later reported, "a sensation."[23] They disembarked with practiced nonchalance, fully aware that the students in the high school building were standing at the windows watching them. The sleigh riders then sauntered merrily for half a block to Murphy's Pig and Whistle Shop, a sweet shop where they had hot chocolate, and more so, relished the display they were creating. They then walked to the courthouse which was closed because of Lincoln's Birthday, but they didn't mind. They continued on Second Street, then took a left turn toward the river and another left to get back to the high school, singing football songs and a few popular tunes most of them knew.

Exhilarated, they were ready for the return trip. No one complained of the cold as they climbed into the sleigh, and by the time they were halfway home, most of the classmates were snuggled together, fully expecting never to forget this great adventure. Around two o'clock the sleigh made the turn into Curwensville where the road took a steep incline. The horses were tiring, and Gunnard Olson suggested the class walk the rest of the way. Jessie said, "But it's cold." What she meant was that she didn't want to ruin her new boots. Joe, disentangling himself from her embrace, gallantly suggested that the boys walk alongside the sleigh and let the girls remain seated. That suggestion was appealing and even more attention-getting for their arrival at the high school.

When Jessie suggested they all sing the Alma Mater, with the girls quartette taking the verses and all joining the chorus, the vote was unanimous. Even Papa heard their voices as the sleigh approached Thompson Street, heading west on State Street toward the school. He stopped his work to enjoy the young people's pleasure and even he had a twinge of nostalgia for his own days of innocence and youth. He called to Mama to come watch with him. "Dillie," he said, as he rapped on the kitchen door, "Come see." She stood on the porch as Papa walked down to the corner of State Street. Indeed, as recorded by Helen Martin in their yearbook, "the home town welcomed us back again."[24]

In the midst of all the activities of the town's youth, another celebration was occurring at the close of a membership and funding drive launched by the Woman's Christian Temperance Union (WCTU). In their Jubilee Campaign, Pennsylvania had made the largest gain with 6,747 new members.[25] Fifty Jubilee meetings were held at luncheons or banquets[26] with Curwensville hosting one.[27] Mrs. John Pifer and her daughter Jessie were among those in attendance. Mama was proud to be a part of the noble mission of the WCTU and kept the banquet program as a treasured reminder. Beyond that, however, she hoped that this movement would make a difference in the lives of her daughters, particularly the impressionable Jessie.

Jessie's future lifetime career was launched even before she was graduated from high school, with the letter of certification/ recommendation from Professor Norris, necessary to enroll in Clarion's summer training program. Prof. Norris certified that she had earned 18 high school credits, two more than the "State Requirement to graduate from a First Class High School."[28] He described Jessie as ". . . a young lady of pleasing appearance, affable disposition, neat and reliable. Her character is above reproach and her honesty has always been unquestioned. She has every promise of making an excellent teacher."[29]

March afternoons and evenings were filled with rehearsals for the class play, cast entirely from the class membership and including 15 speaking roles. Directed by the high school faculty, "Miss Somebody Else," a comedy in four acts, was presented by the Senior Class at the Opera House on Friday evening, March 21, 1924. All four acts of the play take place in the Tuxedobrook Club House[30] with Jessie playing the role of Celeste, a femme fatale. Her appearance in the cast photograph is striking and exotic, and, even three-quarters of a century later her perfect oval face and fine features are clearly evident, her hair stylishly designed with a large "spit curl" centered on her forehead.

Every senior who did not appear on stage served on a committee in a total class effort. At Jessie's suggestion, the stage committee asked the Florida Fruit Market, which had opened the week before, to donate fruit for the table in the Club House. Music by school talent was featured between the acts of the play, a long-standing practice for the school and abandoned only when a new high school was built in the mid-fifties. Immediately following the play, a Senior Class Dance was held at the Legion room. All seniors were invited. Jessie chose to wear her costume from the play and made even more than her usual dramatic entrance.

The Cast of Miss Somebody Else

Even though Jessie believed the world revolved around her, her importance was diminished for a day or two when on April 18, Mama received a telegram from Tom Wayne, Ruby's husband, sent from Canton, Ohio.[31] The message was only eight words, announcing the birth of eight-pound John Pifer Wayne, named for Papa. Jessie liked the idea of having a baby nephew, but had no idea of how fond she would become of him and of the role she would later play in the life of John Wayne, United States Navy.

Near the end of April the yearbooks were delivered. The thought of holding the actual book in hand had everyone anticipating for weeks: "What will it look like?" "I hope we didn't make too many mistakes." "Do you remember if we used that photograph of Kathryn Kephart and me?" "I just know the jokes we selected are going to look old." And when it arrived, there was no doubt that this was "the best yearbook ever." The class poem, so carefully crafted, was pored over for references to any person or activity each had been affiliated with. Nonetheless, despite the initial total focus and concentration, most of the class would read the poem only once.

The classmates—all young, untrained writers—were pleased with their own work, and, indeed, the yearbook featured all of the seniors in several sections, a personal profile, a class history, social events, favorite recipes, and the class prophecy. Jessie marked the pages where her name or photograph appeared.

Senior Profile:

Jebbie, Dainty and sweet, Pretty and neat;
Combine them with work which she does not shirk.

Senior Class Prophecy

. . . Now cupid is shooting his arrows so keen,
Has Mrs. a lot of the once senior queens,
Pifer, Bixler, Leib have taken vows,
And with their young husbands they're all having rows.

Also noted in the *1924 Echo* was the graduation of Mary Alice Thompson with the Class of 1923 and a notation that she had returned with her own class to take special work before enrolling in college. Mention was also made of Joseph Errigo and Kathryn Kephart who were advancing from the Class of 1925 to graduate with the Class of 1924. Mary Alice, Kathryn, and Joe would continue as friends and play a role in Jessie's later years. Kathryn Kephart would attend Normal School for the summer of 1924, and the following school year Joe would enter a four-year program to study pharmacy, while Mary Alice was being sent first to Linden Hall for a semester and then to Drexel Institute in Philadelphia where she would complete a four-year degree in home economics.

Kate also was told that she had completed the required number of credits to be graduated with this class. However, because she was only sixteen, she chose to return to high school the following year and take two classes, French and math.

Graduation announcements were mailed in early May. Jessie was pleased to recognize the seal heralding the announcement as being the embossed design of their class ring.[32] The design notwithstanding, she had ordered more announcements than she used, forgetting that Mama had cautioned her not to send to anyone who would think that she was soliciting gifts.

Class Night was held on May 29, 1924. This traditional special evening for the class, their families, and their friends, consisted of a program of speeches, music, reading of the Class History and Prophecy, and ending with the Class Will. The Senior Girls Quartette made its usual appearance, and Kay Wrigley reported on the class treasury, noting that any remaining funds after graduation expenses would be donated to the high school. As Kay was also the unofficial class historian and had authored that section of the yearbook, he read the sanctioned published account, but added more detail and humorous anecdotes than had appeared in *The Echo.*

Following the program was a social, which in later years was expanded to a full day with the same kind of program held in the morning, followed by an afternoon of games, a picnic, and a dance—all for class members and senior faculty only. The social for the Class of 1924, limited to three hours, was held at the Legion room in the Dwyer Building, where the after-play party had earlier celebrated the success of the Senior Class Play.

Jessie's first graduation gift was sent to her by Mr. and Mrs. William Shields, Papa's twin sister and her husband. Jessie was pleased with the gift, *The Girl Graduate: Her Own Book.*[33] The book was designed as a keepsake with pages designated for the class flower, motto, yell, prophecy, invitations, and all other memorabilia and minutia surrounding a girl's graduation from high school.

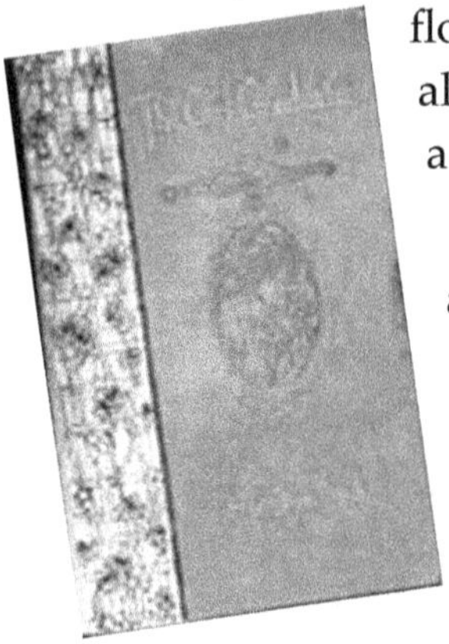

She entered the date she received the book, along with the class flower, colors, and motto; names of teachers; and class officers. She took care to get the autograph of every member of her class. More in typical Jessie fashion, however, the actual saved mementoes are pasted pell-mell throughout the book, with clippings, invitations, paper napkins from special restaurants, programs from plays, and train ticket stubs glued in without written dates, indicative of her lifelong impatience with maintaining orderliness.

While it is likely that she received gifts from her older sisters and her mother's sisters, under the entry for "The Presents" Jessie has listed only two, a wardrobe trunk and a watch, both of which are likely to have come from her parents. Her watch, a gold metal Hamilton, was a treasured possession, as wrist watches were not common especially for persons of little means. Mama had saved for that gift for more than a year, knowing that the following year she would be purchasing one for Kate as well. The trunk, while expensive, was a necessity, since Jessie would need it when she left for Clarion State Normal School in June. Ruby had taken her own wardrobe trunk with her to Ohio and, while Mama had hoped she would offer it for Jessie's use, she had not and with the new baby to care for, Mama rationalized that Ruby could not be expected to think about trunks.

Jessie, like many graduating seniors throughout modern school history, found it difficult to believe that her public school life was coming to a close. Excited at all the attention and eager to begin a new life with college and teaching, she still felt a sense of impending loss at separating from her friends, many of whom she had known since childhood. The term "life passage" would not have occurred to her, but she found herself in the middle of such a one on the morning of June first when it became very clear to her that graduation was real.

Baccalaureate was held first and in two days Jessie would be graduating. She had been fidgety all day and when she tried to remember the lyrics to the song she would be singing at the Commencement Services, she became alarmed. By noon, even Mama asked, "Jessie, what is wrong with you?" Jessie, of course, would admit nothing. Perhaps she would feel better, she thought, once the ceremonies began.

Baccalaureate Services were held that evening in the Presbyterian Church, Jessie's home church, which pleased her because its service was familiar. What she didn't realize is that this was pure chance, as Baccalaureate Services alternated between the Presbyterian and Methodist Churches, the two largest in town. Once the class began its solemn processional, Jessie's fears vanished and she walked in with her classmates, smiling confidently. Jessie's notation in her graduation book under *Baccalaureate Sermon* was typically Jessie: "Everybody feeling great. All seniors present but one. Date with John Wright."

ALMA MATER
FROM "GREAT RED DAWN"
ARR. GERTRUDE ERHARD
Curwensville High School
RIT. A TEMPO
WHERE THE SUSQUEHANNAS SILVER WAT - TERS GLIDE.
THOUGH THROUGH THE PASSING YEARS OUR FEET MAY ROAM,
WHERE GLEAMS NATURES BEAUTY FROM THE MOUN - TAIN SIDE,
FAR FROM THY PORTALS DEAR OLD HIGH SCHOOL HOME,
OUR AL - MA MAT - TER STANDS IN GRAND - EUR FAIR
STILL OFT AT DUSK OUR FANCIES FAIN MAY ROAM
CLAI - MING THE LOVE OF ALL WHO ENTER THERE, HAIL, OH
BACK TO THE SCHOOL WE NE'ER SHALL CEASE TO LOVE,
HAIL, OH CURWENSVILLE HIGH SCHOOL, MAY THY
GREY STONE WALLS HOLD FAST.
LOY AL THOUGHTS OUR MEM' RIES SEND THEE
AS THE DAYS GO FLEET - ING PAST.
WHEN WE SEE THY BANNERS WAVING BLACK AND
GOLD TO THE WINDS FLUNG FREE,
HOW OUR HEARTS LEAP IN FOND RE - MEM -
BRANCE, CUR-WENS-VILLE, DEAR OLD HIGH, FOR THEE

Commencement Exercises were held Tuesday evening, June 3, at eight o'clock in the Strand Theatre. By this time, walking in a procession seemed natural and Jessie was looking forward to the main event, the theatre sure to be filled with parents and friends. Led by the class officers, the Class of 1924 entered to the strains of "Unfinished Symphony" by Shubert, performed by the McKinley Orchestra, well-known in the area. To no one's surprise, the salutatory address was delivered by Joseph Errigo and the valedictory by Dorothy Bixler who had maintained the highest grades for four straight years. There were four orations and music by the Senior Girls Quartette.[34]

Despite their decorum during the processional, many of the graduates could not contain their exuberance following the recessional. Immediately following the ceremony, without even looking at their final report cards which had been distributed with their diplomas, they hurried to the event which marked them as adults—the Annual Alumni Banquet, held immediately following Commencement. The banquet committee used the 1924 class colors in the program, purple paper with gold print, and the menu items reflect the specifics of graduation, such as Commencement Cake. It was also this culminating event which marked the last appearance of the Senior Quartette.[35]

The final event to mark the close of the 1924 school year was the Annual Alumni Public School Picnic, held the following day at Irvin Park. On the way home from the picnic, Jessie turned to Joe and several other classmates who all were in high spirits and declared with great conviction,

"Look out, world. Here we come!"

Chapter 3

The Co-Ed and the Working Girl

Their hearts were young and gay, not realizing they were on the cusp of the greatest time in American history, a time that would change the country like nothing before or since . . .

Jessie could not have fully appreciated that history would consider her and her generation of women as ground-breakers. As she was not one to philosophize about her own life or to reflect upon her place in an historical context, she probably did not realize that she was one of the first females to be both a "co-ed" and, soon after, a "modern working girl." Without being consciously aware of the situation, Jessie was living on the threshold of the greatest time in American history. Behind her was a stable family, which, while not at all wealthy, had provided a secure childhood in which she did not have to leave school, as many of her classmates had done in order to help support their families. She was part of the first generation of middle class Americans, half of whom would complete high school; she had a circle of social friends with personal freedom far beyond what previous generations of women had enjoyed; and her family was not pressing to arrange a marriage or to even suggest she should find a husband. Ahead of her, Jessie had college and freedom to live away from home while attending classes; a job to give her a measure of financial independence; and the opportunity, in time, to choose marriage or remain single.

Living at home while she was working would, of course, be expected, for single women did not live alone; however, she would still have her own bedroom and, with any kind of luck, in time, maybe even an automobile. Jessie thought she had most everything she could want.

Many people say they were born ten years too early, or in the wrong century, or in the wrong place, but Jessie clearly fit the 1920s profile of "Recent Social Trends" (1932) which documented the "wholly unparalleled democratization through the nineteen-twenties of aspects of American life: of education, with a vast multiplication of coed colleges; of transport, long an index of aristocracy, but now available to the masses with the Model T and its successors; of dress and fashion, an obliterator of traditional marks of class . . .; of recreation, through the movies, the radio and the park systems; and of the marketplace."[1] Jessie would be taking her place in a democracy in which one person's dollars were as good as another's.

During the 1920s, educational spending increased markedly at all levels and historians noted this trend as the largest mass education drive in human history. The number of new university and college buildings increased and new educational equipment, such as laboratories, libraries, gymnasiums, and athletic fields, were added. Many communities also took on expansions to accommodate the increased number of those completing high school.

While Jessie and her schoolmates had just missed the local building boom of 1925 when the Locust Street Building was expanded by eight rooms and a gymnasium was fashioned out of its basement, they had watched with curiosity when part of the basement of the high school was excavated in 1922 to create new classroom space. The high school had had a football team since 1912 and played its games in the area known as the football playing lot and the Riverside baseball field. As there was no yearbook annual until 1922, sports records are not readily available; however, the fact that playing fields were maintained is evidence of community interest in a town with a population of only 3,200.

The greatest bottleneck in American education, however, was teachers' salaries, which had risen during the war less rapidly than had prices. The most obvious result was that many men left the public high school classrooms, with the exception of a few devoted souls and those holding such specialized jobs as athletic coach, teacher of woodwork, or principal. As more women sought a college education and job opportunities, salaries in areas women entered began to stagnate and a trend began which continues even today: when women become predominate in an occupation, pay increases do not occur, and men leave that line of work. Even so, many young women found teaching an appropriate and safe occupation and families encouraged their daughters to become teachers.

As young people found more educational opportunity they also experienced more freedom. Co-ed education provided situations in which young men and women learned to be more comfortable in one another's company, and women became more confident of both their academic ability and their independent status. This comfort between the sexes also led to their becoming more open in displaying their new-found self-governance, shocking adults with the close embraces of the modern dances and the promiscuous physical contacts of "necking." Parents especially were horrified at what they viewed as indecorous parties and were appalled at the extent of gate crashing, an action unheard of by previous generations. Further, adults recoiled at the free conversation about sex. Many wondered if the younger generation was obsessed by the subject, as its members openly discussed the ideas of Sigmund Freud and devoured the current confession magazines, sex-filled movies, and books filled with sexual passion.

Silk stockings, high-heeled shoes, permanent waves, and one-piece bathing suits—all were becoming standard among young women everywhere as an emerging fashion industry made it easier for social classes to resemble one another. This leveling encouraged women to believe in equal opportunity.

Jessie's idea of equal opportunity was, for the present, limited to attending college and being able to do what other young people were doing. She likely didn't fully appreciate the additional freedom afforded her in being permitted to attend Clarion—a state-supported school, rather than the more traditional Grove City, the college her mother had selected for the two older girls. Like most young people, and beginning with her generation, she took all privileges for granted.

The Clarion State Normal School catalogue listing of faculty reflects that many held only a bachelor's degree and some had no college degree; its Summer Session for teachers was overseen by a local school superintendent. The catalogue is replete with photographs of dormitory rooms—which by today's standards would be considered austere but to women like Jessie they were luxurious.

Not surprising, none of the history, geography, or organizational structure of Clarion mattered to Jessie Beverly Pifer, member of the Freshman Class at Clarion State Normal School in the summer of 1924. What was important was that she was, with all that implied, a college student. Jessie was as excited thinking about being on campus and living in a dorm as was her friend, Mary Alice Thompson, who was leaving in August for Linden Hall in Lititz where she would spend a semester before enrolling at Drexel Institute in far-off Philadelphia.

Jessie had been packing her wardrobe trunk for weeks, long before graduation and she had the house in an uproar. The trunk was prominently displayed—in an open position—in the front room, as there was no space in Jessie's bedroom to accommodate the trunk as well as the items to be packed in it. Mama was a tad annoyed, but had to agree with Jessie that there really was not a place for anything of that size in any other room in the house. Mama could not recall how Josephine and Ruby had managed to pack their belongings, but she distinctly remembered that they had not set up a packing station in the living room.

Jessie had been saving tissue paper for padding her clothes at least since Christmas of her junior year in high school. Of course, not all of it had been saved in one locale; rather, there were sheets and pieces of sheets of tissue paper in the upstairs hall cabinets, in the attic, in the dining room sideboard, in a box under Jessie's bed, and even under the cushion of the easy chair in the dining room. Jessie had read or heard from older friends that in packing, dresses should be filled with tissue paper as if they were being worn. By the time she had come to preparing the third dress, however, she lost patience. "Mama," she wailed, "do you think it really matters about using the tissue paper? Look how much time this is taking. And if I wrap everything like this, it won't all fit in the trunk!" Her eyes filled with tears of exasperation. "Why don't you ask Kate to help you," Mama offered. Fearing Kate would notice that she had packed some items jointly owned and used by Kate, Jean, and herself, Jessie resisted the offer of assistance. "I'll finish it tomorrow," she hastily replied.

Finally, everything was packed and hauled to the Pennsylvania Railroad passenger and freight station. Mama had arranged for the trunk to be transported by a drayman. There at the station, Jessie and her trunk, along with another piece of luggage—a canvas bag that had belonged to a friend of her mother's—waited on Monday morning, June 16, 1924. Jessie stood, with ticket in hand, anticipating a great adventure. Kate and Jean had accompanied her to the station, even though Jessie had expressed that this gesture was not necessary. She didn't want to be seen as part of a family group. She would change trains in Clearfield, taking the Franklin and Clearfield branch of the New York Central Lines to DuBois, and then to Clarion. Jessie Pifer at eighteen could hardly wait to board and looked forward in eager anticipation for the first person to inquire of her destination.

At the Clarion depot Jessie was met by a porter who transported the trunk to the women's dormitory. Clutching the Summer Session calendar in her hand, Jessie was filled with excitement and bravado. She knew no one, but her naturally gregarious personality soon assumed her grand dame hostess role in greeting all the later arrivals. By the end of the day most of the young women had arrived in the dormitory and friendships immediately began to form. The following day classes were organized and an orientation was held for the largest summer class (to that date) ever to attend Clarion's Summer Session for teachers.

Following a get-acquainted luncheon, a group of girls on Jessie's floor decided to explore the campus and the town. While too naïve to realize that the town of Clarion was quite accustomed to having new college students, this band of co-eds tried to act as if they had always been part of the college scene. Their stopping to buy postcards at Corbett's Drugs and Stationery and posing for photos, however, was a sure sign to everyone that these shoppers were freshmen. Congregated and giggling on the front steps of the County Courthouse, the girls were approached by a group of Clarion High School students, carrying their class pennant announcing "CHS 1925." One of the girls in the college group lived in Clarion and provided introductions. As expected, Jessie immediately caught the eye of the handsome president of the Clarion High School Class of 1925 and son of a prominent town family.

William L. Fowler was self-assured, a letterman in football, basketball, and track, and was about to lead his class for the third time as its chief officer. Bill would become the first of many in Clarion smitten by Jessie Pifer, but he remained one of her long-time favorites, one she would continue to date for several years to come, and who loaned her his high school yearbook (which, characteristically, she never got around to returning).

The following day after the exploration of Clarion and on her way back to the dormitory, Jessie was hailed by one of the other young men who had been with the local crowd the day before. "Hello!" he said. "I just happened to be running an errand and thought I might run into you. I'm John Ditz, in case you don't remember all our names from yesterday." "I remember," Jessie replied. "You are the one who has the car with the odd name." John laughed. "Would you like to go for a ride some day in that car?" Jessie said she would think about it, as she wasn't sure she knew him well enough to ride in his car. The following year she would remember this conversation as she read his profile in Clarion High School's 1925 yearbook: "Ditz is the 'Sheik' of our class. His car, the Chalmers, is the envy of every boy, and it is the ambition of every girl to claim a ride."

Jessie's dorm mates were awed. She hadn't been in town two days yet, and already the two most eligible boys in the senior class at Clarion High School were vying for her attention. Before the summer was over, Bill and John would have come nearly to blows over the affections of Jessie Pifer. After one particularly harsh argument, strong words were exchanged and John called Bill by a pejorative term. He immediately regretted it, as Bill and he had been best friends since childhood. John wrote a hasty note of apology on the back of an order sheet from the Clarion

Dry Cleaning Company and sent it to Bill through a mutual friend. Bill later gave the note to Jessie:

Dear Bill, Please forgive me for calling you that, not that I want to apologize for taking the liberty to do so. John Ditz.

Back at the dormitory her second day in Clarion, Jessie looked over the post cards she had purchased, remembering she had promised to send a post card to Mama to tell her she had arrived safely and was settled in her room. Unabashed at her own forgetfulness, she wrote a quick note and set the card aside to mail the next day. There wasn't time to go to the post office, if she wanted to be fully prepared for the social planned for that evening. Having noted months ago that the CSNS colors of purple and gold were the same as her own class colors, she had borrowed a scarf in those colors from a high school friend. For her first college social, Jessie donned a black dress, knotted the scarf around her neck, and strutted down the hall, confident that she would be an attention-getter.

The following day Jessie paid the $60 fee with a cashier's check she had brought for that purpose and kept the receipt for Mama. She also filled in her schedule and was issued her Summer Session student ID card.[2] A photo of the class was taken, and that photo remains, details still crisp, revealing a group of eager young people standing at the launching of their adult life.

Born for the life of a fun-loving coed, Jessie relished being a trend setter, even though it was only on a small college campus, little known except by those in the surrounding counties. Like most who attended Clarion State, Jessie had a very limited wardrobe, but unlike most of her contemporaries, she had a flair for accessories, both bought and found objects. None of the Pifer girls were skilled at sewing, a fact most people were surprised to learn since their mother had made most of their clothing when they were children. While Jessie could not stitch anything more than a bunch of flowers onto a belt, she made up for this lack of skill by ingenuity. If a piece of costume jewelry broke she would take the remaining part and glue it on a hat or belt or coat. She was also known to simply wear the jewelry piece, missing stones or not.

The *bon mot* was her métier. She had a keen eye and ear for current and trendy words, especially for slang, and she enjoyed watching people's reactions to her use of the language. Not a strong academic student despite a keen intellect, she found her quips kept her in center stage. "Neat" is one of the many slang terms she introduced to her friends who had known the word only as meaning "tidy."

The Summer Term students were kept busy with a full schedule, including the required assembly every morning. Jessie and other first year students found themselves taking basic courses such as English Fundamentals, Health I, Primary Methods, and School Efficiency.[3] A simulation letter she wrote for a class was a contract to teach at Keewaydin Primary School. The teacher's comment on her work is "Good, although probably the time would be given." Jessie promptly rewrote the letter, including the time of the opening and the closing of school. Another assigned exercise was an invitation to a dinner guest. These she saved, along with a sample of an exercise in printing (rather than cursive writing) in which she received a "Fair." (Her handwriting was beautiful, so much so that it seemed almost a shame to expect her to also print well.)

Also remaining from that first year at Clarion is a composition book with a sparse variety of notes on design; how to hang pictures, complete with handwritten diagrams; basic notes on the Renaissance, similar to what today's junior high student would write; building a doll house stage set, complete with dimensions; a list of commercial firms for art supplies (including the well-known "Vinney [sic][4] and Smith," makers of Crayola Crayons);

Jebbie with Schoolmate

a list of reference books for art; styles of alphabets and letters; a listing of recommended art equipment; a description of scissors, noting to use blunt ended ones in primary grades; and uses of clay which included the notation of "use natural clay found in the neighborhood."[5]

Not every minute at CSNS was spent in classes, however, even though the summer program was intended to be compressed and intense. Jessie was popular with everyone, as the *Girl Graduate* book she had taken with her to Clarion reveals. She and her friends had many good times, some recorded through mementos and annotations, others only implied. Jessie, like countless others before and since, kept such souvenirs as a paper napkin with the date, June 23, 1924, and signatures of Lula, Audrey, and Jebbie.

Jessie did the required work, but did not agonize over the material many were trying to memorize. True to the prevailing attitude of the time which was that only the equivalent of one year of teaching methods was needed to teach elementary school because teaching at that level was considered to be simple,[6] Jessie was fully confident that she could teach in an elementary school, based solely on the premise that she had completed public school. "What could be so difficult teaching material we already know?" she asked her friends who were more diligent in their studies than she. "I certainly can teach from any books the township schools have." Earning good grades was not a priority when one was as confident in one's own ability as was Jessie Pifer.

To the credit of the institution, Clarion did provide activities and events to "round out" the college experience for its Summer Term students. Jessie took full advantage of these offerings, immersing herself in all cultural events and leading a very full social life, both on campus and off. While not all of the activities in which she likely participated are recorded, near the end of the term Jessie attended the Second Annual Recital by Nathan Aaron, Violinist, assisted by Nancy Canan, Pianiste.[7] This recital evidently was one of campus prominence, as it boasted its own printed program, complete with program notes, an event special enough to find itself memorialized in Jessie's *Girl Graduate* book. [8]

Three days later, on a Friday, Joe Errigo, along with his friend Wayne Holton, drove from Curwensville to Clarion for a double date with Jessie and her roommate. Such a visit created quite a stir in the dormitory, as Jessie intended to ride back to Curwensville, unchaperoned, late at night with the two young men, to spend the week-end at home. It was nearly a scandal, as Jessie did not have written permission from her parents to leave campus and travel with the young men. When she returned to the dormitory around nine o'clock to pack and realized that she might forfeit her entire summer's work and be expelled for leaving with these two friends, she decided the trip home was not worth the risk. Jessie knew she was perfectly safe with Joe who had been her best pal and protector for many years. He agreed, however, that it would be better for her to stay on campus. Jessie recorded this adventure under "Jokes and Frolics," rather than in the section for "Dating"[9] in her *Girl Graduate* memory book.

This interruption of plans did not, however, deter her the following week from going home by train to attend a swimming party on August 13 and the Clearfield County Annual Picnic the following day. She returned to Clarion on the evening train in order to be present for a review for exams the next day. Classes ended on Saturday following exams, but the students were expected to remain for the Exhibition of Summer Health Classes on August 18. Most students did not leave for home until the day following the exhibition, giving them two weeks free or to prepare before they began their first terms as teachers.

During this time Jessie experienced two milestones: receiving her teaching assignment for the 1924-25 school year and opening her own bank account. The new Curwensville State Bank had opened for business on August 9, welcoming between three and four thousand visitors. With initial cash deposits exceeding $100,000, this modern bank was attractive to new customers. Even though her parents thought she should open her account at the National Bank, Jessie liked the idea that she personally knew the president of the bank, H. J. Thompson, father of her friends Howard, Jr. and Mary Alice.

Holding her first Teacher's Contract made Jessie feel very grown up. The contract assigned her to "teach in Fairview for 8 months, at $85 per school month, to be paid monthly; . . . reserving the right to the Board of Directors for the time being to dismiss the said teacher at any time whatever, for any of the causes specified in the 1208th section of the Act of May 18th, 1911… ."[10]

Jessie would board at the homes of members of the school board, depending upon who had room for the schoolmarm. This arrangement was typical for the township and rural schools, even though Irishtown (location of the Fairview School) was not more than four or five miles from Curwensville. There was no public transportation and certainly Jessie had no car. A few of her friends were lucky to have schools that were close to a train stop and, if the schedule worked in their favor, they could live at home and take the daily train.

Jessie was nineteen years old and weighed 110 pounds when she began her first year of teaching, a career that would continue for more than forty years. Her school was a one-room, barn-like building "in the middle of nowhere," as she described it to her friends. There was no paved road, as the school was perched on a knoll near the edge of a farmer's field. The only access was to follow the path that had been worn into the field for the past thirty years. The clay-like ground was always either a sea of mud because of rain or dusty from lack of it. Two small buildings were located near the school house, one for coal and the other an outhouse. A tiny porch served as the entrance to the school and atop the structure was a bell whose rope hung down just inside the door.

Also inside the door was an offset with a shelf for lunch pails and hooks from which to hang coats. Jessie called this the cloak room based on her own experience with larger rooms in the town schools for this purpose. In the back corner of the room stood a pot-bellied stove, which did not always radiate enough heat to warm the room. On very cold days, Jessie would sit by the stove and have the children gather round to keep warm even though they would become scorched on one side and remain chilled on the other.

On each side of the room was a row of windows to admit light; there was no electricity, so on days when it was very dark, reading was difficult. In addition to the lack of electricity, the one-room school house had no running water. Worse, there was no well either, so water had to be brought from the farmer's well across the field. Jessie minded this most of all.

With all eight grades in one room, sometimes grades were combined for their lessons. A teacher had to rely on older or more advanced students assisting the younger ones, as he or she could not possibly teach every subject in every grade for the time needed for each subject. Jessie's counterparts in town considered themselves lucky to have only one or two grades, even though there were as many as 50 students in some of their classrooms.

Jessie needed to muster all of her authority, theatrical skills, and bluffing techniques to keep order day after day, especially since some of the students were taller—and, she suspected, older—than she was. She had to handle all discipline problems, as she was the sole adult in charge of 35-40 children of various ages and varying abilities. Most of them were respectful of her position, and all knew that if they were disciplined in school, they would face additional punishment at home. Jessie began developing what her family later would call her "teacher tone," a kind of authoritative assurance. This worked most of the time with her students, and only occasionally would she have to resort to paddling. By the end of October, there was no doubt just who was in charge: Miss Pifer had arrived.

And so, in a manner of speaking, had Mrs. Pifer. By November of 1924 Matilda Pifer had spent four years garnering the courage to go to the polls, fearful that she might not fill out the ballot correctly. In that time she became weary of hearing John fuss about women voting, "Women are so easily flattered. Wives will vote just the way their husbands tell them to and daughters will follow their fathers' orders. So what is the point in their voting?" Other times in exasperation he would exclaim to Matilda, "If you would vote for the opposing candidate, it will only serve to cancel out my vote." At first these explanations sounded reasonable to Matilda, but as she thought about his words she saw the flaws in his argument.

On the morning of the national presidential election of 1924, she dressed in her second best dress, pinned her hat firmly to her hair, donned her coat and gloves, and walked a short block to the polling place. Somewhat nervous, she was determined to see this through. She had not told Jessie, who had been coaxing her mother to vote and could hardly wait to reach the age of 21 herself, as Mama was fearful that she might change her mind.

At the polling station, she was greeted by the Democratic Party representative who showed her a sample ballot. She nodded her understanding, and walked directly to the booth where she placed an "X" beside the name of John W. Davis. "Well," she thought, "that wasn't so difficult." When Jessie came home at the end of the week, her mother casually mentioned the election and Jessie replied, "Mama, I am proud of you." Although only 52 percent of registered voters had voted in this election Matilda Pifer was justly pleased that she was one of them.

Schools typically closed for two weeks at Christmas, beginning December 20 at which time the teachers were required to attend Teachers' Institute, a three-day, county-wide series of meetings held in the county seat. Jessie and some of her classmates from Clarion had been looking forward to seeing one another, making plans to get together during the holiday, and comparing experiences as new teachers. And all were relieved to have a few days break from the students.

Christmas 1924 was different for Jessie, as for the first time she had money of her own. After contributing to the household, Jessie still had money to buy some of the clothes she had wanted. Disappointingly, however, there still was not enough to buy the raccoon coat for which she longed. That first Christmas as a working girl she was generous with Kate and Jean, paying for half of the cost of Kate's class ring and buying a coat for Jean. Mama was pleased with her brood, now nearly all of them adults, with Ruby and Josephine married, Jessie employed, Kate in her senior year, and Margaret Jean a freshman.

Sixteen-year-old Kate was still timid but she had developed several close friendships that had originated in her first year of high school when six girls had formed a secret club. They had taken a vow that none of their members would ever reveal what the initials of the TDS Club represented.

Intuitively intelligent, Kate always said she had lacked the confidence to reach her full potential (although it must be remembered how limited opportunities were in a small town, isolated from many cultural events). Even her modest wardrobe reflected her conservative style. In a snapshot of Kathryn Kephart and Kate, taken during their junior year, shortly before Kathryn's early graduation, Kate is wearing a dress unadorned, dropping slightly gathered from the shoulders, obviously homemade, while Kathryn's dress is very full with four wide ruffles circling the skirt, obviously store-bought. In her own handwriting on the back of the photo, Kate had written the names of the two best friends.

Kate was still very young to be a senior in high school, and she was barely seventeen at her graduation in May 1925. Her senior portrait reveals a shy young woman, with short hair and a very simple, long-sleeved shift, probably made by her mother on her treadle sewing machine. Kate's thick brunette bob (not frizzed with a curling iron like Jessie's) is held in check with a plain barrette, and she is wearing the same pearl necklace earlier seen in Jessie's senior portrait. Later, Margaret Jean's graduation portrait in the Class of 1927 (Jean entered the fall of 1926 with standing as a senior) would show a bashful, smiling young woman in a hand-detailed, two-toned shirtwaist dress with small decorative buttons. Her hair, like Kate's, is cut short but not bobbed and she wears no jewelry.

By the end of 1924 it was estimated that there were 25 million new cars on the road and 50 million telephone conversations a day in the United States, although the Pifer family was not among those with either cars or telephones. Jessie dreamed of having a car, but it was completely out of the realm of possibility at that time. She had, however, started her campaign for Papa to consider installing a telephone. Jessie had hoped to convince her father by Christmas that having a telephone would be good for his business, but she had been unsuccessful.

Following the Christmas holiday Jessie resumed her life as a rural school teacher, returning home on week-ends, where the only single bedroom in the house was still kept for her (Kate and Jean now sharing the room once occupied by Josephine and Ruby). The winters were long and cold, and the first Friday in February, the weather was so bad that Jessie could not find a ride home from Irishtown to Curwensville for the week-end. She would miss the special birthday dinner Mama would be preparing on Sunday in honor of the joint birthday anniversary of Kate who would be seventeen and Jean who would celebrate her fifteenth birthday on Wednesday, February 11.

Because Jessie did not have a great interest in reading and did not sew, the time she had to remain at the school director's home on week-ends was interminably slow in passing. She spent most of that February week-end at a table in the parlor of her hosts, correcting papers, preparing Valentine's Day and Easter art projects for the students, and trying to avoid prying questions from the school director's wife. Mama had always impressed upon the girls to "not tell your business," and Jessie was beginning to appreciate the wisdom of that advice.

At the same time Jessie was designing simple hearts and messages for her students to make valentines for their families, Clarion's John Ditz, one of her constant stream of suitors, was purchasing a box of candy and a card to present to Miss Jessie Pifer. The following week-end was Valentine's Day and he and Jessie were looking forward to an evening together. While Jessie was not wild about John, she anticipated their time together as much preferable to cutting out red hearts and white rabbits while sitting in the company of an inquisitive wife.

Fortunately the weather broke and the following Friday Jessie had her borrowed canvas suitcase by the door of the school, barely able to wait until her ride would meet her at the end of the school lane. She had never been so eager to get home, not because of John but because she believed she could not spend another hour in Irishtown or the Fairview school. "Fairview, indeed," she thought. "The school barely has any view, let alone one that is fair." The first thing she did upon returning home was to take a long, leisurely bath, something she had not been able to do for two weeks. She silently thanked Mama for this luxury she had had the foresight—and her savings—to install following the Great War.

As arranged, John Ditz arrived at seven, candy and card in hand. The valentine was unusually beautiful in an understated way. It was soft pink in tone, the cover at least an 80 lb. card stock, the inner sheet of complementary quality, and the envelope lined in silver embossed foil. A pink ribbon threaded through and held the inside sheet to the cover, and the message, spare in language and subtle in expression, was underscored by the handwritten closing, "I love you. John."[11]

The following day Jessie helped Mama ice the birthday cake. Their Aunt Jessie had sent birthday postcards to both Kate and Jean, although only the one to Jean remains because Jessie had borrowed it from her to copy the verse and neglected to return it. More important to Kate, however, was the Valentine she received from Bubby. She kept it among her few mementoes:

If I could find a garden
Where all the Sweethearts grew
I'd look 'em over – every one,
And then I'd just pick you.[12]

Just as he had done for Jessie the year before, Professor Grant Norris wrote a verification and recommendation, dated March 6, 1925, for graduating senior Katherine Pifer about whom he said,

The Co-Ed and the Working Girl

. . . Miss Pifer could have graduated last year, but she preferred to stay in school another year and perfect herself in her academic course. Her marks are comparatively high and she has always maintained the confidence and appreciation of her teachers. She is a young lady of promise whose scholastic attainments, Christian life, amiable disposition, and good moral character, all recommend her to any home and community. . . .[13]

On Saturdays and some days after school Kate worked at Sheridan's Sweet Shoppe, often referred to as the Sweet Shoppe, located in the newly constructed Odd Fellows Building, easily identifiable by the brickwork spelling out in five foot high letters "IOOF." Only a short walk from the Pifer home, the Sweet Shoppe was the closest thing to a meeting place that the young people had, although they usually just stopped by to purchase a drink or ice cream, as few were allowed by their parents to linger.

Jessie's interests no longer centered around her high school, except in instances where she could give advice, whether or not it was asked for, to her two younger sisters. She had tried to impress upon both of them the importance of joining the Literary Society. Dutifully, Kate signed on, later confessing that she was terrified of reciting and had joined the organization only because there were so few activities in which to participate. One can only imagine her stage fright, tempered by her pluck to fulfill her commitment, when she delivered her oratory.

Jessie was full of advice for Kate on how to produce a yearbook since she herself had spent a few minutes on her assigned pages in the *1924 Echo*. Kate had been made editor of the Humor Section and was sure she had been assigned this post only because Jessie had been one of the two humor editors the previous year. Kate always maintained that she was not one for jokes and had no repertoire of canned humor. Others did, however, and the tradition of jokes continued until yearbook staffs in the mid-1940s finally realized that jokes become dated much more quickly than photographs. Jessie also advised Kate to make sure she wrote her own senior profile if she wanted it to be correct. Kate, of course, would never ask and, just as Jessie had predicted, Kate's senior profile was not accurate.

The class prophecy for the 1925 graduates was written more to flatter its writer than its readers, with no attempt to acknowledge possible future accomplishments by classmates. The activities section of the book further reveals the lack of understanding that a yearbook should put its graduating class in a positive light. It begins with "...the social events of the Class have not been as numerous as of some of the previous classes" and continues in the same vein: "... Our only social activity during our Junior Year was a banquet. ...Thus far into our Senior Year we have not had any social activities, but before the year is completed we are sure our class will have enjoyed many activities such as dances, socials, banquets, etc."[14] Even Kate said, "Jessie, our class needed you to liven things up!"

A tone of apology continues in the description of the 1924 football season of six wins, four losses. Since the wins included three shut-outs, including one game in which Curwensville scored 53 points to their opponent's scoreless showing and, in fact, members of the Curwensville team were loaned to their opponents to complete that game, it is surprising that the article is so negative. The entire account bears repeating for its harshness, but the following provides its flavor:

> "Almost from the beginning the team was handicapped by injuries, misfortune, and all the bad luck that ever falls to the lot of a football team.
>
> "The season opened with a game designed to show the merits and weakness of the team rather than to boost Curwensville's first football record. In a game filled with mistakes and fumbles.... [Yet the score was Curwensville – 33; Falls Creek – 0].

> "... followed a series of four games all of which showed clearly the weakness of the line.
>
> "Toward the end of the season outside influences did much to break the morale of the already weakened team.
>
> "In the final game of the season, team morale broke entirely and our ancient enemies from down the river were able to top off the year with a wonderful victory." [Astonishing that a win by arch enemy, the larger town of Clearfield, would be described as "wonderful."]

Jessie encouraged both of her younger sisters to become involved in their class plays, although that advice was moot since nearly every member of the small classes was needed to fill the roles. Therefore, even with her shyness and professed aversion for being on stage, Kate played the role of Miss Dollie DeCliffe in the Senior Class Play, "Aaron Boggs, Freshman."

At her graduation held in the Strand Theatre on Thursday evening, May 28, Kate tried not to be perturbed at the misspelling of her name in the program. Instead, she focused on remembering this final time her class would be together, keeping her tears in check as she sang with the Senior Quartette. Baccalaureate had been held the previous Sunday and the Annual Senior/Alumni Banquet was celebrated at the conclusion of the Commencement Program. The following Friday, May 29, the Alumni Public School Picnic was held at Irvin Park. Jessie, of course, made as large an entrance as one could at a picnic, asking all within range of her voice, "Where is the section for the young alumni?"

Two weeks later on Sunday June 14, Jessie, Kate, and Jean attended the Flag Day celebration and the dedication of the newly installed War Memorial "to veterans of all wars." A memorial tablet on the stone pedestal lists the names of 203 veterans of what now was being called the World War. Because of a broad fund-raising campaign, the whole town felt ownership in the project.

The following week Kate went to stay with Josephine while attending teacher training courses at the Pennsylvania State College's branch campus in Altoona, because she was not one to venture into the unknown by living on a college campus. She wanted the safety and familiarity of family. Josephine, nearly 30 years of age, was pleased to have her little sister live with her since her husband Droz frequently was away on business. Kate usually went home by train on the week-ends, likely to see Bubby who was working for his father's water company in Curwensville. This was made easy by Mama's suggestion to give Josephine and her husband privacy and time together when he returned on Friday evenings.

Jessie, on the other hand, could hardly wait to return to Clarion and was relieved when her sister chose not to attend the same college. As a returning collegian Jessie was even more confident, and she made it known to all that she was a second year student and an experienced teacher. She had packed hurriedly, with little of the elaboration demonstrated in her trunk stuffing of the previous year. Upon her arrival she went directly to the women's dormitory. Luxuriating in her surroundings, she quickly crafted a card to tape on her dormitory room door: Jebbie B. Pifer, 148 Becht Hall. She wanted all to know that she had arrived.

Her student ID card declared it was "certifying that Miss Jessie Pifer has satisfied all the requirements for registration."[15] Newly added to the information distributed to all students was a booklet, *Songs of Clarion, 1925*. This provided the lyrics to school pep songs, including these specific to Clarion State Normal School: "The Purple and the Gold," and "Western Pennsy S.N.S."[16]

In late June Jessie received a post card from East View Grove Park Inn in Asheville, North Carolina. The message, dated June 27, 1925, asks her to "write to an old friend" and is signed "Bill." The handwriting suggests that this is Bill Fowler, who recently had been graduated from Clarion High School and had started to work in his father's company. He told Jessie that he had stayed in Clarion that summer because he didn't want to lose her to any of the "new men on campus" at Clarion, even though he was slated to enter the University of Pennsylvania in Philadelphia in September. Jessie fully intended to keep Bill's interest, but not to the point of spoiling dates with any other young men. Nearly twenty, Jessie was in no hurry to settle on only one "fella" (another of her favorite new slang words), especially one at a distance.

While Jessie had earned an "A" in her bluebook exam on July 13, her term report grades issued on August 22 averaged "C." Good grades evidently still were not a priority for her, as she went home on August 13 for the Clearfield County Sunday School Field Day.

On August 24, after returning home from the Summer Term, Jessie received a letter from Albert Heston, written on August 20 in Coalport, Pennsylvania but mailed from Augusta, Ohio on August 22 with a return address of Mechanicsville, Iowa:

> *Dear Miss Pifer, I can't remember of ever being so disappointed as last night when you couldn't go out with me. Generally "blind dates" are—well, you can imagine how I, a perfect stranger, would naturally feel toward them. But here, in Pa. blind dates[17] are always good. Just seems all of my friends here have plenty of wonderful girls on whom they can pass off the western friend. So after seeing you last night in the light of a date and later finding you were unable to go, the evening was ruined.*
>
> *However, if next year I do get back in the area do you suppose we can arrange a date for at least one night? Perhaps I might at least hope so.*
>
> *Sincerely, Albert Heston, Jr., Mechanicsville, Iowa.*

It may have been this letter that led Papa to forbid Jessie from dating traveling salesmen. A family story relates an incident in which Papa would not allow Jessie to leave the house on a date, saying, "They are all the same and I forbid it! I won't have you going out with any horse thieves!"

On the same day, John Ditz (Clarion sender of the pink valentine) was writing from the Hotel Statler in Cleveland,

Dear Jessie, Saw a ballgame yesterday and a rather risqué musical comedy called "Little Jesse James." Things aren't going too well. I'm in a bad humor and Dad and I have been arguing right and left. This is a terrible city to drive in due to the extremely large traffic and poor system of management, and also to the fact that people cross the street just wherever and whenever they feel like it. Sorry that I couldn't take you home yesterday; however, I will probably get over next week to see you. We are going home Friday. Be good and don't flirt too much with other fellows.

As ever, John

Jessie apparently responded (a chore she did not always relish) and ten days later John wrote again,

Well, I guess Shef and I are going to the races, anyways we have ordered our tickets. If we do go, we will stop to see you of course. Shef says to date you and your sister up for that night; however, I will write again this week and let you know for sure. Kindly write soon. As ever yours, John

Jessie received this letter late in the day, as she had been attending a Teachers' Institute in Clearfield that continued into the evening. The Institutes had moved that year from the December dates to August, in advance of the opening of school, a time much more palatable than Christmas week. Jessie was beginning to look upon John as a good friend rather than a romantic interest, and liked his suggestion of a double date.

Labor Day saw another community event at Irvin Park with family picnics, local musical groups, games, and fellowship. Children as well as teachers took a lot of good-natured kidding about school opening the following day. That evening, Jessie had a date with John Ditz and the next morning she headed out to her new school in Hepburnia. She felt light-hearted because she had found a ride from Curwensville to within walking distance of the school and would not have to board with any of the school directors. She looked forward to having more freedom by not being cooped up every evening in a director's home.

During the 1920s, college football attained glory, and stadiums began to dominate the campuses. Clarion State fielded a team and found itself with the beginnings of a sports industry. The outdoor game of football attracted larger crowds than a basketball gymnasium could hold and colleges began to build their football programs by erecting large stadiums with parking lots. Another factor increasing the popularity of college and professional football was the phenomenal Red Grange, born in Sullivan County, Pennsylvania and considered the greatest college football player of all time.

Jessie sought opportunities to attend games at what she now called her Alma Mater, even though Clarion State, fifty miles west of Curwensville, was still "small potatoes" (an older slang term Jessie revived) compared to nearby Penn State College, the same distance to the southeast. She sometimes found a group to travel with and could hardly wait to show off her new wardrobe, especially the brand new possum coat she was buying on the payment plan. How she loved that coat and herself in it. She hadn't had it a week before she arranged to have her photo taken wearing the coat, her hair bobbed stylishly, and her lips painted in the current, provocative "bee stung" style. She did not show the portrait to Mama until much later and decided not to show it to Papa at all.

The fall of 1925 found only one daughter still attending public school. Jean was entering her sophomore year, as Mama had held her at home an extra year after seeing how difficult it had been for Katherine as a five-year-old first grader. She was glad that Kate remained at home, her closest friend, sister, and birthday mate.

Since Kate had begun school at an early age, she now found herself a teacher at seventeen, feeling relieved that she had not been graduated a year earlier, as Professor Norris had suggested. Her first school was Driftwood, a rural area near the Susquehanna Bridge at Hogback. Just as Jessie in her first year of teaching, Kate boarded with a family during the week. The bedrooms were not heated, the lighting was by oil lamps, there was no indoor plumbing, and everyone went to bed very early. This was not a very pleasant situation compared to teaching in a town and living at home, positions typically earned after many years in the country schools. Kate's students became fond of the shy and gentle "Miss Pifer." Kate noted that while often the boys in eighth grade were much taller than she was, they were kind and respectful.

As a letter dated September 8 reveals, Jessie continued her friendship with John Ditz. His personal stationery was as fine in quality as the valentine had been—deckled, monogrammed, and of good weight. He wrote:

A Couple of "Fellas"

> *It does seem odd to be writing after seeing you last night, but I'm in an awful humor. I could eat snakes alive tonight. ... Didn't do anything tonight except hang around. Been listening to the radio ... a fine orchestra at the Mayflower in Washington. Just finished reading a couple of stories in the* Saturday Evening Post.
>
> *I'd like a date for some night soon with you. I think the coming Sunday night would suit me fine. Would any other night suit you better? Bill [Fowler] has another job now. He is working for the gas company helping to lay the new lines.*

The surprise here is that Bill Fowler did not go to the University of Pennsylvania as planned; rather, he found he preferred employment, and his parents could not dissuade him. Jessie still saw him occasionally, but not as a serious suitor.

On September 17 Jessie heard from (F. X.) "Terry" McGovern. From Sinnemahoning, Pennsylvania, he wrote,

Dear Jessie: I certainly was sorry that I couldn't see you during my stay in Curwensville a few months ago, more especially since I wanted to extend my birthday greetings in person. I didn't send you a card on July 9th for I imagined you were in school, but I was wishing you a happy birthday anyway. If you have no further use for a hand book on chemistry that I gave you, and if you can find it, may I have it? If you use it at all, don't hesitate to keep it, but if you don't need it why it would come in handy to me. [As casual as Jessie sometimes was, he probably never got his book back.]

John Ditz also sent her a letter on the September 17,

Well, things look as if we would be over Friday night. If anything turns up to hinder us, I'll call you Friday morning. Bill Fowler is coming along.

The fall term couldn't go fast enough for Jessie. She could barely contain her excitement at the invitation she had recently received to spend the entire Thanksgiving vacation in Philadelphia. Jessie didn't even know anyone in Philadelphia, but she had been corresponding with her friend, Mary Jane Thomas from Clarion, whose brother attended the University of Pennsylvania and, as luck would have it where Jessie was involved, the brother had met Jessie in early August. Like almost every other young man who ever met her, George L. Thomas liked what he saw. He had convinced his sister that she and her friend Jessie should come visit him at Penn over the Thanksgiving vacation.

Mary Jane, who had been smitten by her brother's roommate, thought this was a wonderful idea, and traveling with her friend Jessie would be the only way her parents might even consider letting her travel to Philadelphia. Thus, an invitation was extended to both young women; reservations would be made at a good hotel, and the college juniors from Penn pledged utmost respect. Jessie was ecstatic. What an opportunity! She was sure she could convince Mama.

She began her campaign in mid-September. Fearing her parents would think her "fast," a term made far too common by fashionable novelist F. Scott Fitzgerald, the twenty-year-old Jessie plotted very carefully. "Mama, you'll never believe what happened! I had a letter from Mary Jane Thomas today. Do you remember me telling you about her? She is as nice as pie (another term which had been gaining popularity)."

"What do you mean, nice as pie?" Mama asked. "How can a person be compared to a pie? There's apple pie, and pumpkin pie, and all kinds of pies. Sometimes you try my patience, Jessie." "It's just an expression, Mama," Jessie replied sweetly. She couldn't afford to annoy Mama and did not want to stomp off as she would like to have done. "What I meant is that Mary Jane was one of the dearest girls on my floor. I met her whole family. She has two brothers and a sister. The sister is married, the younger brother is in high school and her older brother goes to college in Philadelphia."

"Does he know Mary Alice Thompson?" Mama asked, remembering she was enrolled at Drexel Institute in Philadelphia.

Jessie's mind was racing. "Probably." The word slipped out without skipping a beat or any basis in fact. "Anyhow," Jessie hurried on, "she has invited me to spend Thanksgiving vacation with her." There, it was said.

"How are you going to get to Clarion? And what do you think your father would say to that? Traipsing off to Clarion for Thanksgiving, indeed."

"Well, I just thought it was nice of her to ask me."

Jessie did not broach the subject again until early October, on a warm fall evening when Papa was away and Mama was sitting in the front room with her mending. "Mama, remember us talking about Mary Jane Thomas who asked me to go with her this Thanksgiving?"

"What do you mean, go with her?" Mama questioned.

"Well," Jessie began. "We would like to travel together to Philadelphia. That's where her brother will be." Mama looked at her quizzically. "Well, as I said, her brother is a junior at Penn, and the Thanksgiving football game is just about the biggest thing ever, and he can get us tickets, and Mary Jane and I can room together, and ride down on the train, and probably also visit Mary Alice Thompson, and see the Liberty Bell and maybe a real Broadway play, and go to John Wanamaker's store, and I promise we will find a church to attend on Sunday."

Mama looked at her grown daughter, her vivacious, beautiful Jessie, who reminded her just a little bit of herself when she was young; Jessie, she believed, was prettier, although not quite as tall as Matilda. Mama was remembering that she herself had had no opportunities at all as a young woman. "Whatever shall we tell your father?" was all she could think of to say.

On Wednesday, the day before Thanksgiving, school closed at 11:30. Jessie told Mama she had made arrangements to come home, but neglected to mention she had planned to hitchhike, a term she hadn't yet heard but an action she had heard about from friends. As she was leaving school, the farmer on whose land the building stood asked her if she was in need of a ride, that he planned to drive his team into Grampian for grain. Jessie felt sure she could find a ride from Grampian to Curwensville, so she gratefully accepted his offer. By three o'clock she was at the train station at the end of Curwensville where she boarded for Clearfield. There she met Mary Jane, coming in from Clarion by way of Dubois to Clearfield. The two friends traveled to Tyrone where they purchased their tickets for Philadelphia at $1.65 a seat.

Pulling out of the station, Jessie was exuberant, "We did it! Philadelphia, here we come!" They arrived at the Broad Street Station where they were met by George Thomas and his roommate Henry Allen, both with bright smiles.

If Jessie had any qualms she kept them to herself as she robed herself in the mantle of a world traveler. George and Henry guided the young women to the PRT (Philadelphia Rapid Transit) which the locals, including all the college students, called the "pirates, robbers, and thieves" line. The fare was eight cents one way, but Henry suggested they purchase the 15-cent round trip and save the token for the ride back to the terminal on Sunday. By now it was midnight, and Jessie and Mary Jane were tired, but excitement overruled any thought of not making the most of every minute of their stay.

When it was suggested that they stop at Horn and Hardart for a late night supper, Jessie could barely wait. She had heard of this chain—32 in Philadelphia alone, and one of which was three stories with table service on one floor, a cafeteria on another, and the automated on a third—and agreed it would be great sport to use the automat. Upon their arrival, trying very hard not to appear a country bumpkin, Jessie calmly said to George, "You go first," never admitting she had no idea how to place the coin, open the little door, and retrieve a food selection.

Registering at the Hotel Bartram, a first class hotel, Jessie couldn't believe she was actually in the second largest city in the country—her first trip, and was staying in a hotel, albeit in one of their smaller rooms, for the first time. Of course it was not her first time away from home, but it was certainly different going from a population of 3,000 to one of over two million. In 1925, Philadelphia held approximately one-sixtieth of the entire nation's population and produced one-quarter of all American-made goods. Broad Street, the main north-south street in Philadelphia, was the longest, broad straight street (fourteen miles in length) in the United States.

None of those facts mattered much to Jessie, Mary Jane, George, and Henry, however. Their heads were filled with the football game they would be attending the next day. On Thanksgiving morning, Jessie awoke first, convinced she had not slept at all. She dressed in her collegiate sports best, complete with her new possum coat and the boots Mama had bought her nearly two years ago. The fellows met the girls in the hotel lobby and the four of them headed for Broad Street to Hanscom's, a popular cafeteria chain and Horn and Hardart's only competition.

On their way to Franklin Field, Jessie could believe for the moment that she was a true co-ed, much like her counterparts at Penn and Drexel. As the four friends entered the stadium on South Thirty-third Street, Jessie was amazed at the size of what was so humbly called a field, as Franklin Field, completed only three years earlier, boasted almost 300,000 square feet. Her attention was also drawn to the sound of a brass band and freshmen in their beanies who were distributing copies of the original Freshman Song and the Frosh Yell. Best of all, Penn defeated Cornell, 7 – 0, leaving the two young couples in an even merrier frame of mind.

Following the game, the foursome decided to have lunch near campus to delay returning to Center City. They chose to avoid running into the crowds dispersing after the annual Gimbel's Thanksgiving Day parade, ushering in the Christmas season. Because all businesses were closed, the young couples knew the parade-goers would likely not linger in the city, but would head to their homes for the traditional Thanksgiving dinner.

After a late lunch in a small diner, they were ready to head back into Center City for sightseeing. Taking the nearly empty PRT back to City Hall, they began their stroll toward the river on East Chestnut Street starting at Broad and Chestnut at Jacob Reed's Sons whose print ads featured tuxedos for $55. At the corner of the next block they paused at Bonwit Teller, an upscale department store, followed by Oppenheim, Collins & Company known for their top quality gifts. Continuing their course, in the next block they stopped to look in the window of Stetson, the country's premier hat maker which had originated in Philadelphia before it moved to the West and became better known for custom made cowboy hats. Jessie insisted they stop at the Chestnut Street Opera House, near Eleventh Street where she read every word on every billboard.

"Come on, Jebbie; we're coming back here tomorrow. You can read all of this while we're in line waiting to go in," teased George.

"But I promised my pupils I would remember everything to tell them! You wouldn't want me to disappoint the children, would you?" Jessie responded in a mock wail.

"Then tell them about Winkelman. You walked right by their store. You'll love their shoes." George ran back and the others followed. He began to read the advertisement in their window, "Hand made women's shoes; it makes the foot more graceful, petite, youthful; the very effects that fashiondom demands."

They began to laugh, as the teasing continued past the Mandarin Café, one of the many Chinese restaurants that were a result of the current fascination with anything chinoiserie. By the time they reached the Corn Exchange National Bank, at Chestnut and Second Streets, they were exhausted with their own laughter. Even George's attempt at seriousness in explaining that the polished brass corn designs in the cornerstone of the building were polished every day to a high sheen only brought more paroxysms of laughter.

"I think we should cross the street before we reach the pier and find ourselves falling in the drink," Henry said, trying to regain his own composure.

Finally, they crossed to the other side of Chestnut, running for several blocks to the Benjamin Franklin Hotel, where they entered and walked down to the ground level just to peer into El Patio which was offering a special Thanksgiving Dinner at $3 a plate, with music later in the evening by Howard Lanin.

Moving on to Tenth Street, they stopped briefly at The Toy Shoppe, which billed itself as Philadelphia's only permanent toy store. The next block boasted Mawsan & DeMany (with its gorgeous fur coats) and Wm. H. Wanamaker (men's fine clothing). Tiring by this time, the group of four paused to view the second floor setting of the Cathay Tea Garden, a famous spot in the City, ending their tour at Hotel Adelphia.

Henry wanted to go back to El Patio for dinner, but Jessie (concerned with the cost), insisted she loved Horn and Hardart. "Wouldn't it be such fun to have Thanksgiving dinner at the automat?" she asked. In addition to its being less expensive, she would make a good story out of this adventure to entertain her friends back home, along with descriptions of the many active billboards she had seen, such as the Sherman-Williams' globe of the world with red lights being lit in sequence as a depiction of paint flowing down over a globe, announcing "We Cover the Earth" and Morning Sip Coffee's lighted billboard on which the coffee cup turned and coffee dripped into the cup.

Friday morning the girls slept in until ten and met George and Henry for lunch at Hanscom's. In response to George's protests that he wanted to take her to a good restaurant, Jessie promised George that she would agree to the Cathay Tea Garden on Saturday night for dinner and dancing since they had theatre tickets for a matinee. Friday afternoon they went to John Wanamaker's, by far the largest department store in the entire United States and home to the largest pipe organ in the world. They arrived in time for an organ and choir concert at 2:00, after which they had a glorious time browsing in Wanamaker's and Bonwit Teller. Neither of the young women had ever before seen a store even a quarter of the size of Wanamaker's.

That evening the four had front row seats in the Family Circle, the best section of the Chestnut Street Opera House (at $1.10 per ticket) to see Willie Howard in *Sky High*. The theatre was sold out. Jessie wanted to gawk at this beautiful opera house with its loge seats, two balconies, and orchestra pit, but refused to betray that fact that she had so little experience in such grandeur. As usual, she relished appearing "to the manner born," and would not give anyone reason to believe otherwise. On the way out of the theatre, she picked up a playbill for the following week, just as if there were no doubt she would be returning to see *My Girl*, billed as the "snappiest musical show in town" with "a corking cast" featuring "The Vanderbilt Girls, the greatest chorus seen on Broadway in years."[18] Following the performance, the two couples found a quiet club which Jessie ever after referred to as "the speakeasy in South Philadelphia."

Saturday afternoon the four were scheduled to attend the Broad Street Theatre whose marquee consisted of a multi-storied vertical lighted sign that could be seen for blocks in both directions of Broad Street. Jessie would have preferred to go to Keith's, a vaudeville theatre, or even the Bijou or Trocadero which offered burlesque, a chorus line, slapstick, and comedy skits such as Mutt and Jeff, but she feared what Mary Jane and her brother might think of such a suggestion. Besides, she told herself, a fraternity brother of George had given him tickets he had not been able to use, and it would put George in an awkward position not to use the seats at the Broad Street Theatre.

Off they all went to see *The Harem*, presented by the celebrated director David Belasco, in the newly refurbished, best-known theatre in the City. By this time Jessie was, indeed, feeling like she belonged to the Main Line crowd, despite her limited wardrobe and utter lack of authentic sophistication. On her way out of the theatre, just as she had done the night before, she picked up the program for the following week's opening of Sidney Howard's *They Knew What They Wanted*. That evening, as agreed, they all had dinner at the Cathay Tea Garden, a large, top-rated Chinese-American restaurant, where they remained until closing, dancing to the music of Billy Hayes and his Garden Dance Orchestra.

Sunday morning, as Jessie had promised Mama, they attended the 10:30 worship service at Asbury University Church on the campus of Penn, made a final stop at Horn and Hardart, picked up their luggage, and headed for the railroad station where Jessie and Mary Jane kissed their dates, and boarded their Pullman car for the return trip to Tyrone where they would change trains and head for home. However, before they arrived at the Tyrone station, Jessie made the acquaintance of Edmund Smith whose address has been immortalized on a slip of paper pasted in the *Girl Graduate*, along with the ticket stubs, playbills, book of amusements, and her hand-written notation in the corner of the display ad for the Cathay Tea Room: "Hot place."

Curwensville was quiet compared to her whirlwind Thanksgiving vacation, but Jessie kept most of the details to herself, telling her family only what a very large place Philadelphia was, with huge stores and even larger hotels, banks, and office buildings. She found local life dreary with all the excitement of the Philadelphia theatres still whirling in her mind.

Christmas, never overly exciting at best, was anti-climatic for Jessie. Because of her Thanksgiving adventure she had almost no money with which to buy gifts. She had purchased some trinkets in Philadelphia to give Kate and Jean, and the only other person she had to buy for was Mama. Fortunately, Kate came to the rescue and agreed to let Jessie add her name to the inscription in the Bible she had bought for her mother. Other than Mama's Bible that later fell to her keeping, the only reminder Jessie had of Christmas 1925 was a gift card from her sister Jean that Jessie used as a bookmark.

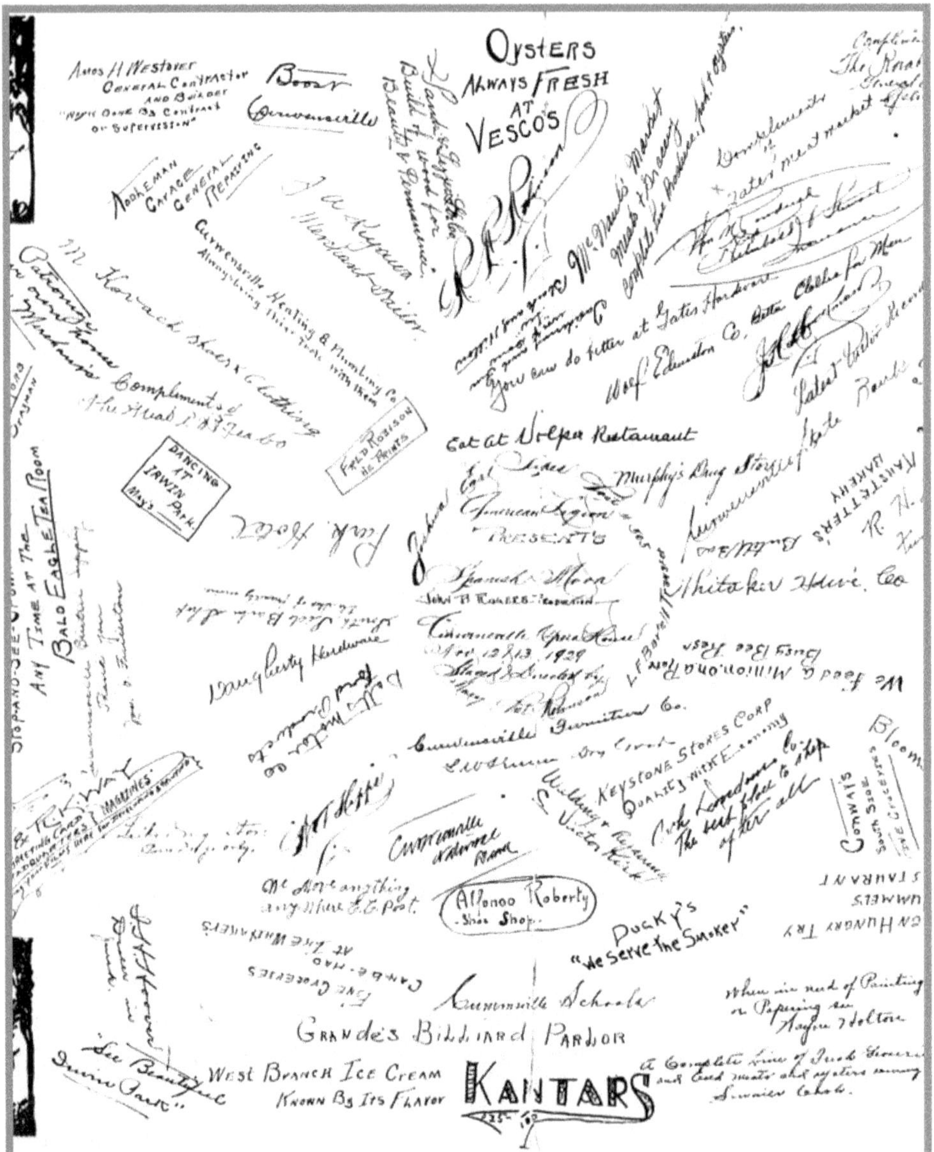

1929 Town Musical "Spanish Moon" Playbill

Advertisers Page

Chapter 4

Marriage and New Families

Modern youth is wild and reckless and radical, we are so often told that we have almost come to believe it. Perhaps it isn't so. Perhaps it is only that the world changes.

Duke, Chronicle, *April 27, 1927 in Fass*[1]

Entering the second quarter of the 20th Century, the United States held a population of 148 million. Memories of the World War were quickly fading, but its after-effects lingered in the form of numerous labor uprisings. A contemporary rise in racial and religious intolerance and discrimination led to immigration restrictions, and in the aftermath of the Sacco-Vanzetti verdict and appeal,[2] the Communist scare was reaching its culmination. Also called the Big Red Scare, this threat referred to the large Eastern European immigration, strongly criticized by some citizens because the immigrants were largely Jewish and, as opponents charged, possibly even Communists. Despite all the reported racial and religious intolerance in the national press, Curwensville remained calm, as most of its citizens were untouched by the immigration restrictions and most everything else on the national scene that did not directly affect their daily lives.

By 1926, Americans were seeking ways in which to spend their ever-increasing amount of leisure time and greater incomes. No longer did religion offer the main emotional outlet for all hard-working men and women as they began to seek other releases. This change in attitude was greatly influenced by a surge in advertising that promoted the idea that no person could spend twenty-four hours a day, seven days a week, tightening a bolt or opening a filing cabinet. Many workers were beginning to believe these marketing techniques that tried to convince the worker that increased earnings should be spent in new leisure—partly to obtain life's necessities and luxuries, including electric refrigerators and automobiles; partly to impress other people with the extent of one's earning power; and partly as an emotional release from humdrum daily chores. In other words, the world of advertising was planting the seeds for the belief that people somehow deserved the better things in life.

For those who did not have discretionary income to spend on leisure activities, one of the least expensive of the new pastimes was crossword puzzles. Interest in this amusement ballooned and the configuration of little squares could be found in every newspaper. Jessie, like many others, got caught up in these puzzles and, even after the craze peaked in 1925,[3] she continued working the ones in the daily newspaper for the rest of her life. However, she rarely finished them (Jessie remained throughout her life unruffled by any task not completed) and left the newspaper lying about the house, roughly folded open to the puzzle page, much to the lasting annoyance of the other members of the family.

Another diversion, which later turned out to be only a passing—although intense—fad, was the game of Mahjong which had begun to sweep the country in 1922, reaching small towns several years later. Jessie spoke of her "friends in college" who dabbled in this game, but none of the Pifer girls became interested. While in later years they described this game to their children as boring, in truth, there was no extra money to spend on something so frivolous as the purchase of a game. Contract bridge was introduced in the

United States in 1926[4] and became very popular among adults. Even Mama, to everyone's surprise, expressed a passing interest in the game in a letter she wrote to one of her nieces, "You will have to teach me to play bridge."[5] Both Jessie and Kate learned to play, but never touched a card in their mother's home because Papa did not approve of card games. Kate enjoyed the skill of the game, but Jessie quickly lost patience with it.

For the first time in history, most life choices were more difficult for single women. Prior to the 1920s, expected behavior was very clear. However, with the revolution in morals and manners sweeping society, single women found themselves in a dilemma. Should they continue to be as ladylike as they had been reared or be modern, sophisticated, and smart? Every young woman wanted to be thought of as "smart," and in metropolitan areas the use of strong liquor and strong language became a mark of sophistication. Of course, this mode of behavior was far milder in central Pennsylvania, more than a hundred miles from any city. The closest to living the fast life Jessie found was the occasional fraternity house party at Clarion or Penn State.

Social freedoms also brought the acceptance of smoking for women. By the late 1920s many women of all ages took up smoking. Among those was Jessie Pifer. Because her parents didn't approve and she hardly could smoke during the day in a school building, Jessie's smoking was very limited to social situations and an occasional cigarette in the backyard during rare times when Mama was away. Despite Jessie's occasional minor breaches of decorum, Mama tried to maintain the kind of household she thought was one of gentility. Propriety was her ever vigilant goal, one she pursued in every daily activity.

One method Mama used to instill her idea of refinement in her daughters was through music that spoke of gentler times. She found appealing some of the music she heard on the radio as she sat by the front window doing her mending during the winter of 1926. She asked Jean to order the sheet music in Clearfield for the popular songs "One Alone," "When Day is Done," and "In the Garden of Tomorrow," all of which she thought appropriate for her girls. Jessie also counted out 24 cents for Jean to purchase "Bye, Bye, Blackbird" and "I Found a Million-Dollar Baby in the Five-and-Ten-Cent Store," because these songs reminded her of the good times she had enjoyed in Philadelphia. This music provided further opportunity for conversation when she would tell friends and, on occasion, her pupils about having been in a store where a 35-cents-an-hour piano player played the songs. She did not, however, tell them that the person embellished the songs with runs and trills that were not written in the printed music for sale, a fact she learned the hard way when she sat at the piano with the music in front of her and tried to replicate what she had heard in the emporium.

Jean, now sixteen, continued to travel to Clearfield by train to take violin lessons at the Susquehanna College of Music, making it easy for her to order the music. She was now accustomed to traveling alone to her weekly lessons, and, in fact, finally began to look forward to them since Chet (Chester Bloom) would walk her to the train station and be waiting upon her return to walk her home. Mama found it a bit easier to find the money for music lessons with Jessie and Katherine now paying board. Even so, she still needed to budget and pay on credit.

In May Jessie and Kate attended the Alumni Banquet, with Howard Thompson escorting both of them as well as his own sister, who was not permitted by her father to invite the young man in whom she was interested. The four of them (Jessie, Kate, Mary Alice, and Howd) were joined by Kathryn Kephart and Merle Smith who were planning to be married that summer. As married women were not permitted to be hired as teachers, the marriage would be kept secret. Kathryn had just been assigned to the South Side School in Curwensville, so the deception would have to be well planned. Most of the evening's conversation centered around guarded references to the pending marriage and good natured kidding—including hints to Kate and Howd that they, too, should follow the example of Kathryn and Merle.

Tiring of this conversation centering on young married couples and Mary Alice's pining for someone she was not allowed to see, Jessie sought more exciting company and soon found it at a table with Joe Errigo and two other male classmates. "Joe," she smiled at him, "always here when a gal needs rescued." Joe, enjoying the role of protector and having no thought at this time just how much he would remain her defender throughout their lives, responded, "Well, Jebbie, I can't imagine that you can't completely take care of yourself, but I am at your service. By the way, where's Katherine?" Joe had always called Jessie's sister "Katherine," from the time he first fell in love with her when they were thirteen. He had not declared his feelings nor had he considered courting her, as both of them knew their becoming more than friends was impossible. He was Italian and Catholic and knew that while his own family would be only disappointed at his choice, Katherine's parents would never approve of her seeing him, much less marrying him. That is just the way it was and he accepted the cultural barriers of the time.

Kate suspected he was interested in her, but at the time did not fully realize the extent of his feelings. Joe was too much of a gentleman to press for a relationship that could never be. But with Jessie, he could kid and be pals and even travel in mixed company with her—so long as it wasn't a date with just the two of them. Everyone knew Jessie wasn't serious about anyone. She was just Jessie, having a good time.

Jessie sat with the three men that evening at the Alumni Banquet, her impatience showing. "What is it, Jess?" one of the fellows asked. "Isn't there someplace else to go? I don't want to listen to these boring speeches," Jessie answered. "Joe promised he would take anyone who wanted to go, to DuBois." "Let's just wait to leave until after the meeting," he said. "Our leaving won't be as noticed once the entertainment begins." During the program following the dinner, the president of the Alumni Association announced, "Curwensville High School now has an alumni membership of 522, the total number of living graduates since the school graduated its first class in 1886. And I am proud to announce that this is the first time our membership has reached the milestone number of 500. All of you should know that we are one of the few high school alumni associations in America—and we may be the only one that does not charge dues for membership." This announcement was met with loud cheering and gave the young people heading to DuBois an easy exit.

In July Jessie returned to Clarion for her third summer, continuing to accumulate credits for her permanent teaching certification. While she was there, the ever-devoted Terry McGovern sent her a birthday card on July 6, so that it would arrive by July 9 for Jessie's twenty-first birthday. Mama had made a cake for the occasion and hid her disappointment when she received a postcard Saturday morning about an hour before Jessie's train from Clarion was expected.

Dear Mama, Some of my friends are holding a party for me on Saturday night at the home of one of the girls who lives in Clarion. I am staying at her home this weekend. See you next Saturday morning after classes. Love, Jebbie B.

With two years of teaching experience behind her, Jessie was even more self-confident and independent, viewing the summer classes as something necessary and the summer social life as very appealing and liberating. Her Introduction to Teaching notebook gives her address that summer as 1075 E. Main Street, two blocks from the campus, indicating that she had rented a room rather than living in the dormitory. Her class notes are meticulously written, very probably copied from the board, and her notebook on Juvenile Literature continued to reflect the very rote-like teaching method employed at the time.

Jessie also continued to carry her *Girl Graduate* memory book with her, and on August 18, 1926 the following message was inscribed,

Dear Jebbie,

Someone said, Gentlemen prefer Blondes, well—they don't know you yet." Johnny, Delta Gamma House, Morgantown, Wva.

Other such endearments include this sampling:

"You couldn't forget a devil like me." John White.

"To attempt to tell you how much I enjoyed your delightful companionship during this summer term would be useless indeed."

"It's no wonder that Joe and the rest of the boys love you when we girls just adore you and envy you, too. I wish you the most success ever."

Perhaps Jessie's popularity among her classmates was the reason her term report of August 20 would, to most other students, have been less than satisfactory. However, to Jessie meeting new friends, particularly Joe Goodwin, was of far more interest than grades. She and Joe, along with an ever-widening circle of friends and acquaintances, always were devising activities by which they could have good times without necessarily being paired. Occasionally a group of these friends would head for Cook's Forest, soon to be the first Pennsylvania State Park acquired to preserve a natural landmark, near Clarion. The old Cook Forest Inn might be their destination, no longer in the best of condition, but available for a meal. From there they could walk to the fire tower for a panoramic view of the forest. If they felt particularly adventuresome and had dressed for hiking, they could find a bluff from which to view the Clarion River.

In contrast to the campus lifestyle enjoyed by Jessie at Clarion, Katherine quietly returned to Altoona to take her courses at Penn State's extension campus. There are, however, no available records of the courses she took as she was not one to save these reminders of days that were not as frivolous for her as they were for the more social Jessie. Kate usually came home on the train on weekends, much as she had the previous summer, and continued to see Howd who wrote to her on a nearly daily basis. Occasionally he would finish his work early in Bellefonte where his father still had business interests and would take the very long way home through Altoona where he would visit Kate. Another memorable date was going to the movies at the Capitol Theatre. Howd never stayed past eleven so that he would get home, he said, before his mother started worrying about him. In truth, it was his father who had set a curfew for his son, even at the age of twenty-two.

Five weeks before Labor Day was the traditional time for the annual Clearfield County Fair, first held in 1860, and most of the county citizens looked forward to its many attractions. Jessie never missed this three-to-four day event, particularly the harness races to which her father had introduced her many years before. Two permanent buildings had been erected on the fairgrounds that spring of 1926—an exposition hall and a grandstand from which the races could be viewed, thus making it possible for the spectators to closely follow the entire race. Jessie had no trouble finding escorts and on the rare afternoons when no one was available, she took herself to the races, striking up a conversation with whoever happened to be sitting nearby, especially if the whoever happened to have binoculars.

That year all county schools opened September 7, the day following Labor Day. Kate, at age eighteen, beginning her second year, had received a renewal of her contract from Lawrence Township on May 27 for an annual salary of $800 for 7½ months of teaching at the Driftwood School. She decided she no longer wanted to board, preferring to pay the train fare and walk to the train stop where she joined Jessie who, new to Lawrence Township, would have boarded the same train near Hyde City.

Jean, Kate and Jebbie

Both Kate and Jessie continued to live at home. To move into a boarding house or an apartment would have been unheard of for unmarried women. While that prevailing practice would soon change throughout America, in the early and mid- twenties in small towns a female adult lived with her parents or other relatives until she married. No exceptions.

By the end of the decade, however, more single women throughout the country began to move out of their homesteads into small kitchenette apartments. This occurred mostly in cities where such apartments were available. In smaller towns, one was lucky to find anything other than a rooming house. Jessie could not have afforded an apartment, even if she would have taken the time to find one, and renting a room held little appeal. She asked herself, "Why would I want to rent a room in someone's house? It would be worse than boarding with the school directors." She was too busy, she said, to take care of an apartment. Besides, at her age, everyone expected she soon would be married. Heaven knew she had more than enough suitors.

Both Jessie and Kate, along with Jean, helped their mother with the housework, although Mama did many of her chores during the week when the two older girls were teaching and Jean was still in school. On Saturdays Kate and Jean often went shopping together, saving Mama a trip to the grocery store. Saturday was the major shopping day when farmers and others who lived outside the borough would come into town and stores remained open into the evening. Saturday also was the day rents were paid and on Saturday evenings Mama, rent in hand from her tenant, often walked to the deposit window of the National Bank, less than a block from the front porch she so much enjoyed.

On the rare Saturday evening that Jessie didn't have a date or other plans with friends, she liked to sashay down the street, tend to the banking, meander down past Kantar's, Lininger's Funeral Home, the Strand Theatre, Kirk Jewelers and the Kirk family home, then cross Filbert Street to Kovac's Department Store. After browsing through the main area, she would occasionally walk the short set of steps to the shoe department where she would invariably ask for some new shoe style that had not yet reached the small towns of Pennsylvania. "Bill," she would say, "aren't you going to get in any of those smart walking shoes?"

Bill Kovach would blush, hoping his father wasn't noticing his obvious crush on Jessie, and say, "Miss Pifer, I will order anything you want." Jessie's typical response was, "Well, let me think about it. I may try the stores in Altoona the next time I am there." She would then flounce out the side entrance, considering whether or not to go next door to Karstetter's Bakery. She knew Mama would not approve and she could hear her mother's voice reminding her, "It just doesn't seem right to spend money on things I can bake myself. It's wasteful." Well, it might be wasteful, but no homemade creampuffs could be as good as the ones made by Karstetter's.

If Jessie heeded Mama, she would decline her own invitation to creampuffs and turn right rather than left to the bakery and walk to the corner to cross State Street to the Park House, and turn left on North Street, actually an alley. By that route she could see into the back yard of the Howard J. Thompson residence on the chance that Mary Alice or Bubby would be around.

Jessie had mixed feelings about the Thompsons. Part of her felt a bit envious of "Tommy" whose father indulged her at the expense of her brother Bubby. She thought of Mary Alice, having a wonderful life as a full-time coed at Drexel, with striking, custom-made clothes—even a real raccoon coat. Jessie tried to tell herself that it was not the coat, nor the shoes, nor the beautifully beaded evening purse that bothered her—even though the coat was just what Jessie would have bought for herself had she been able to afford it. And Mary Alice's coat had even come from the fine Bonwit Teller Department Store in Philadelphia. "It's a wonder she didn't go to Mawsan & DeMany," Jessie sulked, recalling the fine fur store she had seen a year ago. She began to think of a way she could get Tommy to invite her to Drexel for a weekend. She certainly knew how to get there by train. "I'll work on that," she told herself, holding her head high as she turned down Thompson Street headed for home.

Kate spent nearly every Saturday evening with Howd. He was most eager to marry her, even though at age eighteen she was not ready. She didn't want the routine of housework and loneliness she saw with Josephine's marriage nor the strain she sometimes observed in Ruby. For now, she was content. She sometimes felt, however, that she didn't quite fit the marriage pattern and wondered if there was another direction she might take with her life. She didn't have anyone with whom to discuss these feelings, since everyone she knew—except, of course, Jessie—thought that being married was the end-all and be-all of existence.

Even talking to Jean about her concerns regarding marriage didn't seem appropriate. Jean envied what she called her older married sisters' "freedom," not understanding that freedom had its own price. On the other hand, Kate could not make Jean understand that there was no need to hurry to grow up to adulthood. She echoed Mama's concerns for this youngest Pifer daughter. Jean was only sixteen, still in school, and, in Mama's opinion, far too serious about Chester Bloom.

Jessie, of course, wasn't the least bit interested in becoming serious about anyone. Joe Goodwin, among many others, still pursued her, but he found a long distance relationship difficult to maintain. From a letter written October 27, 1926:

> *For the love of Mike, how can anyone get you on the phone? I have tried, by actual count, seven hundred and forty-six times. I was in Dubois Sunday but again couldn't get you on the phone and, as I didn't have a car, I couldn't come to Curwensville. May I come over to see you over the weekend? If I may come, I will be there at about seven-thirty or eight o'clock Saturday evening. Will you call me up Friday at six o'clock and tell me whether I can come or not. Please let me come.*
>
> *Love, Joe Goodwin*

While there is no record assuring that Jessie returned Joe's call, his interest in her remained. But Jessie was far too busy to worry about writing to someone in Detroit or wondering if he would be able to reach her by telephone. There were stockings to buy and dresses to hem, for by the middle of the decade the amount of fabric in a woman's outfit had decreased by half and had gone from amply cut ankle-length dresses over such underpinnings as corset covers, envelope chemises, and petticoats to dress styles that were designed to make the wearer look as pencil-slim as possible and were worn knee-length over silk undergarments or the new artificial silk fabric, called rayon.

This new fabric was also available to purchase as yardage. Jessie bought several yards the first time she saw it in the dry goods store in Altoona and carried it home, not to sew with it herself, but to talk Mama into making her a new dress. "Look at how pretty the print is, Mama. It reminds me of that silk dress Aunt Rosie had. Do you remember it?"

Mama remembered. Rosie had made a point of telling them it was imported silk and very delicate. It obviously had been hand sewn with great skill—and expense. "Jessie, you know I haven't done much fancy dressmaking, but I'll try if you will help."

"Oh, Mama, of course I will," was Jessie's immediate agreement. She did help to pin the pattern to the fabric, the pattern she had borrowed from Mary Alice's cousin Marjorie Wall. However, because the material was smooth and kept slipping off the dining room table, Jessie gave up in frustration.

Mama admitted, "This is the most difficult material I have ever tried to work with. Jessie, you will have to hold it level if you want the seams to be straight. See how it pulls." Jessie liked the drape of the silk-like rayon fabric and wanted the seams loose rather than tight, so she had no choice but to assist in the production. She chose not to follow her mother's suggestion that she hand sew the dress, however, and some of the seams were, indeed, pulled.

Mama, like most who knew Jessie, found it hard to deny her requests. Jessie not so much pleaded her case as trusted that her needs would be met. One would not call her selfish and she was not presumptuous. Her family and friends would simply throw up their hands and say, "Well, you know Jessie," as they did her bidding. When the dress was finished, the result was not as satisfactory as either of them wanted.

One of the difficulties with rayon, as Jessie discovered, is that it could not be easily laundered; it had to be very carefully hand-washed in cold water. The garment then had to be rolled in a towel to absorb the water because wringing the fabric led to wrinkling and it was very difficult to press out the wrinkles if they had been wrung in. In addition, the material was easily scorched, even with the electric irons by then found in 90 percent of households, and sometimes the fabric simply melted. It was best to have rayon garments cleaned professionally and that cost money.

While one would assume material that required dry cleaning would gain stature as a fine fabric, such was not the case with rayon, and the phrase "cheap rayon dress" became a staple phrase of derision. On the other hand, stockings and lingerie made from rayon gained great popularity because these items were more easily hand-washed than were dresses, wrinkling was less of a consideration, and the fabric also more easily conformed to the shape of the body—particularly hips and legs—than did cotton.

Women, especially young women, had gone from daytime stockings mostly made of black, brown, green, or blue cotton or lisle to silk or rayon stockings of a flesh color. Less fragile and not as expensive as silk, rayon flesh-colored stockings were a hit and soon became as standard as the short skirt that allowed the stockings to be noticed.[6]

Despite a very limited income, Jessie did her best to look less like long-curled Mary Pickford, the embodiment of innocence, and more like Clara Bow, the new "It" girl. While not realizing that she was standing at the edge of history's sexual revolution, Jessie and her friends were part of a great wave of social change that went beyond appearances. As social historians describe it, ". . . the atmosphere was different then: there was an air of novelty and self-conscious experiment about the relaxing of the code which was intensely exciting to the participants and shocking to observers who were out of step with the changes."[7]

At this time the average American was working ten to twelve hours a day, with no health or job security, and while there might be a car in the driveway there was often no bathtub in the house.[8] Every third home, however, had a radio, two thirds had electrical service, and forty percent had telephones; scheduled air transportation services also had been established. Cross channel passenger air lines had begun in both England and France in 1919, but commercial aviation was slow to get under way in the United States for emerging airlines, even with the aggressive support of Herbert Hoover, then Secretary of Commerce.[9]

The first regularly scheduled passenger service, between Boston and New York, did not begin until 1927. That same year young, handsome Charles A. Lindbergh made a daring and grueling flight across the Atlantic in his *Spirit of St. Louis*. When Lindbergh landed his plane in Paris he was utterly surprised by his reception, with crowds at Le Bourget smashing fences and lifting him from the cockpit. Upon his return to America four million people in New York showered him with praise and a ticker tape parade. Lindbergh's "self-reliance, slim good looks, and unabashed honesty meshed with the American craving for a myth, for a hero who could lift the national imagination."[10] In 1928 Amelia Earhart became the first woman to make a non-stop transatlantic flight and young women everywhere began imitating her favored style of wearing jodhpurs.

Despite the ballyhoo of these airplane exploits and adventures, few householders in Curwensville were seriously considering flying in airplanes. Even though flying held a fascination, a large number of Americans had not yet even ridden in automobiles, and airplanes appeared to be far too risky.

Those who could afford to purchase an automobile continued to weigh the matter very seriously, and those who were attune to fashion were waiting with great anticipation to see Henry Ford's new automobile design. Ford had stopped making the Model T and had recently introduced the Model A in response to the public's request for a variety of styles and colors.

By this time the closed car had replaced the open model and the number of automobiles in the nation had increased to more than 20 million. The motor car became a room on wheels—storm-proof, lockable, and parkable all day and all night in all kinds of weather. The closed car was in effect a room protected from the weather and could be occupied at any time of the day or night and moved at will into a darkened byway or a country lane.[11]

The automobile thus offered an almost universally available means to young people of escaping temporarily from the supervision of parents and chaperones, as well as watchful neighbors. One could jump into a car and drive off at a moment's notice—without asking anyone's permission—to dance in another town twenty miles away, enjoying a freedom impossible in one's own neighborhood.

Of more immediate interest than automobile traffic to most local residents in the mid-1920s, however, were "the talkies"—talking pictures, the single most technological advance in the entertainment industry. Movies grew into a vast industry which drew millions of people into the theatres, with the average moviegoer attending more than once a week.

The advertising for movies promised sensationalism, much to the consternation of Mama and other parents who objected to the billboards suggestive wording. Churches throughout America openly protested and strongly criticized the motion-picture producers. As a result, Will H. Hays, Postmaster General, was installed by the government as the arbiter of morals and of taste, a so-called legal watch dog. The surprising result of this monitoring was even more movie advertising—innocuous enough to calm the churches, but promising enough to attract the patrons.

In the early spring of 1927 Katherine agreed to marry Howard and consequently would not be eligible to teach after finishing the spring term, since married women still were not permitted to teach in public schools, the rationale being that (1) the women now had someone to support them and (2) to continue to employ married women would be keeping jobs from men who had families to support. While Kate's friend Kathryn Kephart had married Merle Smith the year before and her marital status kept a secret so that she could continue to work, Katherine and Howard decided against secrecy, agreeing that Kate would no longer teach and would work only if she chose to.

Wearing a peach silk pongee dress with a smoked dropped waist for the occasion of her marriage, Kate had no regrets at not having a church wedding as she and Howard stood in the office of the Justice of Peace in an early evening in June, with Kathryn and Merle Smith serving as witnesses. Kate would like to have had her sister Jean as her attendant, but Jean begged off, convincing Kate that Kathryn Smith was a more appropriate witness.

Marriage and New Families

Kate and Bubby set up housekeeping in a second floor apartment of a private home on Walnut Street and later moved to an apartment in the two-block retail business part of town where Kate began life in earnest as a young married, going about town, visiting, and running errands. Kate soon found steady employment in the Sweet Shoppe and also babysat the youngest child of her husband's Uncle Tucker, himself the youngest of the entrepreneurial Thompson brothers.

Jean Pifer had had a busy senior year as a member of the orchestra as well as the basketball team (only the second year for the sport) while her beau, senior Chet Bloom, played on the football team, a sport begun in Curwensville in 1912. The yearbook suggests that Jean and Chet were serious about each other and by the end of the school year, it became evident that Margaret Jean would not be following her sisters' path to becoming a teacher. Mama came to this disappointing realization after learning the secret Jean had shared with Kate, asking her sister to tell Mama.

This news only added to Mama's sadness about Josephine who, properly married and well of an age to have children, longed for a family. Josephine, never envious, felt only compassion for her baby sister, a little more than half her age, when Mama confided in her that Jean was "in the family way." Josie briefly harbored the idea of offering to take Jean's baby and raise it as her own so that Jean could perhaps continue her education, but only once did she even hint at the possibility—when she told Droz of Jean and Chet's haste to be married.

And haste it was. Two weeks following the corroboration of Mama's suspicions, she arranged for the marriage of her youngest child and Chester Bloom to be performed by Justice of the Peace John A. Dale, who recently had conducted the same marriage ceremony, but not under the same circumstance, for Jean's sister Kate. Mama hoped Justice Dale would be discreet.

This same summer Jessie spent her final term as a co-ed at Clarion, completing her required courses and earning eight credits.

The fall of 1927 marked Jessie's assignment to the South Side School in Curwensville, a post she had sought as a matter of both convenience and prestige. There, a group of young women teachers and all graduates of Curwensville High School, formed a bond of friendship that endured until the death of the last of them.

Two months before her 18th birthday Jean became a mother with the birth of Chester Eugene, the second grandchild and second boy of the offspring of Mama's girls. From the outset Jean was, as her sisters before and after, fiercely protective of her children. Having no experience with babies except when Ruby brought Johnny home to visit from Canton, Ohio, and not very self-assured herself, Jean turned to her mother for assistance. Mama was patient, and with her own family grown and Ruby living at a distance, she greatly enjoyed helping Jean learn to care for Gene, as the baby came to be called.

In 1928 radio speakers replaced individual earphones in home radios, allowing an entire family to gather around the radio to hear news broadcasts. The speakers made it easier for the young people as well, for they no longer had to place the earphones in a metal washtub in order for everyone to hear music broadcast for dancing. By the end of the decade, radio sales totaled over three-quarters of a billion dollars annually, and radio advertisers found they had struck pay dirt.[12]

Radio advertising was only the beginning of a major advertising industry. Dramatic changes were noted in all print material, including yearbooks and programs, as well as magazines which were steadily gaining popularity in all households. Slogans and promises, as well as the exploitation of consumers' social fears, were rampant and advertisers did their best to take advantage of the public's fears and uncertainties. Such slogans as "Four out of five lose. . ." suggested that if the right toothpaste were not used one would get pyorrhea. "Often a bridesmaid but never a bride" played on the fears of young women that they might have unpleasant breath from not using the right mouthwash, a product only beginning to be promoted. Nonetheless, these admonishments barely affected Jessie, as she had such self-confidence that she knew those fear tactics weren't meant for *her.*

The cosmetic industry caught up to Jessie's earlier schoolgirl use of Tangee lipstick and by the late 1920s the vogue of both rouge and lipstick spread swiftly to the smallest villages and the braver (or bolder) high school girls. It is estimated that by the end of the decade three-quarters of a million dollars was being spent by American women on cosmetics and beauty shops.

Along with aggressive advertising, the 1920s also saw the heralding of salesmen as the brightest hope of American business. The consensus among manufacturers was that if an item could be produced, it could be sold and a good enough salesman could sell it. Young, ambitious men were recruited into sales (including many of Jessie's acquaintance who corresponded with her "from the road"). Contests were devised and large sales conventions organized, all to teach salesmen the tricks of salesmanship in an atmosphere of revivalism with the idea that they would go back to their territories with renewed vigor.

Also in 1928 the first motion pictures in color were exhibited by George Eastman and color television was demonstrated as a strong possibility, indications of the greatness to come in leisure activities for Americans. While still Secretary of Commerce, Herbert Hoover was an early promoter of technology and the previous year had his face and voice transmitted to New York over three telephone wires in the first public demonstration of television.

Curwensville High School's Class of 1928 wrote the name of its yearbook on the cover in French in tribute to Colonel Lindbergh's flight, much as graduating classes in the early 1940s would play on patriotism, the Class of 1958 would use a science and space theme following the Russian launch of Sputnik, 1960 would dedicate their yearbook to the new states of Alaska and Hawaii, and 1964 would make their yearbook a tribute to John F. Kennedy.

The Sixty-fifth Annual Session of the Clearfield County Teachers' Institute was held August 27-31, 1928 in the High School Auditorium in Clearfield. The fee of $3.50 included membership in the Pennsylvania State Education Association (PSEA), a subscription to the *Pennsylvania School Journal*, and a copy of the Institute Song Book. Jessie smiled when she saw her father's favorite poem, "Snow Bound," listed as one of the selections all children should read. County certificates were awarded to eighth grade students who had read and prepared a written report on ten books. Also included in the program was information on how to display the flag, classroom lighting and ventilation, "Beatitudes for the Teacher," and banalities from a meeting of the PSEA.

The program section of most interest to Jessie Pifer was the listing of all teachers in Clearfield County. Two names, in addition to her own, are noted with a handwritten check mark: Philip Mannino and John Stodart. John must have been of special significance, for his name in his own handwriting also appears on the back cover of Jessie's bound program.

New advertisements in the Teachers' Institute program more than doubled the pages of the publication.[13] These ads included one for car storage at 50 cents per day to those attending the institute. While this was a high price for those earning only five or six dollars a day, it was assumed that if one could afford a car, he could afford to store it safely. The Institute was changing with the times and, as Jessie's friends would say in jest, it was going "big time."

Marriage and New Families

Following Labor Day weekend, Miss Pifer returned to her teaching post. She enjoyed being in a building with three other teachers and was becoming quite comfortable with the fact that she did not have to perform janitorial duties as had been part of the contract at the rural schools. Even lunch became easier when shortly before the end of the school year Whitaker's Grocery Store, a handy place to purchase made-to-order sandwiches and packaged goods such as crackers and cookies, opened on Susquehanna Avenue, a short walk from the South Side School.

In the fall of 1928, on the national scene, Herbert Hoover was elected president, his first elective office. Hailed by Franklin Roosevelt in 1920 as a wonder after he had been one of the Americans instrumental in rebuilding Europe following the World War,[14] President Hoover was inaugurated on a cold, chilly day in March of 1929, just as ingredients for a global recession were gathering.

The literature of the decade portended a darker period in the country with Hemingway's *A Farewell to Arms,* Remarque's *All Quiet on the Western Front,* and Wolfe's *Look Homeward Angel,* all three books darkly brooding. In contrast, the best songs of the year were the lively "Singin' in the Rain" and "Tiptoe Through the Tulips," but both were eclipsed by "Stardust," likely the most popular song every written. Silent films had run their course as the public stopped attending any movies that didn't have sound.

The Depression, which nearly everyone later blamed almost exclusively on the crash on Wall Street, had had its real beginnings much earlier and was far more complicated than any one person at the time realized. When speculation in the market began to get out of hand, neither the federal nor the state government did anything effective to check it. What most people did not realize is that the speculative market had become so huge that the mechanisms that were supposed to make it self-regulatory would become mechanisms for compounding the catastrophic results.

Once it started, there would be nothing and no one to stop the rush toward economic disaster.

Nothing could have prepared Americans for what was to come, and the majority of them spent this last spring of innocence enjoying events that never again would be taken for granted. Only those personally involved in the businesses noticed the collapse in automobile sales and the fall of housing starts and manufacturing output.

The Pifers, especially Mama, were more anxious that spring about the pending birth of Ruby's second baby than they were about the market. Mama didn't like to be so far away and kept hoping Tom would invite her to Ohio. However, the senior Waynes had offered to their son that they would be traveling to Ohio in June and would arrive to spend some time visiting and to help with the new baby. Ruby was not particularly pleased, as she would have preferred her own mother to anyone else's mother.

As she always did, Ruby let her husband know her feelings. "If Mama can't come this time, Tom, I am not going to have this baby." Tom had no answer. "But, sweetheart of mine," Tom would cajole, "I can't tell Mother not to come when they haven't been away from the farm for five years." Ruby stared at him, silently, hoping he would sense her wrath. Then she leaned in toward her husband. "Of course," she sneered. "The last time they were able to visit us for a month was when Johnny was born!" Then she began to cry. Tom couldn't bear to see her cry so he ran to fetch their son, knowing nothing he could say or do would change his parents' plans.

Mama prided herself on not interfering in her daughters' marriages, so, instead of going by train to Canton, Ohio to help that household, Mama signed up to go on the church jitney bus to the Dedication of the Tablet Marking the Place Where the First Church Was Built in Clearfield County, at McClure's

Cemetery in Pike Township, the area surrounding the borough of Curwensville. On Sunday, June 9, 1929 Jessie joined her mother on the excursion more out of boredom than interest, even though her own Sunday School Class had helped contribute to the cost of the marker for this church being honored as the origin of the Curwensville Presbyterian Church. Many of the women on the bus complimented Jessie on her devotion to attending the service of the local church's founding:

"Dear, it was so sweet of you to accompany your mother."

❖ ❖ ❖

"My sister Hazel's daughter is visiting us in July; won't you help introduce her to some suitable young people?"

❖ ❖ ❖

"So all your sisters are married now and have left home?"—none of which Jessie wanted to hear.

Like many young people of the day, Jessie was torn between her religious upbringing and the religious skepticism that seemed to accompany the new, relaxed social code. She liked to count herself among young men and women who prided themselves on their modern-mindedness. "One has a right to enjoy oneself," she thought, "and taking a ride in a car on a clear Sunday morning is much more fun than going to church." Stinging because Papa forbade her to accept dates on Sunday mornings, Jessie was disgruntled that many of the young men she knew could be found on the golf links rather than in their pews. She muttered to herself, "No wonder the church is losing hold of the brighter members of my generation." Why was it, she questioned herself, that her friends could plan an all day event on Sunday and she couldn't go until after Sunday dinner, typically served between 1:00—1:30 p.m.

That June Jessie would rather have been in Ohio, visiting and helping with Johnny during the weeks Ruby would be recuperating from the birth of her second child. She had written to her sister months prior, offering to spend the summer, but in May she realized she had forgotten about the summer courses she had to take. She procrastinated in telling Ruby that she would have to renege on her offer to come to Ohio to help and was greatly relieved when Mama told her, "I hope you weren't counting too much on going to Ruby and Tom's in June since I had a letter from her and the Waynes are going to be there."

Summer Sessions offered by Pennsylvania State College began the second week of June in State College and Jessie took an early train on Monday morning, arriving in plenty of time for registration. Even though Penn State's education extension courses for college credit were held at several convenient locations throughout the state,[15] including Clearfield, Jessie, ever the co-ed even at the age of twenty-four, preferred to be on a college campus. She was familiar with Penn State because she had attended a few fraternity parties following football games, invited by friends of Howard Thompson, and had been invited several times for special week-ends.

Jessie reveled in these fall and spring weekends—part of what often has been called the mad, bad, glad era of campus life in the late 1920s—almost as much as she had enjoyed her trip to the University of Pennsylvania in Philadelphia, even without the houseparties, in the fall of 1926. While not as much a "party girl" as those more accustomed to the high life, Jessie could hold her own with the youth who "endeavored to unshackle themselves from what they disdained as the old-fashioned ideas and values of their parents and grandparents."[16] Mama would chide her, "Jessie, every time you come home from a weekend at Penn State your skirts are shorter."

During the summer session of 1929, where nary a whisper of the impending Depression was heard, Jessie roomed at the Phi Sigma Kappa House, converted for the summer to a campus boarding house for women. Jessie loved telling her friends that she was staying at a fraternity for the summer—and not explaining any further unless pressed. Her two classes each met for eighty minutes a day, five days a week, for six weeks, which tied up more than half of her day and half of her summer. One can only speculate that she fully partook of campus life, although historically Penn State during that time is said to have been much tamer than many of the other colleges.

During Jessie's time at Penn State, Thomas J. Wayne, Jr. was born, despite Ruby's expressed threats not to give birth. Jessie was pleased for her sister although she could not imagine having two small children, or any children for that matter. Of course, there was plenty of time to make such decisions. Ruby had been 27 when her first child was born and 32 with the birth of her second son. Jessie at age 24 didn't consider herself near old enough to think about marriage and a family, even though both her younger sisters were also married. Jessie was having too good a time that summer at Penn State and was satisfied to be kept informed about all her sisters through Kate who wrote to her with regularity.

On July 11, 1929 Kate wrote:

> *You certainly have some address! How do you like 80-minute periods?*
>
> *Do you have any use for my text book? It's nice you have all p.m. off, especially these terribly hot days.*
>
> *Mama said you might wonder why we didn't write but there isn't much to write about. We moved last Wednesday and are nearly fixed up except the windows of which there are 21. I like it much better and so does Bubby. It is real large and we also have a phone now. It is to be connected this week so I do not know our number yet.*
>
> *Mama made me a dress yesterday, figured pique, while I straightened up the third floor for her. I hope you can eat the cake I sent for your birthday. I think the cake was good enough, but had doubts for the icing.*
>
> *If anything interesting ever happens I will write and tell you about it.*
>
> *Lovingly, Kayran*[17]

That something interesting occurred soon enough in the person of Baby Donald D. Bloom, the second son born to Margaret Jean and Chester Bloom, providing the fourth grandson for Mama.

The Annual Clearfield County Sunday School Field Day celebrated its eighth year, continuing to be one of the largest community events of the summer. Most local businesses closed for the day. The printed program in its 32 pages lists all officers, committees, events of the day, and a preponderance of advertisements, part of the growing national trend.

This year the program of competitive events for cash prizes was restricted to those who held Sunday School membership. Nearly fifty solo and group performers from the member Sunday Schools entertained throughout the day, along with invited guest performers from Pittsburgh and the New York Central Chorus. However, by early afternoon, Jessie was asking herself why she had cut two days of classes to come home.

Early in September the stock market began to collapse. It quickly recovered only to fall again, rise, and fall yet again until on the morning of October 24, it broke wide open. The leading bankers of New York met to form a buying pool to support the market and for a few days there was a rally, but it soon became obvious that nothing could stem the tide of potential disaster. On October 28 the Stock Exchange collapsed and U.S. securities lost $26 billion in value. On Tuesday, October 29, more than sixteen million shares of stock were thrown on the market by frantic sellers and John Kenneth Galbraith called this "the most devastating day in the history of the New York stock market and it may have been the most devastating day in the history of markets."[18] It was not until more than two weeks later on November 13 that order was restored—at least to the market, but the depression that followed would go on for years.

Most people in Curwensville weren't paying a lot of attention to the event of order being restored to the stock market that day, as

Marriage and New Families

November 12 and 13, 1929 were the dates of the town's annual musical production, "Spanish Moon." The Opera House was filled for the show's two-night run, as everyone in town knew someone in the cast. Jessie had a featured role as Valera, billed as a Spanish vampire, who had one featured number (that did not include a vocal solo), "Lady of Lisbon." Jessie loved the part because it was exotic and she was well cast in the role. Evelyn Williams Milligan recalls the show with fondness and some amusement, "None of us could dance very well."[19] The playbill itself is notable in that all the advertisers' names are handwritten on its cover much as one would sign a souvenir program.

The winter of 1929-1930 provided an interlude in the country's history, with most people simply waiting to see what the future had in store. Publicly the nation's leaders asserted their confidence in the future. President Hoover announced that business was fundamentally sound and that it could look forward to the coming year with greater assurance. Top executives in both government and business reassured the nation that the recession was only temporary and that the worst was over. Everyone could only hope for the best.

Taking stock of the 1920s, historians note this time as the decade of women gaining their freedom—freedom to work and to play without the restrictions that had bound them heretofore to lives of comparative inactivity.

Yet Jessie Pifer seems to have been born expecting freedom. She had always lived by her own rules—not at the expense of others, but simply by who she was. She wasn't overtly rebelling; she was just living her own life. She was responsible, a good daughter, and had not brought any embarrassment to herself or to her family. In her own early twenties, she held a good job, certainly one with the highest respectability in a small town, and with a new decade on the cusp, Jessie Beverly Pifer looked forward to all life might yet offer.

Chapter 5

Life is Not a Bowl of Cherries

No one can possibly have lived through the Great Depression without being scarred by it. No amount of experience since the Depression can convince someone who has lived through it that the world is safe economically.

attributed to Isaac Asimov

A retrospective on the 1920s shows that a totally unparalleled democratization of nearly all aspects of American life occurred during that decade in education, transportation, dress and fashion, recreation, and the marketplace. As a result, democracy as a *way of life*, rather than as a philosophy, became entrenched in the nineteen twenties as America became a leader in world affairs. Automobile sales boomed to nearly 4.6 million and nearly 43.3 percent of the world's manufactured goods were made in America, a barometer that America had become the greatest financial and creditor nation in the world.[1] From the view of some historians, it appeared that with this economic boom ordinarily restrained, Americans were happily enjoying a profitable economy and learning about the wonders of investing in stocks and bonds. In reality, however, in a population of 120 million, there were 1.5 million investors and only around 600,000 speculators,[2] not at all the entire nation.

In the last year of the decade, the number of investors reached its peak as stock prices zoomed out of sight and credit was stretched close to snapping, the like of which would not be seen again for eighty years. The breaking point occurred on October 24, 1929, the day known in history as Black Thursday, when the stock market crashed. Speculators rushed to unload their stocks as the market took a sickening plunge, but most were too late. Within weeks the 1.5 million investors had lost $30 billion—a monetary amount equal to almost a third of the entire year's Gross National Product. Amid the panic sweeping banks and brokerage houses that had financed the investing spree, the realization dawned on the American public that the nation had experienced the most devastating financial collapse in its history.[3]

Early in 1930 a "wait and see" attitude concerning the economy prevailed and many of the events of the year were not at all reflective of the terrible times yet to come. Rather, in many quarters there was a sense of normalcy, an interlude from worry with only occasional flashes of concern. There was even a flicker of national pride when on the morning of May 1, 1931, President Hoover pressed a button in Washington and switched on the lights of the Empire State Building in New York City. Topped by a steel tower designed for mooring dirigibles, the skyscraper was the loftiest structure on earth and had been put up in a single year at a cost of $52 million. However, not even that excitement could reverse the course of events.

The tailspin of the economy began that summer of '31 and continued until mid-1932 when nearly 12 million people—about 25 percent of the workforce—were unemployed. Soup kitchens and breadlines became common in the cities, and shanty towns began to spring up. Before long, as the country started to blame President Hoover for their plight, the jobless began to call these collections of makeshift buildings "Hoovervilles." On cold nights the homeless covered themselves with newspapers, mockingly called their Hoover bed sheets.

Farmers were particularly hard hit and those who could not pay their mortgages faced foreclosure. In angry frustration they dumped milk on the highways and allowed their crops to rot in the fields because prices for milk and grain did not cover the cost of hiring the workers needed for harvesting. Many unemployed men of all classes sold apples or, in desperation, went begging in the streets. Resorts were empty and Pullman trains often made their scheduled runs without a single passenger. People recalled the words of former president Calvin Coolidge who a year earlier had made one of his characteristic understated comments, "The country is not in good condition."[4]

Near the end of 1932 the entire economy was snowballing downhill as consumer buying declined sharply and the public, leery of banks, hid their currency in home safe-deposit boxes or under their own mattresses. During the next several years every business in the country suffered and employees were furloughed. Unable to find other jobs, many of the jobless defaulted on their installment payments and were forced to use their life savings for daily expenses. Without unemployment insurance or Social Security, many workers had nothing to fall back on except to move in with relatives or try to find some kind of work just to survive.

When this all began in 1930, the Depression hit most families in Curwensville in a subtle manner when the demand for goods and services began to gradually decrease. Fortunately for most of the people of the town, life's important events continued to be focused on the family and friends, rather than job losses. The inexpensive pastime of contract bridge gained popularity because it cost nothing and because many pastors no longer decried against card playing, or at least had stopped inveighing against contract bridge, rationalizing that it was more a game of intellect than chance. In truth, many of them didn't want to speak out against one of the few free pastimes parishioners could enjoy.

Jebbie ❖ Vamp to Victim

At this time in her life, and the economy for the moment aside, Matilda Pifer was content with how she had reared her girls, and when she saw how happy Jean was at age twenty with two fine little boys, she had no regrets. She trusted it would be only a matter of time before Kate started a family and she continued to hope that Josephine, too, might be blessed with children. Jessie seemed to prefer the freedom of a working girl and Mama knew better than to suggest she begin to think of settling down in a marriage. Jessie was having a good time, had a steady job, and did not appear to be serious about anyone in particular. Mama knew Jessie could have her choice from a large number of suitors, not all of whom she approved. However, Jessie did not ask Mama's opinion. Mama believed that Jessie occasionally confided in Ruby and, for many reasons—Jessie foremost among them, Mama wished Ruby didn't live so far away. Sometimes she felt that half the people she loved lived too far away.

At the end of January, Mama heard from her Aunt Agnes, her mother's youngest sister, who lived in Cincinnati, Ohio. The letter was in the form of a small notebook perforated on three sides, which caught the attention of the entire family:

> *Dear Dillie,*
>
> *I received your letter and was so glad to get it. I think of you all every day and wish I were with you. Can't we get some place where we can earn some money?*
>
> *...Glad Jessie is getting along well with her school. Yes, you are right. The children have it nicer than we did, but I am glad. I look back sometimes and think we had it pretty hard but we are too far along now to think of it. I am so glad the babies are coming along so nice. I feel some days that I would like to get up and start home.*
>
> *...I am not as content as when I had my own home and Orville. I can not get used [to] being without him. He took a part in everything. Now my dear, write me soon. You know the circle will be broken some day.*
>
> *Love to all, Aunt Agnes*[5]

Life is Not a Bowl of Cherries

Mama missed her aunt as well as her sisters and, while she didn't often have the time to pine for them, on this cold January day she became nostalgic, remembering with fondness the aunt who had stepped in to help care for the five Smith sisters when their mother died. As she recalled how difficult it must have been for Aunt Agnes to take on such a responsibility, suddenly and unexpectedly, Matilda Smith longed for her mother.

"Mama," she cried out. "I miss you so. How you would have enjoyed my five girls. It would be almost like having your own five again—Lennie and Jessie, Rosie and Ella, and me. My Jessie is so much like me. She may be a little more headstrong than I was and I certainly never had the opportunities she has had, but I watch her and see myself in her. I am so proud of all of them, Mama, and I think you would be, too. Certainly there have been some disappointments and while John hasn't been the best provider, he is kind, and I am satisfied with the life I have made. If I could change only one thing in my life, Mama, it would be to have you here. I miss you so much and with each passing year I miss you more." She sat at the small kitchen work table and wept, unaware that Jessie had come downstairs.

Little did Mama know in January that two months later one of her wishes would come true. She wrote to Josephine, "... if I had known, I never would have wished for this. Why do you suppose she did it? Did she say anything to you about it?" Mama was speaking of Jessie. Her beautiful middle child, Jessie Beverly, had eloped. And Mama didn't really know who this new husband was. Jessie had not talked much about him, Mama had met him only once, and Jessie's sisters didn't seem to know anything in particular about him. "Why would Jessie elope?" Mama kept asking herself. But she had no answer.

Jessie had called Kate on a Friday evening from Greenville, the seat of Mercer County, saying, "I'm on my way to Mercer to be married at the Justice of the Peace."

"Where? Who?" Kate asked. "Jessie, what are you talking about?" "Why are you in Mercer County? That's practically to Ohio. I thought you were going to visit Ruby. How did you get there? We thought you were taking the train to Canton. And what do you know about this man?"

"Don't say 'this man'," Jessie said, an edge to her voice. "You know who he is, Kate."

"Well, yes, but not very well." Kate agreed.

"Just do me a favor and go up and tell Mama, won't you?"

"But, what will I say?" Kate pleaded.

"Tell her I am getting married this evening and that I'll see her Sunday night. Harry will drop me off on his way to Harrisburg. I'll see you sometime next week."

"What about school?"

"Well, if you would be a dear and also teach for me Tuesday and Wednesday, I can go with Harry to Harrisburg. (Kate had already offered to teach on Monday for Jessie, thinking she would be taking the train from Canton to Curwensville on Monday.) Would you do that, Kate? It would be so nice to be able to take a little wedding trip. I know you said you would teach for me on Monday when you said I could stay an extra day at Ruby's, so it would just be a couple more days. You aren't working at the Sweet Shoppe until Thursday, are you? Please, Kate? I could stop and see Mama on our way to Harrisburg and pick up some other clothes."

"Then when you get here you can tell her yourself that you got married, can't you?" asked Kate. "I don't know what she'll say. I know she'll be disappointed that you didn't tell her what you planned to do."

"Kate, I have to go. Will you do this for me?"

What could Kate say? She was scheduled to work on Tuesday at the Sweet Shoppe, but knew she could make other arrangements and teach for Jessie for three days. What Kate wanted to say to her sister, but didn't because she had not shared her suspicions with anyone, was, " . . . but I can't teach for you; I think I am expecting a baby!"

Two weeks later, Jessie, still living at home while her new husband was on the road working as a traveling salesman, sent out her wedding announcements. She had chosen the same typesetting style she had liked so well in the calling cards she had selected six years before when she was graduated from high school.

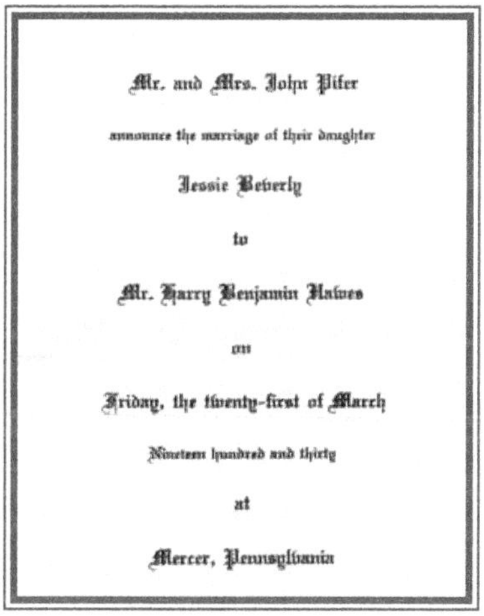
Mr. and Mrs. John Pifer
announce the marriage of their daughter
Jessie Beverly
to
Mr. Harry Benjamin Hawes
on
Friday, the twenty-first of March
Nineteen hundred and thirty
at
Mercer, Pennsylvania

Joe Errigo was as surprised as anyone at the news of Jessie's marriage but was too much of a gentleman to ask her why she had decided as she did. He was also preoccupied in the flurry of opening his own drug store which he called The City Drug Store. It opened April 30, 1930[6] and Joe didn't see Jessie until she stopped in his store in mid-May. "Mrs. Hawes, welcome!" Joe greeted her. "You have broken all our hearts." Jessie laughed, but did not respond. After school closed in May (she finished the term), Jessie moved with her husband to his home town of

Cherry Tree. The practice of hiring only unmarried women had relaxed, but teaching jobs were not easy to find in the shadow of a pending national Depression, and Jessie was having difficulty finding a position in or around Cherry Tree. She wasn't too worried about working, for, as she told her mother, "I have a husband to take care of me."

Harry Hawes had promised Jessie a good life with him, a house, travel, nice clothes, and status. He had big plans to open his own business in a field related to the sales job he had. The kind of life Harry offered appealed to the adventurous Jessie and she was happy to spend most of the summer just enjoying her new station as a married woman. As she wasn't keen on spending time in Cherry Tree with nothing to do, occasionally she went on the road trips with her husband. She soon tired of that, however, as there was nothing for her to do while Harry was calling on clients.

Jessie talked Kate into visiting her, although Kate's baby was due in late October. She said to Kate, "When the highlight of my summer is asking you to come up by train for the Golden Anniversary of the Mt. Pleasant Quinquennial Reunion, you know I am bored."

Kate and Howd agreed to drive to Cherry Tree for one day of the three-day event as much to see Katherine (Pifer) and William Shields as to visit with Jessie. Katherine, the Pifer girls' aunt, and her husband played a major role in the celebration, the tenth every-five-years-reunion of the community, and Jessie and Kate enjoyed their visit with each other as well as seeing both Aunt Katherine and her younger sister Aunt Margaret (Maggie) Pifer Jourdette. It was evident from the program that the Shields played a predominant role in the community, such so that Jessie couldn't help remarking, "If you took the name 'Shields' from the program, there would be hardly anyone left."

As Kate and Howd were leaving, Jessie pleaded with her sister to come back to visit as soon as she could. Jessie looked so sad that Kate promised she would do her best. Howd had taught her to drive and she knew she could use the car to visit her sister, but she was beginning to feel uncomfortable as her pregnancy progressed.

Harry's being gone from home so frequently gave Jessie time to think about why she had married him. First, she reasoned, she had been bored with her life in Curwensville. Her social life had begun to slow down and she attributed this to several reasons, although she had not set them in her mind in any order: none of her friends had any extra money to spend on social activities, an increasing number of her friends were marrying, and she didn't belong to the Country Club which more and more was becoming the only spot in town for recreational and social events.

What Jessie was beginning to realize is that it was the best and the worst time to be a single woman. Magazines were beginning to extol marriage and family life, even though hundreds of thousands of young people who wanted to get married could not afford to. The marriage rate per thousand population was falling, from 10.14 in 1929 until it would reach a low of 7.87 in 1932.[7] Nonetheless, it seemed that marriage had become more highly prized as an institution, and according to a survey conducted by *Fortune* magazine, "Sixty percent of the college girls and fifty percent of the men would like to get married within a year or two of graduation."[8] Many college administrators were said to have noted that college girls of the nineteen-thirties were more eager for early marriage than those of the nineteen-twenties. The Depression seemed to have made some of them more respectful of security.[9]

In contrast to Jessie's pessimistic outlook, when Kate took stock of her situation she felt blessed, even though she found it difficult to believe she was expecting. After three years of marriage she had almost resigned herself to being childless. Her pregnancy was fairly uneventful except for being uncomfortable during the summer heat in the tiny apartment. She and Howd began talking about renting a house, saying it would be so helpful to be in a larger place before the baby's expected arrival. Kate also spent many Saturdays alone, as the Curwensville's Fireman's Club had formed a Drill Team and Howd was a very active participant.

As one of the founding members, Howd was instrumental in finding interested men to join the team, and he himself never missed a practice. Kate would not have expected or asked him to miss either a practice or a parade. She knew how important this was to her husband who—too young to have been in the World War and whose father denied him permission to join the Boy Scouts, finally could at least be part of a uniformed group. In its first year, the drill team took several first prizes.

The following Sunday, Kate's last public outing prior to the birth of her child, she and Howd went to the Park Hotel Tea Room which had opened earlier that year. Following the meal, Howd suggested they take a drive to New Millport, only a few miles from Curwensville. On the return trip, he said, "Just one more quick stop, Kate, if you're not too tired. I have a surprise for you."

Several blocks into (the) South Side of Curwensville, Howd turned right on Hill Street and stopped at the second house. "What do you think?" he asked. "Mama said it will be available sometime after the first of the year. Papa owns it so the rent will be reasonable. You'll have a back yard and be close to the park. Would you mind living on South Side?" Kate responded enthusiastically, pleased to soon have her own home, while hiding her disappointment at living so far from the center of town.

Early Halloween night Kate's labor pains began and her daughter was born at home, shortly after midnight, under the watchful eye of Mrs. Bornhoff who assisted at many births in town. As this was the first female grandchild in her family, Kate gave her child the name of "Matilda" for her own mother and the middle name "Kay," by which she would be known.

Life is Not a Bowl of Cherries

The following year was notable to the Pifer family as the year Kate moved into her first house. Jessie continued to live in Cherry Tree where she still held hope of finding a teaching position, as it did not look like Harry was going to get his business established as quickly as he had hoped with the economy so bad. She had not taught the school term of 1930-31 and while she didn't miss teaching, she did miss the salary. She worked part-time in a grocery store but did not like that work. Harry's commissions were not as large as they had been the first nine months of their marriage because of the Depression and his clients simply did not have the money to buy anything except necessities; in addition, a number of them faced losing their businesses completely. Worse, Harry had hinted that if things did not soon improve financially, the young couple would have to move in with his parents. This did not please Jessie at all.

"If I wanted to live with someone's parents, I would have stayed home," Jessie wailed. "I miss my friends, you are always on the road, and this place is even smaller than Curwensville." Without Harry to drive, Jessie had to rely on the train or bus to go home occasionally. Cherry Tree was only about 30 miles from Curwensville, but it took a good hour by bus, which was a bit less expensive than the train. "There is nothing to do here, Hal," Jessie fussed. "I think I'll go home for awhile this summer." "What about your work?" Harry asked. "Well, I've been meaning to tell you, but Mr. Waisl said he doesn't need me this summer because his daughter's husband is out of work and they are coming back to Cherry Tree. I am supposed to check in with him in the fall and see if he needs me."

In June Jessie returned home for a two-month visit just in time to help Josephine pack. She and Droz were moving to Curwensville and Josephine couldn't wait!

In August Jessie returned to a displeased husband. He berated her for leaving him, telling her that her absence embarrassed him in front of his family and friends. Jessie, not accustomed to being questioned—husband or not, told Harry that if he couldn't provide for her he should find a better job. This began a standoff between the young couple, with Harry demanding that Jessie be satisfied with his earnings and Jessie responding that the life he was providing was not the life he had promised. Jessie's letters to Kate bemoaned her circumstance and hinted at a situation of growing volatility. Kate tried to cheer up her sister, but was at a loss as to what kind of advice to give her. Jessie also telephoned occasionally, but because Hal complained at the charges, Jessie felt constrained to limit her calls.

By early spring of 1932 the situation with Jessie's marriage was no better. Her letters and calls began to include tales of what Jessie termed "Harry's mean streak." She never elaborated on what this might mean, but in late April a call from Jessie awoke her sister Kate in the middle of the night. Through tears Jessie asked, "Can you please come get me? I need to get out of here. Now." Kate alerted her husband, giving hurried instructions about Baby Kay, and headed to Cherry Tree and Jessie's apartment. The sisters had agreed that Jessie would watch for the car and come out of the apartment so that Harry would be less likely to hear her leave. Two hours later, the sisters were back in Curwensville.

Jessie had brought nothing with her and Kate gave her several dresses, "to tide you over until you decide what you are going to do." Jessie stayed with Kate and Howd for several days and after many long telephone conversations with and promises from Hal, she decided to give her marriage another chance and returned the next week-end to Cherry Tree.

Despite attempts at reconciliation, by June Jessie had decided to move home. What she had hoped would be more status and independence as a married lady had resulted in disappointment. Her husband's commissions had not yet begun to match what he had claimed to Jessie when he had asked her to marry him and there was no indication that Harry would make any effort to keep his more recent promises to her. Further, Jessie still had not found a teaching position or any other job that provided steady employment. Mainly, she simply could find no reason to continue her marriage. She asked Mama—or rather told her in a letter—that she would be coming home the following week, for good. There was neither time nor any point to Mama's attempting to refute Jessie's plan. While concerned as to how she would explain her daughter's return, Mama was not going to deter her from coming home.

Two weeks later Jessie arrived by New York Central Railroad, with luggage and a few boxes. As she stepped off the train, she was glad to find Mr. Korb, a familiar drayer who would transport her heavier items. Even so, this was a mixed blessing as Jessie realized that he would quickly spread the word that Jessie Pifer seemed to be returning with all her belongings. His own daughter Mildred, yet unmarried, would no doubt relay the information among the young crowd. "Good," Jessie thought. "That will save me the trouble of explaining." She hoped she would not run into her father before seeing her mother, and was relieved to find that his drilling machine was not in sight as she neared the house. Jessie entered through the back door as was the custom for family members. "Hello, Mama," Jessie said. Mama had been thinking for days about what she would say upon her daughter's arrival. Her response was clear in both tone and meaning, "Welcome home, Jessie."

The first thing Jessie did after unpacking the next day was to go to the County Superintendent of Schools to put her name on the list of those seeking teaching positions. Strapped for money, she had only one pair of silk stockings. She debated going bare legged, but decided she had to risk wearing the stockings, hoping she wouldn't snag them on the train to Clearfield. She still could not withdraw any of her small savings, as the

Curwensville State Bank had not yet re-opened. Mama smiled to herself as she reminded her daughter that the Curwensville National Bank had reopened, the first in Pennsylvania to do so after closing during the worst part of the Depression,[10] but her concern for Jessie kept her from making an issue of Jessie's choices of either banks or husbands.

Jessie was hopeful that she would be assigned to a school, for she was beginning to feel the pinch of not having her own money to purchase a few stylish dresses. The length of hemlines was dropping again,[11] and Jessie could lengthen her hems only a little as the hems didn't have enough fabric to be let down to the fashionable length. Dress styles also were changing and Jessie didn't sew well enough to be able to redesign her dresses by adding ruffles, bows, and other embellishments. To make matters worse for one who had very little sewing skill in tailoring, waistlines of the thirties dresses had returned to their natural place. Even Mama wasn't sure how to reconstruct the basic outline of a dress of the twenties to one more modern.

Thwarted in her attempts to re-invent her wardrobe, Jessie decided she at least could let her hair grow since the short, shingled style was fading in popularity; nevertheless, she also knew to have it look its best required a good haircut to even the length. She bemoaned that she didn't have the 50 cents required for a cut and she couldn't bring herself to ask Mama for the money when she wasn't able at the time even to pay board. Further, Mama's renter was having trouble paying the rent which meant Mama would have to find that amount in order to pay the mortgage on the double house. With her world turned upside down, Jessie was disquieted. "This is not the way things were supposed to be," she said to herself. The assumptions of her world had failed.

As Jessie looked around at the lives of her friends it appeared that all of them were either happily married or heading in that direction. In particular, she couldn't help but compare her "lot in life" with that of her classmate and Kate's sister-in-law, Mary Alice Thompson. Jessie liked Mary Alice—everybody liked Mary Alice, but at times Jessie couldn't help but contrast the advantages her friend and classmate enjoyed.

Jessie was right about one thing: Mary Alice did live a privileged life in comparison to most of the young women in Curwensville. Her father was a successful businessman and enjoyed providing the niceties for his only daughter. Despite appearances, however, she lived just as much a sheltered life as Jessie did, even though she spent a semester at a girls' preparatory school following high school and then four years later earned a bachelor's degree at Drexel Institute in Philadelphia. It hadn't occurred to Mary Alice that part of the reason for her father sending her so far from home to attend college was as much to meet the right young men as it was for an education. And he made sure that she did meet people of whom he approved. Mary Alice's interest in a local young man was another one of the reasons her father decided she should not remain in Curwensville where the crush might develop into something more serious.

While at Drexel, Mary Alice became reacquainted with William Jackson, Jr. whom she had met when they were children. Both the Jackson and the Thompson families encouraged the friendship between Bill and Mary Alice, and the term arranged marriage was whispered about by some who knew the families' hopes. However, there was no rush and upon graduation from Drexel, Mary Alice, her cousin, and another friend embarked on a cross-country trip in the new car Mary Alice's father had given her for her college graduation.

Upon her return from the west coast, Mary Alice taught home economics at Clearfield High School for a year or two while a long distance courtship from Philadelphia continued. In 1932 Mary Alice accepted the marriage proposal of William K. Jackson and moved to Philadelphia following their wedding trip. The

Jacksons' only child, a son named for his father and paternal grandfather, was born in September 1934. Several years later, in 1939, the Jacksons returned to Clearfield where Mr. Jackson became general manager of Mid-State Theatres and Moshannon Valley Theatres, which together included 15-16 theatres.[12]

Even by the time Jessie and many others in small towns began to be affected by the economic depression, President Hoover remained at a loss as to how to help the country. He seemed to resist anything that smacked of handouts (redolent of his own background as an orphan) and acted as if he did not believe the government should become involved in the economy because most situations would self-correct.

Doomed to be blamed for the Depression, President Hoover valiantly but futilely continued to lead his country even as the Democrats found and supported "a rising star" in the person of Franklin D. Roosevelt, governor of New York. His supporters promoted "FDR" as champion of "the forgotten man,"[13] with the implication that Hoover had not helped the middle class out of the Depression.

With interests more keenly focused on her family than on the political scene, Ruby wrote from Canton, Ohio on May 19, sharing stories of daily life with her young sons, describing plans to fix up the house, and looking forward to a visit from her mother. After reading this letter, Jessie decided she would go to Canton to visit Ruby. Approaching Mama she said, "I think I might as well go help Ruby with the boys while she is redecorating. Besides, it is likely I will be teaching this fall and won't be able to go with you and Josie and Kate at that time. I am sure the State Bank will reopen soon and I will have the money for my ticket." Mama offered to lend her fare and suggested she go soon in order to be back in time to help Josephine with her moving, knowing full well that Josephine would have most of it to do.

Life is Not a Bowl of Cherries

Near the end of June, Josephine and Droz returned to Curwensville to the house they had purchased on Meadow Street, a large house so designed that they could rent out part of the second floor in order to help with the mortgage payment. Droz's company had reduced its size, letting a number of salesmen go and Droz himself had had some very anxious moments, half-expecting to be given a pink slip. As a veteran of the World War he strongly believed consideration should be given to those who had served their country, but that attitude was not pervasive in a country with so many unemployed.

Nineteen thirty-three saw the worst year of the Depression. It also marked the inauguration of the thirty-second President of the United States on March 4 on a day of dreary weather, attended by a delegation of businessmen from Curwensville.[14] Even with banks throughout the country collapsing, Franklin Delano Roosevelt braced himself on the podium proclaiming, "The only thing we have to fear is fear itself."[15] On March 7 he announced a four-day bank holiday, essentially closing all banks in the nation, and on March 9 he called Congress into special session to launch what he termed a "New Deal."

Mr. and Mrs. H. J. Thompson had spent Inauguration Week in Pittsburgh, perhaps not attending the actual inauguration ceremony after Mr. Thompson's defeat in his bid for election as State Senator.[16] As president of the Curwensville State Bank, his first concern at the announcement of the bank closings was to return home as soon as possible. Even though the State Bank had been closed for several months, plans had been made to reopen and, in fact, his trip to Pittsburgh included meeting with federal bankers. While the banks did reopen as scheduled, by the end of the year there were to be 4,004 bank closures, 25 percent unemployment, and a shutdown of 31 percent of the nation's productive capacity.[17]

President Roosevelt appointed the first female Cabinet Member in the person of Frances Perkins as Secretary of Labor, a move ridiculed by some but praised by many others. Another major appointment was that of General Hugh S. Johnson to administer the program known as the National Recovery Administration, or NRA. This position involved organizing thousands of businesses under fair trade codes drawn up by trade associations and industries. While these negotiations were taking place, Congress passed legislation that set a 40-hour week for clerical workers, a 36-hour week for industrial workers, and a minimum wage of 40 cents an hour. This legislation also abolished child labor and guaranteed that trade unions could organize and exercise the right of collective bargaining.

The new NRA program was voluntary. However, businessmen who accepted the codes developed by the various trade associations could place a NRA blue eagle symbol in their windows and on the packaging of their goods. In essence, this made the NRA plan compulsory to conduct any profitable business.

In Curwensville a well-attended mass meeting was held to prepare for a large NRA drive to be inaugurated the following Monday. *The Curwensville Herald* announced that "Every man, woman and child in the borough who is interested in national industrial recovery will make it a point to be in attendance."[18]

Soon approximately 23,000,000 people nationwide worked under the NRA fair code. However, violations of codes became common and attempts were made to use the courts to enforce its rules. In 1935 the Supreme Court declared the NRA as unconstitutional because many of its codes were an illegal delegation of legislative authority and the federal government had invaded fields reserved to the individual states.

A more palatable program for most of the citizenry was the Federal Emergency Relief Act which appropriated $500 million for direct relief to states, cities, town, and counties. By January 1934 the Civil Works Administration (CWA), an outgrowth of the Act, had over four million people on its rolls building roads, schoolhouses, airports, parks, sewers, and other public works, including the Locust Street School in Curwensville where a little theatre stage was built and the gymnasium enlarged as a CWA project.

One of the most laudable efforts of the first hundred days of FDR's presidency was the creation of the Civilian Conservation Corps (CCC), established as a great conservation movement to help stem the Great Depression and restore the nation's natural resources, as well as serve as a device to give unemployed young men useful work and to help divert them from drifting into subversive organizations.

As a result, 17 million acres of new forests were planted, numerous dams were built to stop soil erosion, and a great deal of other useful outdoor work was performed in federal and state parks. Projects near Curwensville included Black Moshannon State Park, 35 miles distance, and Parker Dam State Park in northern Clearfield County. S. B. Elliott State Park, a 318-acre park entirely wooded with magnificent stands of maturing oak and maple that dominate the mountaintop, was the CCC project located closest to Curwensville, and was the most popular of the nearby state parks in the 1940s for the Pifer girls and their families with its cabins, pavilions, roads, and trails.

Even with the Depression—or perhaps because of it—Howd and Kate were offered a larger home for purchase. It too was on South Side, but was closer to town. Howd's father had acquired the property through a mortgage foreclosure, and his mother was willing to help underwrite the cost of purchase with her own funds. Kate struggled with gaining a house that someone else had lost because of the Depression, telling Howd that it didn't seem right to benefit from another's misfortune. It was a difficult decision, even when Howd assured her that the house would be put on the market if they turned it down and would not be returned to the original owner regardless of any choice they made.

This house on Schofield Street was much larger than the young couple's home on Hill Street, with bigger and better appointed rooms. It was far from luxurious, but a nice "step up" with potential. Kate particularly liked the roomy kitchen and large pantry where the sink was located and where there also was a Hoosier-style cabinet. What the Thompsons could not have known in advance is that the very best thing that the move would bring was exceptional neighbors.

In these dark years of the Depression, the well drilling business decreased, but did not completely close down. What the situation did affect was the frequency by which John Pifer needed to travel to find work. Thus, at age 65, without a pension plan or sufficient savings, Papa was back on the road. In the summer of 1933, he wrote from Ontario, Canada; Michigan; and Wisconsin.

Later in the year (October 19), John received a letter from his brother Joe in Oregon, which reflects that John had been out on the road yet again:

> *I arrived at Frank's 11 p.m. the night after we parted at Waterloo, Iowa. Rode the bus all the day, stayed in Kansas and Missouri about two months, then on to Kansas City, Topeka, Wellsville and Ottawa. Might as well have gone East with you folks as nothing developed here. Was up to the farm a couple times, but most of the time at home in Portland and nothing to do. Getting to feel worthless. [Joe was at this time seventy years old.] Sold a few logs the last month. Mighty small profit. I'll get through the winter then I will have to go on the farm in spring.*[19]

As 1933 was drawing to a close, Josephine felt a quickening, a sign which confirmed her highest hopes. At age 38 Josephine was in the family way. Mama stood in a state of disbelief, but one of great joy. "Oh, Josephine," she beamed. "I can't think of any better Christmas gift for any of us. My prayers have been answered." Privately Mama held great concern because of the age of her oldest daughter, but would not spoil Josephine's moment for anything. Her memories of the visit Josephine and she, along with Kate and Kay, had made that fall to Ruby's home were still vivid. It had been a poignant scene as Josie played games with the children of her younger sisters. She didn't talk much any more about having a family, but now the following summer it was to be a reality with the birth of her son whom she would name Noel Franklin Hamilton. This made an almost perfect picture for Mama; all of her married daughters now had families.

Mama had long ceased to think of Jessie as being married and by the 1934-35 school year Jessie herself had nearly forgotten Harry Hawes. She was back to both her life of teaching and her maiden name. Because she had been absent from teaching in Clearfield County as a result of her marriage and moving to Cherry Tree, she found herself starting over in a rural school at Bridgeport where she would remain for the next decade.

Bridgeport School, in Pike Township, was perched atop a hill above the Crescent Division of North American Refractories Company. Jessie greatly wanted to purchase an automobile since there was no public transportation to the school, two and a half miles from her family's home, but she did not have enough money. There had been no salary increases since she had begun teaching in 1924, and as late as 1938 her contract offered only $800 per year.

"I would rather walk than board with any school director," Jessie cried to her sisters. "I don't want to be trapped there five days a week. And, besides, I would still have to find a ride at the beginning and the end of each week."

Josephine suggested that Jessie check with the bus service and perhaps the bus might stop at the foot of the hill or at the refractory. Thus, Jessie became a regular on the bus run and on occasion when she missed the bus and started walking, various kind souls on their way to work at the Crescent Division would stop and offer her a ride. Occasionally, and more often when the workers got to know her and watch for her, some of them would go out of their way to drive her the remainder of the distance up the hill to her country school. After a time, the men at North American would kid one another about courting "Miss Pifer." There were several with whom Jessie became friends, although these friendships went no further than Jessie's being grateful for a ride. One young man in particular may have looked for her daily, hoping to be the first to offer her a ride. Jack Mohney would later figure more prominently in Jessie's life.

The Sunday School Field Days continued to be a highlight of the summer with every Sunday School in Clearfield County participating. There was a parade in the morning, and a Pentecostal Banner was presented to the Sunday School with the most cars at the rally. After the death of one of the founders, however, this Field Day celebration lost its momentum and ceased operation shortly after the 1938 events.[20]

The Clearfield County Fair, on the other hand, had suspended operations during the Depression because of economic conditions. It reopened in 1937 when the James E. Strates Shows made their first of thirty some appearances on the midway. The following year the Clearfield Volunteer Fire Department took over management of the Fair and began to expand the offerings to a full week, opening with the first fireman's parade ever to pass by the grandstand.[21]

Near the close of 1935, H. J. Thompson purchased the local Strand Theatre, earlier that year destroyed by fire. He remodeled the building and renamed it the Rex Theatre, a name he thought appropriate—Rex meaning King—as it was the first of a chain of theatres he was soon to own.

The following year was marked by disasters for Curwensville, first with destruction by fire, then by flood. On a bitterly cold

Life is Not a Bowl of Cherries

Friday night, January 25, 1936, with the temperature at zero or below, a kerosene heater exploded in a barbershop, the fire quickly spreading in an easterly direction throughout the next two blocks, buildings quickly covered with ice from the water used to fight the fire. At least ten businesses and four homes were lost in the devastation at an estimated total cost of $90,000.[22]

Fire was followed by a flood in the spring. Precipitated by a quick spring thaw, the flood centered its destruction in the lower Filbert Street area and lowlands bordering Anderson Creek, particularly at its junction with the Susquehanna River. The flood reached the Covered Bridge at Schofield Street, the Irvin Hill Bridge by the Susquehanna House, and the Filbert Street Bridge, flooding all the surrounding lowlands, and, in effect, separating both Irvin Hill and South Side from the central area of the town. Because the houses on Meadow Street were in the floodplain, most basements were filled with water and the flood waters threatened to reach the first floors. Among those evacuating were Josephine and Droz with their little son.

Kate and Howard also were prepared to evacuate because the meadow behind their home was flooded and the floodwater encroached into their basement, rising about two feet before the flood abated. When the waters receded, several items not belonging to them were found in their back yard, in particular a long, sturdy wooden bench. There was no way to discover its owner, so the bench remained with the house.

After such a ruinous winter and spring, by fall the townspeople of Curwensville were ready for something good to happen. And it most definitely did in the form of high school football. The Curwensville Golden Tide became the Western Pennsylvania Football Champions of 1936. This squad of only 30 players (from a high school population of 300, counting both sexes) had won eleven games in their regular season. Excitement reigned throughout the immediate area and traveling to Kingston,

Pennsylvania for the state championship was the main topic of conversation in the town for the two weeks between winning the Western Championship and playing for the state championship. This event brought the town together in a frenzy of support for the players and pride in the town itself.

On December 5 a trainload of fans, including Jessie, traveled to Kingston (a distance of about 180 miles), a town of 21,000, seven times the size of Curwensville. Many viewed the excursion as the highlight of Curwensville sports history. Not so curiously, perhaps, the yearbook's glowing account of the game never mentions that Kingston won, 7-0.

Fire returned to Curwensville early in 1937 when flames broke out in the furnace room of the Presbyterian Church, and again the firefighters had to brave the cold of winter to quell the blaze. The damage to the church amounted to $6,500, a considerable sum in the 1930s. Repairs and rebuilding, however, began early in the spring and a Re-Dedication Service was held on October 3, 1937. Choir members included many familiar names but not that of Jessie Pifer, further evidence that Jessie, a former soloist, never sang again after the mid-1920s.

Nineteen thirty-seven also saw the completion of the Golden Gate Bridge, the death of millionaire-philanthropists Andrew Mellon and John D. Rockefeller, the Hindenburg dirigible disaster by fire, and the loss of Amelia Earhart on a flight over the Pacific. Locally, Clifford Kelly, a classmate of Jessie's, opened Kelly's Shoe Store providing competition for Kovach's, the only other shoe store in town. Of interest to the Pifer family that year was the birth of Kate's second daughter, Judith Evelyn, her middle name in honor of their neighbor who was to be a most positive influence in the lives of Kate's middle daughters.

Life in the Thompson household would soon be different than it had been prior to 1937. For the first six and a half years of her life Kay had been an only child, and while the family was not well-to-do, their daughter was indulged with toys most children in those days didn't have. For example, she had a cast iron toy coal stove whose little burners lifted off just like real stoves of the time. She also had a round, child-size "ice-cream parlor" -style table and chairs made of black wrought iron with composition seats in gray trimmed in blue. One of her other special toys was an outsized wicker doll carriage that was large enough for her life-size doll, whose name was Gorgeous. The doll became Kay's dearest treasure. During the summer and fall of 1937 she would bundle up Gorgeous while her mother dressed baby Judith, and mother and daughter would take a walk with their babies in nearly matching carriages.

1938 brought with it the House Un-American Activities Committee, the Lambeth Walk, and the Benny Goodman band, foreshadowing the "big band" sound, soon to be a major influence on American music. The Pulitzer Prize for literature that year was awarded to Marjorie Kinnan Rawlings' *The Yearling* and for drama to Thornton Wilder's "Our Town."

For the general worker in business and industry, the important matter of the year was that the 40-hour week became the standard. Offices began to close on Saturday mornings, providing the foundation for the concept of "free" week-ends. Retail stores that remained open on Saturdays began arranging rotating schedules so that their employees also would work only a 40-hour week.

The event for which 1938 is most remembered, however, occurred on Halloween Eve with the radio broadcast of a fictional radio drama, Orson Welles' "War of the Worlds." The program was so convincing that, despite announcements to the contrary, many listeners believed that the world actually was being invaded by Martians. As a result, a short-lived but intense panic gripped the country.

Six days following Halloween and five days after her seventh birthday, Kay's initial welcoming of a sibling to her family may have been tested, when baby Jo Ellen arrived on the scene. Both Kay and I, then a 20-month-old toddler, remember the day Jo Ellen was brought home from the hospital (as if that is where one found babies). Kay had rushed to the door when she heard the car pull into the driveway. I recall standing at the top of the stairs and watching the arrival of the new infant into the household, as I held the hand of Ann Zwolski, a high school girl who helped my mother with the children.

With the addition of this baby to the family, Kate couldn't help but compare herself to Mama who herself had not expected to start a "second family" with the birth of Jessie a number of years after her two older daughters had been born. Already with this third child Kate had surpassed her three sisters who had one, two, and two children respectively. Further, Kate was the only one with daughters, all the more reason to think she was cut in the pattern of her own mother and her mother's mother. However, at nearing age thirty-one Kate wasn't sure she would look forward to two more children to match her mother's five.

As Howd and Kate entered the house with the third baby, he said to her, "If the babies keep coming, we shall have to find a larger house." Kate laughed and said to her husband, "Just remember that if Mama had stopped at three daughters, I wouldn't be here!" She was beaming as she reflected on her healthy family, the only concerns in her life being the far-off rumblings of war.

As the clouds of conflict gathered on the world's horizon, Kate was only one of most Americans who were very uncertain of what the future might hold. Hitler had been collecting European countries from the time he had met with his foreign minister and top generals in November 1937 and had announced his plans for acquiring new territory for Germany in Europe's heartland. In only one year's time Hitler had brought under his rule Austria and the Sudeten Germans. Then in 1939, breaking solemn promises he had made to heads of state in Europe, he moved his army into Prague, dividing the remainder of Czechoslovakia into two German satellite states.

At the same time, Japanese militarists were beginning their aggression in an aim to build an empire in East Asia. As part of their plans they made a concerted effort to drive American and European missionary, educational, medical, and cultural activities out of China. In 1939 the Japanese captured Shanghai and proceeded to make life intolerable for Americans and Europeans in the international settlement.

Then, suddenly and without warning, on September 1, 1939 Germany attacked Poland. Two days later Britain and France declared war on Germany and the British dominions followed suit shortly, in effect beginning another World War and changing life forever—in Curwensville and in the larger world. Ruby and Jean, in particular, felt fear grip their hearts because each had two sons who possibly could be called to military duty if ever the United States entered the War and if it should last long enough for the boys to enter the service.

Since the war had not yet affected the United States, expansion construction began at the Patton Building during the school year of 1939-1940. The basement was entirely excavated and three classrooms were created in the space to help accommodate the increasing size of the school population. Fire escapes were erected on the exterior and partitions put in the west annex rooms. In addition, a "little theatre" stage was constructed in the basement of the Locust Street Building.

One indication of the slight upward trend in the economy was that by the late 1930s nail polish, first advertised in 1936, was gaining popularity with those who could afford it and who had the chutzpah to wear it. Jessie longed to be among those with bright red nails, but still could not afford any extravagance and could think of no rationale to convince her mother otherwise.

Another sign that conditions were beginning to return to normal and that society was again gaining attention was the advent of traveling speakers who provided lectures on the etiquette of cigarette smoking. One very popular speaker, sponsored by Philip Morris & Company, toured the country, speaking to clubs, department store employees, nurses, and charm-school students, convincing them of the advantages of smoking.[23]

As the decade drew to a close, Christmas 1939 brought difficulties both in finding and in having the money to purchase gifts. One comfort to Kate was that toys could be passed down to each child since all three children were girls. Each child had her own section under the tree so that on Christmas morning it would be clear as to what gifts belonged to which child. These items were neatly arranged in a semi-circle with each child's gifts collected at the same spot. This arrangement also made it possible not to have to wrap every gift, particularly in times when wrapping paper was at a premium.

Kay was nine, Judith nearly three, and baby Jo Ellen a little more than a year old—all three at ages in which Christmas would be exciting, both to them and their doting parents.

Early that morning big sister Kay led the procession down the staircase which opened directly into a large hall where the Christmas tree stood, with all its lights shining. Kate followed, carrying Jo Ellen, and Howd walked down the stairs with Judith. Kay was silent. Noticing this, her mother asked, "What's the matter, Kay?" Their oldest daughter looked at her parents, surveyed the gifts, stepped back and drew an imaginary line on the floor. She then answered their question, "I remember when *my* presents came out to here." These words would haunt her family in later years when they reviewed their shared childhood, looking for clues to Kay's expressions of entitlement.

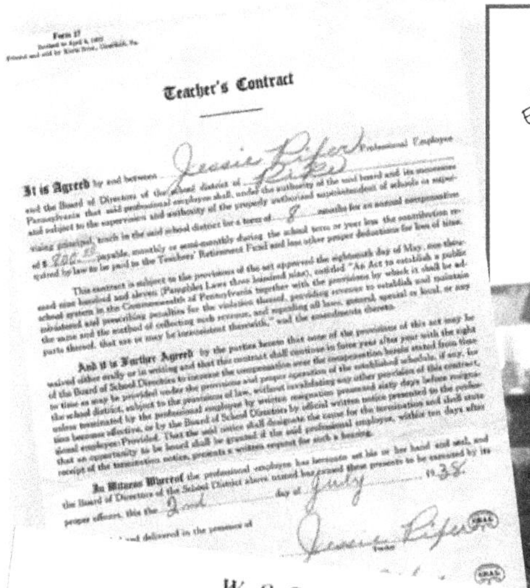

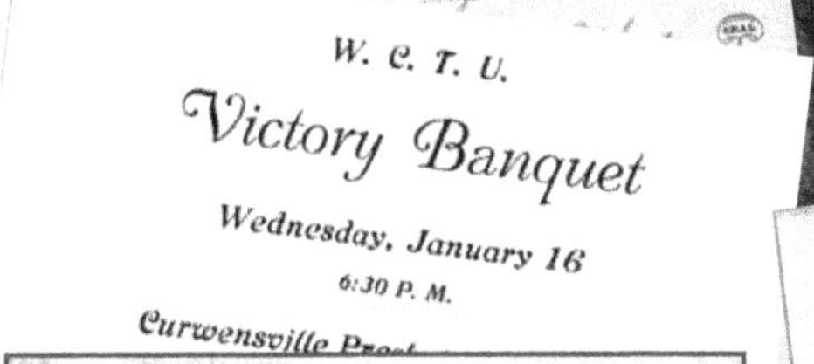

Jebbie
Early 40s

Kay, Judith and Jo Ellen
Easter 1944

John and Joseph Pifer

Jebbie with the author, age three

Chapter 6

For the Duration

The world war that began in Europe and Asia in the thirties was the greatest single tragedy in the history of mankind. Death and suffering, hatred and terror, consumed the souls of millions of people. The cost is beyond calculation, the arithmetic is stupefying, but the neatness of the round figures defames the chaos and the agony. . . . more than 50 million people lost their lives, perhaps 20 million of them civilians.

—*Harold Evans*[1]

Despite all of the destruction to lives and property that wars bring, the Second World War remains unique in the history of the United States in that it captured the spirit of an entire country. The impact of World War II is perhaps followed only by what happened in the fall of 2001 with its compelling horror and patriotic aftermath of a single day's mass destruction that became known simply as 9/11.

Historians suggest it was the economic hardships of the Great Depression that steeled the country's resolve to get through the adversities of WWII. While that spirit of determination perhaps has been identified more clearly in retrospect, persons of any age who lived during that time will say that people banded together and the whole thrust of living focused on the war effort: factories retooling to produce military goods, women joining the Armed Forces, children collecting tin cans, and patriotic music being heard everywhere. It was an intense time, but the people were quick to share what they had, and were instilled with a deep sense of service to others.

Everyone, young and old, soon realized that the way of life they had known was now forever changed. With factories concentrating on the needs of war, the entire population of the country found they could make do with what they had. Rationing became a way of life and coupon books determined both menus and wearing apparel. More than factory production, however, was the dedication of an entire generation.

Jessie, Kate, and Jean at this time were all in their thirties—old enough to realize the seriousness of military conflict, yet young enough to be transfixed by the excitement of a nation at war. During the earlier World War, these young women had been children of thirteen, ten, and eight, and had not been directly affected. Their memories of that earlier war were vague, only impressions of there being a few young men from town referred to as "doughboys" who forever after marched in the annual Memorial Day parades. The young Pifer sisters, however, were familiar with some of the World War I songs they occasionally would come across in Mama's piano bench, including their favorite, "Over There."

During World War I there had been no radio broadcasts from the front lines to keep the citizens informed on the war's progress, and in 1918 Europe seemed very far away. During the evenings of those war years the Pifer family had sat at the dining room table after supper as Papa opened his newspaper and read aloud accounts of the battles in places with unfamiliar names. The girls had barely paid attention to these accounts, as the war was something very formless and quite unrelated to their daily lives.

Thus, at the outset of this new World War the younger Pifer sisters had no frame of reference for warfare. They didn't need to give much thought to their classmates or husbands being called to battle because of their ages, and they had neither brothers nor uncles who might go to war. Among the three of them—Jessie, Kate, and Jean—were no sons old enough for service. Jean's older son was thirteen and she comforted herself based on the short duration of that first World War. It never occurred to any of them that this new war actually would last long enough that he would be called to military service. Even the oldest Pifer grandson, Ruby's son, John Wayne, was barely sixteen in 1940.

Early in the decade, people's daily lives remained fairly routine. In the schools there was little discussion about war (or any other current event), as immediate news was not widely available and many parents and teachers were not comfortable with in-depth discussions of contemporary world events because of their own limited knowledge and a general belief that children were unaware of world events and concerns.

Most households in the Curwensville area did not subscribe to any major newspaper, preferring the local weekly or *The Clearfield Progress*, a daily. A few bought *The Grit*, a folksy weekly broadsheet aimed at rural and farming communities. However, it was community and family matters that were uppermost on the minds of most citizens. Jessie was occupied with her school and Jean, Josephine, and Kate with the care of their children.

Movie theatres were doing a brisk business in the 1940s, particularly with films showing the separation of families, and several extraordinary films of 1939 which were Academy Award contenders: "Good-bye Mr. Chips," "Stagecoach," "The Wizard of Oz," and "Gone With the Wind." These outstanding films of 1939 did not make it to Curwensville until early in 1940, because studios printed only a certain number of copies and small towns had to wait their turn.

The Pulitzer Prize in Literature in 1940 was awarded to John Steinbeck for *The Grapes of Wrath*, published the previous year. More than by movies, novels, and plays, however, the last year of the depression is marked by a song forever after identified with Kate Smith and World War II. Although "God Bless America" presents a difficult voice range and requires exceptional vocal power to deliver, it led the many memorable songs to come out of the era in both popularity and longevity.

The first stark reality of the world condition, however, was one that hit the hearts of wives and mothers in the form of the Selective Service Act of 1940. While this Act prohibited draftees from serving anywhere outside the continental United States, the very fact of its activation was enough to create alarm. By fall, the Burke-Wadsworth Act ordered the conscription of all males between the ages of 21 and 35, leading to induction of 800,000 draftees into the armed services. Many citizens saw this Act as a signal that Washington was expecting war, and by 1941 the impression that war was inevitable pervaded all thinking.

While it was clear that most of the American people did not want war, the voters still overwhelmingly supported President Roosevelt. Nevertheless, the reality was that the country was low on war supplies and was grossly unprepared to go to battle. Robert Sherwood later summed up the national temper when he wrote that World War II was "the first war in American history in which general disillusionment preceded the firing of the first shot."[2]

Jessie had purchased a car "on time" in the late 1930s and that summer of 1941 she decided that she was financially able to get out and have some fun. Thus, she planned two vacation trips, one to the Philadelphia area in June and the other to Atlantic City in August. In mid-June, Jessie and her friend Jean Boyce took the train to Philadelphia. No one questioned her trips as everyone knew she preferred to shop in a city, and her flamboyant tone was convincing when she said she enjoyed "doing the theatres."

With a choice of 380 single screen theatres in operation during this heyday of movie theatres in Philadelphia, Jessie and Jean chose the Aldine at 5th and Chestnut, described by *The Philadelphia Inquirer* as a palatial wonder. Jessie was also determined to see the other two "largest and grandest" theatres, so the second night in the city the young women attended the Earle at 11th and Market. Big bands played the Earle on a regular schedule and, while Jessie loved to dance, hearing Cab Calloway in person on stage was an agreeable substitute. Jessie also insisted that she and Jean go to the Mastbaum Theatre the following afternoon so that they would not have to "dress to the nines," according to Jessie, as they would if they attended an evening performance.

When the two young women entered the Mastbaum, Jessie, who had been told that the Fountain Lobby was almost as well-known a meeting place as the eagle at Wanamaker's, wanted to let anyone within earshot know that she was a sophisticate and said a little too loudly to Jean, "I like to meet my friends here when I come into the city," as if she were a frequent theatre-goer. Both women were in awe of this huge lobby with its two grand staircases and eight free-standing Doric columns, but Jessie wouldn't allow herself to gawk. "Jean," she asked, "shall we take the elevator to the eighth floor lounge?" Jean, silent in the presence of such grandeur and Jessie's assumed confidence, could only nod in agreement, then soundlessly follow Jessie's lead.

The fourth and last day of their trip, after breakfast at Horn and Hardart, the young women took a streetcar to Willow Grove Park, a grand amusement park north of the city. The pleasures there ranged from renting a row boat in a man-made lake and the Venice amusement ride—in which passengers rode in gondolas guided under a bridge where a mechanical man tipped his hat to the customers—to the public band concerts. Jessie held a blurred remembrance that John Philip Sousa conducted concerts at Willow Grove. Always aiming to appear cultured, she asked, "When will Captain Sousa be conducting?" The attendant kindly replied, "I am so sorry, madam, but Mr. Sousa's last appearance here was in 1926, a few years before he died."

In August Jessie went to Atlantic City with two other single women. This time she drove her car so the ladies could take what they needed for the cottage they had rented. Jessie loved the beach and was a good swimmer, even in ocean water. At the famous Steel Pier they saw headliner entertainment, including Tex Beneke and his orchestra. Jessie wanted to go to Club Harlem, but her two friends hesitated, even though Jessie tried to assure them that they would be perfectly safe. What bothered them, the women said, was being without escorts, but they said they would consider going on their next trip to the shore. As they made a final trip to the Boardwalk to purchase salt water taffy before departing for the drive home, the trio agreed they would make this an annual event, if war didn't prevent it. Nine years would pass before Jessie returned to Atlantic City.

Heading back to the classroom a few weeks later, Jessie was glad she had taken her trips that summer. She sensed the tension prevalent in a country anticipating war, noticing it even in her students. She also was glad she had had a telephone installed that spring, over the grumblings of her father, "We don't need one of those contraptions, Jessie." "Papa," she replied. "If we should go to war, then probably no one will be allowed to buy a telephone. Also, it will help your business if people can telephone you. The ringing won't be that bad and if it rings when we are all busy, why, we just won't answer it! And think how nice it will be to be able to talk to Ruby." Thus, the Pifers became among the growing number of townspeople installing telephones.

December 7, 1941 was a quiet Sunday afternoon on the Eastern seaboard when news of Pearl Harbor began to leak. At first there was nothing definite, but by evening families were gathered around their radios waiting for any news. Most sat silently through the programs of Jack Benny, One Man's Family, and Edgar Bergen and Charlie McCarthy, waiting to hear what their president would say about this frightening event on his regular Sunday evening Fireside Chat. That evening, however, because he was meeting with his national advisers, President Roosevelt was unavailable to address the nation.

Mrs. Eleanor Roosevelt, the president's wife, replaced him at the microphone, addressing the country from the viewpoint of a mother who had three sons in the war zone, one in military service on a destroyer and two in coastal cities in the Pacific. "I feel as though I were standing upon a rock and that rock is my faith in my fellow citizens," she stated with confidence in her voice.[3] Everyone felt a commonalty with the President's family, all of them dealing with thoughts of their own sons, husbands, and brothers, and perhaps even themselves in danger should the United States go to war.

The following day at noon, 60 million Americans were at their radios to hear Franklin D. Roosevelt speak briefly and simply to his Cabinet, both houses of Congress, and the Supreme Court, "Yesterday, December 7, 1941—a date which will live in infamy—the United States of America was suddenly and deliberately attacked by naval and air forces of the Empire of Japan." His speech concluded with these words, "I ask that the Congress declare that since the unprovoked and dastardly attack by Japan on Sunday, December 7, 1941, a state of war has existed between the United States and the Japanese Empire."[4] The resolution passed and the United States was at war.

Young men rushed to volunteer for military service and, once trained and transformed from civilian life to fighting men, the GIs became the world's best fed, clothed, armed, and educated soldiers.

Wartime was difficult for everyone and American citizens coped in various ways, although many children of that time recall that "grown-ups all seemed to have a sense of purpose."[5] Wives and parents could do little more than wait and worry, following the news as best they could and trying to imagine what their loved ones were experiencing. Mama, who always sought solace in her

Bible, expressed sadness in the margins of the Book. Earlier she had written "Dear Rob (Robert Heighes, her sister Jessie's son) died July 22, 1941, Los Angeles, Cal." and on December 29, 1941 she had noted, "Had a letter from Lennie today. She is so sad of our Billy (Lennie's grandson) and the war."[6]

Many different levels of rationing soon went into effect. Some items, such as sugar, were distributed evenly based on the number of people in a household. Restaurant owners and other merchants were accorded more availability, but had to collect ration stamps from customers to restock their food supplies. Other rationed items, such as gasoline or fuel oil, were available only to those who could justify a need.

Red stamps were used to purchase rationed meat and butter, and blue stamps were used for processed foods. To enable making change for ration stamps, the government issued "red point" tokens to be given in change for red stamps, and "blue point" tokens in change for blue stamps. The red and blue tokens were about the size of a dime and were made of thin compressed wood fiber material, because metals were in short supply.[7]

In the initial years of rationing, worn automobile tires had to be turned in before ration cards would be issued for replacements. However, as the war dragged on, the task of finding replacements was pointless, because rubber was so scarce that no new tires or recaps were available. Further, because of rubber shortages, the government confiscated all tires in excess of five per car owner. If a person's automobile blew a tire and he had no spare, the car either sat out the war or the car owner would try to find a spare tire from a relative or good neighbor.

Needless to say, there was very little "driving for pleasure," even more so after the president placed a ban on pleasure driving after a number of oil tankers were sunk by German submarines. Nationwide gas rationing was ordered and coupon books issued. With gasoline rationing in effect, passenger traffic on the

Pennsylvania Turnpike, which had opened in 1940, fell by more than 70 percent. It was also understood that should it become necessary, the Turnpike would be commandeered and used strictly by the military.

Because of the country's fundamental need for milk and produce, farmers were given unrestricted purchasing privileges for gasoline. Many of them, however, did not need all the gasoline that was available to them and they became clandestine retailers of the commodity the government made available to them. A story is told of a local farmer who sold his unlimited supply of fuel from a storage tank inside his barn. The barn featured a Dutch door with an overhang so when "customers" drove up, the farmer could pull the pump hose over the half door and into the car's gasoline tank. Jessie was delighted to discover this fuel supply as she certainly did not want to have to ride the bus to school again.

By 1942 sixty percent of all civilian food items had been rationed and the hardships from the lack of goods were felt in earnest. Hoarding of items increased as consumers began to fear goods would not be available again for years. One of the oddities of behavior during this time was people who hoarded coffee not because they particularly enjoyed the drink, but only because it was scarce.

Evenings in many households consisted of listening to the radio and, during the first year of the war, the number of listeners increased 20 percent overall.[8] Parlor games also rose in popularity; sales of checkers and chess sets zoomed; and sales were up 1,000 percent for playing cards. A 1942 survey showed that card games were played in 87 percent of American homes.[9]

Light reading predominated in early 1942. Later, when books about America's fighting men began to appear, many were heavily censored and conveyed only glimpses of the real trials of combat. Because of her students' interest in the war, Jessie read some of the accounts of life on the home front to them, carefully omitting sections that might be upsetting to children in the early grades.

The most popular adult books included *They Were Expendable, Into the Valley, Guadalcanal Diary,* and *See Here, Private Hargrove*. A favorite of many readers was *The Robe,* and by 1945 that book had sold 2,000,000 copies. Not surprising, however, the best seller of the year was the *Red Cross First Aid Manual*.

Paperback books, first introduced in 1939, increased in sales and the Armed Services Edition program published cheap paperback copies of a size that would fit in a man's pocket. At the height of the program 40 titles a month were being sent out and, throughout the war, around 100,000,000 copies were distributed to servicemen free of charge.

The most pervasive intrusion in Curwensville during the war years, other than rationing, was the Civil Defense program with its air raid wardens patrolling the streets, making sure all windows were covered during an air raid drill. Most wardens were men too old for active service, but dedicated and dependable nonetheless. Blackouts, complete with the warden's cry of "Get those lights out," became a familiar occurrence in many towns. Blackout curtains, light-opaque window shades, blackout candles, and lighted blackout canes became familiar to everyone.

Other national civilian defense organizations included the Civil Air Patrol who worked on the East Coast.[10] Enemy U-boats are presumed to have come off shore on the East Coast when flashes of explosions appeared against the night sky and flotsam and jetsam appeared at Cape Hatteras and as far north as the Delmarva Peninsula.

State Guard units were geared up to provide assistance should there be an attack. These units included draft-age men with deferments and men too young or too old for the draft. Among those many state volunteers was Howard V. Thompson, fulfilling his lifelong desire to be part of a military unit. To help keep the attention of the townspeople focused on the war effort, the Guard sponsored dances held once a month in the armory located in the small town of Hyde City, four miles from Curwensville.

Jessie, always ready to dance, attended many of these events, although most of the guard members had wives or sweethearts and Jessie got tired of "borrowing someone's husband" for a dance. Of course, the husbands were quite willing to dance with the good-looking Jessie Pifer, but not all of their wives were keen on this. Jessie still could have had the pick of the lot—married or unmarried—were she interested in pursuing such, but she clearly was not.

On the morning of August 19, 1942 Kate told her husband, "It's time for me to get to the hospital," and shortly after being admitted, she gave birth to their fourth daughter and last child. Kate already had selected the name "Nan" when Howd asked his wife if she would consider naming this child for his mother. Thus, the new baby was named Elizabeth Nan, and would use the middle name Nan much as her oldest sister, named Matilda Kay for her maternal grandmother, was always known as Kay.

Christmas 1942 was somber in most households throughout the United States, and pastors tempered their Sunday Christmas sermons with concerns for those away from home, serving their country. There was a shortage of most goods and families had to make do with what they had rather than buying new. Even Elizabeth Thompson sewed by hand pima cotton undergarments for her granddaughters. This was a surprising gesture by this reserved woman who had never had to make any of her own clothing. Kate was moved by this kindness, for lingerie was a luxury not manufactured during wartime and there was a scarcity.

Nylon would not be used again for stockings until after the war. This left only cotton for hosiery, not at all pleasing to American women.

Jessie and her elementary teacher colleagues discussed ways they could help the children make something in school that they could give to their families as Christmas gifts. The problem was that there were no school funds budgeted for materials and they could not tell the children to ask their parents to purchase materials, because not all of those families could afford to. Jessie came up with an idea ahead of its time. She made a list of the factories and stores in town and considered what supplies they might be willing to donate to her classroom. She started with the hosiery mill that had been retooled to make parachutes, and she began to design something that could be made from the white nylon used for the parachutes. She had asked persons who worked there if there might be any leftover fabric and what size it might be.

Encouraged by her findings, she went to the factory manager on the Friday after Thanksgiving and asked if she could have some scraps for her school children to make Christmas gifts. The manager, taken by her earnestness (and, no doubt, good looks) gave her a large box of scrap fabric with enough material to share with any other teacher who might want to use it. A volunteer mother taught the children to stitch the fabric into handkerchief holders and tree ornaments.

While Jessie was hustling for scrap material, our mother was making an inventory of what toys might be recyclable that Christmas. She decided to paint some of Kay's toys—a small doll carriage and a wardrobe, and to have new doll clothes made for one of the dolls I no longer played with. She would use these as gifts for Jo Ellen, feeling confident that her four-year-old would not recognize the old toys in new wrappings. Whether Jo Ellen did or did not notice the refurbished toys was irrelevant, as both Kay and I clearly recognized the items and lamented on the unfairness of having our toys given to another.

While rationing of meat had begun early in 1942, the crisis of the

1942-43 winter saw butchers' display cases gradually emptied. Steak was the first to disappear and soon not even hamburger was to be found in most meat counters in the East. Spam also was found among the items rationed beginning in February 1943. The meat shortage continued into the years following the war, resulting in meatless days, usually Tuesdays and Fridays, when housewives reverted to the "food stretchers" and meatless dishes they had learned to prepare during the Depression. These meals required even more ingenuity when cheese, often used in those meatless dishes, was also rationed. As a result, eggs became one of the most abundant meat substitutes. Because butter was rationed, the use of oleomargarine increased.

Fuel oil rationing was instituted during the icy winter of 1942-43. A formula determined that each consumer could buy about two-thirds of what he had used in 1941, an amount established as sufficient to keep a home at sixty-five degrees.[11] Most people in Curwensville, including all of the Pifer households, still were using coal, and as much as they tired of shoveling coal and the resulting infiltrating coal dust through the house, they were glad coal was not yet rationed.

Reflective of the times, the *1942 Echo* dedicated the high school yearbook to classmates in their country's service and to all "who are sacrificing so that liberty may not perish from this earth."[12]

The best-known national war-time organization for high school students was the Victory Corps.[13] The Class of 1943 dedicated a sixteen-page section of their 92-page yearbook to those serving in the armed services, despite the need to shorten the publication because of the scarcity of paper and ink.

Concern for soldier moral and homesick draftees prompted the YMCA, YWCA, Salvation Army, National Catholic Community Service, National Jewish Welfare Board, and Travelers Aid Society to form the United Service Organizations (USO). Through their efforts recreational centers sprang up in every American town near a military base or major transit point, offering movies, dances, hot food, a room to write a letter, and even in some places, a shoeshine. By 1943 these canteens had sprung up around the country affording citizens an opportunity to "do something for the boys in uniform."

Depending upon the town and the number of volunteers, the canteens became popular social clubs for young people, particularly young women who could do their part by befriending the troops, yet be protected in a safe environment. In larger communities near military bases local families invited "the boys" to their homes for holidays or a Sunday meal. And weekly buses filled with young women and the omnipresent chaperones headed for dances on the bases. Few parents complained about their daughters supporting the war effort, so the buses were usually full of willing volunteers.

Many of the larger canteens supplied space for volunteers to knit blankets, scarves, and gloves or to help the Red Cross in rolling surgical dressings, packing supplies, or collecting cigarettes for the boys "over there." USO canteens were also collection sites for scrap metal, newsprint, and other materials for recycling. The Hollywood Canteen in Los Angeles and the authentic Stage Door Canteen in New York City became the major attraction for servicemen on leave because of their location and being featured in movies. There servicemen could get free food and beverages and could dance with starlets or converse with stage luminaries serving as volunteers. There was always a line waiting to get in, and once inside, the boys in uniform could—at least for a few hours—put aside thoughts of war.

Increased radio listening, as well as the availability of records, made everyone—especially young people—more aware of music than most ever had been before. In the larger cities, adults enjoyed nightclubs with their large, lively crowds and much of the public could name the largest clubs in New York City. Most of the larger hotels had nightclubs with live bands, all of which concentrated on producing smooth, slick, jivey sounds or slow, sweet fox-trots that seemed reluctant to end and disunite clinging partners."[14]

For those still in their twenties these years were a particularly exciting time to live, work, and play in New York City. Young women recall dinner dates and dancing nearly every night of the week, with a seemingly endless number of military men on leave who did not know if they would ever return from battle, but who wanted memories of good times to carry them through the European war trenches.[15]

Young people were committed to doing their part to win the war, and the 1942-43 school year saw an all-out victory effort at the high school level. The Tri Hi Y collected clothes for the Red Cross, repaired and distributed toys to needy children at Christmas, sold defense stamps throughout the year, and helped the VFW sell poppies for Memorial Day. The younger children packed boxes of small toys and supplies for the Red Cross to distribute to the Allies, and many students made a great effort to gather as much milkweed as they could find to be used as a replacement for scarce kapok in the lining of life jackets.

Individual and community Victory Gardens flourished, reaching an estimated 20,000,000 at the peak of the war, and producing 20 percent of all vegetables grown in the United States. This allowed for more of the commercially grown vegetables to be used by the military.[16]

A proliferation of volunteer "victory speakers" sprang up to speak at rallies, civic clubs, schools, and social clubs, much as they had in World War I; patriotism was at a fever pitch everywhere. Much of this was the result of an enormous push that year for War Bond Drives to be held across the country, from large cities to small towns. Hollywood personalities were instrumental in bringing publicity to these efforts, and personal

appearances by movie stars would guarantee a large turnout for the selling of many bonds. Hollywood bond drives included entertainment by major stars, although just the appearance and a short speech by a celebrity was guaranteed to raise thousands of dollars.

The Third War Loan Campaign of September 1943 was a major effort, with bond rallies scheduled concurrently throughout the United States. It was this drive, under the chairmanship of William K. Jackson, which brought the largest turnout to Clearfield on a clear, cool night. On the program were three from Curwensville: Fred Robison, the popular ventriloquist, Anthony Sorrento, a young, talented baritone who resembled Frank Sinatra, and I, a six-year-old, wearing an Uncle Sam top hat, corduroy slacks, and my cousin Bill Jackson's hand-me-down tweed coat. I sang "Over There," the crowd-pleasing tune from World War I.

It wasn't easy to work a full shift and also run a household, but because workers were badly needed and parachutes were essential to the war effort, Kate had agreed to work for the cause. Earnings were good and growing—at least until President Roosevelt froze wages, salaries, and prices to forestall inflation. The wages were still more than Kate had ever earned and it gave her some independence and money to pay for piano lessons and other niceties for her girls, as well as starting her own savings account. What she had not counted on, however, was that by 1944 people were not allowed to leave any jobs related to the war effort. Everyone was working, young and old alike. Even John Pifer, at age 75, thought about what he might do, and one day, without preface, said to Jessie, "I wonder if the government has need somewhere for a well driller."

For the Duration

The scarcity of manufactured goods continued without relief throughout the war years. Automobiles were not being built, toys were very limited in availability, and the clothing shortage increased with each successive year, with men's suits in particular being hard to find.

As might be expected, women's clothing styles were simplified and accessories that possibly could change the look of an ensemble became popular. Designers were limited by the kind and amount of fabric available and by a keen awareness that buyers were looking for versatility and durability. Pinafores, jumpers, three-piece outfits, dickeys, jabots, and turbans were all created to provide a bit of fashion—or at least variety—without using much fabric.

Full skirts, knife pleats, and patch pockets were banned from new clothing being manufactured and shoes not only were rationed but also were limited to six colors: black, white, navy blue, and three shades of brown—when they were available. Painted on stockings in the form of leg make-up replaced real stockings, except for those who didn't mind wearing cotton hosiery. The application of leg make-up required a steady hand, and for those who preferred a seam line, a willing family member was pressed into service to draw the line from the back of the thigh or knee (depending upon the length of the skirt) to the heel. The disadvantage of leg make-up was that it often rubbed off on one's clothing or on the furniture, and in the rain or heat of summer the make-up frequently streaked or smeared.

Ruby found a trademark that wouldn't change with the times. She loved turbans and claimed them for her own, continuing to follow that style for the remainder of her life. On the other hand, Jessie enjoyed experimenting with accessories and had, long before the war, assumed a style of her own with unexpected combinations. She sensed she could get away with almost anything so long as she strode with her natural air of self-assurance.

Because rationing was hard on everyone, a sense of camaraderie in doing without goods and services prevailed among the citizenry. Anyone over the age of six or seven during the war remembers standing in line for almost any purchase while clenching a ration coupon book. Families would sometimes work in shifts as mothers who also had pre-school age children at home sent their school age offspring to stand in line at the meat counters until time to leave for school. Even though it was sometimes disquieting for the child, the mother knew the child would be safe among the adults waiting in line.

Before the end of the war canned goods were added to the list of rationed foods, then came the five percent tax on everything to help pay for the war effort. It would have been considered unpatriotic to complain, particularly when the government had so cleverly named this tax the Victory surcharge.

A motto, "Use it up, wear it out, make it do, or do without," was coined to encourage the public to tolerate half a decade of rationing. More encompassing, however, was the stock answer to almost every question as to how long the shortages, the rationing, the blackouts, and the boys overseas would continue. It was always the same: "For the duration." *Everything,* it seemed, was for the duration.

The inconvenience of the scarcity of goods and services was, however, minor in the face of the personal losses suffered by many families whose members were serving in the military. Despite all the patriotic slogans, wives still longed for their husbands, children missed their fathers, and mothers pined for their sons. As the fighting intensified in North Africa, and for the first time casualties started to mount up, of all those who suffered losses, the noblest were the Gold Star Mothers, mothers who had lost sons in battle.

Mama Pifer prayed for the safety of all the young men, grateful again that she had daughters rather than sons. More than once she expressed remorse to her daughters that she and her sisters—all at least in their 60s—were still living their lives, while young men were losing theirs. Later in the year, on December 6, Mama wrote in her Bible, "I'm sick. It has rained all afternoon." Many people were not feeling well that winter, as immunity systems were strained by the stresses of war.

An epidemic of infantile paralysis also struck that winter resulting in 1,200 deaths in the United States and the crippling of thousands more. No cure or vaccine had yet been found, although the trials for penicillin were showing that it was successful in the treatment of chronic diseases. Of even greater benefit, penicillin was being used in the treatment of thousands of wounded soldiers, while on the home front it was rationed by a triage committee at each hospital.

Near the end of 1943 a rhythm to wartime living was developing and many more people were interested in reading accounts of battles. Magazine journalism flourished as the number of reporters in the field increased. Many readers relished the in-depth reports arriving from the battlefield, vividly illustrated with the new photo-journalism *Life* had pioneered in 1936. Publishers also found that the war news was the story that sold newspapers and the Normandy Invasion alone was covered by 400 reporters.

Going to the movies and reading books increased as families sought ways to pass the time waiting for the boys to come home. Books with a war theme and those nostalgic of home were particularly successful. Best-sellers in 1943 included *God is My Co-Pilot, Thirty Seconds Over Tokyo,* and *Guadalcanal Diary.*[17] Two of the most popular films that year were "Jane Eyre" and the Academy Award-winning "Casablanca." The biggest record and sheet music seller in the country that year was "There's a Star-Spangled Banner Waving Somewhere," although its hillbilly origins kept it from being counted in the popular tabulations of success.[18]

By November 1943 another bleak holiday season loomed as nearly every American family had one of its members "away in the war." Christmas catalogues were restricted in the number of pages allotted to them and many listed items were stamped with the words, "Sorry, not available." Thus, even those who had money found that many items could not be purchased. Parents became ever-increasingly creative in finding gifts for their children, because children did not understand that Santa could not produce items tagged "Unavailable." When one of a series of government orders prohibited the use of traditional toy materials such as steel, tin, rubber, and lead, manufacturers had to substitute cardboard and wooden toys.

Many families shared their Christmas lists on the chance that one family member would find an item one of the others might be seeking. Jessie offered to drive her three sisters to Altoona to shop, a generous offer considering gas rationing.

Winters were cold in the mountainous region of Curwensville from November through March, and usually there was a lot of snow, allowing for great sledding. The older girls took turns pulling Baby Nan on a sled on sunny afternoons, sometimes "the whole way up" to the tannery and back. They all loved to go sled riding after school and into the evening. The evenings were the most fun because very few cars interfered with sled riding on Schofield Street. Those more daring began their toboggan ride from Upper Schofield (at the very top of the hill), taking a forty degree turn, crossing an intersection, and traveling downhill for a total of nearly a quarter mile.

Another winter activity that attracted both adults and children was ice-skating on the pond between the town dump and the tannery. Perhaps "pond" was too generous a term. "Swamp" might have been more accurate, as there were no definite borders between the frozen water and the shoots of sumac and other striplings. Bramble bushes and other scrub growth, some overgrown, made the area frightening at night for young children, but provided hidden nooks for couples looking for a spot of privacy. Of course, there were no restrooms and if one had a need, he or she just had to go home and, if a child, chance not being permitted to return.

Jessie and her friends—at least those who had ice skates, for none were available for purchase during the war years—occasionally would meet to go skating, particularly on a Friday evening or Sunday afternoon. The women found plenty of company among one another, although the shortage of male companionship was quite evident. There was no such thing as an eligible man, as they were all either married with families, serving in the military, or older than what would appeal to most of Jessie's friends still in their thirties. "For the duration" took on new meaning.

It was ice skating at this pond that Kate's oldest daughter's natural grace was first noticed. Even at the young age of twelve she had developed a style that had first shown itself in dancing school, but the poise came with skating. While she had long given up on piano lessons and did not have a strong singing voice, she was a gifted dancer. Ice skating, roller skating, tap-dancing, and any kind of social dancing—she could perfect the steps with very little practice. In ballroom dancing she could follow any lead. She had her mother's style, but with much more confidence, some would even say chutzpa. Others said her outspokenness reminded them more of Jessie. Like her aunt, Kay would soon develop a unique style that would seek no quarter or approval. Her manner of dress, vocabulary (particularly her apt nicknames and terms for people and situations), and her general insouciance would more and more suggest her aunt's personality, but, as was later noted, with far less regard for others.

Her younger sisters accepted, as children do, that Kay, as the oldest, held special privileges. She had her own large bedroom, one that had been remodeled for her, complete with new hardwood flooring, a vanity table and bench, and its own closet. While her bedroom was off-limits to her younger sisters, Kay would make up bedtime stories that engaged the girls. All in all, Kay spent a good deal of time with her young siblings, taking them with her when she palled around with her own friends, and creating many games and interesting pastimes to entertain them.

Kay was also resourceful in finding ways to earn a bit of money and one summer set up a comic book stand on the front porch steps, which provided four display levels. She charged three cents for comics that were a bit shopworn and five cents for those in good condition. No one in town had the size collection Kay Thompson did, and word soon spread that good comic books could be purchased from her at half-price.

Later, I also set up a comic book stand (on the less desirable two-stepped side porch), but I was quickly put out of business by Kay who not only claimed exclusivity, but also told me it would be illegal to have a second comic book business at the same address. Soundly dejected, I gathered up my comics and stacked them back on the bookshelf in the dining room.

Kay's entrepreneurial ventures continued both in the household and among her friends when she periodically sold items she no longer had use for. She would display these on a table in the large foyer or on the dining room table where her younger sisters had first dibs—to purchase. I longed for some of these "grown up" and very appealing items, and my limited resources would invariably end up in the cash box of my older sister.

Kay's other money-making scheme consisted of cutting strips of paper about five inches in length, numbering them, and then folding the edge of each strip in neat rows across the closed Venetian blind in the window of the foyer. The object was for the buyer to pay a fee, select a number, and receive the prize that matched the number (this all neatly kept in a notebook). The prizes were for the most part trinkets that in most households would have been given by the older to the young children as a matter of course. Nonetheless, we children were engaged and Mother saw these games as ways to entertain us during the long darkness of the war years.

As might be expected considering the comic book venture, one morning while Kay was on errands with our dad, I painstakingly made my own strips, gathered my own knick-knacks to be sold, and set up shop. Upon Kay's return, I proudly displayed my handiwork, hoping I could interest her in items I considered my own treasures. Containing her annoyance for the moment, Kay leaned in toward the closed Venetian blind and separated the slats. "There is a state police car coming down the road; he must have seen the folded-over tops of the strips through the window. He'll probably stop and arrest you for gambling," she said calmly. Terrified, I snatched the strips from their display rack, and ran to the small bedroom I shared with Jo Ellen, crushed at being "busted."

By 1944 everyone was "hunkered" down for the duration when rationing with its accompanying shortages of goods and services increased in severity, making a normal life difficult for anyone. Millions of Americans relied on the radio as their primary source of war news and NBC was devoting 20 percent of its airtime to news, compared with 3.6 percent in 1939, while 30 percent of the airtime at CBS was given over to the news.

With so many men overseas, America's wartime industry relied heavily on women to keep up its frenetic pace. Between 1940 and 1944 the number of employed women rose from 12 million to 18.2 million[19] and at the height of the war years, women made up more than one-third of the civilian workforce.

College enrollments throughout this time also reflected the paucity of young men, and during 1944 more than 80 percent of the journalism school graduates were women. The campus population was decimated by the draft and there were no college deferments in those days. Some colleges dropped football entirely. Jessie had to forego watching any horse races, sulky or otherwise, as horseracing was the only sport to be banned during the war for non-essentiality to the war effort.

In 1944 the federal amusement tax was raised from 10 to 20 percent while the cost of living rose almost 30 percent. Wages, for the most part, were frozen, and the result was a further "tightening of the belt." Teachers, already underpaid, watched their incomes steadily fall further behind prices, and scores of thousands abandoned their profession for better-paying jobs,[20] particularly in the factories.

Scarcity of goods continued—and in some areas increased—with shortages of candy, ice cream, and chewing gum, as well as meat, butter, fats, and canned goods. Even though America's farms, orchards, pastures, and ranges were producing record amounts of vegetables and meats, the Lend-Lease Act[21] and armed forces demands added an increment of 25-50 percent to a civilian demand already swollen by increased purchasing power. By early 1944 shipping overseas of canned goods had increased in amounts approaching one-half the entire production of the United States.

The wildly popular singer Kate Smith went on a successful marathon tour selling war bonds, and all across the country people continued to collect scrap metal and newspapers. Iron, steel, rubber, nylon stockings, and cooking grease were also collected, as well as tin cans whose tops had been removed by a can opener so that the cylinder of the can could be stomped flat. Households were asked to save tinfoil, string, and toothpaste tubes along with the tin cans. One of the more ingenious ideas of recycling came from the record industry. Not able to get shellac from which records were made, the manufacturers turned to salvage. In the Philadelphia area RCA Victor dealers posted signs offering two cents each for old records, regardless of condition.[22]

As expected, books and plays continued with a war theme

and John Hersey's timely *A Bell for Adano* won a Pulitzer Prize in 1945. Jean Paul Sartre ushered in the theatre of the absurd with *No Exit*, while Tennessee Williams wrote *The Glass Menagerie*. Songs of 1944 included "Don't Fence Me In," and the following Big Band numbers: "Swinging on a Star," "Sentimental Journey," and "Accentuate the Positive."

Jessie loved to dance and enjoyed the socializing promoted by clubs, either local or some distance from Curwensville, which she preferred. Not that her conduct was unbecoming in any way, but rather that it was difficult for a teacher to participate in activities others could take for granted. The Sunset Ballroom in Carrolltown, a large structure built just for dancing, was the closest to a nightclub atmosphere most people in central Pennsylvania ever experienced. Sunset booked most of the Big Bands of the day and had no trouble filling their hall.

That summer Howard's State Guard unit was sent to Indiantown Gap, a military facility not far from the state capital, for two weeks training. Jessie suggested to Kate that they visit him during the weekend his unit would be stationed there. Kate reluctantly consented to go after Jessie convinced her that such a short trip would be a welcome break and, as she said, "I need to use up my gas coupons." One of the Zwolski sisters stayed with the children, so in July the two women headed south to the state capital. They arrived late Friday afternoon and took a room at the Harrisburger Hotel, close to the Capitol Building and twenty-five miles from the military training base.

Howard had hoped to have a pass for Friday night to join "the girls" in Harrisburg. However, they found a message waiting for them at their hotel that he could not leave base until noon on Saturday. Jessie said, "Well, we'll just have to make the best of it," as she began to page through the hotel listing of restaurants. "Let's have a light supper across the street, look around the town, and then find a place that has a band," none of which Kate would have done on her own. On their way out of the hotel, Jessie asked the desk clerk where he would recommend two young women might safely go out for a drink on a Friday night. "Without a doubt, ladies," he quickly replied, "I recommend the High Hat Club, directly across from the Pennsylvania Railroad Station. For dinner and dancing, you might want to try the Hawaiian Room at the Warner Hotel."

Following that advice, the sisters headed to the Warner. As they were leaving the lobby of the Harrisburger, the desk clerk said, "If you don't want to go through the lobby, there is an entrance to the Hawaiian Room off the alley." (Twenty-five years later in Harrisburg on business, Kate recalled that evening, ". . . the Warner where Jess and I had such a good time."[23]) By dessert, Jessie had made friends with a group of young people at the next table who, in turn, introduced them to a table of Army officers from the Army War College in Carlisle. Later in the evening, it was suggested that the newly formed troup move on to the High Hat Club to wrap up the Friday night festivities there.

The High Hat Club did a brisk business because it had the best location in town, across from the train station, a natural stop for soldiers leaving the station and heading for the bus stop where they would board the bus for Indiantown Gap. The nightclub was large enough for bands and was known as the best place in the city for fun and dancing. A gal never lacked for a dancing partner there. With Jessie's vivacious personality and ability to banter with anyone, the two women had a good time meeting and dancing with some of the soldiers, both regular Army and those in the Guard.

The following morning Jessie and Kate did some shopping, with a special stop at Troup's Music, the largest music emporium either of them had ever seen. At one o'clock they headed to the bus station to meet Howard and a friend he had brought to make a foursome. The sisters had made a bet with themselves that Howd would ask them to drive to Gettysburg, 45 miles south, and when he framed the sentence, "Jess, why don't we all . . ." they broke out in shared laughter. When the men offered to take them to dinner at the Gettysburg Hotel, they accepted their fate and headed to the Civil War battlefield, with Howard reminding them that he and Kate had honeymooned in Gettysburg seventeen years earlier.

Continuing routine traditions was one way the adults kept life as normal as possible for the children in the face of the stark reality of the ever-present war. Wives and parents could do little more than wait and worry and follow the news, trying to imagine what their loved ones were going through. In their letters home, some men found ways to code their whereabouts such as mentioning the time of day that the readers could then interpret as longitude and latitude. Every family eagerly watched the mail for letters, which offered at least a temporary reassurance of the writer's safety. Many kindly mailmen would make an extra home delivery, in addition to the regularly scheduled twice-a-day service, if a letter arrived at the post office from a serviceman. Everyone, however, dreaded the unexpected knock at the door announcing the delivery of a telegram that began, "We regret to inform you...."

The school children were little affected by all of this turmoil, even though they held a sense of sadness. Stories of war were vague to their understanding, as was the loss of life. Their experiences in wartime were limited to packing the Red Cross boxes and buying war stamps, with only periodic doses of reality with the deaths of adults close to them.

Nineteen forty-four was a particularly difficult year for the American military as they pressed their campaigns in both Europe and the Pacific. There were rumors of a major continental offensive in France having been planned for more than a year when General Dwight D. Eisenhower was appointed to command all Allied invasion forces of soldiers, sailors, aviators, and supporting services of 2.8 million men. His target was a 40-mile strip of beach along the Normandy coast, and it would mark the first time since 1688 that an invading army would cross the English Channel.

On the morning of June 6, 1944, the assault fleet of 600 warships and 4,000 supporting craft, freighted with 176,000 men from a dozen different ports, crossed the Channel. The attack itself was considered magnificent from a military point of view, even though it resulted in many casualties on both sides.

On the Pacific Front other heroic efforts were occurring on the thousands of atolls and islands sprawled so widely that General MacArthur had at one point superimposed a map of the United States on a map of the Pacific to show the vastness of the area and the difficulty of moving troops quickly. Following a valiant six-month stand on Bataan and Corregidor, MacArthur was ordered out of the Philippines to command the forces in Australia in resisting the feared Japanese onslaught from the north. Two and a half years later, General MacArthur returned after a brilliant plan referred to as "leap-frogging the islands," culminated in a major three-part battle for the Leyte Gulf. The second part of the three-part strategy was the Battle of Surigao Strait—a smashing night victory and the Navy's revenge for Pearl Harbor. This victory left the United States Navy in complete command of Philippine waters, the result of which the Japanese Navy no longer could pose a serious threat.

Jessie knew that Johnny Wayne was stationed "somewhere in the Pacific," and every time the phone rang, she jumped. She was almost afraid to answer, fearing it would be Ruby with bad news. Jessie had loved Johnny since she had first set eyes on him as an infant. While she wasn't particularly enamored of children, Jessie was close to Johnny who had been born the year she had been graduated from high school. He had spent the summer between his junior and senior years working in Curwensville with his grandfather, and Jessie, who usually had no patience with laundry or any other household chores, chose to hand wash Johnny's shirts, a task she continued any time he visited. In a way, Jessie viewed Johnny as the child she might have had. She faithfully corresponded with him from the day he left Ohio in the spring of 1942 to enter the Navy until the day he returned from service in 1945. They were more like cousins than aunt and nephew, and even though Jean's sons, Eugene and Don, lived in Curwensville and Jessie was fond of them, no one held a place in her heart like Johnny Wayne.

Jessie saved Johnny's letters to her, although only one remains. Written November 8, 1944 and postmarked November 12 with the return address of San Francisco and stamped with *Passed by Naval Censor*, Johnny had written across the top margin of his letter to Jessie, "P.S., I don't think it wise to tell Mother of these battles. She'll only worry."

The body of the letter began,

> *At Sea.*
>
> *Dear Aunt Jeb,*
>
> *...The Naval battles took place in the Surigao Strait between Leyte Gulf and the Sulu Sea. I don't believe I've ever seen a Fourth of July any more beautiful. It took place in the early morning. Still dark. When the ships started firing at each other the guns left long white arches to their targets. It seems the whole sky was covered with lines like July Fourth sky rockets. The only thing I didn't like was the Japs were firing back at us with guns, just as big. One Naval Battle that big is enough to last a man a lifetime. After it's all over maybe I can tell you more about the Island for your school teaching. ...One of these days we'll stroll down the street in Pa. Three pages is the limit, Jeb.*
>
> *Love, John A. Wayne S'16.*[24]

Jessie rejoiced at this good news, full of hope that with this victory over the Japanese Johnny might not see any worse action. But Okinawa was yet to come.

During the 1944-45 winter, the bitterest in years, an acute fuel shortage left Americans in the eastern half of the country shivering in their homes. Overburdened railroads, manpower shortages, and blizzards were to blame. A brown-out was ordered throughout the nation, and the use of neon signs was prohibited. Stores closed at dusk. Throughout the east coast some schools were closed for lack of fuel and businesses went on short weeks. Downtown shopping areas in cities were empty and dark at night and a midnight curfew was imposed on bars and nightclubs.

Those living in Curwensville were mainly affected by rising costs for the coal most families still used to heat their homes. Many whose heating systems had pipes only to the first floor, relying on a dispersal system though a ceiling vent to heat the second floor, vowed they would install new systems following the war. Jessie offered to her parents to help purchase a new furnace system after the war, but her parents demurred.

By this time, Jessie was earning enough to rent her own apartment, but with her parents aging, she quietly accepted the responsibility for remaining in the homestead. She also understood that Mama counted on her contribution to the household expenses. No discussions were held among the sisters as to how to care for their parents as they aged; rather, it was an unspoken understanding that Jessie would handle things.

This winter of 1944-45 was also severe in Europe, making it difficult for the final military press. In the Pacific, the Japanese kamikaze attacks on the U.S. Navy off Okinawa in 1945 were successful; seven carriers were damaged and there were 12,000 American casualties—the price America paid for winning this island, in addition to the nearly 7,000 Naval and Marine losses at Iwo Jima. This news, along with many other stories, including the German breakthrough in the Battle of the Bulge in Europe, was not released to the public.

Among those lost in the waning days of European battle was

Pfc. William K. Jackson, killed in action at Duren, Germany on February 23, 1945, during the counter-offensive following the Battle of the Bulge, as he attempted to cross the Roer River with Company I, 413th Infantry of the 104th Timberwolf Division. He was survived by his wife, Mary Alice Thompson Jackson, and their ten-year-old son, Bill.

Even as German resistance crumbled and victory appeared certain, President Roosevelt, returning in February 1945 a sick man from the Yalta Conference of the Combined Chiefs of Staff, went to his winter home in Warm Springs, Georgia, to prepare for the inauguration of the United Nations at San Francisco. There he suffered a cerebral hemorrhage which brought instant death. That evening the presidential train, bearing his body, began its journey home to Washington where it arrived the following morning. The next day the body of the President was borne to Hyde Park for burial in his mother's rose garden.

Within the next three weeks, Italian partisans killed Mussolini, Hitler committed suicide, Berlin surrendered to Russia, and Germany signed an unconditional surrender. Thus, the war came to an end in the West. Three months later, after meeting at Potsdam, President Truman and Prime Minister Winston Churchill presented Japan with an ultimatum to surrender. The alternative, Japan was told, would be "prompt and utter destruction."[25] Japan refused to acknowledge this challenge and on July 25 the United States gave the order for the dropping of atomic bombs. On August 6, 1945 the first was dropped on Hiroshima, wiping out the Second Japanese Army, razing four square miles of the city, and killing 60,175 persons. Three days later, a few hours after Russia had declared war on Japan, the second bomb exploded over Nagasaki, killing 36,000, most of them civilians. Emperor Hirohito surrendered on August 14, 1945, ending the war in the Pacific.

The surrender did not, however, mean that all the troops

would come home immediately or that others would not be sent overseas as part of their tour of duty. Early that spring Eugene Bloom, much to his mother's dismay, had enlisted in the Navy. At the time of his enlistment the war was by no means over and even should it soon end there was no guarantee that harm would not come to him. Jean was heartbroken when Eugene's brother Donald said he planned to follow the same path as soon as he was graduated. She suspected that her sons had talked to Jessie about these plans because they seemed to know more about Johnny Wayne's war experiences than they could have known otherwise.

While my sisters and I sensed an air of relief and celebration that the war was over, the summer of '45 was exciting to us not so much because of the end of WW II, but because of a chicken coop. The order Dad had placed a year earlier for material to build a chicken coop was finally filled and the lumber was delivered in early May. With the growing shortage of building materials he would not have been granted permission to build much else; a chicken house was one of the few constructions that could be viewed as helping the war effort. And had he waited another year, lumber prices might have been prohibitive.

The chicken coop, approximately 8′ x 12′, did not take long to construct. It looked like a playhouse and that is just what we were permitted to use it for all summer long. No more playing under the porches this year. Here was a real playhouse in which even an adult could stand upright. Mother said all of us could share the space, but with Nan not yet three and Kay nearly fifteen, in actuality, the playhouse was completely owned by Jo Ellen and me. Bliss it was.

In the fall of 1945, Armistice Day, originally established to commemorate World War I, took on a greater significance as the country realized that once again they had paid a high price for liberty. And even though Eugene Bloom was on board a Navy ship heading for the Pacific, the anxiety was much less than when Johnny Wayne had shipped out. When Jessie received word that Johnny was on his way home, she marked that day on a corner of the blackboard as well as in her heart.

Sisters Kate, Jebbie, Josie and Jean

Chapter 7

Out of a World of Darkness

...1945 was the watershed year of the 20th Century. One kind of world ended, another began. Roosevelt died, Hitler committed suicide, Churchill was voted out of office. The United Nations was founded. ...The end of the WWII was a time of huge celebration and thanksgiving, but it was also the point at which mankind saw, as never before, its own capacity for evil.

—*David McCullough*[1]

Regardless of the chaotic end of the World War II era, the years 1945-1950 were probably the last time Americans would ever have a chance to bask in the powerful aftermath of winning a major war. The words of Winston Churchill best summarized the situation when he said that America was "at the summit of the world."[2] Among all the warring nations of World War II, America alone emerged with its territory inviolate, its people not displaced, its farms producing in abundance, its industries gearing up to satisfy material needs, and its confidence unbounded. And, to add to this confidence and sense of security, the United States alone possessed the atomic bomb. Life was good.

According to military veteran Marion Rivers Nittel, reflecting fifty years later on this post-war era, it was "the last time in the history of our country when a full-blown spirit of true patriotism was in every heart."[3] Historian William Chafe says of post-war America, "Rarely has a society experienced such rapid or dramatic change as that which occurred in America after 1945."[4] The upbeat theme of this period was prosperity, and social analysts congratulated themselves on a nation capable of almost anything.

The feeling of confidence was further highlighted by a communication system that was only beginning to realize its impact on public opinion. During World War I the public had had to rely largely on newspapers, but by 1947, 34.8 million of the 38.5 million households had at least one radio receiver.[5]

World War II also was the first war to bring to the public a sense of the immediacy of combat. From the very beginning with the bombing of Pearl Harbor, the country was very much engaged in directly participating in the war effort. Nearly everyone was involved: the fighting men, men at home who served in the guard units or civil patrols, women who took jobs formerly held by men, volunteers who knit caps and blankets, citizens who collected for the scrap drives, and school children who bought war stamps and packed toiletries for the Red Cross.

Journalists in particular made this war personal in a way not seen since Matthew Brady's photographs of the Civil War. They provided stories of individual heroism and wrote many descriptive accounts that put names to faces. Even the visual images which convey the end of World War II stand in stark contrast to that of any other warfare until that time. While the ending of the Civil War is visualized as Confederate soldiers returning to a devastated South and the end of World War I as doughboys marching home in parade formation, the close of World War II is vividly captured through photographs of crowds in Times Square, of soldiers returning on ships, and of many informal public displays of affection. Also new with the Second World War was an attitude of wanting to resume life as it was before the war. Ambassador Averell Harriman commented that after the war most Americans just wanted to "go to the movies and drink Coke."[6]

The editorial staff of Curwensville High School's *1946 Echo* expressed more serious sentiments than a picture show and a soda pop, perhaps because their most clear memories of growing up had been defined by the shadow of war. They optimistically declared: "The Class of 1946 Steps Out of a World of Darkness and Violence into a World of Light and Peace." Many Americans shared the anticipation of peace, and most people sincerely believed that *this* time the world had been made safe for democracy.

On VJ Day slightly more than 12,000,000 American men and women were serving in the military with approximately 7 million of them in foreign countries or at sea. Deciding the best and fairest way to discharge individuals was debated among the military leadership until it was suggested to ask the men themselves. The results led to the order of discharge based first on overseas service, followed by number of dependents and then time in the military and age of the individual. This plan offered the servicemen the first faint promise of "coming home."[7] A Gallup poll in June 1945 reported that 73 percent of the public felt the established point system to be fair.

The nuclear bombing of Hiroshima and Nagasaki provided an unexpected quickening in the pace of demobilization. Nonetheless, the best plans were still complicated by the need for the U.S. military to remain in place for peace-keeping duty. Regardless of the delays, everyone focused on coming home—whatever that might mean for each individual—to a steady routine of life where even the mail was delivered on schedule, twice a day.

Curwensville was a microcosm of what was happening throughout the entire country, where in thousands of small towns men and women were returning home—some to resume their lives and some to discover that home as they remembered it no longer existed, either because they had changed, people they knew had changed, or the town had changed. However, most veterans headed home with the goal to create a better life.

President Truman instructed federal agencies to give preference to veterans in hiring, an order that has continued into the 21st Century with bonus points still being added to the scores on civil service tests. Because government field site jobs were filled by civil service, many returning veterans took the Civil Service Test and found better jobs than they had left. Jessie's cherished nephew, Johnny Wayne, home safe and sound, entered a degree program at Ohio State University, but after a year joined his father at Timken Roller Bearing Company.

Monetary discounts for veterans began to appear both in expected areas such as a half price subscription to the *Reader's Digest* and in unlikely places such as the private plane manufacturer who offered to place any serviceman "at the head of the line" to purchase a plane, an offer of limited appeal.

Tom Brokaw wrote that, overall, the veterans came home and, "…went back to work at their old jobs or started small businesses; they became big-city cops and firemen; they finished their degrees or enrolled in college for the first time; they became schoolteachers, insurance salesmen, craftsmen, and local politicians. They weren't widely known outside their families or their communities. For many, the war years were enough adventure to last a lifetime. They were proud of what they had accomplished but rarely discussed their experiences, even with each other."[8]

While the GI Bill brought a college degree to within reach of millions of persons who otherwise would have gone directly into trades or blue-collar jobs, it also had a more profound implication in that after the 1940s a college degree came to be considered an essential passport of entrance into much of the business and professional world. While this expectation certainly raised the standard for entry into the teaching profession, many of those who, like Jessie, lacked a four-year degree found themselves not receiving the same kind of increments in pay as their degreed colleagues did.

The unprecedented college enrollment by veterans also created challenges for the higher education institutions. In the fall of 1946 half the student body at Franklin and Marshall, a small but prestigious liberal arts college in Lancaster, Pennsylvania, were veterans. Most colleges welcomed the revenue from increased enrollments, but trustees found themselves faced with major building needs—in some, if not many, cases having to find factories or other buildings no longer needed by the government, dismantle the buildings on site, and then reassemble them on campuses. Administrators also had to scramble to hire additional faculty; and the entire university system had to deal with a philosophical dilemma—how to treat the returning veterans, now students, who, for the first time in history, were from social classes other than the elite.

The fear that veterans were not taking their classes seriously and were hurrying through their courses just to finish early turned out to be unfounded. In June 1947, when asked by a reporter from *Time* magazine, a student at Indiana University responded, "The main problem of everybody is to catch up. We're all trying to get where we would have been if there hadn't been a war."[9]

Most veterans also were older than the typical college student and they were all business in the approach to their education. Many accelerated their programs, taking heavy course loads. The majority of colleges were pleased to find students who wanted to finish early, as it meant a faster turnover in enrollment. On the other hand, class sizes increased and there was the problem of whether or not to charge additional tuition to those who carried more than 18 credits a semester.

The President of Queens College warned that to permit anyone to finish a degree in fewer than three years was a disservice to them. He called acceleration deceptive, stating that one must *live* with ideas in order to understand them.[10] In the opinion of many academic pundits, nothing would ever be the same on college campuses. On that they were right.

For the most part, these veterans in their early twenties were mature beyond their years. Kent Forster at Pennsylvania State College, commented, "They raised questions in class and had pretty critical comments to make, based on their own exposure to life in the armed forces. ...One simply dared not go before a class without having something to say."[11]

A survey found increased enrollments of up to 580 percent in teachers' colleges, 125 percent in agricultural and engineering colleges, and 280 percent in arts and sciences.[12] The practical problem on the college campuses was where these numbers of students would live, attend classes, and study. The housing situation, in particular, is best described as being a mess. On many campuses, veterans and their new families lived in villages of house trailers, Quonset huts, plywood houses, and old army barracks that had been hauled to campuses and converted into civilian housing.[13]

As expected, the aftermath of war had a profound effect on the general economy and after the war many factories had to lay off workers. Women were especially hard hit by the layoff and in 1947 pink slips were handed out to almost two million working women. Within only two months, factories had retooled and began churning out consumer goods at a record pace, but almost all the new jobs went to men.

After Congress lifted wartime price and wage controls in 1946, the cost of almost everything shot up dramatically—often by more than 100 percent. Again, teachers and clerks, who did not set their own salaries, were caught in the whirl of rising prices.

This increasing leveling of income emphasized the rise of mass markets and led to mass production: "Not only did all classes of Americans drink the same water, stroll in the same parks, and send their children to the same schools, but also they stored their food in the same refrigerators, cooked on the same stoves, read the same books, and saw the same plays. Their clothes and automobiles varied in cost but not much in appearance."[14]

With the rise of mass marketing and production, it became more difficult to purchase distinctive items, particularly clothing. The number of dressmakers decreased as mass production increased and caused hardship not only to the trade but also to those who did not sew. Fortunately for Jessie and Kate, Mrs. Buterbaugh, a seamstress who lived on Filbert Street, continued to make one-of-a-kind items. Part of the fun in going to Mrs. Buterbaugh was that the fabric remaining from a garment was available to make matching hat bands for the ladies and dresses for the children's dolls.

To add to the sweetness of winning World War II, and in some persons' eyes almost equal to the victory, the 1945 Curwensville High School varsity football team enjoyed its most successful season, undefeated and untied, with only one team scoring against them. The stadium was packed for home games, with nearly the entire town coming out in support of the team. Many elementary students wore their season passes on a cord around their necks so as not to lose them, and every sports fan sought to wear something in the school colors of gold and black. Those who had them from the few former championships wore their prized miniature gold footballs on a chain. A proud editorial staff devoted six pages in the yearbook on the details of each game. Life at Curwensville High School was upbeat and everyone basked in the reflected glory.

Gearing up for peacetime when the only combat was on the playing field, people felt a renewed need for community. As the men returned to their homes, most town events and celebrations were reinstated and new ones initiated. These involved mainly civic organizations and schools, with the adults "making up for lost time" and the children taking it all for granted.

One such case of community spirit was the flurry of activity in promoting a teen center which, while primarily for the young people, would also serve as a meeting place for several civic organizations. Another activity, which became an annual event for many years to follow, was the town's Halloween Parade. Grade level classrooms, Boy Scouts, adult groups, high school bands, and adult organizations all participated.

By the end of the year most of the United States faced a "housing shortage of unparalleled magnitude," in the words of a government study.[15] Much existing housing was in ill repair, with scant materials and few skilled workers available, and few new houses had been built. Even towns the size of Curwensville could not offer enough housing for veterans, and families saw "No Vacancy" signs wherever they turned. Jessie convinced her mother to raise the rent on the rented side of their double house by $3, and Howard joked to Kate that had he known how desperate people were for housing, he would have advertised his new chicken coop for rent.

This vast housing shortage provided the perfect opportunity for developer Bill Levitt, who created Levittowns where very small houses were built on site in a type of assembly line. Some 17,000 houses were built in the first Levittown and 82,000 people quickly moved into these houses with four-rooms-and-a-bath.

Tract housing became a way of life for many veterans, even though some of them saw these as resembling the military world they had just escaped. The houses, income levels, clothing, and behavior all resembled government issue. Even the children appeared to be interchangeable, as if drawn at some supply depot.[16] With only one car in most families the women were left isolated during the day in a world of children and other mothers.

Because the new suburbs physically separated women from the workplace, one of the most influential results of tract housing was the break that occurred in the progress some women had been making professionally. Add to this the women factory workers who had been fired, and an opportunity was ready-made to create something for women that would take the place of employment. Magazine advertisers eagerly stepped in, began glorifying staying at home, and created a pseudo-career called "homemaking," particularly located in suburbia.

Since magazines stood to gain revenue through advertising household and personal products created for women, *Ladies' Home Journal, Redbook, McCall's* and *Mademoiselle* took it upon themselves to explain how women should live, dress, and consume, pushing the idea that they could best find fulfillment as homemakers.[17] It would not be until later that this focused campaign to domesticate women was seen for what it really was: the creation of a targeted market by which *to sell products* for the lifestyle advertisers were convincing the women to emulate.

Popular magazines and emerging television programs glorified dutiful mothers, reinforcing the post-war definition of the American woman as one who did not work outside the home. Those who did work found themselves being described as hard and aggressive, competitive with men, and doomed to a life of loneliness.

Thus, girls in these new suburbs were reared in homes in which mothers had no careers. Daughters were educated to get married while boys in the family were to learn the skills critical to supporting a family. If young women had ideas of a professional career, the real world did not give them much encouragement.

Early in 1946 price controls and rationing were lifted and after years of hearing "Don't you know there's a war on?" citizens were eager to buy again. Only one thing stopped them. The cost of nearly everything shot up dramatically, often by more than 100 percent.[18] The food price index jumped 16.1 points the first week controls ended and, with the lifting of rent controls, increases were reported of from 15 to 1,000 percent. By fall the control system was in near collapse, resulting in shortages and the resurgence of a black market.

Another problem occurred when government contracts for war supplies ended and hundreds of thousands of workers found themselves jobless, with many remaining so until the factories were retooled for manufacturing consumer products. Only then were workers rehired in the new jobs and soon found themselves among the rising number of eager purchasers. Between 1945 and 1950 Americans bought 5,500,000 passenger cars; 5,076,800 houses; 20,207,000 refrigerators; 17,549,000 vacuum cleaners; and 5,451,000 electric ranges. During those same five years, American technology gave the world the long-playing phonograph record ($33^{1/3}$ rpm to replace the 78), automatic transmissions for automobiles, electric clothes driers, and garbage disposal units for kitchen sinks, as well as whimsical items such as the hula hoop.

The most highly regarded literary work of 1946 was Robert Penn Warren's *All the King's Men,* winner of the Pulitzer. Other notable works that year included John Hersey's *Hiroshima,* Arthur Miller's play "All My Sons," and Eugene O'Neill's "The Iceman Cometh." The best film of the year was "The Best Years of Our Lives," based on the story of three returning veterans faced with the uncertainties of coming home. It was nominated for eight Academy Awards. However, the best-selling nonfiction was Betty MacDonald's *The Egg and I,* an account of life on a chicken farm.

The *1946 Echo,* indirectly Curwensville's social history, featured the Maietti family with its four military veterans—three sons and a daughter—returning home from the war and their mother on the porch greeting them. The yearbook also affirms that the Senior Literary Society continued to thrive, but had changed in format. Rather than recitations, the new Literary presented a one-act play, along with several specialty numbers. Sophomore Literary offered two one-act plays with a variety of musical interludes. Kay Thompson played the role of Claudia Bennett in "A Close Shave." Well-dressed in every photograph in which she appears, Kay sports a suit in one group picture, with her hair in the upsweep hairstyle popular in the fashion magazines. The yearbook also announced the razing of the Susquehanna House, contrasting the closing of that era with photographs of a new era of mandatory chest X-rays for all school children.[19]

The year 1946 also saw inflation rise 6.5 points, and a record 4.6 million of the labor force (one in ten) go on strike, encouraged by the first big post-war strike the previous December in which 195,000 men had walked away from 95 General Motors plants. The 1946 strikes, added to the earlier GM strike, resulted in shortages in housing, cars, refrigerators, stockings, sugar, coffee, and meat. Standing in line at the meat counter again became the norm.

Of greater interest in the extended Pifer family that year of 1946 was Jean's pregnancy. At age 36 she found herself expecting a baby, and on December 15 a daughter, Janet Lynn Bloom, was born. This baby's brothers were 17 and 19. The birth of a girl also meant that the Thompson sisters now had a female cousin.

The fall of 1946 saw Jessie reassigned to the school at Locust Street, a move she relished after traveling to Bridgeport for several years. One of the first things she did was initiate an after school activity for her third grade youngsters which included her niece Jo Ellen Thompson. Miss Pifer's Key Club operated one day a week for children to sing and learn more about the piano. This was part of a nascent trend to offer enrichment activities to children who might not otherwise have such opportunities. The school and the town were on the move.

As part of the post-war surge in civic pride, the Presbyterian Church began a capital campaign called the ROSE (Restoration, Organ, Sunday School Renovation, and Emergency) fund. Jessie took an active role in this project, along with other members of the congregation, and by 1949 a new two-manual pipe organ was installed and in the early 1950s new carpet was laid and the outdoor bulletin board was erected. These improvements continued through the late 1950s with the addition of a two-car garage, and in 1960 total electric heat was installed.

Nineteen-forty-seven saw the arrival of the Bell Laboratories transistor, the forerunner of yet another soon-to-be revolution in technology. This year also marks the date that a United States airplane first flew at supersonic speeds. In contrast, a reenactment of the journey on a raft from Peru to Polynesia was undertaken in 101 days by Thor Heyerdahl to prove his theory of the prehistoric migration to that island.

Tennessee Williams continued as a dominant playwright with "A Streetcar Named Desire." *The Diary of Anne Frank* rivaled *Hiroshima* in its personal account of the effects of war on the individuals. And on the stranger side, the sighting of flying saucers was first reported in this country at about the same time as the fashion designer Christian Dior unveiled his "New Look."

With the new styles Jessie continued to be inventive in dress and her niece Kay seemed to be following in those footsteps. Whether it was a British soldier's tam o'shanter, capes, Indian moccasins, or simply being the first in a small town to start a trend—both women had a knack for using every available fashion resource, even though neither of them could sew a stitch. From hairdos down to shoes, they were able turn everything that struck their attention to decorative uses. While it was said that college girls with their freshness of looks and mold of figure allowed them to get away with almost anything,[20] the coeds had nothing over either Jessie, in her early 40s, or Kay at age 16.

In general, times were good in the late 1940s. By 1947 more than one million veterans had enrolled in college under the GI Bill and others were taking advantage of a lesser publicized part of this GI Bill that granted loans for building homes or establishing businesses. These loans helped many young entrepreneurs "to make up for lost time."

One such veteran in Curwensville opened a restaurant on Filbert Street. Jessie was one of its first patrons and she coaxed Kate into going with her for a spaghetti dinner, a dish both of them were only beginning to appreciate, as it was still considered foreign and this restaurant was the first in the area to offer it as a menu item. With great anticipation, they ordered spaghetti "with sauce." Jessie took the first bite and looked incredulously at her sister. "Kate, taste this and tell me what you think." Kate complied, put her bread on its plate and, with her fork, lifted the spaghetti, covered with sauce, to her mouth. "Good heavens. Is this what I think it is?" It was. The newest restaurant in town, with obviously no cook experienced in Italian cuisine, was topping spaghetti with plain tomato sauce, straight from the can, with not a hint of onion, garlic, or oregano.

Radio was still the king of entertainment in 1947, despite its being called "corny, strident, florid, insane, repetitive, irritating, offensive, moronic, adolescent, or nauseating."[21] However, even its detractors must have been listening to it, as there were 8.5 million radios in use in automobiles, in addition to the millions in homes, and 21.6 million in stores, hotels, and institutions.[22] With listening patterns expanded by the war, people began the habit of switching on news broadcasts and then forgetting to turn off the radio when the news ended. Thus, in many households the radio remained turned on most of the day and evening.

People found the broadcasts filled in lonely hours and they

planned their days around the programming, often feeling a sense of personal friendship with the characters on the soap operas that were gaining popularity. Many young children, not understanding that the sound was broadcast and carried only one direction, believed that they could interact with the radio, especially when they saw adults directing conversation to the electric box. Initially there were very few radio advertisements. However, it did not take long for station owners to realize the revenue to be earned from commercials, and advertising increased dramatically.

Radio had the most adverse effect on live musicians, particularly the Big Bands. Many people no longer would pay to hear live music when they could hear it for free on the radio. Radio essentially led to the demise of bands such as Woody Herman, Benny Goodman, Tommy Dorsey, Les Brown, and Jack Teagarden, even with their traveling to small venues such as the Sunset Ballroom in Carrolltown, Pennsylvania, a favorite haunt of many, including Jessie. Some bands were able to keep afloat by reducing the number of players, but in doing so they were no longer Big Bands. Others looked to the possibility of appearances on television, but musical variety shows would not appear until the next decade.

While there were only 10,000 television sets in the entire country in 1941, by 1948 70 television stations were on the air nationwide. By the following year Pittsburgh had its first station and in January1949, the city's WDTV (KDKA-TV) went on the air as the "golden spike" that joined the New York and Chicago systems. This major event was celebrated in a special broadcast from Pittsburgh's Syria Mosque. Of local interest, although no one in Curwensville had a television set, was the appearance of Slim Bryant and His (Georgia) Wildcats, a very popular guitarist group.[23] Of greater notice to Curwensville residents, however, is that Slim Bryant earlier in the year had made a personal appearance at the Rex Theatre.

During the next decade television air time would be extended from ten o'clock to midnight and complaints were voiced that there weren't enough programs to fill the time available. Advertisers had the answer and commercials quickly began to intrude on the television programming just as they had on radio.

A major appeal of television was the audience it provided for major events, particularly sports, one of which occurred on June 19, 1946, when an estimated 100,000 viewers watched Joe Louis in a knockout. This marked the beginning of broadcast-on-location even though by mid-1948 only one American in ten had viewed an actual television program. This same year the Republican Convention was televised to an audience of ten million, and the following week the Joe Louis – Jersey Joe Walcott heavyweight fight was broadcast on both television and radio where it set a new high in the ratings.[24] This event occurred on Noel Hamilton's 14th birthday celebration, and Jessie, Jean, Kate, and all the children found themselves in Josephine's kitchen, eating cake and Dixie ice cream cups with the pictures of movie stars under the lids, and listening to the prize fight on the radio.

Following the 1946 football season, noted for the Golden Tide's scoreless tie with Clearfield,[25] the Junior Class presented its class play, "Brother Goose," at the Locust Street Theatre, with Kay Thompson playing "Rose Lenore, a sophisticate" a role made for her flair. Stylishly dressed in the appropriate fashionable ensembles (all her own clothes, but embellished by artificial flowers and other accessories borrowed from her Aunt Jessie), it was the delicately scalloped black suede medium-high heeled sandals that were most coveted by her sixth grade sister.

Donald Bloom, Jean's younger son, was graduated from high school that spring of 1947 and promptly followed his brother into military service, and for the same reason—to fulfill what he saw as an obligation, to choose his service branch, and to enter college through the GI Bill. The *1947 Echo* was the first Curwensville yearbook to use spot color throughout its pages and Kay was mentioned in the Senior Class Will as a recipient of a senior bequest: "I, Beulah Hipps, leave my frequent hunting expeditions to Kay Thompson." At the time, her sisters didn't understand the innuendo. I clearly recall thinking, "But she doesn't have a gun."

The summer of 1947 marked a more relaxed time as memories of the war began to fade. The weather lent itself to porch sitting and Jessie often joined her sister Kate in late night conversations on the capacious porch of the latter's home which Kate's family had purchased in March 1946 on lower Thompson Street. Often their laughter could be heard by the girls playing in the backyard, or, late into the night through their open bedroom windows, the girls would hear the quiet talking from the porch. Occasionally in the evenings the children would join their mother and aunt, sitting quietly and listening to their conversations.

One evening the telephone rang and I was sent into the house to answer the call. A gentleman asked to speak to Beverly. I, of course, assured him that no one of that name lived in our house. The man repeated the telephone number he had been given and asked me if I was *sure*. I agreed to inquire of my mother and aunt and quickly ran to the door, asking if they knew anything about a "Beverly." Kate and Jessie both maintained they would have no idea who Beverly might be. It was not until years later that I realized that Jessie frequently gave a false name to interesting gentlemen she might meet, along with the telephone number of her sister Kate, and that it would be natural for Jessie to use her middle name for this purpose. However, in typical Jessie style, she promptly had forgotten and the hapless gentleman caller was left in perpetual perplexity.

Not so with Mary Alice Thompson Jackson. Two years after her husband had been lost in the war, she was introduced to a handsome pharmaceutical salesman—a Texan by birth. After a whirlwind courtship Mary Alice and former Capt. Bradford B.

Crunk were married and two years later moved to Texas to his family's ranch, much to the consternation of her father.

Also in the lingering summer of 1947, John Pifer drilled his last well. He was seventy-nine years old and found he no longer had the stamina for the job. He was pleased, however, that among his final clients was the Department of Highways for whom he drilled 95 feet for $190 and placed 16 feet of casing at $20 for a total of $210. There was no fanfare or retirement dinner for John Pifer; he simply came home one day and told his wife that he thought that after drilling wells for 63 years it was time to rest.

That fall, of the 2.2 million Americans returning to or entering college, half were former members of the armed services.[26] With the overcrowding on campuses, many colleges increased the size of their extension services, particularly in areas for which the courses did not require a laboratory or other resources necessitating attendance on campus. Courses for teachers needing additional credits were among those that became almost exclusively delivered "off campus." Clearfield was a central population site and from 1948 through 1951 Jessie was among the many teachers who took Penn State courses offered in Clearfield.

Like resident students at most colleges, Penn Staters, including a high population of veterans, became more involved in issues that affected their lives off the premises of the university. "Blue laws" were being debated on many campuses, and in State College, a quiet conservative town, a controversy over Sunday movies erupted. Many townspeople regarded this as a moral issue while most students saw it as an issue of freedom. A former burgess told students the ban on Sunday movies was for their own good. This riled the students as well as some townspeople, and the issue soon found itself on ballots. While the proposal for Sunday movies was defeated 282 to 252 in 1947, a few years later Sunday movies became prevalent throughout the nation.

Kate, much like her parents and sisters, privately believed the theatres did not need to be open on the Lord's Day, but as her husband's family business included theatres she was careful not to get into such arguments. Howard agreed with her, but for different reasons. Sunday movies at the Rex Theatre meant working seven rather than six days a week, and he, along with his daughters, would be sweeping theatre aisles every day.

It was a cold winter that year and the ice on the Susquehanna had frozen. A few skaters ventured on to the solidly frozen areas near the shoreline and other sections where the river did not run deep. Many more skaters went to Anderson Creek. Kay was among these, but the younger girls preferred sled riding and coming inside to the popcorn their mother made on the stove.

Danger was never far away from youngsters in the wintertime, and Jessie was furious one day when a young boy who had crouched between two parked cars ran out behind her car as she was slowly making her way up Locust Street one afternoon to deliver materials to Marion Snyder who lived on George Street. This boy, as many like him in the winter time, had grabbed the rear bumper of the car, hooking a ride. Jessie didn't see him until she started to make a left turn onto George Street. Frightened as well as annoyed, she stopped the car with the intent of grabbing the boy and taking him home to tell his mother what he had just done. By the time she was out of her car, however, the boy had run off. Jessie was visibly upset by the time she reached Miss Snyder's home, as only the week before a fourth grader, Larry Bowman, had been hit by a car at the corner of Thompson and Meadow Streets where he was sled riding.

That terrible accident had affected everyone in town, but particularly the school children. Jessie took Lucy Bloom's class in with her third graders so that Mrs. Bloom could accompany two representatives from Larry's class to his funeral held at the home of his grandparents with whom he lived, an experience I will never forget. The death of a classmate was difficult for the fourth graders, but at that time there was no available counseling—or even thoughts of the possible need for counseling. Schools didn't have guidance counselors or anyone else skilled in discussing any tragedy with children. It was the teachers who were left to deal with situations and most had only their good sense on which to rely. They really did find themselves in *loco parentis*.

The following year memberships in local social and civic clubs reached an all time high, spearheaded by veterans returning from a culture of war where one's life could depend on one's comrades. They sought to join groups, clubs, and organizations in civilian society where they would find a replacement for what they had lost when they left their military unit. This trend spilled over to the general society as people joined groups to get ahead, meet other people, learn something new, and, in some cases, simply to fill their lives.

Despite the stated beliefs of the Pifer girls that they were independent and not interested in social clubs, Jessie decided to join the Daughters of the American Revolution (DAR), a patriotic society of "old America" that offered a hierarchy, an element that appealed to many. Jessie traced her descendency to one Charles Clifford and on April 17, 1948, she officially became part of the DAR. She loved belonging to this organization, one believed to convey status, and she devoted herself to it, eventually rising to the office of chaplain.

Also in April of 1948, DAR member Pearl O. Weston, Dean of Women at Pennsylvania State College, became distressed over the increasingly casual attire in which coeds appeared at meal times. She issued a directive stating that coeds were not to enter the dining halls wearing "raincoats, jeans, shirts hanging out, kerchiefs on the head, bedroom slippers, pajamas, bathrobes, nightclothes, shorts, or halter-style dresses." As there was a growing trend toward more casual dressing, this was a battle college deans were not going to win. Monitors could not be found to oversee these orders and Miss Weston's directive had to be rescinded.[27]

The general population, however, was not going to get upset about something so frivolous as fashion, because conditions in Europe were much more serious than worrying about what coeds wore to the dining halls. Few who saw the *Life* magazine photograph of an Austrian boy hugging a pair of shoes given to him by the Red Cross will ever forget the joy in his face. Impoverished people throughout Europe also received food, clothing, and other desperately needed goods through the Marshall Plan—a huge, economic aid package for Europe developed by Secretary of State George C. Marshall. A London newspaper called the aid "the most. . . generous thing that any country has ever done for another."[28]

The late 1940s were years of contrast and change on the local as well as the international level. Curwensville High School's 1948 yearbook was the first in recent memory to depart from the traditional black cover and was printed in a medium blue with an embossed figure of two students standing at the edge of a horizon. Blue spot color was also used throughout the pages of the book, although the advisor may have overlooked the book's being designated as the 24th edition.[29] The annual was dedicated to the townspeople for their generosity to the school in raising the money to install stadium lights. As this school year marked the first time in Curwensville that football games were played under the lights, a group picture of the senior class was posed in the stadium as if they were all watching the game together, cheering on the team. The effect was spoiled, however, as three of the seniors were looking at the camera instead of the field.

Kay Thompson, Class of 1948, was known as a beauty. She was slender, with long dark hair always stylishly arranged. She had flair, designing most of her own clothes which then Mrs. Buterbaugh was able to create often without a pattern. She outdid herself with a prom gown unlike those worn by any of her classmates. Kay's one-of-a-kind gown, in an era of puffed sleeves, was two-pieced with a plaid taffeta skirt and a yellow, cuffed off-the-shoulder taffeta blouse. She went to the dance unescorted because she was dating a 1942 graduate and only high school students were permitted to attend the prom.

Kay was popular, although with a certain perceived aloofness that seemed to be part of being a Pifer. She spent many Sunday afternoons at the Clearfield roller rink where she was a skilled skater. Having done well in the commercial course, attending college held no interest for her. Like many young women of that time, Kay held the Miss America pageant as a distant dream, but there was no available pathway open to her to reach such a goal. Contestants had to have backing, and in small town Curwensville, while there were words of encouragement, there was no financial support. Kay therefore decided to set her sights on a career in dancing or modeling. While she did not resemble her aunt Jessie in physical appearance, there was a definite resemblance in manner.

Kay's high school activities included Gymnastics Club and the Victory Corps as a freshman; Literary as a sophomore; Mixed Chorus and Class Play as a junior; Camera Club as a senior; and Tri-Hi-Y and Girls' Chorus, sophomore, junior, and senior years. The Senior Class Will held this entry: "I, Kay Thompson, leave my original vocabulary to Fritzie Smith." The difference between Kay and Jessie is that Jessie was quick to adopt new slang words while Kay was adept at coining clever—and sometimes cutting—descriptors of people.

Kay's sisters, while intrigued with their older sister, found their idol in head majorette (Joyce) "Fritzie" Smith who gave baton lessons to any young girls who were interested. Every one of Fritzie's aspiring twirlers, whether or not they had any skill, had visions of wearing majorette boots and leading the band.

Kay was only seventeen and a half at her high school Commencement where her class presented a Choric Drama (speaking choir and short skits), "Unto Us the Living," in which Kay had a featured role. Following graduation, she was determined not to remain in the small town that she found so provincial. Her mother, however, would not permit her to leave home until she was eighteen, so she continued to work fulltime at Murphy's Drug Store. During the parade season Kay and Peggy Way traveled with the Rescue Hose and Ladder Company Drill Team as banner carriers, properly chaperoned by Kay's father, a founding member of the drill team. That year the team won the state championship.

By the end of summer it was widely known that Penn State was back to full power as a football presence. Jessie was ready to cheer on the Nittany Lions, pleased that in a small way she was a part of the College by virtue of taking summer courses. Daily passenger rail service to State College had been halted in 1946[30] and the bus service on Saturday did not align with the game times, so Jessie either drove her car to the games or had a date who would drive. The College accepted a bid to the 1948 Cotton Bowl, becoming the first school in Cotton Bowl history to field a team that included African-Americans.[31] Jessie's yearnings of going to the bowl game, however, had to be satisfied by listening to the game on the radio.

As Christmas drew near, Mama began to be affected by what was still being called "melancholy." She spent a good part of her day sitting at the window in the front room. Jessie bought her a sturdy Windsor rocking chair, but Mama preferred the upholstered chair, worn though it was. She would say to Jessie, "Keep the rocking chair for yourself, Jessie. It won't be long before you will want some nice things of your own for the house." Mama sat at the window, making notations in her Bible. Most poignant is her entry dated December 10, 1948, "I'm so lonely."

The 1949 Sesquicentennial, the largest celebratory event ever undertaken by the community, was a great deal of work, but it brought the citizenry together in planning and delivering an extensive list of activities and celebrations. It did not go unnoticed that Curwensville's celebration in 1949 of its 150th anniversary occurred the same year as the dismantling of the covered bridge, a landmark dating from its construction in 1868. There was no movement to "save the bridge" as everyone accepted that it was unsafe. All that was left for the venerable old bridge was to serve as the insignia for the Sesquicentennial.

One of the major undertakings in the preparation phase for the celebration was the fitting of the football stadium to seat an expected 4,000 persons for each evening's performance. In addition, approximately a dozen food sales booths were erected throughout the town and fifty new picnic tables were added to those already available in the park. Borough crews cleaned all main and side streets with a fire hose and painted curbing and parking meter posts. Curiously, it was not until two weeks prior to the celebration that the Girl Scouts canvassed homes for sleeping quarters "in an effort to determine how many are available for use by visitors during the week."[32]

Included in the week's events were daily street fairs and activities, with a parade every day, and a gigantic fireworks on the Fourth of July in the football stadium, along with other special attractions held there every evening. One of the innovations of the committee was to offer a different program each day. Every storefront in town had a window exhibition, many choosing to show "then and now." There was something for everyone that week and, blessed with good weather, the town was packed every day, a feat never to be repeated.

Special religious services opened the Sesquicentennial Week on Sunday, July 3. The town's Catholic Church conducted a field mass at the stadium, a first for the congregation; a united service was held mid-afternoon at the same place; and a concert was held in the evening with the Curwensville Community Band accompanying the Curwensville Male Chorus. Veterans Day,

July 4, featured baseball games, a giant parade (including 12 fighter planes of the Pennsylvania Air National Guard), a band and a drum corps competition, an Army chemical warfare sham battle—including an exhibition of weapons and materials devised and used in World War II, an aerial acrobatic act, and the daily fireworks.

Industrial Workers Day offered guided tours through all Curwensville industries along with a parade of the town's industrial output, floats from the various industries, equipment and trucks from industries, and marching units of the town's labor organizations. Picnics at Irvin Park were also a highlight of July 5. Founders and Merchants Day, July 6, focused on displays of relics and antiques with women store clerks wearing long dresses and matching sun bonnets while men displayed "appropriate whisker trimmings."[33] That day featured Hillbilly bands and competition square dancing with music provided by the popular Slim Bryant and His Wildcats. The largest firemen's parade in the history of the borough was held the evening of July 7 along with a full program in the stadium.

The final day of celebration boasted an appearance of Pennsylvania's Governor James H. Duff and featured open houses at all school buildings with special displays, alumni reunions with an alumni ball that evening, a parade featuring the schools, an all day outdoor program for school-age children, a basket picnic following an address by the Governor, and a dance for teenagers in the evening. A finale at 10:30 p.m. in the stadium closed the week's events.

Jessie was featured on the float whose theme was The Little Red Schoolhouse. Still very attractive (and turning 44 this very week), she dressed as a turn-of-the-century schoolmarm, with a backdrop cutout of a red, one-room schoolhouse, and a scene of a typical day in a schoolroom. It was one of the hits of the parade, partly because it was such a fitting setting for the popular Miss Jessie Pifer. Kantar's presented new settlers and Murphy's Drug Store's float depicted an 1899 pharmacy, with old-fashioned booths and ice cream parlor tables. Jo Ellen rode with Aunt Jessie on the bank's float, I was on Kantar's, and Nan and Flossie Murphy, two darling little girls, stole the show on Murphy's.

By the end of June Kay had convinced her mother to allow her to enroll in the Barbizon School of Modeling in New York City. Kate was reluctant to see her young daughter go to New York yet didn't want to prevent her from following her dream. Kay had been corresponding with the school since the previous fall and believed she had enough information to make her own choices. She had applied for admission, complete with a portfolio of professional photographs, taken by local photographer Jimmy Loddo who had opened a photography business with help from the GI Bill.

Townspeople were not surprised at Kay's choice, although no one else in town had ever thought of modeling as a career possibility. Jessie was encouraging of Kay's decision and offered to pay her first month's expenses. More importantly, she did her best to allay her sister Kate's fears of sending a child to the big city. She even suggested that Kate accompany Kay to see her settled in and to visit both school and the hotel.

Kay had made reservations to live at the Barbizon Hotel for Women, one of the earliest residential hotels for women moving to New York City. The hotel was known for "creating an environment that reinforced the values of the families from which the women had come."[34] Codes of conduct and dress were enforced, no men were allowed above the lobby floor, and prospective tenants needed three letters of recommendation to be considered as residents. Kate found the hotel to be all that it had advertised and the modeling school to have what she described as "a veneer of professionalism," although a bit too slick. She tried to convince herself that it was only her motherly concern, but she did not like the city at all. She spent three days with Kay, and came to the decision that she could not leave her daughter alone there in New York City. Without protest Kay returned home with her mother.

As part of agreeing to come home willingly, Kay garnered her mother's promise that she could go to Philadelphia at the end of the summer and audition as a dancer in one of the many theatre stage shows. This was more palatable to Kate than leaving her eighteen-year-old in New York City, even though Jessie couldn't help but express her disappointment over the lost opportunity in New York. Kay, still optimistic in finding an exciting career, asked Jessie to accompany her to Philadelphia, perhaps believing that Jessie would not be as likely to drag her back home.

The experienced Jessie (who had been to Philadelphia a grand total of six times) enjoyed watching Kay's first experience with Horn and Hardart. Jessie also took Kay to some of the stores, notably Lit Brothers where Jessie purchased a hat trimmed to specifications, a specialty for which the store was known. Jessie telephoned Kate their first night in the city to report to her that Kay would do fine in Philadelphia. She accompanied Kay on several auditions and celebrated with her when she was offered a position as a member of the dance chorus at the Trocadaro, a production theatre which had a second theatre in Atlantic City.

Kay quickly found a roommate who also had been newly hired and Jessie felt confident that all would work out. Kay would remain in show business, as Jessie liked to call it, for a full year, first in Philadelphia, and then the following summer in Atlantic City. Kate had mixed feelings about this decision, but trusted her sister's judgment. She also respected Kay's desire to be a performer and realized that Kay certainly could not find a career as a dancer in Curwensville.

While it was difficult to see her first-born leave the nest, Kate realized that the world was changing rapidly and that her daughters, each in turn, would have to seek a line of work. She also knew that opportunities were limited in Clearfield County and she vowed she would encourage all of them to seek a career elsewhere. Despite the societal trend to praise the housewife, Kate was convinced her girls should be prepared to make their own way in life. Career choices were limited, but she wanted her daughters to be able to support themselves, much as her own mother had done with Kate and all her sisters. It had taken Jessie many years to earn a respectable salary, but she certainly was proof that a single woman could earn a living.

Teachers were still earning less than industrial workers, and it was said that only a devoted educator could resist the lure of a job assembling radios or running a drill press where one could earn a much better wage. Of even greater long-run importance was the growing difficulty of attracting able young women and men into the still underpaid profession of teaching.[35] Fortunately for the country, many educators like Jessie could not see themselves working in a factory and opted to remain in a position "respected by the community." Jessie, in her twenty-fifth year of teaching, earned $2,166.68 in 1949 and paid $223 in taxes on that amount. More surprising, however, is that while her income had increased by only $370 from 1924 to 1943, it increased almost $1,000 between 1943 and 1949.

As the post-war period drew to a close, the size of the average home decreased while its equipment improved. The big, old-fashioned houses tended to be cut into apartments while the building industry encouraged a trend toward ranch houses all on one floor with multipurpose rooms. None of this interested Jessie, except the new pressure cookers. She bought one despite Mama's fears that it would explode. Also new was frozen food. While it had little appeal to many Americans, Jessie decided it would be worth trying and she began, as most new consumers did, with frozen vegetables.

As more and more young families moved to the suburbs, large stores and mail-order houses established branches in suburban districts near housing developments. A new area of Irvin Hill opened for development, as did an area which was called Temple Heights, presumably because it was on a hill behind the Masonic Lodge.

In 1949 a study of favored leisure-time occupations by *Fortune* magazine showed that reading of books was the fourth most attractive recreation for women but only seventh for men. The favorite of both was listening to the radio, second for men was viewing of sports and for women was needlework. Visiting was third with both. The male list continued with cards, movies, books, magazines, records, and handicraft, while women listed movies, magazines, cards, records, outdoor sports, playing musical instruments, and watching outdoor sports. With the advent of popular television, legitimate theatre fell drastically in the poll and revenue from movies began its downward trend.[36] However, there still were not enough homes with television sets to make television viewing a contender for a spot on the list; thus the rated popularity of radio remained high. By 1950 there were only 1.5 million television sets in the United States, but one year later that number would increase tenfold to approximately 15 million.

In September 1949 Russia tested an atomic bomb, throwing a dark shadow over any hopes for lasting world peace. This fear led some families to seriously consider building a bunker or some kind of shelter that they were told would protect them from an atomic bomb. The publisher of the Chicago *Tribune* had already built himself a bomb shelter, one of the first. Five months later President Truman announced that America was building a hydrogen bomb, and the nuclear race was on.

Thompson Sisters

PREVIEWS
REX
THEATRE
CURWENSVILLE, PA.
HOWARD V. THOMPSON, Manager
PROGRAM OF HITS FOR NOVEMBER 1946.
NOV. 1st.
FRIDAY,
Night Train to Memphis
With ROY ACUFF & HIS SMOKY MOUNTAIN BOYS
NOV. 2nd
SATURDAY,
'Song of Old Wyoming'
With EDDIE DEAN and JENNIFER HOLT
NOV. 3-4th
SUNDAY and MONDAY,
MAUREEN O'HARA · DICK HAYMES · HARRY JAMES
DO YOU LOVE ME
in Technicolor
A 20th Century-Fox Picture
TUESDAY,
Paramount presents
"THEY MADE ME A KILLER"
with ROBERT LOWERY · BARBARA BRITTON

Matilda and John Pifer

REX THEATRE
CURWENSVILLE, PA.
COMPLIMENTARY
Pass
Acct
Good Until
NOT GOOD FRI., SAT., SUN., HOLIDAYS OR SPECIAL ATTRACTIONS
Subject to Federal Tax
Manager

Curwensville Boro School
Grade 3
1949–1950

Chapter 8

The Best of Times, The Worst of Times

...that grayness of the 1950s with (its) unimaginable restrictions.

—Daniel Day-Lewis[1]

The 1950s are viewed by many as the best times possible, although historians describe that view as a veneer, assessing much of the decade as repressive to women and teen-agers. Small towns were admired as ideal places to rear a family, and Curwensville was considered a safe and happy place to live—as long as you weren't a Communist, did not believe in progressive education, subscribed to the belief that the family was centered around the father, and weren't an unmarried adult female.

Historian William Chafe describes this decade as a period of transition,[2] because so much of what became characteristic of life in the second half of the 20th Century had its roots in society's new-found obsession with suburban living, transportation by car, television, rock music, and paperback books. These trends, along with the struggle to end racism, were to become and remain dominant social issues through the 1960s.

The 50s decade was also one of shifting focus from production to consumption, from saving to spending, from city living to suburbia, from blue-collar to white-collar employment, and, indirectly, from an adult to a youth culture, laying the foundation for the dominance of society by youth. Yet for all the connections this period of history has to every society that followed, the fifties remain distant in people's frame of reference. Typically the decade is regarded as quaint, for much of what was perceived as shocking and troubling in the 1950s seems quite tame and inoffensive today.

Women in particular were in conflict with societal norms of the time. Just as conditions for the full emancipation of women were ripe following World War II—both in the job market and educational institutions, society's ideas of women's place began to change in the early 1950s. Part of this was caused by the returning war veterans and their need to regain their place as breadwinners and protectors of the family. However, a greater reason for this change in outlook toward women can be attributed to the need of manufacturers to market new consumer goods to women in their prescribed roles as homemakers, not as business and professional women. America was viewed as the richest and most successful nation on earth—a nation where all citizens could anticipate living the good life, defined by a well-equipped house in the suburbs, a new car or two, and a good white-collar job for the husband. In such a world, the role for women needed to be framed as one of full-time wives, mothers, and *consumers* who would produce well-adjusted and successful children.[3]

This period also marked the first time in history that middle-income American families could dwell in comfort and, with only minimal inflation during most of the decade, a life of relative leisure seemed to be within the reach of the middle class. For the first time ever in history, most people had time on their hands, and "leisure" soon became the new operative word. Some universities responded to this societal phenomenon by creating academic departments of Leisure Studies.

Americans began to believe that they could be rich in material goods by using the growing trend of buying on the installment plan. The new pre-fabricated houses and gleaming cars could make the middle class worker feel successful—so long as he could convince himself that both house and car were tasteful (meaning not differing greatly from others on the block) and mid-priced (a four-door Kaiser sold for $2,289.99 in 1951[4]). And for the first time, working people began to play golf and join country clubs, where their membership payments, just like their car payments, could be made on the installment plan.

In 1950 the typical new house was only 894 square feet in area, usually with two bedrooms, one bath, no garage, and few built-in appliances,[5] but as the decade continued with the advantages of both money and time to spend in these homes, middle-class Americans could concentrate on building houses with more conveniences. They could raise families and fulfill aspects of themselves and their children which heretofore had not been possible, such as taking music or painting lessons, golf lessons, or traveling. Cooking on a charcoal grill also became popular. The grill, however, was the only household area in which men participated. All other household responsibilities were the purview of women.

The design of houses began to change to reflect a family-centered home. For those who could afford it, the main room in a house was no longer the living room or parlor, but a room especially created for the purpose of family togetherness. These new family rooms provided the perfect place for the television sets advertisers were promoting. Few persons saw the irony in the fact that watching television detracted from family conversations and interaction.

The ideal 1950s woman was expected to strive for the family concept that *McCall's* magazine termed "togetherness." A family was considered a single perfect universe with no conflicts, contradictions, or unfulfilled ambitions: a single unit with its aspirations twined. The model husband was designated leader and hero; the wife was his mainstay on the domestic side.[6] Most women of the fifties could not have dreamed of the coming women's movement that would bring so much upheaval—and so many benefits—in the sixties and seventies.[7]

Adults taught by their own example that life was safer if one had no expressed politics. Teachers did not express reactions to the current headlines (either thinking they were protecting their young students or not wanting to be criticized for expressing opinions) and most teachers did not discuss the Korean War or Communism. Therefore, without fully understanding the reason, youth watched the adults excavating for underground fallout shelters, once called bomb shelters, under the specter of Communism and the growing evidence of extensive Soviet espionage throughout North America. Soon full-blown "red hysteria" was sweeping the nation as citizens and their elected officials reacted both reasonably and unreasonably.

Frightened and angered by the thought that Communist spies might be among them, the federal government had enacted the Loyalty Order for federal government employees in 1947. Its watchdog, the House Un-American Activities Committee, enforced the order that required government officials, college professors, and others to sign "loyalty oaths"—declarations that they were loyal Americans and had no Communist sympathies. Many of those who refused to sign, including 120 professors at the University of California-Los Angeles, lost their jobs.

This order was followed by the Internal Security Act (The McCarran Act) of 1950 which called for severe restrictions against Communists and the registration of all Communist organizations and individuals. The act also forbade entry into the United States of aliens who had belonged to totalitarian organizations.

By the fall of 1950, after California had established a new loyalty oath for all state employees, there was talk of these oaths for state employees everywhere, even among the teachers in small towns like Curwensville. At the time there were few teacher unions in Pennsylvania and fewer still in small towns. Teachers held a kind of understood "tenure," so that it was not easy to dismiss a teacher arbitrarily; however, regulations regarding teachers and their employment were determined by the Pennsylvania Department of Public Instruction (DPI), a state agency, and if the state legislature or DPI called for loyalty oaths as a condition of employment, teachers would have to comply.

Jessie and her teaching colleagues worried about what they would do if they were asked to sign a loyalty oath, particularly when, in the neighboring state of New York, about three hundred teachers, most of whom had taught for at least fifteen years, were dismissed from the New York City public schools after the Board of Education and the Senate Internal Security Subcommittee delved into "subversive influences" in the schools.[8] Many Curwensville teachers saw no dilemma in signing the oath, while others, especially those who had served in WWII, were offended that their loyalty to the country would be questioned.

Jessie, ever the pragmatist, said she couldn't imagine the government would bother itself with small town teachers. Nevertheless, she did not relish the town discussing teachers in terms of their loyalty—or anything else for that matter. As she once had remarked to Kate, she now repeated to her fellow-teachers, "There are no secrets in a small town. I can't imagine anyone on this faculty being a Communist and our not knowing it. You can't go to hell at midnight without someone you know seeing you."

Unable personally to have an impact on world affairs they didn't understand, most citizens simply sought pleasure in their everyday lives through entertainment. Popular reading for 1950 included science fiction—particularly Ray Bradbury's best-selling *The Martians Chronicles* and John Hersey's *The Wall*. Major films that year were "Sunset Boulevard," and "All About Eve," nominated for a then-record 14 Academy Awards. In music, silly songs abounded, but more serious music was redeemed by the cool jazz of the period, a style that had evolved from earlier bebop.

Buying on the installment plan continued as a popular means to purchase items for which one did not have the cash; however, this kind of purchasing plan would soon decrease in appeal with the advent of what would come to be known as credit cards. Although never owning a credit card of any kind during her entire life, Jessie later remembered telling her teaching colleagues about a man she had dated who belonged to the Diners Club. She had told her friends that she hoped she was giving them accurate information as at the time she wasn't sure how a card possibly could work like cash. "Where does the money come from?" she had asked, "and how does the restaurant get its payment?"

That same summer Matilda Pifer turned 78 years old, in a time when only eight percent of the population was over 65.[9] By fall she was feeling "poorly" and again wrote in her Bible that she was lonely. She did not seek medical attention nor did she consider telephoning her sisters to talk about how sad she was feeling. Even though the Pifer family had had a telephone for a number of years, Matilda still was not at ease using it. She had not ever placed more than a handful of calls, and while she would answer the telephone when it rang, she was not adept at conducting a conversation without seeing the speaker in person.

It was also during this period that Matilda decided to write a Will. The Will, still intact, is in her own handwriting and bears the signatures of no witnesses, yet when she handed it to Jessie to read and to put away "for the right time," Mama held no doubts that her five daughters would honor her last wishes. That was just the way things were done and the way her father and her grandmother before her had written their own wills. It was a matter of family trust, and the daughters all knew they would deal with her wishes when the time came, silently grateful that she had expressed them in writing.

In many schools that year tempers were a bit stretched with the threat of loyalty oaths in everyone's thoughts. In addition to that disquieting possibility, Jessie and her colleagues (national as well as local) also had to contend with a public that was becoming nervous about a movement called "progressive education." *Life* magazine devoted an entire issue to what they called "the crisis," while highly respected journals such as *The Saturday Review* ran a series of articles cautioning the public to be wary of extreme attacks against the schools.[10] Additional criticisms of schools were soon added to the mix of complaints: overcrowding, the growing need for scientists and technicians, the shortage of adequately trained teachers, and the possibility that there might indeed be communist subversion in local schools.

Throughout the country teachers whose loyalty was questioned or who supported the National Education Association (then the closest thing to a teachers' union) were fired. Even small towns felt the reverberation when local school board members were asked if any teachers belong to subversive political organizations.

When a board member came to visit the elementary schools in Curwensville, the teachers, including Jessie, heretofore welcoming of the members, were now wary and some could barely conduct their classes. Nothing like this had ever happened to them before and it led to a sense of unease and mistrust between teachers and the school board that continued for some time.

Fortunately for all, the school board of the newly formed Curwensville Joint School District had more important items on their agenda than visits to classrooms, namely the long-planned-for school jointure. In September 1950 student enrollment doubled with the addition to the school district of various small towns and townships surrounding Curwensville, resulting in the reshuffling of teaching assignments. Jessie and her fellow teachers held their collective breath, each afraid she would be assigned to a country school in one of the townships in the jointure.

Once both teachers and students discovered that they had much in common with their colleagues from Grampian, Lumber City, and Heburnia, friendships began to form, and by the end of the first year of the jointure, the Class of 1951 proudly noted in their yearbook that they were the first class to be graduated from CJHS. Not all alumni of CHS, however, were pleased when they saw the Commencement Program announcing it as the *First* Commencement.

The first yearbook of the jointure, the *CJHS Echo,* featured the school's new courses, including art, physical education, and home economics. A chapter of the new national Future Homemakers was formed, its stated purpose, "to prepare each girl to take her place in the home and in society." Out of the 42 girls in the Class of 1952, 17 of them majored in Vocational Home Economics.

The high school's meager library holdings were generally limited to the classics, although occasionally a few contemporary titles were added. The librarian was very conservative, and no questionable books were ever placed on the shelves. For example, J. D. Salinger's legendary *The Catcher in the Rye* was published in 1951, but most teen-agers in small towns did not hear of the novel until they got to college. Some of them borrowed their parents' copy of Herman Wouk's *The Caine Mutiny.* A few older teens understood the importance of Rachel Carson's *The Sea Around Us,* but none were likely to be allowed to read James Jones' popular *From Here to Eternity.*

Through the efforts of the businessmen in town, *The Curwensville News* began publication in 1950, the first time Curwensville had

had a newspaper since manpower shortages had closed *The Curwensville Herald* in March of 1944. The newspaper continued until 1955 when it was discontinued for lack of support.

In addition to planning the school jointure, leaders from most of the service organizations in Curwensville had been meeting to strategize how to pay the large debt incurred with the Sesquicentennial celebration of 1949. That event, while successful in the eyes of those involved, had been costly and the debt cloud hung over the entire community. The leadership committee wanted an activity that would rally the town in the way the Sesquicentennial itself had and would also raise money to pay the debt. The committee favored some kind of musical entertainment, recalling the town operettas that had been popular during the 1920s.

A minstrel show using local talent was suggested and immediately took fire. The result was a full house for each performance with strong, complimentary reviews in the newspaper: "From the time the curtain opened in the Locust Street Little Theatre until the last song had been sung …the program unmasked one of the largest parades of local talent ever viewed by area citizens."[11] Many, including Jessie Pifer, who had been featured in the earlier operettas, helped behind the scenes.

Jessie's third grade students loved her. She was described as a "marvelous breath of fresh air" by a former student who still remembers the sterner teachers in first and second grades. "I was so busy trying to prove Mrs. X and Mrs. Y wrong about their saying I could not be very smart. I can never recall joy or laughter in their classrooms. Miss Pifer, however, was absolutely the perfect teacher for me. She is the person who allowed me to know that I could be successful in school.[12] She was someone who could praise what you did well and help you learn to do better. No wonder I thought I had died and gone to heaven when I arrived in third grade and experienced Miss Pifer's warm, caring, and fun-loving ways. I can still recall thinking how beautiful she was. I loved her clothes, her hair, her gentle, yet lively style, and she was always so positive. I can remember the classroom, and how she entered the room each day, greeting all of us, and treating us as though she truly looked forward to seeing us. Her love of clothes is something I recall so vividly. Part of going to school every day was wondering what she would be wearing, whether she would wear the suit with the fur collar, what fancy earrings she might wear, and whether her shoes would be the same color as her dress or suit. What a gift she was!"[13]

Another child a few years later and now a teacher herself, remembers as a first grader being traumatized by Mrs. X who once lifted her out of her seat by her hair, sending her home to retrieve a book she had forgotten. She also recalls being struck on the knuckles, a common practice in Mrs. Y's room. Miss Pifer was different. "She was so classy," recalls this former student.[14]

Jessie enjoyed a good time and the companionship of interesting men, although she remained discriminating in her choices. She liked the attention of men, but did not suffer fools. More than once she had been compared to Barbara Stanwyck, or at least the characters the actress played in the movies and, like those characters, Jessie was adept at dodging unwelcome advances. She would assess her gentlemen friends quickly, separating those who were worth her time from those who were, as she termed it, "muscling in" on her. The latter she would dismiss with a withering look of disdain. While her posture remained erect and her stride strong throughout her lifetime, her good friend Joe Errigo once described her as having a "seen-it-all slouch" when she was sizing up a fancy talker to see if he was on the level.

Joe Errigo remained a close friend, continuing to look out for both Jessie and Kate, letting it be known without having to say it that he would always be there when they needed him. It was recognized that Joe had always had a fondness for Kate and would have done anything for her, but it was Jessie he could kid with, because Jessie knew where his heart was. He often would address her as "Miss Stanwyck," or, if she were acting particularly outrageous, he might say something to this effect, "Jess, sometimes you remind me of Bette Davis, the way you sling yourself around as if you are obeying some inner law of your own." Which was precisely the case with Jessie Pifer. She could be bold and even brash, but could also, in a moment, change from cold detachment to beaming acceptance.

Jessie was true to type and, while considered unique in her own community, she was behaving as did many cosmopolitan adults of her generation. A study conducted of those who had been youth during the 1920s showed that in middle age many behaved as though they were thoroughly unfettered, as if for them authority didn't exist. They stood with their own generation and considered themselves citizens who were free "to behave as outlaws whenever they pleased."[15]

This generation, Jessie notably among her more conservative family members, seemed to believe that there wasn't any point in planning for the future. Not only did Jessie relish the unexpected, but also she was optimistic about what might lie ahead. There was a sense of unending time; whatever one wanted, there would be plenty of time to achieve it. Worrying for those of Jessie's generation—and disposition—almost seemed to be a sin, not only because it wasted energy, but because to deal with apprehension was thought to be unreasonable.

This side of Jessie was both exhilarating and at times exasperating to her nieces. The children, who passed the crackers and cheese or were told to "get Aunt Jessie a fresh glass of ice water," would often feel colorless in comparison to this fanciful creature of an aunt who still lived as though something wonderful would happen in the next twenty minutes.

On the one hand, Aunt Jessie insisted on good manners. Her five nieces were expected to be ladylike and were held to a practice of courtesy that Jessie and her friends did not even expect from each other. From the children's perspective, Jessie was strict, an attribute Kate called "Jessie's teacher attitude." It was, however, more than her teaching manner that caused this position. Rather, it was her personality and ever-present sense that the way in which her nieces and nephews conducted themselves reflected on her personally and professionally.

On the other hand, her generation's optimism held forth when difficulties arose. Jessie assured her nieces, and in particular Kay, that somehow, somewhere, sometime, things would work out as they ought to. She often told Kay that a gifted person deserved a fine life; indeed, the world owed it to her. Little did Jessie realize how well she imprinted this notion of *deserving* onto Kay and that Kay would demonstrate and capitalize this feeling of entitlement.

Kay's own sense of privilege began with little purchases for herself which she rationalized to her sisters that she should have because she deserved them. Her husband indulged some of these "fancies," as he termed them, but he also tried to explain to her that they were on a budget and couldn't always afford these extras. Kay began to complain to her family that she could not indulge her baby daughter or herself in the same manner she had been indulged as a little girl, "before the others came." She seemed to grow increasingly dissatisfied with her situation, suggesting to her family that there should be more to her life. She missed the glamour of the stage and before long began to rail against the stultification she was feeling. She mentioned to her mother that her sisters seemed to be having a better time as school students than she was as an adult.

The year 1952 suggested a kind of larger-than-life attitude, producing the brilliant literary work of Ernest Hemingway (*The Old Man and the Sea*), John Steinbeck (*East of Eden*), and Edna

Ferber (*Giant*), with these latter two novels becoming major movies starring James Dean. Hit movies of the year were "High Noon" with Grace Kelly and Gary Cooper and "The Greatest Show on Earth" which won the Academy Award the following year. The Awards ceremony itself was first televised in 1952 and had the single largest viewing audience in television history to that date.

Producers saw the results of this television exposure and realized that nominated movies could be assured of box office results, even when the number of television sets in January 1953 stood at only 21 million.[16] What temporarily fascinated the public, however, was the first 3-D movie, "Bwana Devil" released at the end of the year.

Jessie's interest in the dashing sulky races never wavered and the Clearfield County Fair, counted among the largest fairs in the state, attracted quality harness racing. Jessie loved these races and attended every day. Her father went with her once or twice during the week, for he, too, enjoyed the harness races and had years earlier introduced his daughter to this event. Frequently she invited her nieces and nephews to accompany her and one or another of them occasionally would go, but the younger ones found the races boring.

One of the more memorable events of early 1953 was the inauguration of President Eisenhower, as much for the fact that it was televised as for his popularity with the public. It was generally agreed that no President since George Washington had entered office with a greater bank of good will. The public schools closed for the event so that the students could watch the ceremonies on television, either at home or at the home of friends. The second televised event for which schools closed was the coronation of Queen Elizabeth II.

A special family event in the Pifer household that summer of 1953 was the visit of Joseph Pifer, older brother of John, who made his 27th trip from Portland, Oregon where he had moved in 1910. Joe was 90, five years older than John. A *Clearfield Progress* photograph taken at the time shows a vibrant Joseph and a very tired-looking John. When Jessie saw the contrast in their appearance and watched their interaction and conversations, she had to acknowledge, first to herself and then to Kate, that Papa didn't look well. Jessie's fears were heightened when for the first time in her memory Papa was not interested in attending the harness races at the County Fair.

Jessie didn't like these visible reminders that her parents were elderly and that soon she not only would have to deal with their passing but also would be alone. She rarely expressed this concern, but she did admit that she dreaded thinking of their growing old. Like Scarlett O'Hara, however, she would rather tell herself, "I'll think about it tomorrow."

At this time Jessie was forty-eight years old and, as middle age loomed, she, like many who reach this time of life, was faced with restlessness, a vague sense of perhaps having missed something. Yet when she tried to identify that "something" there was nothing she could name that she would have changed in her life, except perhaps less responsibility for her aging parents. She didn't like to think too much about the future and thought of herself as still vibrant. While she continued to feel a stirring that made her uncomfortable, she felt and looked good, and by September was ready for the school year to begin.

With the return of fall, Curwensville maintained a variety of activities for the teen-agers and adults alike, one of the best being football games at Riverside Stadium. The town was proud of its record of victories against arch-rival Clearfield, the neighboring town at least three times its size. Headlines following this game were especially sweet: "Curwensville Scuttles Bisons, 26-0."

In 1954 the minimum hourly wage increased to one dollar and the average suburbanite was earning an estimated $6,500 per year. Teachers were making considerably less and, after thirty years in the classroom, Jessie was earning half that, approximately $3,500.[17]

At Shippingport, Pennsylvania, about two hours from Curwensville, ground was broken for the world's first non-military atomic power plant which would open three years later, two months following a reported UFO sighting near the plant. In Pittsburgh, not far from Shippingport, Jonas Salk began inoculations against polio and shortly after, mass inoculations occurred throughout the nation.

Reminders of Communism resumed a place in the public eye during 1954, when the McCarthy witch-hunt for subversives culminated in televised hearings seeking to prove Communist infiltration into the U.S. Army. A study that year revealed that 19 percent of Americans considered that the danger from Communism was "very great," 24 percent that it was "great," and 38 percent that there was "some danger." In addition, many more of those polled thought the danger from Communists lay in the spreading of their ideas rather than in actual sabotage or espionage.[18]

Conditions became so tense in many schoolrooms throughout the country that some teachers removed maps of Russia. The U.S. Congress, in a reactionary step based on a growing religious fundamentalist movement, changed the wording of the Pledge of Allegiance by adding "one nation under God." By the end of the year, however, the public, as well as Congress, finally became disenchanted with the "red scare," and many zealots began to feel a bit foolish.

Even with the fading fear of Communism, the nation's public schools continued in the headlines following the ruling by the Supreme Court that segregation by race in public schools was a violation of the 14th Amendment. Segregation was not, however, an issue in Curwensville with its less than one percent minority population. What the local schools did share nationally was a steadily rising school enrollment which jumped by 30 percent during the decade. New classrooms could not be constructed quickly enough to meet the need.[19] The Curwensville Joint School Board congratulated themselves on their own foresight with the new junior-senior high school under construction.

Although television was still a novelty to most Americans in the mid-1950s, 29 million households owned a television set; another two years would pass before Jessie would buy one. The daily paper was still the medium of choice for Jessie, as well as for most other Americans who subscribed to 1,768 different daily city papers.

Ernest Hemingway won the Nobel Prize for Literature and Charles Lindbergh (*The Spirit of St. Louis)* the Pulitzer Prize for 1954. Teen-age readers were buying William Golding's *Lord of the Flies,* and teen-age French writer Françoise Sagan became a literary sensation with her *Bonjour Tristesse.*

In the spring of 1954 Jessie's unspoken fear of the death of her parents had to be faced when, after an illness of five weeks, John Pifer died of a stroke on May 3. In her grief, the first thing Jessie thought of was the news photo of Papa and his brother Joseph. She was convinced that this picture showing a very tired John Pifer had been a warning. Jessie found Papa's death especially difficult because she had lived with her parents nearly every day of her life.

A month after her father's funeral Jessie packed a suitcase and left Curwensville to spend the remainder of the summer in Massachusetts as a counselor at Camp Dibble, a tobacco processing farm that employed teen-age girls and boys to work the farm and teachers to serve as chaperones. She didn't discuss this decision with her sisters except for asking them if they would take turns keeping an eye on their mother, seeing to her needs while Jessie was out of town. The sisters thought a tobacco processing farm a very odd choice for Jessie, who typically enjoyed her quiet summers away from children and who had no great need for the small amount of money she would earn as a camp counselor. They could only assume that Jessie felt the need to get away in response to the loss of their father. They readily agreed to take care of Mama, allowing Jessie to grieve in her own way.

In mid-September Jessie made what she called her "regular run to Gettysburg" to take Noel back to college, this time for his junior year. Leaving Curwensville early in the morning, she didn't mind the drive (more than four hours each way) and dinner mid-afternoon in one of the several good restaurants in the small, quiet town of Gettysburg. She also was very much aware that Josephine enjoyed personally overseeing her son's return to college. On this particular journey they also drove around the battlefield and finished the last roll of film left over from the Camp Dibble anomaly.

The following week, Jessie took her mother to The Golden Yoke, a pleasant, white-tablecloth restaurant in Luthersburg, close to DuBois, and a place Mama preferred the few times she would agree to have dinner out. The next day Mama wrote to Ruby of her loneliness and her concern for Jessie: "I must get used to not having John come in. Jessie took me to The Golden Yoke for dinner last week. Jessie misses her Father coming in. The other girls have their own homes, but she has no home but this."

The grandchildren were busy with their own lives: the Wayne sons and Eugene Bloom married and working; Don Bloom and Noel Hamilton in college; Kay Thompson Brunetti with her new baby and new home, now complete with Boots, a black cocker spaniel; Jo Ellen and I respectively entering our junior and senior years of high school; and Nan, the youngest of the Thompson sisters, beginning seventh grade. Janet Lynn Bloom, the youngest grandchild and her mother's delight, was in third grade.

Jessie couldn't help noticing how much my school experiences imitated school events that she had encountered at the same age. Jessie didn't say anything to me, but she did remark to Mother how similar some of the experiences seemed to be. Jessie laughed when one of her teaching colleagues noticed that I, like my aunt thirty years earlier, liked to be at the helm of the school activities in which we were involved. Like our Aunt Jessie, all of Kate's girls were in the town musical productions and class plays, took piano lessons, attended the football games, attended dances, performed in concerts and festivals, and had a variety of boyfriends.

Jessie was particularly reminiscent when fall brought football season with its attendant hoopla, culminating in the end-of-season game between Clearfield and Curwensville. Attending the evening pre-game pep rally and, bundled up against the November chill, Jessie found herself wishing she had kept her possum coat. Other spectators, many thinking of earlier pep rallies, included men of various ages wearing their letter sweaters or championship football jackets, self-consciously shifting their weight from one leg to the other, recalling battles fought long ago. Many of the high school girls, most of whom had walked to the football field, wore car coats (the irony lost on them) and brightly colored silk head scarves, both as a fashion statement and to guard against the dampness from the river only yards away.

Following the rally, the band and cheerleaders led a snake dance from the stadium on to the highway, in a single file conga line, weaving from one side of the street to the other, cheering as they headed up the main street. Jessie drove home by way of South Side to arrive ahead of the paraders in time to park her car in the driveway and join those along the parade route in front of the City Drug Store, cheering and waving as the teen-age revelers noisily wove their way through the center of town heading for Spinelli Motors where a smaller pep rally would be held.

As the crowd passed by the corner of Thompson and State Streets, Jessie was startled by her sudden recollection of how her father had stood at the same spot, watching a horse-drawn sleigh pass by on its way home from Clearfield, filled with the laughter and songs from the members of the Curwensville High School Class of 1924. When the cheering from Spinelli's subsided, Jessie could hear the crowd singing the Alma Mater, just as her classmates had sung it going though town three decades earlier. She noticed Joe Errigo at her side, and the two classmates joined in the chorus, remembering....

In December, Mama again wrote in both her Bible and her journal, "I'm so lonely." Her melancholy was increasing, but Jessie, busy with school and coping with her own sadness over the death of her father, could offer little solace to her mother.

The last week-end in April 1955 Jessie made plans to visit Ruby. Mama wasn't up to going but encouraged Jessie to make the trip by herself as she sensed Jessie needed to get away. Mama likely realized that she herself was sad most of the time and that Jessie would enjoy seeing Ruby and her boys, particularly Johnny and his growing family. Torn between wanting to see Ruby and having reservations about leaving her mother alone, Jessie called her sister, "I just don't think I should go, Kate." Convinced by both Kate and Josephine that she needed a change of scene and that they would look after their mother, Jessie set off with mixed emotions.

"They were right to tell me to come," she told Ruby, as they talked and laughed late into the night. "It is good seeing you and the boys. This is just what the doctor ordered." And they laughed even harder at the poor joke. That was what was so much fun with Ruby, everything led them to paroxysms of laughter.

Jessie arrived back home early Sunday evening, May first. "Mama knew," she thought, as she made the turn on Thompson Street. "I did need to visit Ruby." As soon as Jessie saw Kate waiting for her on the porch, however, she felt a cold chill. "It's probably all right. They would have called if anything had happened," she told herself. But her unsteady gait up the steps revealed the quiet terror in her heart. Kate's face said it all. "Oh, Kate," Jessie cried out, "It's Mama, isn't it?" Kate could only nod as the tears filled her eyes. "I never should have left her," Jessie sobbed. "Jess, dear sister, Mama slept away. Josie and I brought an early supper and we found her lying on the sofa, very peaceful. We thought she was asleep."

Ruby came from Ohio the next day and among the sisters they made sure that Jessie was not alone that first week. After Ruby and Tom left for Canton, however, Jessie sat by herself on her mother's wide swing on the front porch. Gazing at the empty chairs there on the porch and not realizing that Kate was standing in the doorway behind the screen, hearing her plaintive sigh, Jessie said aloud, "Now I really am alone."

Despite the grief all five sisters experienced at the loss of their mother, Kate would not allow a pall of gloom over the spring school activities of her daughters.... She did not speak to the girls of the depth of feeling at her loss—either at the time or later, but did her best to keep their lives as normal as possible despite her personal grief. Like most of their generation, the Pifer sisters kept their emotions in check. Their children never saw them cry, nor did they ever see them hug each other or openly show affection for their own children, much as they obviously loved them.

Jessie, remembering her own high school years and the excitement of graduation, did her best to not hang a cloud over the celebration of my end-of-year activities and graduation. She offered her car for my use during the last two weeks of school, a service she offered to all her nieces and nephews. She arranged to get a ride to her school and had already canceled all evening engagements for the month because of her own bereavement.

The Best of Times; The Worst of Times

Amidst all the flurry of the usual end-of-school activities and the exclusive events for the graduating seniors, the new high school was finally completed. The Class of 1955 was to have only a few days of occupancy and we found ourselves wondering why the school board didn't just wait and move into the new building in September. It would have been so much easier for us, we thought. However, a new school belonged to everyone and with twenty years in the planning, the town wanted to celebrate and make the move a special event. Thus, near the end of May, a Moving Day was proclaimed to both symbolically and in reality have the entire school walk together from the old high school to the new. The elementary schools closed at noon and the townspeople lined the street along the route the students would be taking.

Through the open door of her kitchen, Jessie first heard the band members tuning their instruments in the high school parking area a block from her house. Then there was a brief silence followed by the strains of the Alma Mater as the entire student body sang farewell in tribute to the Patton Building. Jessie began to sing along quietly as she stood at attention on the porch, ". . . may thy gray stone walls hold fast, Loyal thoughts our memories send thee, As the days go fleeting past. . . ." Thinking of her sisters, each in turn, and the memories of high school she had shared with them as well as her classmates and parents no longer living, tears welled in her eyes. She had not expected the leaving of the Patton Building to affect her in this way.

Composing herself, Jessie turned to watch the parade of high school students, led by the marching band, as they filed past her house, beginning the march to their new building. Jessie waved from her porch as they passed. All motor traffic had been re-routed, as this was a long-awaited day in Curwensville.

Jessie spent that long, quiet summer of 1955 on her porch and began the practice she would follow for the next thirty-five years, inviting passers-by (all known to her) to "come up and sit awhile." While the offer was hospitable, not many people had the time or inclination to stop and sit, as most were either on their way into town on errands or on their way home after work. Nonetheless, some responded to her invitation as they sensed Jessie's loneliness since the death of her parents. In July she turned fifty, not a happy prospect from her point of view. She shrugged off well-wishes, not wanting to be reminded of her age.

Like others in her circumstance, Jessie did very little cooking and found the newly marketed TV dinners suitable for her needs. After tiring of balancing a plate on her lap, she took the next logical step and purchased a set of TV trays, beginning the routine of taking most of her meals in front of the television, rarely missing the evening news.

Even though she began to fret about returning to school that fall, she knew she needed to get back into a better routine, hoping that would help her out of her doldrums. What she had not expected, however, was yet another national focus on teachers, this time unmarried ones. Many women who had entered teaching in the 1920s under the condition that if they married they would lose their jobs now found themselves being scrutinized and criticized for being single. A widely read book advised that "the family is the unit to which you most genuinely belong. . . . The family is the center of your living. If it isn't, you've gone far astray."[20]

Family living author Paul Landis added, "Marriage is the natural state in adults" with implications that not to be married was unnatural. Further, he said, "Except for the sick, the badly crippled, the deformed, the emotionally warped and the mentally defective, almost everyone has an opportunity to marry."[21] In addition, a book by Ferdinand Lundberg and Marynia Farnham written in 1947 began to be widely touted. These authors also considered the single person to be warped and defective. They had very specific—and extreme—ideas about unmarried adults and what should be done with them: Bachelors of more than thirty, unless deficient, should be encouraged to undergo psychotherapy.

Far more dangerous than the single man, however, they said, was the unmarried woman. Farnham and Lundberg suggested (emphasis theirs), "*all spinsters be barred by law from having anything to do with the teaching of children on the basis of theoretical (usually real) emotional incompetence.*" ...Worse, they said that a great many children had been damaged psychologically by the spinster teacher who "cannot be an adequate model of a complete woman." Children, the authors believed, modeled themselves after their teachers and to hire a spinster teacher would only perpetuate future generations of incomplete spinster women.[22] Even though Jessie had been married for a brief time, she was angered by this implication of unmarried teachers' inability to be good role models.

Unfortunately, unmarried women became the object of somewhat condescending pity or disdain, as the repeated use of the term "old maid" in magazines suggested. Even though Jessie lived the life she chose for herself, there was always the second-guessing, and given her already bereaved and unsettled state, this kind of criticism made her very uncomfortable as she was already noticing signs of what later would be identified as anxiety.

Criticism of educated women, however, was also the tenor of the times, regardless of how offensive this was to all educated women. The criticism was particularly confusing to young women desiring a college education when they read that "the more educated a woman is, the greater chance there is of sexual disorder, more or less severe."[23] To then also have these words cast up to them by persuasive young men added to young women's uncertainty of their place and identity.

When *House and Garden* reported that suburbia had become the national way of life, it became the norm to marry young. By 1955 the average age of marriage was twenty years for women and twenty-two years for men (down from 20.4 for females and 22.9 for males in 1951).[24] Nearly one-third of all American women gave birth to their first child before reaching their twentieth birthday. Almost one-half of all women married while they were still teenagers, and two out of three white women in college dropped out, mainly to get married, before they were graduated. As a result, a declining proportion of college women prepared for professions or pursued advanced degrees, because *not* marrying as soon as possible was suspicious. Thus, holding fast to the idea of a career became an uphill battle for young women.

Jessie saw her niece head off to a four-year college, although because of my lateness in applying to Penn State, I spent my freshman year at a satellite campus in nearby DuBois. While Jessie likely held a passing thought of how easy it seemed for me since my education was being paid for my Aunt Mary Alice, she never expressed these thoughts; in fact, she obligingly offered her car to transport this new freshman to her lodgings 22 miles from Curwensville.

DuBois Center offered a number of clubs and social events, although they were localized and engaged mainly those few students who boarded in the small dormitory or in private homes. Students at the Centers were told we were welcome to attend events at the State College campus but most of us did not pursue that privilege because of a lack of transportation and the distance of 65 miles. Thus, I didn't think it particularly odd that Kay suggested we accept an invitation a younger friend of hers had extended to attend the Alpha Phi Delta house party on main campus. I did, however, wonder why a twenty-five-year old mother would be interested in going to a fraternity party.

It later became clearer that Kay had started to make choices in her personal and social life that perhaps were not supported by her husband. Kay loved to dance and while Albert was also a good dancer, he did not share her passion for dancing. They began to grow apart and soon separated, much to the chagrin and embarrassment of both families. Mother's entire life and example-setting had been one of order and dignity, and she, like most of her contemporaries, believed in living what writers were calling a "decent life."[25] She also believed in and demonstrated self-denial in the interest of her family, and she did not relish having to deal with gossip about her oldest daughter.

During the second half of the decade, a number of changes occurred in government regulations. The postal service upset a number of citizens when mail delivery was reduced from twice to once a day and in 1958 the cost of a postage stamp went from three cents to four, although still less than half the cost of a telephone call which in 1951 had doubled in cost from five to ten cents. Some of the citizenry questioned the decision of making "In God We Trust" the official motto of the United States, believing it to be a violation of the Constitution.

By the end of 1956, in a time when modest wages went a long way, there were 16.6 million families with more than five thousand dollars in annual earnings after taxes. By 1959 there would be 20 million such families—virtually half the families in America who viewed this as a comfortable wage. Jessie, with thirty years experience, was making $3,900 in 1956, although by 1958 her annual salary reached $4,756 before taxes. The following year in larger cities and their suburbs teachers with a bachelor's degree would be starting at $4,000.[26] During this same year, for the first time the number of white-collar jobs outnumbered blue-collar ones and America officially became a post-industrial, service economy with a new managerial class.

By the mid-fifties 22 million women were employed in a

third of the nation's jobs, although most of them were poorly paid and sparsely promoted. At the end of 1956 *Life* paid tribute to the working woman, adding to the general and deliberate stereotyping of women: "Household skills take her into the garment trades: neat and personable, she becomes office worker and saleslady; patient and dexterous, she does well on repetitive, detailed factory work; compassionate, she becomes teacher and nurse."[27] (This author is struck by the similarity of tone and style in Alexander Black's *Miss America*, a patronizing, stereotypical view of women of the 1800s cited in the Introduction.)

While Jessie's niece and Kate's popular daughter Jo Ellen was enjoying her senior year, she was also making plans to go to Washington, DC to work for the federal government. The FBI had paid a visit to Curwensville Joint High School in February to speak to pre-selected students about a career in this government agency. Mr. James Bonsall had recommended Jo Ellen as his "best student—without reservation"[28] and she was accepted by the FBI without having to take their screening test. Kate didn't like to think of sending her seventeen-year-old to the nation's capital, but she had an innate sense that leaving town provided the best chance for her girls to have a brighter future.

Spring again had Jessie ready to loan her car, this time to Jo Ellen for the last two weeks of school, but Jo Ellen had not yet applied for a driver's license despite being among the first to take driver education when it was inaugurated at the new high school. Early June brought Commencements, with Jo Ellen's graduation on June 1, and Noel's graduation from Gettysburg College on June 3. Jessie, Josephine, Mother, and I made the trip to Gettysburg for the occasion, to share in Josephine's obvious pride. Her joy was lessened, however, knowing her son would be entering the service to complete his military obligation begun in ROTC (Reserve Officer Training Corps).

Summer of 1956 brought The Four Lads to the County Fair as the featured attraction. Kay had been separated from her husband for nearly a year and she was openly dating, waiting for her divorce to become final. She went on several double dates with me, including the County Fair and Sunset Ballroom where a program billed as "TV Discoveries of 1956" showcased, among others, the then almost unknown Pat Boone.

A year after her mother's death, Jessie was still upset that she had not been there to say her good-byes. She couldn't bring herself to address the final matters in settling her parents' estate, although this was not unusual because Jessie was well-known for letting things slide if she didn't want to deal with them. One of her other habits was visiting her attorney on the spur of the moment without having scheduled an appointment. It was as if the thought of calling in advance had not occurred to her, or that she expected an attorney to see her at any time she would stop in.

A letter from Attorney Morris Silberblatt written to Jessie October 23, 1956 confirms her disregard of protocol. In the letter, he first asks her for all the final bills against the estate of her mother and her father. He then notes that he needs to know the worth of their property to determine the final worth of the estate. His tact and consideration for his client is also evident by his careful choice of words: "Let me know when it will suit you and I will try to arrange that when you do come here that I can see you. If I know in advance that you are coming here then I will keep other people away from that time. I would not want you to come in here when I cannot see you. That is one of the reasons why people call me for appointments."[29] Many years later had this letter been available it might have proved useful in supporting the fact that Jessie's calling on attorneys without an appointment was quite common and simply her way of doing things, and not a sign of mental decline.

A second letter from her attorney, also dated October 23, is in reference to the estate of John Pifer. Apparently Jessie did not respond to either of these letters as a third arrived three days later. In this letter Mr. Silberblatt reminds Jessie that there will be a legal notice in the newspaper in reference to her mother's estate. He asks again, in rather direct terms, for a complete list of her mother's debts. He also suggests that if other members of the family want to come along with Jessie he will be glad to talk to them as well, as "very often, the members of a family do not understand what is involved in the handling of an estate." He further asks the value of the real estate.[30] Again, this is an indicator of Jessie's typical avoidance in dealing with legal matters.

She did, however, at the urging of Kate and Josephine, have her dining and living rooms painted and repapered. She also contracted for repairs to her furnace and paid a fifth of the cost (divided among all five sisters) for a much needed new furnace for the rental side at 410 Thompson Street.

In Washington, DC that fall Jo Ellen was adapting to city living where she resided at the Meridian Hill Hotel for Women, took her meals in its cafeteria, and rode the bus to work. At seventeen she was the youngest employee of the Federal Bureau of Investigation. Understandably, she was frightened living alone in the capital, but also realized there was no choice. She could not easily return home and had to make the best of Washington, not unlike her Aunt Jessie and her own mother who had had to board in school directors' homes when teaching in rural schools.

At the same time I began my sophomore year on Penn State's central campus in State College. While Jessie was faced with having to deal with her parents' meager estates and Jo Ellen was battling her homesickness, I was doing my own adjusting to an only slightly lesser degree of loneliness with dormitory living and the formidable size of the Penn State campus. I too was homesick.

The Best of Times; The Worst of Times

By spring 1957 Kay had been at Kent factory for well over a year. She worked the day shift and left her daughter Kim with our mother who took care of the child until Nan came home from school at which time Mother left for work at the Dimeling Hotel. Nan watched the little girl until Kay arrived from work around 4:30. Nan also often baby sat on week-end evenings when Kay began to spend time at local clubs where there were good bands. Kay just wanted to dance. The Cha Cha had recently been introduced and Kay was the first in the area to master it. Her response to any criticism of her lifestyle echoed the earlier words of her aunt, even though in a way not intended by Jessie, "Why shouldn't I? I deserve it."

Kay maintained a keen interest in her younger sisters and attended many of their activities. One of the most exciting family events of 1957 was Jo Ellen's becoming a finalist in the Miss Washington, DC contest. Kay and I borrowed Jessie's car for the trip to Washington for the finals. Kay, while very supportive of her sister, could not help but voice "what if," for she herself had always dreamed of being a beauty pageant contestant, and saw in her sister what might have been, had her own life taken a different turn.

Kay continued to spend time in social events with her sisters, including a football game with me at Penn State where the Nittany Lions played against Army. She resumed the use of her maiden name which placed finality on her status as a married woman.

On September 2, 1957 the relative tranquility of the early to mid-1950s—regarded by historians as a brief happy moment in American life, albeit bland, moral, patriotic, conservative, and buttoned-down—was broken by the Battle of Little Rock Central High School. There the National Guard, under orders from Governor Orval Faubus, seized the school building to prevent the enrollment of nine black young people. The sight of federal troops called out by President Eisenhower at the behest of the mayor of Little Rock evoked the resentment and rage that this southern region had cultivated since the Civil War.[31]

While the public was still reeling from Little Rock, a greater fear arrived in the form of a "beep, beep, beep" in A-flat coming through radios and televisions. The signal, frightening to those who heard it, came from several hundred miles above the Earth, generated by a 184.3-pound aluminum sphere the size of a beach ball.[32] This was Sputnik I, the first Russian space satellite.

Responding to public pressure to surpass the Russians in space as soon as possible, the federal government began pouring money into education, particularly math and science. The most far-reaching impact of the National Defense Education Act came from Title III, for strengthening science, mathematics, and modern foreign language instruction. The effect of this act on American education was monumental, especially in elementary education—most importantly affecting elementary teachers, most of whom who had had no training in teaching science.

The reaction of Jessie and her colleagues to this national act and all its implications ranged from nonchalance to something akin to panic, as most were all too well aware of their shortcomings in science content and teaching techniques. School districts began to insist that their elementary teachers attend workshops or take college courses in the teaching of science, and Penn State began offering courses at Clearfield and DuBois.

Earlier this same year writer/housewife Betty Friedan had begun working on an article for *McCall's,* a reminiscence on the 15th anniversary of her graduation from Smith College. She had expected to profile families on "togetherness," but what she unexpectedly found among the classmates she interviewed was a strong dissatisfaction with their lives. *McCall's* turned down her article, dismissing it as not accurate because it did not demonstrate a positive impact of family togetherness.

Smarting at this reaction, Friedan decided to write a book on her findings that the dissatisfaction felt by the women she interviewed was caused by what they were reading in popular magazines. What stunned her was that these magazines, which in the late thirties and forties had been reporting optimistically on women moving into the professional world, dramatically changed their focus around 1949. At that point their writers began to portray women as having no need to exist on their own; rather, they said, a woman's only role was to be a reflection of her husband and his career. Friedan concluded that it was the magazines that had created a fantasy world of the perfect family *as a promotion to sell their magazines and the products they advertised.*

Jessie may not have been aware of these studies, but the profile Friedan drew of women was in many ways parallel to the disorientation to life Jessie herself was beginning to feel by the spring of 1958. Jessie had been one of those women who knew how to take care of herself and make it on her own. With the new social focus in the 1950s in which a woman was expected to subsume her own identity to that of a husband, Jessie, who always had known who she was and content in being single, began to have doubts. She didn't like having to question her life.

She also was annoyed at the thought of having to be bothered taking science classes and she was tired of giggles from students and snide remarks from adults and the media about "old maids." She saw her nieces and nephews growing up with families of their own, and a creeping uneasiness began to overtake her on occasion when she realized that she was becoming the older generation in her family. While she preferred to live alone and welcomed the solitude, the house seemed empty at times. Holidays were becoming oppressive, and there were fewer interesting men to date. In addition, there was an ambivalence of new possibilities in the world in general, but she didn't feel young enough to take advantage of them.

On the other hand, Jessie was strong and independent. Most of the time she was quite satisfied with her life and didn't want any changes. She finally told herself—and mentioned in passing to her sister Kate—that she was not going to give in to these foolish notions she was having. She continued to enjoy both horseracing and football, and particularly followed the professional football games recently brought to television. She enjoyed watching the Colts' quarterback Johnny Unitas and the Giants' halfback Frank Gifford who reminded her of her nephew, Johnny Wayne.

Aside from spectator sports, Jessie had become active in her church and the Daughters of the American Revolution, having risen to chairman of the junior division where in April 1958 she conducted a discussion on "Our Heritage." Her faithful attendance and involvement in both the church and the DAR added to the status she enjoyed as a teacher.

"I'm making a comfortable living, I like my home, I can come and go as I please, I have respect in this town, and people still view me as a stylish presence," she thought, as she tightened the new, dangle earrings on her earlobes, slipped into her Springolator sandals—knowing her legs were still good, picked up her new straw handbag, and headed to Leitzinger's Department Store to look at their Rose Marie Reid swimsuits. She felt like having a cigarette just to confirm her own independence, but decided that could wait until she returned.

Kay also had spent the winter living alone, but she was hatching a new idea to follow a career she had earlier considered but had not pursued, that of an airline stewardess, at the time considered a glamorous job. Kay sent for information and began formulating a plan. The requirements were that one be young, single, slim, attractive, and female. The prerequisites were largely the same no matter which airline one hoped to work for. The life of a stewardess was touted as exciting, and many young women from small towns found the allure appealing, an opportunity to "take a fling at the big, bad world."[33]

This was very much what Kay wanted to do, even though it was highly competitive with only three to five of every 100 aspirants chosen for the six weeks of training. Nonetheless, she was resolved. She fit the profile as defined by a career stewardess who had flown for TWA for three decades, "These women almost to a person . . . left home, college, or other jobs because they couldn't stand the drudgery of an ordinary life."[34] In the late 1950s airline stewardesses were almost on the same level as movie stars and people admired them as they walked through the terminals in custom-fitted uniforms. Kay did go to Pittsburgh for an interview, but that is where the dream ended.

Mother had her emotional hands full for an entire year, beginning with the double wedding of Jo Ellen and me. She also had to deal with her oldest daughter who announced she was leaving for California with Robert Walker, recently divorced. Kay had decided to leave her daughter Kim with her ex-husband and his parents and begin a new life.

Years later Kate admitted mixed emotions over Kay's choices—both trepidation that Kay was going into the unknown without a job with someone she may or may not be marrying and relief that her first-born would be taking her lifestyle with her away from Curwensville. Thirty-five years later, Kate admitted to her three younger daughters, "I was embarrassed by Kay's actions and was glad she was leaving." On the other hand, it was inconceivable to Kate that any mother could go off on an adventure not knowing when she might ever see her child again.

Nearly unbearable for Kate was the loss of her sister Margaret Jean. The second week of December Jean was in the midst of planning a birthday party for her daughter Janet Lynn and ignored the abdominal pain she was experiencing. The day after Christmas she was rushed to the hospital. A burst appendix led to peritonitis and on December 30, at age 48, Jean died. This loss was devastating to Kate, as not only was Jean her sister closest in age—they shared the same birthday of February 11 two years apart—but was also her best friend. Kate would continue to mourn deeply for Jean the rest of her life and never really got over this loss. The following year I would name my first born Jean in honor and memory of my aunt.

As the 1950s decade drew to a close in 1959, John Galbraith's *The Affluent Society* provided Americans a good profile of who they were, while Vance Packard's *The Status Seekers* revealed a profile of Americans as others saw them. The European Common Market was in its fledgling year, and the American Express credit card made its debut. America's economy was more secure, although the threat of science supremacy of Russia was the deciding factor in Alaska's becoming the 49th state, followed by Hawaii the next year, making an even 50 states in 1960. Americans cheered when the nation regained some of its defense status with the U.S. nuclear submarine, The Nautilus, passing under the icecap at the North Pole.

Perhaps the greatest cultural change of this decade was that at the beginning of the decade television had been essentially unknown in most households. As the decade ended, 86 percent, or 46 million, of the country's households had television sets, and average Americans were "watching the tube" almost six hours a day.[35]

Jebbie's 40th High School Class Reunion

1964

Chapter 9

Winds of Change

Whether we like it or not, this growth of national consciousness is a political fact The wind of change is blowing through this continent.

—British Prime Minister Harold Macmillan[1]

While every decade serves as a bridge between the periods which precede and follow it, the 1950s probably had further reaching economic influence on society than did most other decades. Its most crucial legacy was the wave of unparalleled national prosperity that coursed through it, so that by 1960 the gross national product had increased by 250 percent and per capita income was 35 percent higher than in 1945, the closest boom year.[2] Continuing the longest economic growth period in U.S. history, the 1960s saw real per capita income increase by 41 percent, resulting in relative prosperity for many workers. This new affluence neatly coincided with the impact of the bumper crop of post-World War II baby boomers coming of age just in time to be indulged by their parents who (many for the first time) found themselves with discretionary income. Thus, the decade of the sixties became a time of optimism, especially for the privileged young who believed there were no limits as to how comfortable and powerful and healthy and happy they could be.

Between 1960 and 1969 the number of Americans ages 15 through 24 nearly doubled and, by the end of the decade, that ten-year age group accounted for more than one-sixth of the entire population of the United States. At the mid-point of 1965, more than half of all Americans were under twenty-five years of age, and a huge majority of these were still in school.[3]

Jessie's generation held a mixed opinion of these youngsters, proud progeny of the war veterans. Jessie's peers found them to be open to new experiences but with a much greater sense of entitlement than any children they had previously encountered in their classrooms. Teachers found this transformation increasingly noticeable with each class as their numbers continued to grow. When enrollment rose to forty children in a class in the last two years of her teaching, Jessie for the first time felt the stress from the demands of a crowded classroom.

The ethos of the 1960s was in large measure confrontational and politically fractious in all areas of society, although the focus fell on the religious community in particular, as people searched for moral answers to political problems. A surprisingly large number of the young in the 1960s were attracted to the doctrine "faith is as faith does" and began to demonstrate their belief that the test of religious faith is the social good it produces. This conviction moved many of them to action in political arenas, and it was these idealistic young who provided the numbers—as well as the energy—for the civil rights movement, the Peace Corps and VISTA, various campus movements, the ecology movement of the late 1960s, and—most vehemently—opposition to the war in Vietnam.

College campuses almost immediately became the centers of debate—followed quickly by turbulence—over the issue of Vietnam. Students sought answers from their professors, some of whom were among the nation's best thinkers and historians. However, regardless of their quest to understand the politics of the situation, most of these young people could not rally the kind of fervor for a war with Vietnam that their professors and other elders had shown against Germany and Japan. Neither generation could fully comprehend the antagonism of the other, with the result that many WWII veterans who had been young and full of nobility of purpose in the 1940s became angry at the young men of the 1960s who saw no nobleness in war.

Possibly the most striking element about the turmoil of the 1960s was that social and political issues did not dramatically affect small town America until the following decade. Its effect was subtle, slowly reshaping society (although barely directly touching anyone over the age of 35) and laying the groundwork for a world no one born before 1941 could have imagined.

Cardio-pulmonary resuscitation (CPR) replaced the chest compression method that had been taught in schools for more than a generation. Public school teachers were encouraged to apply this new technique, but training was not mandatory. Thus, very few, Jessie among them, chose to volunteer to learn a method that required breathing into another person's mouth.

Jessie, never a regular smoker, continued to enjoy her occasional cigarette, although she never smoked in public or in the presence of her nieces and nephews. Like many others, she viewed smoking as an adult choice and made no apologies for smoking in her own home. By 1966 Congress required manufacturers to place a warning label on each pack of cigarettes: "Caution: Cigarette Smoking May Be Hazardous to Your Health." Never one to think that health hazard warnings were meant for her, Jessie continued to smoke, albeit infrequently.

In January 1960, I was graduated from Penn State with a B.A. in English Literature. Nan, following graduation from fun-filled years of high school, left for Washington DC where she was exempted from the usual interview process with the National Security Agency based solely on her sister Jo Ellen's proven

performance. Nan thrived in DC, and several years later the sisters laughed when Jo Ellen found herself being introduced as "Nan's sister."

During that same spring, Josephine's son Noel, living in Framingham, Massachusetts, became engaged to Karin Gustavsen whom he brought to Curwensville early in the summer to meet his mother. In August I flew to Boston to visit Noel and Karin. Upon my return, Jessie asked me if I had visited Camp Dibble, the tobacco farm where she had worked as a chaperone in the mid-50s and which was located outside of Framingham where Noel lived. I had not and found myself apologizing for the oversight.

In September 1960, at 26 years of age, Bill Jackson, son of Mary Alice Thompson Crunk and cousin to the Thompson sisters, married Rosemary Keating, a Penn State classmate and home economics major. Bill enjoyed telling his family and friends that a home economics degree was a pre-requisite for his choice of bride, just as it had been for his father.

The mood of Christmas 1960 was an unfamiliar one for Kate, as it was the first time in 30 years she was without children living at home. Even though Nan and I visited for a few days, Jo Ellen remained in Washington and Kay in Los Angeles. Kate realized with a sudden sadness that an era had passed and there was no one to whom she could express the waves of longing she was experiencing. Jessie, childless, could not understand the emptiness of a house once filled with children. Adding to the holiday sadness was the lingering mourning for her sister Jean. This bereavement still weighed heavily on Kate's heart, even though she kept her grief private, the deep loss ever present. Josephine likely sensed

Kate's quiet anguish, but she had her own concerns with her husband Droz's terminal illness to face and Noel's wedding only three weeks away.

On the morning of January 13, 1961 Noel Hamilton's family—Josephine, Jessie, Mother, and I—made the trip to Boston by train for his wedding. A photo taken on that occasion shows the three Pifer sisters in jewel tones with Mother's hand on Josephine's arm as if in support. Josie, remembering her own marriage at an even younger age than her son on his wedding day, admitted her sense of sadness to Kate, but said that she could hardly argue that Noel was "only" 25. What troubled her was her conviction that she would now see even less of her son and would not be close to any grandchildren, an accurate premonition.

One week later, on January 20, John F. Kennedy was inaugurated as the 35th President of the United States. Many citizens, including Jessie, who had been so taken with this vibrant Democrat that she had volunteered one evening at the county campaign headquarters, watched this televised event and years later could still recount the processional walk to the reviewing stand, the top hats, and the late January sun reflecting from the new-fallen snow, casting everything in brilliant relief.

Kennedy at 43 was the youngest person ever elected President of the United States, and Eisenhower, the out-going President, held the designation as the oldest chief executive in U.S. history. It struck Jessie as she watched the ceremony that she was midway between the ages of the two presidents and very much a part of the history both had experienced.

Nineteen-sixty-one was to be a turbulent year for the country with the Bay of Pigs incident, construction of the Berlin Wall in Germany, and increased tension when Russia resumed nuclear testing and Kennedy responded by ordering the U.S. resumption of nuclear testing as well as advising families to prepare fallout shelters.[4] Also during this year the Congress of Racial Equality sponsored freedom riders, interracial groups seeking to end segregation on interstate bus routes in the South; Malcolm X advocated for the separation of the races; Russia sent the first man into space; and Alan Shepard became the first American astronaut.

Television was called "a vast wasteland" when the chairman of the Federal Communications Commission asked for more educational programming from television networks. Ray Kroc bought out the McDonald brothers, launching an empire identified by golden arches. However, the action that year which would have the most divisive results throughout every level of American life was the sending of 4,000 servicemen into Vietnam.

That summer Jessie served as a delegate to the national DAR convention held in Constitution Hall in Washington, DC. She continued to try to interest her nieces in applying for membership to the organization to which she was devoted, but she met with no success. What Jessie failed to realize was that her nieces, by not joining, were very much like their aunt who at their age also was not at all interested in club memberships.

In December Howard V. Thompson and his sister Mary Alice Crunk, through a lawsuit against their father, were awarded Mid-State Theatres, Inc., founded by the Thompson family in 1925. They divided the properties and, while this division appeared to be amicable, it placed a strain on the relationship between Howard and Mary Alice. It also added to the rift between Mary Alice and her heretofore adoring father and it compounded the nearly lifelong, never-explained estrangement that already existed between father and son.

Despite Mother's own inner strength where her daughters were concerned, she was bothered by the dysfunctional relationship between her former husband and his own father and the effect it might have on her children. She was particularly concerned about the changes she observed in Kay and the lifestyle she had chosen.

Winds of Change

Her oldest daughter seemed to have changed from the once sweet-tempered child who, for the most part, had been very helpful with her three younger sisters. However, there had been incidents that Kate was now recalling when Kay intimidated them: the times she frightened the little ones by pretending the Wolf Man was hiding in the hedges as they walked home from the movies; taking her sisters across the dangerous—and forbidden—swinging bridge; daring them to cross the train trestle bridge where the water flowed beneath; and telling me that the police might arrest me for imitating Kay's schemes of selling discarded trinkets.

Mother tried to ignore these troubling recollections, focusing instead on the great deal of time Kay had spent with us as children and the many games she had devised to entertain us: forming our own Necco Camp with activities and excursions in the woods near our house, taking me with her when she was with her own teen-age friends, and spending hours huddling by the radio with the three little sisters listening to "The Inner Sanctum," a program that in retrospect seems odd for children to be listening to.

Yet, all in all, Kay seemed to have changed. As a teenager, she had developed wanderlust, always harboring a desire to be **someone**. While she had made very precise plans to go to New York City, then Philadelphia after graduation and, later, on a far more complicated journey that led her to California, Kay seemed to lack a specific plan of education, training, or apprenticeship that would take her to the kind of life she so desired.

Mother also worried about what she saw as an edge to her daughter that she could not understand, considering Kay's upbringing. While beautiful and stylish as a young woman, Kay's panache grew into a California style of flamboyantly colored caftans and tunics. In some ways she was coarse, using language that other family members found uncomfortable. She was witty, but her clever comments often were sarcastic with a sharpness to them, sometimes to the point of being hurtful. Most disturbing, however, was Kay's attitude, echoing what her Aunt Jessie had told her years before, that somehow, somewhere, sometime, things would work out as they ought to and that "a decent or gifted person *deserved* a fine life: indeed, the world *owed* it to her."

Kay definitely acted like she thought she "deserved" whatever it was she wanted and believed that she was "entitled" simply because she was Kay. She told of many instances when she had bargained her way out of paying full price, haunting the stores until an item was reduced to a price that suited her, or finagling ways to pay less for services, including legal, medical, and dental bills. There were a number of other instances, suggestions offered, comments made, and actions reported by Kay that, according to Mother, concerned her and thoughts of these incidents returned time and again to haunt her.

Kay apparently was well thought of at TWA, earning several promotions and commendations. She particularly was enthralled with opportunities to work with the television and motion picture industry, including hosting Trans World Airlines dinner parties for celebrities.[5] She was now among the "somebodies," even attending the Academy Awards, a lifelong ambition. But it didn't seem to be enough. For some reason Kay appeared to feel cheated, as if someone or something had not worked out for her or that the world was out of sync for her.

Max Lerner, professor and syndicated journalist, explains why certain individuals find themselves in tune with their times or at odds with it and why some thrive in their culture while others seem to feel betrayed by the principles by which American culture lives: freedom and acquisition. Lerner clarifies that there always have been a number of people who feel themselves left out of the operation of these principles, or who are too much in a hurry to wait, or who feel resentful because other persons seem to start with an unfair advantage. These persons, therefore, seek some equalizer, feeling justified in tearing down the accepted bond of social relations.[6]

Such a description fit Kay, whose desire for freedom was in conflict with the constrictions of small-town morality by which she was reared. As Kay herself admitted, "I'm the type that wants everything right now."[7] According to Lerner, such individuals grow up expecting great things of life, and they are disappointed if they don't achieve them.[8] Worse, they truly believe in the American idea of a natural right to happiness and material success because, as they tell themselves, "I deserve it." This apparently became Kay's credo as she sought recognition, happiness, and, most of all, secure material success at the expense of all else.

Kay unfortunately suffered from ulcers as well as cluster headaches and was willing to try new medical drugs, always sending information to her family about new treatments such as Elavil. This is not to suggest that she used medications recklessly; rather, she had such debilitating pain that she occasionally would check herself into a hospital. She attributed these ailments to tension in her job and stress in driving the Los Angeles freeway 60 miles every day. Her family blamed much of her stress on her passion for constant traveling. In June of 1965 she wrote,

> *Bobby was in Mexico when I decided to put myself in the hospital. I should have gone sooner but you know how you keep putting things off. I was discharged on Sunday but didn't go to work until Tuesday. I'm so washed out and sleepy all the time. No wonder I'm living on pills. I was finally diagnosed as having vascular headaches related to migraine. I'm also allergic to something in the Los Angeles air and I can't breathe right.*[9]

Historians could well have been describing Kay as they defined the sixties as a period of hard-edge skepticism, particularly in those persons trying to carve out a new life for themselves. The worlds such persons were creating often made it difficult to know what was true. According to Nora Sayre, "You met people who didn't seem to believe what they themselves were saying; I especially encountered that in California. There, contempt for the past was paramount."[10] This was Kay, who loved this California lifestyle where the past was irrelevant and she had the independence to live her life outside the scrutiny of a small town.

The year 1962 brought more triumphs and turmoil to the decade. Triumphs included John Glenn's circling the globe three times; Polaroid's first colored film for its instant cameras; James Meredith's enrolling at the University of Mississippi; and the Nobel Prize for Medicine and Physiology for determining the molecular structure of DNA. The turmoil included the military stand-off in Cuba, thalidomide as the cause of birth defects, and the political manifesto of Students for a Democratic Society, criticizing the American political system.[11]

This year also held events that were yet to be determined as either triumph or turmoil. Controversial and troubling to both scientists and the general public were Rachel Carson's *Silent Spring* and the Supreme Court's ruling on prayer in public schools as a violation of the First Amendment guarantee against state establishment of religion.

Successful films of 1962 were "Lawrence of Arabia," "The Miracle Worker," "Phaedra," and "The Manchurian Candidate," while important books included Michael Harrington's *The Other America,* James Baldwin's *Another Country,* and Katherine Anne Porter's *Ship of Fools.* Despite these thought-provoking offerings for the general public, most of what was written in the popular magazines specifically for women continued to be aimed at married women and women who presumably (and that meant *every* woman) *wanted* to be married. No attention was yet being paid to the single working woman—independent and often single by choice.

Winds of Change

One of the most dramatic changes ever to happen in Curwensville occurred in 1962 when ground was broken for the Curwensville Dam as part of the Susquehanna River Flood Control. This major project required the relocation of the New York Central Railroad and the entire town of Lumber City, as well as many other homes on the valley floor, all destined to come under water. When completed, the Curwensville Lake Recreational Area offered swimming, unlimited power boating in the 700-acre lake, and a major warm water fishery.

Curwensville residents remember with particular pride that they joined forces with surrounding townships in a show of support against naming the area "Clearfield Dam" for its neighboring town, county seat, and staunchest football rival. Despite increased traffic and dust in South Side during construction of the dam, the new Elementary II School (completed in 1961), located next to the high school building not far from Irvin Park and down river from the construction, held its annual school production under the direction of Miss Jessie Pifer.

Two minor events, one national and one personal, also occurred in the fall of 1962, both of which later would have a major impact on the life of Jessie Pifer. Nationally, membership in the Social Security System had opened to teachers in the early 1960s when it became optional for tenured teachers and mandatory for all new hires to enroll. Because it was highly recommended that all teachers sign on for this program, Jessie did. She agreed that it was likely she would receive more in lifetime payments than she would contribute during her remaining years of service. Social Security would be a welcome supplement to her state teachers' retirement plan that she believed would be adequate for her living expenses.

Jessie considered her savings and stock in the Curwensville State Bank as being sufficient for other supplemental or unforeseen needs. She liked to say her savings were "for a rainy day," a phrase that became familiar to her family. True to the American culture at the time, Jessie Pifer did not speak in terms of "growing old." She was not extravagant in her lifestyle and was confident that she would be prepared for her own rainy day.

The personal event that would change Jessie's life was the death of the wife of a gentleman she knew casually. In late December she sent a note of condolence to the widower, a man who would come to affect her life in many ways. John P. (Jack) Mohney responded to her note of sympathy and thus began a lively correspondence which quickly evolved into a courtship:

> ***Jan. 4.*** *Sorry that I have not had time to answer and thank you for the two consoling cards I received from you. …It has been many years since I last saw you and although I had been in Curwensville for the last three years, it was the first time I had gotten to say hello.*
>
> ***Jan. 8.*** *Well, so I met you again after all these years. You did not remember those rides of long ago that I gave you to your school in Bridgeport, but I did. I think you're still a darn nice girl and I look forward to a date in the near future. I am all by myself so any time you're so minded we can have a meal or date together. Gee, Jesse, you don't know how much I appreciated seeing you.*
>
> ***Jan. 23.*** *This was a very enjoyable evening and I hope you feel the same about it. I vote for more like it, but we must still get out where we can cut a rug or two and put away a big steak. …I am thinking about you.*
>
> ***March 3.*** *Darling, I want to take time and tell you I don't know when I have had a more enjoyable time. I knew from the day I first saw you, you were for me. When I received those cards I knew you were a real friend, for no one else even thought of me.*
>
> ***March 10.*** *Darling, I just arrived home from being with you; sure had a most enjoyable evening. It will be a long time till Wednesday. Jessie, can't restrain any longer, must ask you a question. Aren't you ever lonely and could live with someone?*

Winds of Change

During the ten years before she met Jack, Jessie had had only occasional dates, content with her work and involvement in the church and the DAR. Perhaps she was lonely living by herself following the death of her parents and may not have relished spending her later years alone. Or perhaps she truly fell in love after being "swept off her feet" at age 58. Since separating from Harry Hawes less than a year after their marriage in 1930, Jessie had had only one other long-term serious relationship and that had ended with the gentleman's death sometime in the 1950s. Because he was not a local person, little evidence remains of his association with Jessie except in the memory of this author who recalls him only as Mr. Shoemaker.

As Jack's letters continued in intensity Jessie began to have second thoughts about a permanent involvement. She evidently told Jack she wasn't sure of her feelings and didn't want to continue seeing him. He replied,

> **March 18.** *As you know, we had a swell time today. I sure enjoyed it, but didn't realize I was going in for the kill. I haven't yet got my feet on an even keel, yet have cried a gallon. But if that's the way you want it, Dear, that's it. You were a real pal and I want to thank you for every thing. I am returning the gifts because I can't have any memories around staring me in the face. I still love you.*

It can be surmised that they were able to resolve whatever the issue was, for four days later Jack was again making plans for the two of them:

> **March 22.** *I expect to see a lot of you, Dear, whether you like it or not for I just can't erase you from in front of me. I love you so. I would like to take a trip with you and come back with you all mine. Maybe I am being what you would call too romantic or maybe too fast, but if you feel as I feel, Dear, I don't think there should be any in-between answers.*
>
> *Your question the other nite to me was why don't I go out and play the field. I seriously considered this at one time, but I didn't think that after finding you, Dear, that I needed look further, for you have been such a pal and I love you for it, and I would do anything for you, dear.*

> ***April 3.*** *I had a wonderful evening last evening. I love you, dear. I could hardly sleep for thinking about you and can't wait till I am with you again.*
>
> ***May 1.*** *I am going to try and not think so much about things, but can't help it some times. That is why I can't stand being still, till I get some place to light and someone to call my own. I can't stand being by myself too long.*

It is likely that Jessie had remarked to Jack about his habit of constant moving. He was in perpetual motion and his impatience and inability to remain at rest bothered people who spent any time around him. Jessie's family could never understand why or how she could tolerate it. As it would turn out, less than a year later, she couldn't. However, wedding plans were being made.

On Saturday, June 22, 1963, Jessie married Jack Mohney in a church ceremony witnessed by more than a hundred guests including Jessie's students—all of whom had been invited to the wedding and many of whom attended in their Sunday best. Jessie, always stylish, wore a sleeveless, powder blue silk shantung, street-length dress, trimmed with satin Dior-style flat bows at the shoulders and waist, a powder blue picture hat, matching shoes and short white gloves. All three of Jessie's sisters and their families, many of her friends, and members of the Presbyterian Church were also present.

Jessie and Jack left for a wedding trip to Florida, returning in mid-July, well in time for Jack to buy box seats for the 1963 County Fair sulky races. Jessie never gave a thought to, or at least never asked, why Jack seemed to have so many free days. They had taken a two-week honeymoon, yet Jack also worked only half days during the week of the Fair, as they went to the races every day. At a later time, Kate would write, "Jack hasn't gone back to work yet."[12]

Lest it be thought that Kate might harbor even a twinge of jealousy regarding Jessie's married state, it should be noted that she spent much of the mid-1960s rebuffing continual offers of marriage from Carl Tagliente, who was devoted to her. We daughters were fond of him and would have been pleased to accept our mother's choice. It took many years for us to understand why she chose not to marry. Mother and "Tag" remained close friends, but through the next fifteen years both realized that they were first and foremost committed to their respective families, Tag to his sisters and Mother to her daughters. He continued in his devotion to her, but Mother was right—for both of them, family came first.

Jack and Jessie settled into domesticity and enjoyed going places together, including dancing, sight-seeing, and occasionally a horse race or other sporting event. On one of those excursions, while heading to the Huntingdon County Fair they were driving near the town of Huntingdon with Jessie at the wheel and Jack in the passenger seat. They had stopped at a roadside restaurant where orders were delivered by car hops. After finishing their sandwiches, the Mohneys kept their yet-unfinished soft drinks and headed back out on Route 22. Jessie threw her cup out the window, not noticing the township police car behind them.

When they heard the siren Jack said, "Isn't it just like the cops to be looking for poor suckers going to the Fair? Good thing you're not speeding." A few seconds later, when Jessie realized the officer was edging up beside their vehicle, she immediately pulled over. "Guess you didn't notice the 'No Littering' sign back along the road," the officer said as Jessie looked up at him. Had she been by herself, she thought, she probably could have talked her way out of this predicament. However, not wanting Jack to try to play hero, she replied, "I am sorry, Officer. We were just on our way to the Fair."

There was no excuse; she had tossed the paper cup and there was no point in arguing otherwise. Jack started to say something about "no way to treat visitors," but Jessie shushed him. She was issued a citation with a fine of $50 + $5 in costs, for a total of $55, a rather stiff fine for 1963. Jessie was so upset with herself that she gave her address as 411 Thompson Street, which some years before had been changed by the post office to 408.[13] A bit subdued, Jack and Jessie continued on to the Fair, trying their best to make light of the offense.

By Labor Day, Jessie was almost eager to return to school with anticipated additional status as a married woman. No longer would she have to endure the jokes about "old maid school teachers," although until she married Jack she had claimed such monikers didn't bother her. It was exciting the first morning of the opening of school as she wrote her name on the blackboard, in her beautiful script—"cursive" handwriting as she would point out to her third graders:

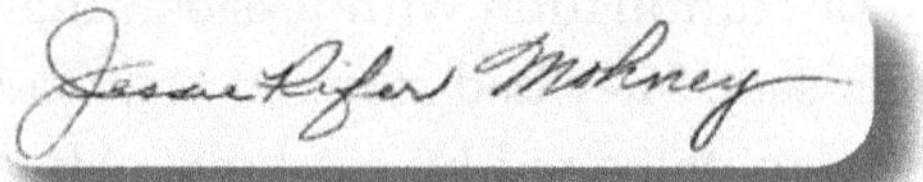

Of course, some students, as well as many adults throughout the rest of Jessie's life, misspelled the name as Mahoney. Jessie took to using her new name very readily and did not feel the necessity of continuing with three names—Jessie Pifer Mohney—a style that was becoming more popular with young people, particularly the increasing number of women professionals.

Jessie enjoyed the first semester, particularly Halloween when her class decided they would dress as gypsies for the town's annual Halloween parade. Teachers had the choice of walking along the sidelines with their group or dressing and parading with the class. Jessie got into the spirit of things and decided she would go in costume.

The result was spectacular. Beginning with a wig of long, dark hair, she carefully selected her costume—rich, vivid colors of purple, red, and green and extravagant jewelry, covering her wrists, dangling from her ears and draping around her neck. The effect was dramatic, such that even though she was entered with her class, she was awarded first place as an individual. [14]

[While winning first place at the Halloween parade occurred in 1953, it was the inspiration for the 1963 program Jessie directed.]

Early November brought the annual Elementary II School program, again under Jessie's direction. All early indicators pointed to this being a typical school year. However, it turned out to be a year of difficulties, both for the entire nation and, later, for Jessie personally.

No one alive at the time will ever forget where he or she was on Friday, November 22, 1963, when the news broke of the assassination of President Kennedy. However, because elementary classrooms typically did not have television sets, radios, or telephones, the elementary principal decided it would be in the best interest of everyone to not notify the teachers of the tragedy until after the children had left for the day. One minute before the dismissal bell was to ring, the voice of Mr. Ammerman came over the public address system, "There will be a very brief teachers' meeting in the all-purpose room immediately following the close of school. Please report there as soon as the children have left your classroom. This is urgent, so please come at once." There was a tremor in his usually calm voice, alarming to the teachers, but not noticed by the students who were busy chatting and gathering their belongings in readiness to board their buses.

That day and for several days following, everything in America came to a standstill; all events were canceled. With government offices closed, Washington, DC became an overnight ghost town and throughout the country all activity halted. Most theatres closed; those that didn't might as well have, because very few people left their homes for the next three days except to attend church services. Pastors everywhere hurriedly changed their Sunday services from a family-oriented, pre-Thanksgiving message to one far more solemn.

The Thanksgiving-into-Christmas holiday season was somber that year, with most of the country still in a state of mourning and bewilderment with the ramifications of the assassination. Nearly every holiday social event was either canceled or the festivities much subdued. Those with weddings scheduled on November 23 particularly found themselves in a dilemma. In Curwensville Edith Wright's large church wedding of November 30 was held as scheduled (because of the difficulty in rescheduling such an event).

Like many thousands of Americans, Jessie found herself "down-in-the-dumps" following Thanksgiving. However, unlike most of those thousands, she continued to feel listless through Christmas Day and into the extended holiday time. (With Christmas and New Year's Day falling on a Wednesday, schools were closed for two full weeks.) During the second week of school vacation, Jessie was still "moping around" as she described it to Ruby. Ruby suggested she come out to Ohio for a visit, but Jack said he couldn't take the time off work and Jessie wasn't comfortable leaving him to spend New Year's Eve alone.

At Jack's insistence Jessie promised to buy a special dress for New Year's Eve and went shopping on Thursday, December 26. She found a stunning dress in the window of Leitzingers and asked to see it. A clerk checked the size and explained that it could not be taken out of the window until Monday. On Saturday, Jessie called to confirm her interest and asked that the dress be held for her. The agreement was made and on Monday she returned to the store. Noticing the dress had been taken from the window display, Jessie waltzed into the Better Dresses department prepared to claim her prize, only to be told that the dress had been sold. One of the clerks told her, "You need to speak to Jennie." Quietly furious, Jessie contained her anger as she explained she had been told the dress was to be hers. "I'm sorry," was all Jennie would say.

Jessie replied, "You are not sincere when you say that; why

couldn't it have been taken out of the window on Thursday when I first asked to see it or on any of the days following?" Jennie responded, "The window trimmer wasn't here." "Well, indeed," said Jessie. "When I had admired a hat last spring the manager of that department was only too glad to get it for me." Jennie again just said she was sorry and "Is there anything else you care to look at?" Jessie glared and, clipping her words, said, "No thank you, not **now** or any time."[14] She marched over to The Fashion Shop and bought a smart (the ultimate criterion for Jessie) dress there, doing her best to hide her anger at Leitzingers. She came home and called Ruby to lament her disappointment, thus giving Ruby another chance to coax Jessie to come to Ohio.

Jessie agreed to leave Curwensville on January 2 and return the fifth. Shortly after her arrival in Canton the two sisters were laughing together like old times. Tom Wayne loved to watch the way these Pifer sisters could communicate with total understanding by merely a raised eyebrow, exchange of glances, or a single word.

Despite their good times, however, Ruby was concerned for her next younger sister and in a moment of levity casually mentioned she looked "run down." Jessie stiffened a bit, then with deliberation tried to assure Ruby, "I'm all right." Ruby knew by those words and Jessie's tone that she was not all right. The morning Jessie was packing to leave, Ruby suggested she might want to make an appointment with her doctor when she returned home. Jessie agreed to consider it, but that's as far as any action went.

In mid-January 1964 we Thompson sisters received word of the imminent death of our father. We found ourselves in a dilemma. Should we return to Curwensville as quickly as possible to say our last good-byes? All of us were working and bereavement leave, particularly for me, was an issue. More than that, however, was the question of being considerate of our mother. She would not be comfortable with our rushing home to see our dying father. In fact, we knew we would be asked why we would want to chance being seen in the company of his wife (and her children) whose very existence we had chosen to ignore. Thus, each of us made her own decision, while preparing for the inevitable.

I chose to grieve by writing a profile of my father, a description that addressed the view I held of his life: sorrow for a talent never fulfilled and mourning for the father we all had lost years before. I began, "There he lies, waiting to find the peace in death that he could not find in life." The tribute concludes, "A sad life. At the early stages a life with potential, but a life browbeaten and discouraged at every turn by an unloving, unforgiving father. So now this life waits for the release of death. The two things he best loved are reflected in his last wish—that he be buried in a uniform and be laid to rest beside his mother." Both wishes were honored.

Shortly following our father's death, Kay began to obsess over his Will. She had earlier had a conversation with him about this and at that time he had indicated his daughters were to be beneficiaries. Kay later visited him in the hospital a few days before his death with the intent of asking him again about the Will. However, he was not able to speak coherently, and she did not have that opportunity.

She then asked Mother to find out what she could about the duties of an executrix in Pennsylvania. At this behest, Mother found herself as a reluctant intermediary in the Will situation, and agreed to meet with Howard's attorney, if I, an even more reluctant participant in Kay's quest, would go with her.

In March, Kay wrote to me, "...I'm still depressed about the whole deal. I still can't believe it. Maybe you could talk to his doctor and get his opinion if he was himself when he wrote the Will."[15] She later continued, "I really didn't think it was his wish to cut us off like that. Maybe he wanted his wife to have it all, or maybe she convinced him that he did. ... I am going to write Liz, however, and ask her where it [the money] is."[16] And she did.[17]

Winds of Change

Earlier that year, Jack had showered Jessie with Valentines, one each day during Valentine's week, and they had taken a special weekend trip to the Poconos, a resort area in the northeastern part of the state. Jack continued to be solicitous to his bride, but his constant presence seemed to be wearing on Jessie who had been so independent for most of her life. She couldn't identify the vague uneasiness that plagued her. She was happy enough with Jack, but often longed to be alone. She admonished herself for having these doubts about her marriage for she did care for her husband. "If only he weren't so 'underfoot' all the time," she mentioned to Kate.

By the beginning of March, however, Jessie had started to withdraw from everyone and everything except school. At the end of that week she said she felt exhausted and took to her bed when she came home from school on Friday, March 6. She arose early Saturday morning, then slept around the clock from Saturday afternoon until Sunday evening. Since she had missed the Sunday morning church service, Josephine took the opportunity to ask the pastor to visit Jessie Monday evening. As Mother noted, "Reverend Clever came up and explained the sermon, but told Josie he couldn't get much out of Jessie. She didn't talk, just sat and listened."[18]

Jack was beside himself with worry and by Tuesday he insisted Jessie seek medical help. She said later that she was almost relieved to go to the doctor just to get away from Jack's constant attention, as over the week-end he had been coming into her room every 15 minutes (as she described it) to see how she was. For the short term, her doctor suggested a change of scene, hoping that Jessie was just suffering from "the winter blues." Jack called Jessie's principal to explain the situation and said he would like to take Jessie to Florida for a few days on the advice of her doctor. They left the next day. According to Mother, "She didn't put up any fuss even about flying. She seemed somewhat brighter, but still listless and has apparently forgotten all about school. So, if the change and rest don't help, then professional help must be the next step."[19]

Jack reported that "Jessie was not herself" the five days they spent in Florida and he was resigned to coming home to seek further medical care. Jessie went through the motions of daily activities, but didn't seem to be enjoying anything, he said. On the 17th she again visited her doctor who prescribed a low-dosage tranquilizer. By the end of the week, however, Jessie was no better and it was advised that she admit herself to the Elk County Hospital in Ridgway, commonly referred to by the locals as simply "Ridgway," the code name for the place where people in the area were admitted when they had a "nervous breakdown."

Jack was overwhelmed with anxiety, telling everyone, "I just can't take her to Ridgway," but there were no other options. Jessie had withdrawn into herself and could not make her own decisions; therefore, as her husband and next-of-kin, Jack was required to take her to the hospital and complete admittance papers. Jessie was admitted on March 21 and remained hospitalized 32 days.

Her condition was diagnosed as acute depression, and at that time patients who were acutely depressed often were kept in hospitals for a far longer duration than they are presently. It was believed that patients needed to be observed for a long period of time to make sure they didn't attempt suicide. Electroshock (ECT), now regarded as a highly controversial form of therapy, was then the method most widely used for depression and was part of the treatment used with Jessie.

Jack could not bear to see Jessie after these treatments, and found it increasingly difficult to visit her, although he did his best, going to Ridgway every Wednesday and sending her letters, including a romantic Easter card. Since the shock treatments lasted only a few weeks, families could keep the ECT procedure secret if they wished. Knowing Jessie would want to keep her condition private, Kate suggested that Jack not mention it to anyone, but she had no way to assure this confidentiality.

Jessie was permitted to come home week-ends and Jack was happy to make the trip to bring her home, although he found it emotionally draining to take her back to the hospital following her visits home. Jessie didn't seem much different at home than in the hospital and, even by the second week-end home and two weeks of treatment, Kate had noted no change in her general condition. She wrote, ". . . [Jessie is] about the same, only she doesn't remember being in Florida. She refused to wash her hair and appears not to care. Jack talked to the doctor who said the listlessness is caused by the medicine and treatment, which is preferable to the condition before treatment."[20] Jack, therefore, decided he would wait and take Jessie back to the hospital early Monday morning where he could take her to the residential beauty shop.

Regardless of Jack's well-intentioned solicitousness, Kate noticed how much his presence appeared to add to Jessie's distress, so she offered to take his place for the mid-week visit. Jack accepted the offer and Kate traded work days at the Dimeling Hotel and made the visits, a distance of nearly sixty miles each way. Jessie seemed pleased to see her, but because Kate was not the official next-of-kin, the staff would not provide her with information as to Jessie's progress.

On April 23 Jack signed the discharge papers and brought Jessie home. Weekly therapy sessions followed for six weeks and Kate took Jessie to these. She knew that Jessie didn't want Jack to take her because it made her nervous to travel with him during the long drive.

Jessie did not return to teaching for the remainder of school year as the thought of the end-of-year paper work was overwhelming.[21] She did, however, meet with the substitute teacher to help determine the students' grades for the year. She also visited her students the last day of school. Because so many of them had been worried about her, the principal thought it would be good for the children to see their teacher and he had arranged for cake and chocolate milk as a treat.

Jessie's first public appearance after her confinement was at the Curwensville High School Alumni Banquet. This also marked the occasion of her 40th Class Reunion. Jessie was attractive and trim in the powder blue dress she had worn for her wedding, her hair was stylishly coifed, and she appeared serene and rested. Few were aware of the extent of her stay at Ridgway and those who were privy to the information did not mention it.

In July Jessie and Jack drove to the New York World's Fair at Flushing Meadow in Queens, New York. At the dawn of the space age the Fair's theme was "A Shrinking Globe in an Expanding Universe." Jack told Jessie she could collect information for her protégés (the term he used for her students), although Jessie noted much of the available material would be too difficult for third grade. They dutifully visited the Hall of Education, but found the exhibits geared to the children attending the Fair, not materials that a teacher might take back to her classroom.

By fall, Jessie was considered "cured" of her depression and she was eager to return to her classroom. She continued in third grade and was welcomed by both teachers and her new class. Jack, still concerned, was overly solicitous and Jessie finally said to him, "Jack, you don't need to follow me around the house. I am fine." Nonetheless, he continued to worry about her health. By Halloween things were back to normal and Jessie again became involved with the annual Halloween parade.

Also by fall Nan had decided to leave Washington and move to California with her high school sweetheart, Joel Edmunds. After returning to Curwensville to repack for the trip to California,

Nan and Joel left early on the morning of October 9. Mother sent her off with not a few regrets, almost exactly five years after watching Kay and Bob depart for the West Coast.

Kay continued to nag all of us about our father's Will, still trying to nudge me to meet with Glenn Thomson, a chore I had been evading. She wrote and telephoned me frequently and also asked Mother to remind me. I simply found the task distasteful and did not want to pursue any interest in my father's Will, and I particularly did not want to raise an issue of our father's mental capacity for writing his own Will. If he had changed his mind about leaving his inheritance from his mother to his children, so be it. It was his choice.

Jessie also was evading meeting with her own Attorney Morris Silberblatt whom she had engaged to settle the estate of her mother. Mr. Silberblatt wrote, "I would appreciate it if you would stop at my office and sign some papers with reference to your mother's estate. I want to get this cleaned up. Your father's estate is cleaned up except the matter pertaining to 10 shares of stock in the Curwensville State Bank. I have a short certificate for same which I have sent to Mr. A.W. Straw and I have also asked for a waiver and I expect to have same within the next few days or so. We have to clean up the inheritance tax on your mother's estate and any outstanding bills. Please come in at your earliest convenience."

What is striking about this letter is that Jessie's mother had died in 1955 and her father in 1954. Apparently by 1964 settlement of the estate was no closer than it had been when Mr. Silberblatt had written to her in the fall of 1956, suggesting she collect all final bills against the estate and that she should make an appointment when she had need to see him [See Chapter 8]. Thus, nearly ten years had passed without settlement of this very modest estate.

Such a circumstance reminds family members who had known Jessie all their lives that Jessie more often than not simply let some matters slide. Her pattern of not dealing with problems that might be uncomfortable or inconvenient was legendary. Then again, such procrastination usually did not result in serious consequences, and Jessie's sisters were so used to her unique character that no one thought it unusual at all. In addition, they respected her position as executrix of their parents' estates and believed this was her personal business, not theirs.

Jack, more practical—and assuming a vested interest as Jessie's husband—pressed Jessie to bring this matter to conclusion, including settling the matter of the deed to the adjoining house. He was of the opinion that the ownership interest Kate held in the house might not be legitimate and he wanted that issue settled as well as the ownership of the bank stock. His concern annoyed Jessie, as she considered this a family matter involving only her sisters and her. The girls had left matters in Jessie's hands, following their mother's wishes that Jessie was to inherit the house in which she lived and the other daughters were to share in the rental income of the house "on the other side." That, however, had changed when in 1957 Howard Thompson, Sr. sold the Rex Theatre and Kate had to vacate the apartment that was part of the building. Kate could not afford to either buy or rent a place, for not only did she lose the apartment, but, with the sale of the theatre, she also lost her job as its manager.

At that time (1957) Kate had discussed her dilemma with Josephine who suggested that her younger sister consider moving into the rental side of the property that had been their mother's and whose ownership was now shared by the sisters. As Kate saw no other options, she discussed her situation with Jessie and called Ruby to ask her advice as well. The three sisters readily agreed that Kate could live in the house. They knew that was what their mother would have wanted. She had written her Will giving their homestead to Jessie and the rental income of the other half of the duplex to the other four girls only because Jessie was the only unmarried daughter and didn't have a home of her own. Thus, Kate moved into 410 Thompson Street with Jessie retaining ownership of 408.

The renters at 410 were given three months' notice after which Kate took on the daunting task of making needed repairs, both structural and cosmetic. As the half house had not seen many improvements except when painting or repairs were made to the entire property, there was much to do. Even though Kate needed to vacate her apartment and move into the double house before all the work was finished, she was grateful to have her own home. It was comfortable and Kate relished the independence it gave her.

In late November 1964 Mother relayed another message to me from Kay relative to the pursuit of our father's Will, "Perhaps you can see Glenn Thomson the Monday after Christmas. Kay says she needs the money and is becoming fearful of not getting it at all."[22] Finally, in December, I could no longer procrastinate in this unpalatable task and I read the Will in Mr. Thomson's office. The Will did not include us.

Early in the new year Kay still could not put the issue of the Will aside and wrote directly to me, vowing to pursue any avenue by which she could contest it. We younger sisters were uncomfortable at her brashness in seeking a way to contest the Will, but didn't openly express this to her because she was the oldest daughter and always her father's "little girl." We three younger daughters found it repugnant to ask anyone—let alone one's father on his deathbed—about a Will, but we had not openly challenged or interfered with Kay's choice to have done so.

Kay would not accept the fact that we did not share her fervor in pursuing a legal course of action and apparently she could not stop thinking about what might have been, or in her own mind, what *should* have been. In late January she wrote, "...I still don't believe it's hopeless."[23]

In June, Kay wrote to Jo Ellen and me, "Last Monday, I talked to Attorney John Gates who reviewed everything and said we didn't have a chance, that Liz had just simply changed his mind or what was left of it." She continued, "I next went to see Elizabeth (Liz) to get her consent to read the hospital records, saying I wanted to know his condition during his last days. I also asked to see his death certificate. I told her I was the only one bothering to find out everything I could about his last days, because I remembered him when he was normal. I feel much better and more satisfied about the whole matter now."[24]

Nevertheless, this failure to gain what she felt was rightfully hers upset Kay greatly. She told her mother that she was always losing out, that their Grandmother Thompson's death had set many unfortunate circumstances into motion. With his mother's death, Howard Jr. had lost his best friend and his defender against a hateful father, leaving him vulnerable in many ways.

Kay lamented that Elizabeth Bennett had ensnared her father after he had turned to alcohol in his despair over his mother's death and, while Kay did not say as much to Mother, it is possible that she partly blamed her for the divorce and subsequent downslide of her father. Still believing that the Will should have been contested and smarting at her perceived loss of an inheritance, Kay let it be known that if ever a similar situation should arise she would be ready.

DAR (Daughters of the American Revolution) Service Award

presented to Jessie Pifer in 1983

Curwensville School District Retirees Honored – 1970

Chapter 10

When the Glow Left the Rose

There were The Roaring Twenties and The Fabulous Fifties, but no such euphonious phrase describes the astonishing era of Viet Nam and its aftermath–unless perhaps The Preposterous Seventies.

—*Dick Cavett*[1]

During the fourteen years from 1965 to 1979, the political times in the United States were troubled. The economy hit a deep rut following a quarter century of post-World War II prosperity and world prominence; America's longest war ended in divisiveness; and a president and vice-president resigned in disgrace. Yet, with all the turmoil, the nation celebrated its 200th birthday as one united country.

The troubles by which the era would be known began in the mid-1960s when the controversy over whether the United States should be involved in the Viet Nam conflict began to roil over into campus unrest and riots. Most college officials were at a loss as to appropriate action to take against protesters. As a result, their reactions were as varied as the kinds of student protests they were meant to address.

In 1964 the University of California at Berkeley placed a ban on political activity only to find itself then faced with the Free

Speech Movement established by its own students, many of them veterans of the earlier Civil Rights Movement. The following year the University of Michigan conceived the first "teach-in," drawing 3,000 teachers and students to public discussions about the war. None of these conversations, however, had any effect on the situation.

In 1968 students at Columbia University took over campus buildings in protest over both the university's involvement with the Pentagon-funded Institute for Defense Analysis and the university's plans to build a new gymnasium in an area of the city where low-income housing was said to be needed. During the same year more than 600 demonstrators gathered at the Pentagon, attempting to levitate it. Although they failed to get the nation's military headquarters off the ground, they did succeed in making a unique statement.

Four other memorable milestones in American social and political history that paralleled the demonstrations generated by the Viet Nam War added to the confusion many Americans were beginning to feel near the end of the sixties. These major demonstrations included the (1) riots in the Watts section of Los Angeles in August 1965 when a clash between black citizens and white police officers spiraled into a five-day insurrection; (2) Chicago Republican National Convention in August 1968 where a riot left more than 1,000 student protesters, anti-war demonstrators, and bystanders injured; (3) Black Panthers' altercation resulting in the death of a policeman in Oakland in July; and (4) Woodstock Nation, an open-air music festival, where between 400,000 and 500,000 gathered in upstate New York in August 1969.

In sharp contrast to the proliferation of riots, protests, and demonstrations, the most significant scientific accomplishment of the century occurred one month before the Woodstock event, when on Sunday, July 20, 1969 Apollo astronauts Neil Armstrong and Ed "Buzz" Aldrin, Jr., in their lunar module *The Eagle,* landed on the moon.

At 11:42 EDT the two men unfurled the Stars and Stripes and uncovered an engraved plaque on the base of *The Eagle. The Philadelphia Inquirer* heralded the event in two-and-a-half-inch headlines: MAN WALKS ON MOON. The lunar landing was viewed on television by an estimated 600 million people, giving Americans, wearied by protesters and demonstrations, something to cheer about.

With such scientific breakthroughs demonstrating America's strength and promise, Jessie and most others of her generation could not understand campus protests or why young men would not be willing to serve their country. Her friends had watched their older brothers go off to war during WWI, their husbands or brothers enlist during WWII, and their sons leave to fight in Korea. They could only shake their heads at this new generation, wondering why the young men would run away or burn their draft cards or take over university buildings through what they were calling a "sit-in."

For those in Curwensville not directly affected by the war, daily life, as it always had, centered on local events such as plays, pageants, and picnics; football games and chorus concerts; Memorial Day parades and speeches; scout fund-raisers and music recitals. In particular, there was increasing community interest in the piano recitals of Mrs. Eileen Brown, with the number of piano and organ students growing over the decade she had been in town. The first recital with only a few students in 1955 had expanded into three evenings of programming by 1965. The names listed on the program reveal a kind of social register of Curwensville and Clearfield surnames.

On Friday, June 11, 1965 one of the final piano soloists was Janet Lynn Bloom. It was a bittersweet evening as Kate blinked back tears, noting the same familiar physical features, voice, and gestures in Janet Lynn that she had known in her sister Margaret Jean at the same age. Kate's voice broke as she whispered to Jessie, "Jean would be so proud."

In addition to attending recitals and school events involving their late sister's daughter, Jessie and Kate helped Chet with Janet Lynn's typical teen-age rebellion against rules. While by no means wild, Janet did struggle with what she viewed as her father's old-fashioned ideas and she turned to her aunts for advice as well as clothes for special school events. Janet wore the same size as Kate who lent her some of her own best outfits and, occasionally, gowns or coats would be mailed or hand-delivered, on loan from her cousins, Kate's daughters.

In many ways the daily life of the extended Pifer family was a microcosm of mid-1960s American society, reflected in such typical events as Janet's school socials, Josephine's trip by train to visit her son and his wife during the Christmas season of 1966, Jessie and Jack bustling about on numerous road trips, Jack planning to retire as early as possible, and Kate, who had emerged as the strongest, serving as the Pifer family's center. Jessie, Kate, and Josephine continued to plan special holiday events so that Janet Lynn would be assured of the family gatherings and support that her older cousins had experienced. "I'll be at Chet's for Thanksgiving," Kate wrote, "with Janet, Josie, Don, and Lorraine."[2]

Kay's reaction to the Pifer sisters' mirth and enjoyment of one another's company was to look for reasons to explain why "Mother is reluctant to come out to California." On November 22 she asked her sister, "Did you ever ask Mother why she is acting funny about coming out?"[3] A month later Kay may have answered her own question: "I know she felt uncomfortable when she was here. Maybe we acted different, I don't know. I do know she makes me nervous anymore and I suppose she senses it."[4] Five weeks following that insight, Kay added this information, "Nan said she thought I had been mean to Mother when she was here.

It's just that she made me nervous at times when she wouldn't come right out and say what she wanted to do. I wanted to take her where she wanted to go but she didn't want me to go out of the way. I didn't want to go to San Francisco at all."[5] Kay did not understand that guests—particularly mothers—do not want to feel beholden, especially mothers like ours, of modest means, but independent.

Independence had always been very important to Kate and, while we daughters were the most important people in her life, she wanted for us to live our own lives. What she had not expected in her own life were the circumstances that had placed her living next door to her older sister. She also could not have foreseen their growing interdependence and compassion for each other, despite their basic differences. Thus, even with Jack's constant presence, Jessie and Kate looked out for each other's welfare, including sharing expenses incurred in the upkeep of the property, such as painting the house and re-shingling the roof.

Kate's world soon revolved around her grandchildren much as it had around her own four children. Even though she worked fulltime, she arranged her schedule to be with each of her daughters after the birth of the children, thus establishing an immediate bond with her grandchildren that continued throughout her lifetime. Each child found a special niche and relationship with their grandmother, whom they called "Kaki," the nickname bestowed upon her by her first grandchild, Kim, and later shortened to "Kak" by the grandchildren who followed.

I frequently visited Mother on the weekends and Kay visited with her several times a year either in California or by coming to Curwensville. However, Kate missed Jo Ellen who did not get home often and she pined for her youngest daughter Nan after she and her husband moved to California in 1964: "I called Nan last night, just felt like hearing her voice…"[6] "Nan sounded a little wistful and said even the rain is not the same."[7]

Nan also mentioned having pangs of loneliness, something she had not expected with her move to California. She had thought about returning to the East and in a letter to Jessie, she promised to come back home, "Joel and I were ready to pack and return to winter wonderland when I called Mother last month. Now we're going to give California another chance, but I feel as if the only change is that we'll be moving East later rather than sooner."[8]

During this same time Kay was having difficulty enforcing the visitation rights she had for her daughter.[9] While Kate made a concerted effort to visit with Kim during the time Kim lived with her father in Curwensville and Jessie and Mother both tried to make those visits special for Kim, the unsteady situation was upsetting to everyone in both families.

Kay loved her daughter, but she often expressed exasperation at the constant need for attention and entertainment Kim's yearly visits to California required: "I haven't been able to keep up on my magazine reading at all. I have a full box of them that are untouched. Did I tell you about my Fourth of July week-end? Friday night, Disneyland; Saturday, down to Joanne's at Long Beach all day; Sunday, Los Angeles Sports Arena to see Herman and the Hermits! I haven't been right since! Last Monday we enjoyed a private guided tour of 20th Century Fox where we visited the sets of "Lost in Space" as well as "Peyton Place." We also had lunch at the studio commissary. Kim was impressed. Yet she still misses Irvin Park![10] I've been taking double doses of Vanquish."[11]

Early in March of 1966 Jessie began to withdraw into herself again, much as she had two years earlier. Jack told Kate, "Jessie won't talk to me, Kate. We didn't have an argument or anything. She just won't say anything. She has been lying on the davenport since she got up this morning. I tried to get her to go for a ride this afternoon or go out to the Golden Yoke for dinner, but she won't even answer me. Come help me. I'm worried." Kate went over and asked her sister, "Jess, aren't you feeling well?" "I'm fine," was the only reply. Kate could tell by the tone of her voice that she was not. Kate suggested she make an appointment with her doctor. Jessie just repeated, "I'm fine." But Kate feared otherwise.

The following week-end things did not appear to be much better, although Jessie had not missed any time at school. Jack told Kate that Jessie seemed OK in the mornings, but when she got home she would just sit and stare at the television or lie on the davenport until time to go to bed. She still refused to see her doctor and Jack said, "I don't know what to do. I kept hoping this would resolve itself."

On Monday after Jessie had left for school, Kate knew she had to tell Josephine before she heard any rumors and, with a heavy heart, she walked the three blocks to her sister's. Before Kate had her coat off, Josie read her sister's face and asked, "What's wrong?" Kate related the sad news that it was possible that Jessie was slipping back into a depression. Josephine looked stricken, but could get only two words out, "Oh, Kate," she sighed, then added, "poor, dear Jessie," plaintive words that were to echo in Kate's heart 25 years later.

Jessie tried her best to convince Kate and Josephine that she was feeling fine—"I'm all right, just a little tired," she said. She readily and accurately answered test questions put to her by her sisters, such as where she had purchased the new flooring she and Jack had installed. She even added facts that she thought would convince her sisters that she was clear in her thinking. On the other hand, she showed indications of mild paranoia in saying, "They are on my back at school."

The following day Jessie asked Kate, "Did you see on TV what they are doing?" Kate quickly replied with what she hoped was a safe answer, "Jess, I haven't been watching television." After three days of similar comments reflecting Jessie's belief that she was being watched, Josephine and Kate went to talk with her after Jack had spoken to the school superintendent. Kate said,

"Jess, we want you to go to Dr. Browne for a check up." Jessie responded with great control and calm. "I'm perfectly all right and I'm not going." Kate then said, "If you are all right, why did you call the superintendent and resign your teaching position?" Jessie replied, "I wanted him to know I'm tired of being picked on."

Jack then left the house and went straight to Dr. Browne to make arrangements for Jessie to be re-admitted to Ridgway before her condition worsened. When he returned he told Kate and Josephine what he had done. "This is the hardest decision I have ever had to make," he said, trying to keep his tears at bay. Steeling himself, he turned to Jessie, speaking firmly but with kindness, "You are going, so get ready." She did not answer him. Jack asked Kate and Josephine to go with him, as he anticipated he might have trouble once they got to Ridgway.

Sunday morning, Kate went over to see if Jessie needed help packing, but she was ready. In fact, Kate noted that Jessie had remembered that her luggage was at Josephine's and had sent Jack for it earlier that morning. On the journey to Ridgway Jack made an attempt at conversation, but Jessie said not one word the entire trip. Kate later said, "Josie cried more this time than she had two years ago, and I didn't know which sister my own tears were for."[12]

"When we pulled up to the hospital entrance, Jessie cried, but she still knew to give me her rings to take home. I was beginning to wonder if we had acted too hastily, but then Jessie said, 'Jack, did you hide that peanut butter?' I knew then from the way she said this that she had brought some home from school and, yes, did need help."[13]

Following a thirteen-day stay in the hospital, Jessie was discharged Easter week-end. Kate told her daughters that Jessie seemed to be doing fine and would be returning to school the following full week after the Easter break. Kate and Josephine were relieved, but wary, even though the doctors at Ridgway had told Jack that Jessie had had only a mild relapse and could safely return to teaching and resume all activities as she chose. After a few days at home she told Kate that she felt "like her old self." There were to be no further episodes, and when Jack's grandchildren arrived in August she welcomed their visit, even joining them when they headed for Jack's camp.

Jessie's remaining at home for a few extra days following Easter eased the transportation problem Kate was facing. Her Ford Falcon was, as she described it, "out for repairs again with either a clogged oil line or a bad oil pump," and with Jessie's car being available, Kate was able to use Jack's car while he drove Jessie's sporty convertible.[14] Kate began looking for another car, not wanting to risk any more problems with the Falcon that seemed to be in for repairs more days than she was driving it. In late April Kate found her dream car, but not at all what she had been looking for, as this car would require a garage.

Chet, who told Kate he would case the neighborhood while on his milk route, found a garage for rent less than a block from 410 Thompson Street. Kate, never known to have made an impetuous purchase, found it easy to rationalize that the walk would be good exercise and that in winter walking the distance would be no harder than covering the car and cleaning the snow off in the early morning hours. She loved that car, describing her decision to purchase it, "I should never have sat down behind the wheel, because I was hooked before I rounded the first corner."[15] This 1966 white Chevy Malibu convertible with red leather interior became her prized possession for the remainder of her days.

In 1967 an announcement was made of the planned demolition of the South Side School. This unexpected news became an immediate concern to everyone (approximately a quarter of the population of Curwensville) who had ever been enrolled in this little school. While questions of its future had not been raised when the school had closed in 1961, razing it hit a different chord in the citizenry. An initial protest began with calls to school board members and a few "letters to the editor," followed by the circulation of petitions.

Teachers who had taught at South Side were asked to serve on a committee being formed to save the school. Jessie attended, but didn't want to chair even a sub-committee. "I don't have any sentimental attachment to the building, just to the students," she said. This brought some pause to the discussion and the impetus of a full-fledged plan was tabled pending the public meeting to be held in the high school auditorium by the school board.

At that general meeting concerning the fate of the South Side School, structural engineers explained the instability of the building, provided cost projections, and responded to questions pertaining to the possibility of selling the building for other purposes. All suggestions for alternative use were cost prohibitive, including an archival or historical society site, as no organization could afford the repairs and upkeep, even if the school building itself were donated to them. Simply put, the building had outlived its usefulness. In 1968 demolition occurred amid some tears, but with acceptance of the inevitable.

Worse, however, was the razing of the iconic Patton Building. After much opposition from the public, in 1968 the Julia Girardi family purchased the landmark that had been empty since 1961 when the elementary classes housed there were moved to the new elementary building adjoining the high school. As in the case with the South Side School, no one had the funds or plans for renovating the structure so that it would meet current building codes. The school board was left with no choice; they couldn't afford to keep the building safe, even with the great sentiment the townspeople held for their school. The Girardis flattened the venerable old building and in 1971 built and opened the Tastee Freeze Sandwich Shop, regarded by most of the community as a mockery of the grand gray stone edifice that had been the alma mater of nearly every adult in Curwensville.

As the 1969-70 school year approached, Jessie knew that it would be her last, just as she had known two years earlier that she had not wanted to close her teaching years by leading some kind of drive to "Save South Side." For many reasons this was a wise decision and made her final year in the classroom a positive one. She did not announce to the students that she was retiring as she believed it was of no concern to them, nor would they understand the concept of retiring from a life's work. Rather, she began her last year in the fall of 1969 as she had for forty-five years, writing her name on the board and instilling self-confidence in the ability of each youngster to learn.

Earlier that same year Kate had embarked on a tour of Europe with Kay. It was the first of many trips mother and daughter would take together, including an ocean voyage on the Queen Elizabeth 2 (courtesy of TWA passes and employee discounts), and an opportunity Kate would be the first to admit that she otherwise would not have had.

To this point there was a history of complete trust between and among Kate's daughters and nothing personal shared between any two of us was shared among all without permission. No one questioned anyone else's choices, and little did we three younger ones ever think that some of those confidences would later be revealed once Kay found the information useful to her own purposes in undermining that earlier trust between and among her siblings. Until this time there also had been no evidence of jealousy among the girls. Certainly we admired skills and sometimes possessions of each other, but basically each was content being who she was and Mother, of course, was proud of us all.

Later, when we three younger sisters tried to understand what appeared to be a drastic change in Kay, we sought answers by looking for earlier clues to both her personality and actions. We easily recalled that her behavior was sometimes abrasive and we remained uncomfortable with how she handled the matter of our father's Will. We also discussed that Kay never hesitated to broadly hint to any of us when she saw something she liked, either in a store or belonging to one of us. More often than not, we purchased the item or gave her what she wanted of ours.

We three previously had acknowledged that Kay always spoke her mind, whether asked or not, and we now were ready to admit to one another that often her remarks were hurtful; we just had not thought about this as being a pattern. We did, however, begin to realize that the one thread that ran through all of these incidents was Kay's basic view of life, that *she* deserved more. Nonetheless, we were not prepared for what began happening in the well-named Preposterous Seventies.

The decade of the 1970s opened with an announcement by the media that nearly every household in America contained at least one television set. This fact became the foundation for what media theorist Marshall McLuhan called "the global village." Once television networks realized the potential advertising market in every household, they began to build what would become a strong consumer base. Advertising first aimed at situation comedies because they were family programs with many viewers of all ages. Two of the most memorable are the "Mary Tyler Moore Show" and the unexpectedly successful "All in the Family." Jessie and Jack particularly enjoyed the "Dinah Shore Show" and the "Tennessee Ernie Ford Show." Jessie also continued her interest in sports, particularly football and horse-racing, and she watched these programs into her eighties.

Undisputedly the 1970s were a time of high energy with "be-ins," "happenings," "teach-ins," mood rings, yellow happy face buttons, streaking, leisure suits in polyester fabric, and pet rocks. The underside of this vigor, however, was the doubt, transition, and troubling times that began for the general public with double-digit inflation brought on by gargantuan spending on the Viet Nam War, government social programs, high unemployment, three recessions, and an energy crisis—not to be repeated until thirty years later in the first decade of the 21st Century.

The nation's long struggle against inflation proved as intractable as the war in Viet Nam, and President Nixon's action in widening that war further undercut public confidence. For example, when Nixon ordered troops across the border into Cambodia, furious protests on college campuses were set off, the worst resulting in the deaths of four students at Kent State in Ohio and two at Jackson State in Mississippi.

Such violence on college campuses was entirely foreign to Americans, and parents who had children in college began to fear for their safety when faculty members and students at more than 400 colleges and universities went on strike. Unrest of this magnitude was unprecedented in the United States, and adults began to wonder what kind of society they had spawned.

Protests continued into the 1970s, even though the most influential social movement of the decade directly affected only half the population. Jessie occasionally remarked to her nieces that they had been born just in time to enjoy opportunities for women that her generation had never considered. "You have so many choices," she would add, sometimes wistfully. Nonetheless, the feminist movement was still a decade or so too late to have full impact on the early career choices of those born prior to 1940, including three of Kate's progeny. Even so, it did open some doors for these women who had been, for the most part, expected by society to become only housewives.

Amidst the turmoil of this decade, many parents were giving more freedom to their young offspring because they were at a loss as to how to explain the world clearly enough to place parameters on it. As a result, youth first expected, then demanded, even more latitude in their individual lives and in their educational institutions—universities, colleges, and then high schools.

As a direct result of changes on college campuses, many high schools in the early 1970s began to reform and expand their programs, offering more electives, along with "mini" courses and independent study programs. Many schools across the nation also began to offer environmental education, first as an elective, and later as part of the required science curriculum.

Of greater impact on public education was the growing trend of more powerful teacher unions. Many teachers began to have second thoughts about their choice to be unionized, sensing that they had traded one problem for another. Unfortunately, there was no turning back, and those, like Jessie, near retirement tried not to let such thoughts bother them as they closed their careers.

In the late seventies, when the graduates of the 1960s began to send their own children to the public schools, they were much more demanding than had been their predecessors or their own parents. They had learned to question the system and to use their collective power of strength in numbers. They also were very adept at bucking the system and challenging procedures, most notably when the system and procedures did not make accommodation for what they believed was their own specialness and, more so, the specialness of their own children. This unprecedented pressure from demanding parents, combined with pushes for curriculum changes and union demands, led to many of Jessie's cohorts expressing that they were glad to be close to retirement.

The dominant national issue of the decade, however, always pointed to the Viet Nam War and the erosion of public trust. Yet with all the complicated political issues of Viet Nam, the war appeared to have little effect on the daily lives of small town

America. The Memorial Day parades in Curwensville during the 1970s continued to honor all veterans, even though few, if any, Viet Nam veterans marched in the parade. Jessie still persisted in inviting parade watchers to sit on her large, shaded front porch to view the band, veterans, firemen, high school speakers, and native-son dignitary who would deliver the keynote address at the services following the parade. On Memorial Day 1970 Jessie was in particularly good spirits when many well-wishers stopped to congratulate her on her retirement.

On June 3, 1970 Jessie Pifer Mohney ended a teaching career that had begun in a one-room schoolhouse nearly 46 years earlier. She had taught for 45 years, missing only the year she had first married, and she would reach her 65th birthday on July 9. Not one to sentimentalize her life, Jessie finished this school year much as she had begun her first in the fall of 1924, with a no-nonsense approach. She had agreed to a cake-cutting ceremony in the school cafeteria during the lunch period, but did not want to further involve her third graders who, she said with both wisdom and a smile, "had their minds on the summer ahead."

A dinner in her honor was held on June 13 with most of her teaching colleagues, as well as the principal, retired superintendent, and superintendent, in attendance. Jack Mohney, who had retired from North American Refractories two years earlier, could hardly wait for both the school year and the retirement dinner to draw to a close. Jessie did not seem to notice his impatience during the laudatory speeches, but Kate, Josephine, and Ruby—all who attended the retirement party for their sister, did. Ruby, particularly annoyed with Jack's behavior, said to Kate and Josephine, "Wouldn't you think he could sit still for half an hour?" At that moment, Kate caught Jack's glance and returned it with a hand motion to sit down, since it appeared to her that he was about to leave the table while the letters from former students and a class letter from that year's third grade were being read.

The following day Jessie told Jack she had decided to drive Ruby home to Ohio and to stay with her for a week or so, adding, "Don't worry; I'll be back in time for the opening of Monday Night Football." Jack smiled and responded in kind, "And here I was hoping you would make it in time for the County Fair. I guess I'll have to find someone else to share the box seats with."

As Jessie drove west toward Massillon, where Ruby and Tom had moved from Canton, she thought about the many times she had gone to Ohio for rest or refuge. Her first visit had been while she was still in high school and she had so wanted the freedom she knew Ruby would allow. There had been many more drives to Ohio since that time, both alone and to take her mother to visit. "Now," she thought, "I am at the age that Mama was when I began to think of her as getting older."

She decided not to share these thoughts with Ruby who was in her mid-seventies and might not welcome such a discussion. She did, however, admit to her sister that even though she looked forward to not returning to school in the fall, it seemed odd to be retiring. "I don't feel older," she said. Ruby, usually quick with a quip, couldn't come up with anything better than "At least you have Jack," hoping it didn't sound too insincere after having discussed with Josephine and Kate that Jack left a lot to be desired.

The death of Aunt Rosanna E. Stormer that fall only added to Jessie's sense of her own mortality, and it was all she could do to attend the service. However, she felt it only proper to accompany Kate in representing the family since Rosanna, born in 1880, was the last survivor of their mother's family of five Smith sisters.

As Jessie had earlier promised Jack, by the time the first televised game of the brand new program known as Monday Night Football was aired, she was fully acclimated to not going to school every morning. Jack was delighted, glad to have the fulltime company of his sweetheart. Their new daily routine became not unlike that of many retired couples and she viewed it as "being like summer year-round." As such, Jessie threw her energies into her position as a deacon of the Presbyterian Church, becoming involved in plans for the construction of the new Manse that would be completed in 1971 at a cost of $48,000.

Nineteen-seventy also marked Kate's retirement from the Dimeling Hotel. Not having anyone to advise her, she had laid no claim to the Social Security benefits of her late ex-husband, even though she would have been entitled to a portion of his earned benefits. Instead, she made do with the minimum amount, based on her own limited time of employment (approximately seventeen years) as Rex Theatre manager and then desk manager at the Dimeling Hotel. At age 62 she was expected to retire and it isn't clear whether or not she made an intentional choice in the matter. Her daughters, like most young adult children, viewed their mother's retirement as time for a rest, not fully appreciating how vibrant their mother was.

Even before retirement, and on a very limited income, Mother had managed to run her household and provide gifts and treats for both her children and grandchildren. Following her retirement, the grandchildren, usually one at a time, visited Kaki for an extended stay every summer. She could be counted on to find interesting things to do with each child in turn and she readily took part in their many enterprises, from worm farms to sand castles. All of them confided in her, knowing their secrets were safe and her support of them boundless.

Considering that Jessie herself was childless, she was surprisingly kind to her sister's grandchildren and welcomed them into her home, giving them school supplies no longer used in her classroom, and regularly entertaining them in order to give Kate what Jessie termed a "break." She made sure her charges would go across the street to greet Raymond, the neighbor who spent his summers on his porch, and that they say "Hello" to Joe Errigo who lived in an apartment in the same block.

Jessie was also very willing to take the children to Irvin Park where they would swim, and she occasionally treated them to an evening at the movies. As expected, she corrected their manners, and constantly offered to prepare something for them from her kitchen. To this day, all one of them has to say is "Would you like a cheese and relish sandwich?" and all go into spasms of laughter. And yet they would not for anything trade the memory of their grandmother's gentle pressure to accept whatever offering was made by their great-aunt and of her never-ending reminder to "Make sure you thank Aunt Jessie."

With a schedule filled with family, neither Jessie nor Kate fell into the typical description of women retirees of that time. They would have taken issue with, or just simply laughed at, all-encompassing descriptions such as historian William Henry Chafe wrote about female retirees:

> ...they are unprepared for the burden of leisure, and helpless when the family web has been broken. They are left almost functionless, with no status and no sense of being useful.[16]

In contrast to Chafe's view, a small number of women's magazines, including *McCall's,* began to change their focus, shifting their orientation toward articles on what women were doing, particularly in women's rights, politics, and social protest.[17] Representatives of the Future Homemakers of America also began to rethink their purpose, admitting that women's liberation had exerted an influence on their 600,000 members.[18]

Shortly after Mother's retirement, Kay began planting seeds for what later would be viewed by the other family members as a long-range scheme. Kay began by telling her mother that she should consider what she would do when the time came that she might not be able to take care of herself. At the same time she began recommending to her three sisters that the four of them talk about optional living arrangements for their mother because "she probably gets lonely there in Curwensville with all of us gone." Every conversation carried the same theme: "We-should-make-some-kind-of-arrangement-for-Mother."

The fact that Mother was in excellent health and that her own mother and aunts all had enjoyed good health, living into their eighties—as had her father and his siblings—didn't seem to enter much into the discussions Kay continued to hold with her sisters. It appeared that Kay wanted a definite course for her mother's future, one that she wanted her sisters to agree with. It seemed she was determined to get this settled even though Kate was not ready to have specific arrangements made for her, yet alone arrangements with an emphasis on any pending old age.

It was not often that all four sisters were in the same place at the same time, so most of the communication occurred one-on-one, in this case between Kay and each of her sisters separately. In most conversations on this subject each of us would just listen, only occasionally asking questions, because none of us wanted to discuss someone else's business, especially when this someone was our mother who was not present. At one time or another, each of the three younger daughters individually had invited our mother to make her home with us but none of the three had discussed our separate offers to Mother with the others.

Kay also began reminding us that some provision needed to be made for Jessie as well. Of course, Jessie's financial situation was much more secure than that of our mother, so there was not the same kind of planning needed for Jessie. It was well-known among the family members that Jessie had prepared for "a rainy day" with both savings and bank stock, in addition to her retirement pension and Social Security. Although none of the sisters except Kay had raised the question as to the amount of Jessie's financial worth, it was accepted among the three younger ones that Jessie would make her own decisions without our input, unless she asked for our help. As Jessie had made very clear to everyone, she did not wish to discuss the matter.

Mother, on the other hand, might need some financial assistance should she require institutional long-term care. However, at that moment, the potential need for additional monetary assistance for Mother was not under consideration. It soon began to annoy Jo Ellen, Nan, and me that Kay kept raising the question of "what to do with Mother." Jo Ellen had long ago offered any help needed as she had been financially subsidizing Mother for years and all three sisters had made it clear that we would either help financially or welcome our mother into our homes at any time.

This "what to do with Jessie and Mother" was a subject Kay revisited with increasing frequency, both in letters and conversations with her sisters. Along with this, she began dropping hints to both Mother and us sisters that she was considering moving back to Curwensville upon her own retirement, although she never verbalized a link between her two areas of interest.

Unaware at the time of what we later would term Kay's fixation on planning their futures, both Kate and Jessie were more concerned about their oldest sister Josephine than they were about their own possible future care needs. Josephine had begun to lose interest in activities and had become forgetful, buying unneeded items at the grocery store one week and forgetting to purchase even necessities the next, even though only a few years earlier she had taken care of two children for her nephew and his wife while they were on an extended business trip to Florida.[19]

When one or the other of her sisters would stop in to visit Josie, they might find half a dozen cake mixes in the cupboard or on the counter. They would half smile to themselves, remembering the many cakes Josephine had made for family birthdays long before cake mixes were available. They never questioned her about the boxes in her cupboard, as they would not want to make her feel embarrassed. In their own conversations, Kate and Jessie chose to assume that the cakes pictured on the boxes looked good to Josephine when she went for groceries, but once home, the effort needed to prepare for baking must have seemed overwhelming.

Mother checked on Josephine daily and at times went to the grocery store with or for her and frequently helped her with the household chores. Among Jessie, Jack, and Mother, meals were often provided for her and a person was hired for the heavier cleaning. Like many other older people who live alone, Josephine found it difficult to maintain interest in daily household activities. Another trait she shared with others is that she had trouble locating the On/Off button on the remote control for the television. Kate tied a rubber band to mark the area at the point below where the button was placed and fashioned a ribbon for Josephine's reading glasses so that if she removed them she would not misplace them. The Pifer sisters were doing what family did, taking care of one another.

In February 1972, my husband offered to convert a building that had been a workshop and stable into a two-bedroom cottage for Mother's visits to Hummelstown and perhaps eventual place of residence. I was confident that Mother would be pleased to have her own newly-built quarters for extended visits, so I began to talk to my sisters about the possibility.

That same year, an era of local school history in Curwensville ended when the Locust Street School bade farewell to its last student. That closing marked the finality of the three school buildings that had provided the educational foundation to most of the population of Curwensville. Locust Street, however, was the only school among the three to be saved from demolition when it was converted to apartments.

The strength of Curwensville Dam was also tested that year when Tropical Storm Agnes hit the Northeast, its rainfall making this storm more than twice as destructive as any previous hurricane in the history of the United States and, to that date, the worst natural disaster ever to hit Pennsylvania. While the Dam prevented flooding of the Susquehanna River in Clearfield

County, Anderson Creek did overflow and cause flooding along its banks, including the basement of Josephine's house on Meadow Street. Her sisters believed the strain of this flooding, coupled with her comments of feeling vulnerable and alone, were the deciding factors in Josie's losing interest in her home and herself.

Mother and Jessie held many worried conversations concerning their oldest sister, then only in her mid-seventies. They had initiated telephone conversations with Josephine's son numerous times during the previous several years, and a year earlier he had made a visit and had approved arrangements for the monthly cleaning service. However, the final time Mother telephoned him to give him information on his mother's status, she said she sensed a detachment in his voice, after his abrupt greeting of, "Hamilton here." She told Jessie, "I will never forget the coldness of his words as we were discussing his own mother."

In September Josephine died peacefully in her sleep and her son came home to attend to the final arrangements, including a memorial service conducted by her pastor. Josephine's three remaining sisters, deeply grieved at the loss of their oldest sister and still mourning the loss of their youngest sister fourteen years earlier, were disappointed that Noel had not asked their assistance regarding details of her memorial service and that neither the date of Josephine's birth nor that of her death is recorded on the memorial card.

The next—and final—time Jessie and Kate talked to Noel was a few months later at the auction of his mother's estate. He had allowed Jessie and Kate to select one item each from the China closet, but Kate had to pay for the mahogany bedroom suite Josephine had wanted her to have.

Kay used this poignant final year of Josephine's life as an example to her sisters of what they might some day be facing with both their mother and Jessie—if they did not do some advance planning and do it *now*. Jo Ellen, Nan, and I were annoyed with what we viewed as scare tactics. We were—and had been all along—very clear in our own minds as to our responsibility and did not need Kay to keep reminding us of an urgency only she held. We certainly understood that family decisions might have to be made on Jessie's behalf. However, that was in the distant future and we agreed that, when the time came, we would assume any responsibility needed, just as we always had.

Over the next several years we all agreed it would be an excellent arrangement for Wally to build the proposed cottage for Mother's use. Conversations continued among us, along with possibilities that, in time, both Kate and Jessie might choose to share the cottage. This arrangement to provide a residence for our mother and aunt seemed to satisfy—for the moment—Kay's behest that something be done—and soon.

Each of us pledged to contribute proportionately to the costs of the materials for construction of the cottage with Wally's also volunteering to do the construction. Work began in 1975 and during the summer of 1976 Wally and I were putting the final strokes of paint on the interior woodwork as the tall ships from around the world sailed into New York harbor, the celebratory highlight of the Bicentennial of American Independence Day. The family agreed that such a celebration seemed appropriate by which to inaugurate "Kaki's Cottage."

The following spring Kate would start her pattern of residing there for several weeks each summer. Beginning in the early 1980s, in addition to the summer visits, she would close her own house for the winter and spend December through March in the Hummelstown cottage. There was always the expectation that some day Mother might make her permanent home there, but no one was pushing because, just as she looked forward to coming to the cottage, so she was just as eager to return to her own home in Curwensville.

In 1974 Curwensville celebrated its 175th Anniversary. However, with memories of the debt resulting from the Sesquicentennial twenty-five years earlier and the current national recession, the town leaders had little choice but to have a more simplified celebration for Curwensville's Centeseptequinary, one that would be locally focused, rather than offering activities that would attract out-of-town visitors. In addition, with the American Bicentennial only two years hence, it seemed prudent to act conservatively for the current celebration.

Not surprisingly, the simplified schedule of events in no way diminished the enthusiasm of the townspeople. Jessie's primary involvement was with the role of the Presbyterian Church in the special Sunday services planned as part of the week-long commemoration of the town's founding. In addition, without mentioning it to anyone, Jessie had her own plan for Founders Day, the day on which most celebrants would wear bonnets and long dresses fashioned for the occasion, or held over from the Sesquicentennial in 1949. On the morning of July 16, as Jessie dressed for this day's festivities, she was pleased with her frock, but unexpectedly found her eyes filling with tears, remembering her mother, Matilda Adeline Smith, who on a bright afternoon in late June, almost exactly 80 years earlier, had been preparing to wear this very dress on her wedding day.

Curwensville's 175th Anniversary was considered not only a success, but also a welcome relief from the morass of the Watergate scandal, when the Supreme Court unanimously ruled that executive privilege did not apply to Watergate. A week later, on July 30, the House Judiciary Committee voted three articles of impeachment against the president. On August 9 Richard Nixon signed a letter of resignation—the first ever by an American president—and he bade farewell to the nation.

While almost no adult in America could ignore the muddle in Washington, Jessie was far more concerned with Jack's health. He had been under a doctor's care for several years for various ailments, most seriously a heart condition. Further, he had experienced a number of medical episodes during the summer and on two occasions had been hospitalized for observation. Finally, very early one morning at the end of September he complained of chest pains and a "kind of numbness" in his extremities.

Jessie called for an ambulance and Jack was taken to the Clearfield Hospital. An EKG confirmed Jessie's fears, which turned to alarm when the doctor told her that the prognosis was not good. For ten days Jessie rarely left Jack's room. When he took a turn for the worse, Jessie remained with him around the clock. Kate spent the final twenty-four hours with her sister in Jack's room, sitting quietly and simply being there for support when at 3:04 a. m. Jack passed away.[20]

Jack's death was hard on Jessie and was a reminder not only of her sister Josephine's passing two years earlier, but also of the reality of now being completely alone again. More than once she said to Kate, "Jack and I had eleven good years together, didn't we?" And Kate always agreed. She, too, held her own thoughts about being alone, but for different reasons. While Kate enjoyed her independence, there were many times she missed having her family nearby. However, at that moment she felt very sad and very sorry for her childless sister.

Kay came to Curwensville that year to spend Christmas with her mother and to visit her two sisters on the East Coast. Kay also came with a purpose—to purchase a burial plot in Oak Hill, the town cemetery. Because Bob wanted his final resting place to be in the Punch Bowl, the National Veterans Cemetery in Hawaii, Kay had decided to buy three burial plots in Curwensville, one for herself, one for her daughter, and one for her mother. On Christmas Day she told her mother of her plan and three days later the two of them purchased this deed, paid for in part by Mother herself. We three younger sisters thought such a purchase a bit out of place during the Christmas season, but we accepted Kay's choice since she seemed to pride herself that this task had been taken care of so efficiently—and so easily.

The following summer (1975), Jessie's first as a widow, Jo Ellen suggested that Mother invite Jessie to accompany her to Jo Ellen's beach house. Jessie agreed to go and the two Pifer sisters drove to Hummelstown where they spent the night, a routine they would follow for several summers. The next day I drove them to Bayberry Dunes and went back a week later to pick them up.

Jessie and Kate at Bayberry Dunes

Mother revealed that she felt a little sheepish that she hadn't told Jessie about the cottage being built for her. She wasn't sure why she hadn't—it just never seemed to be the right time to tell Jessie that her daughters were providing a home for her, whenever she wanted to use it. Having waited to tell Jessie turned out to be even more awkward, as Mother would now also have to explain why she hadn't told Jessie earlier of her plans. Later, in describing this scene, Mother said, "Even after all these years, I still felt like the baby sister."

The dynamic between the two sisters was typical but complicated with the natural evolving dependence Jessie and Kate had on each other following the deaths of Jean and Josephine, and the obvious differences in income. Jessie's side of the double house was larger and had more amenities than Kate's, with its driveway and garage, an enclosed back porch, and a bigger, far more comfortable front porch complete with their mother's swing and sturdy, cushioned wicker porch furniture. Even the view was better from Jessie's side and there was more space between the next house and her side of the duplex.

The issue, however, was not the quality of the respective sides of the double house but that sometimes Kate felt she needed to justify to all her sisters that the expense of improving the home in which she lived totaled more than the rent income they would have earned. Other dynamics of the relationship between Kate and Jessie included the fact that it was Kate and Jean who had been best friends with far more in common than Kate and Jessie.

Conversely, Kate was very proud of her daughters and felt blessed that she had a family to depend on. Thus on the one hand Kate felt more fortunate than Jessie, while on the other hand, she felt just a little resentment. The same could be said of Jessie. More than that, however, was the obvious question in the back of the minds of both of them: "If one of us is no longer here, on whom will the other depend?"

In August 1977 Jessie and Kate made a long, sad journey to Ohio to be with Ruby whose son Tommy had died at age 48. Jessie could not stop saying how young he was and how unfair it was that he should be taken, and it was all Kate could do not to scream, "Tom is the same age as Jean was when she died." It was such comments that Kate found so exasperating in her sister, even though Kate realized it was her own perpetual grief and sense of loss she herself had carried for nearly twenty years that created her frustration, and not anger at Jessie. In total, Jessie and Kate were sisters with all the love and complex situations found in most sibling relationships.

As the decade grew to a close, the final assault of the nationally tumultuous nineteen-seventies came when on Wednesday, March 28, 1979, the worst fears held by the critics of nuclear power were realized. On that day began a series of events at Three Mile Island, less than ten miles from Hummelstown, by which the core of a nuclear reactor came very close to meltdown. The residents were alerted by an announcement that broke into the regular radio programming that there had been an "incident" at Three Mile Island. No details were available, but listeners were told there was no immediate danger. Residents were, however, advised to "stand by, close their windows, and stay indoors."

Later in the morning, it was announced on radio and television that while no schools were officially closing, any parents who wanted to pick up their children at the local schools could do so. It was, however, strongly suggested that the children remain in school and that parents not interrupt classes but report quietly to the offices if they insisted on picking up their children early. Unknown to me because I was with my own high school students at the time, my son was the only child in his elementary school whose parents had not picked him up early. Years later he told me how frightened he had been as his classmates left, one by one, and that he had been the only one left, holding a terrible, unspoken fear that "something had happened to the world."

The next six days were anxiety-laden for everyone in the country, but especially so in the area around the nuclear power plant at Three Mile Island. Emergency evacuation centers were being identified at destinations fifty miles from the reactor and routes to these centers were hastily being planned, even as to which towns should evacuate in what order. Most of the citizenry didn't know what to do nor whose advice to follow. Many were reluctant to leave their homes for fear of looting, and others packed up their valuables and left town as soon as they could.

Only later was it known that the rest of the country was getting news information far more frightening than what was being broadcast to central Pennsylvanians. The local tactic was to keep the population calm and, while no one would ever admit to withholding information, the residents were not being told how potentially dangerous the situation was. Official announcements from the government and its Nuclear Regulatory Commission took on an air of calm with messages that everything was under control. In reality, Middletown, the town closest to TMI, was fast emptied of its citizenry as people fled in fear.

An eerie calm prevailed among those who stayed, and the entire situation was later described as surreal. Most people were not aware at the time how close to a nuclear disaster they were living through in the shadow of the giant cooling towers. And at the time, no one really wanted to know. To those for whom the 1970s was at best confusing and at worst chaotic, TMI was a fitting way to close out the decade.

Chapter 11

While the Storm Clouds Gathered

Despite the opinion of the young who would call this decade exhilarating and liberating, the 1970s was a tired replay of the vibrancy of the 1960s. The youth of the 70s originated nothing and the best they could claim as their own is that they closed the era of flower children and Viet Nam, thus settling for being the caboose, rather than the locomotive, of change.

—*Adapted from Tad Friend*[1]

By the end of 1979, most people were tired of hearing the rallying cry of the seventies, "Do your own thing," and they were bored with long hair, platform shoes, hot pants, leisure suits with their large patch-pocketed, loose fitting jackets and bell-bottom slacks; and they were sick of looking at—let alone wearing—anything that was made of polyester double-knit. Most of all, they were completely weary with the ubiquitously smiling "happy face," and even those who used the phrase would agree with Jessie Mohney's statement that "Have a nice day" was the flattest expression she had ever heard.

When the 1980s dawned, the country was primed for political revolution and a sweeping away of all that the 1970s had been. The Republicans ran a likeable cultural populist as their 1980 presidential candidate and President Ronald Reagan suited the times, seeming to know that the American people needed an optimist. Yet, by the end of 1981, a year after his election, America was in its deepest depression since the Great Depression fifty years earlier and Reagan himself had been the victim of an attempted assassination.

In 1981 the appointment of Sandra Day O'Connor as the first woman Supreme Court Justice marked what many thought would be a dramatic historical change for women, even though the following year the country fell three states short in ratifying the proposed constitutional amendment granting women equal rights. "On Golden Pond" was the surprise hit movie of the year. Beth Henley won the Pulitzer Prize for her drama "Crimes of the Heart," and "Dream Girls" captivated Broadway. "Dynasty" made its debut on television where 28 million households had switched to cable television. Drawing the largest viewership that year, however, was the real life story of a princess who married her prince charming—the wedding of Lady Diana Spencer to the Prince of Wales.

What was later to be known as the technology age arrived this same year when IBM introduced its first personal computer. Yet for another ten years, this new technology would make not a ripple in the lives and work of most people in small towns. And it held no interest at all for those in the later years of their lives, Jessie included. "I have my Royal typewriter," she would say.

One of the worst occurrences of the early 1980s was the report of a strange malady that had begun to strike homosexual men. Unknown in areas outside large cities, initially there was no term for the affliction or for those who were its victims.[2] "Something dreadful is happening here," wrote a family friend who was living in New York City. He described an illness that was making its victims weak and unable to fight off infections of any kind. The fear and concern were clear in this young man's voice as he described how helpless he felt and how worried he was for everyone in his circle of friends.[3] He told of those who were dying from this yet-unidentified illness, a growing epidemic that did not even find an official name until May 1983 when "acquired immuno-deficiency syndrome," or AIDS, was named the No. 1 priority of the U.S. Public Health Service. Only then did the public realize the seriousness of this illness.

Likely unaware of such national concerns as AIDS, Jessie filled these days of her eighth decade as she had filled her summers for many years, sitting on her shaded porch, either alone or with friends she had hailed to "come on up and sit for awhile." She attended the monthly DAR meetings and continued—although in an abbreviated capacity—her service as deaconess in the Presbyterian Church.

The early 1980s were generally tranquil at 408-410 Thompson Street as both Jessie and Kate, in good health, enjoyed visits from Kate's daughters and their families, and assistance from Don Bloom, always faithful in checking in on his aunts. He particularly made a point of visiting Jessie since she had no children of her own and he was her only other relative still in Curwensville.

Don humored his aunt, overlooking her eccentricities, and usually agreed to her insistence that he sit down and have a sandwich. In a word, he was good to Jessie, and he and Lorraine would occasionally deliver meals to Jessie and Kate and/or invite them to their home. It was particularly a comfort to know that when Kate was out of town visiting her daughters Don could be counted on to see to Jessie's needs.

At the end of the school year in the spring of 1981, Nan and Joel sold their home in the high desert, packed their belongings, and drove East with their two sons to reunite with the family. It had taken her fifteen years, but Nan did make good on her promise to Aunt Jessie to "come home."

As each of Mother's five younger grandchildren neared the age of sixteen, they held interest in her Chevy convertible. From the time they were small she had taken them for rides with the top down, and all of them have vivid memories of the red leather interior of the Chevy Chevelle Malibu, dreaming of themselves in the driver's seat. However, it was Shayne, the oldest of the five, who had been completely captivated by "Kaki's convertible" and who would often sit behind the wheel, pretending he was taking his cousins on a great adventure.

To Shayne this was more than pretend, because from the time he was six, Mother had promised him that when he turned sixteen she would give him her car. Of course, at the time of the promise she had anticipated that she would no longer be driving. On the contrary, as Shayne's 16th birthday approached the fall of 1981, Kate was still very much in need of her car and found herself in a quandary.

She shared her dilemma with Jessie, ending with "I don't know how I am going to explain this to Shayne." "Kate," Jessie reassured her, "let me think of something." What Mother did not realize is that Jessie saw in Shayne's personality many of the same qualities she had most enjoyed in her nephew Johnny Wayne forty years earlier, and by October Jessie offered an unexpected and generous solution. "I am going to buy a car for Shayne," she announced one morning as she leaned over the banister separating their two porches to hand the previous day's newspaper to her sister. "But, Jess," Kate began, "you don't need to do that. That is far too generous." Jessie brushed off her sister's protest with a dismissive, "But I want to."

What Mother did not know is that on a trip to the DAR's Constitutional Hall in Washington DC earlier that summer, Jessie had been part of a private tour of the site in the Constitution Gardens to be immortalized the following year by a memorial to those who had given their lives in the Viet Nam War—a black granite wall inscribed with the names of 57,939 Americans killed or missing in action. Unexpectedly shaken by the stark reality of the heretofore unheralded loss of young lives in this war, on the return trip to Curwensville Jessie began to take more of a personal interest in her grand-nephews.

Mother's predicament gave Jessie her first opportunity to do something for Shayne and she began her search for a new car. Nan, surprised yet pleased at her aunt's kindness, nevertheless insisted that a new car would be too extravagant for a new, young driver. "Aunt Jessie, while Shayne is thrilled with your offer to buy him a car, we just can't accept a new one. Shayne would be just as happy with a used one. Let's wait a little while, maybe until spring." By early May, Shayne was behind the wheel of his very own car, a pre-owned sporty Chevrolet Monza Spyder.

Kay's reaction to Jessie's unprecedented generosity surprised her sisters. While first expressing pleasure for Shayne's gift and "luck," as she phrased it, it soon appeared to the family that Jessie's kindness had stirred an unexpected response from Kay. In a birthday card sent to her aunt in the spring of 1982 Kay wrote, "Sure was nice of you to get Shayne a car,"[4] but in conversations with Mother and me, Kay's resentment was noticeable, as several themes emerged in her questions, with emphasis on the last: "Why would Jessie buy Shayne a car? Why do you suppose she did that? She never bought anything like that for me."

Kay's reaction to Jessie's gift was particularly troubling to Mother because only the year before she had handwritten a Will in which she had bestowed her property at 410 Thompson Street to her firstborn. This decision was based upon Kay's assurances to her mother that she wanted to return to Curwensville upon her retirement, "You know the other girls won't ever want to come back here to live and I do." While it was likely that the three younger daughters would not return to their home town, it was Kay's declaration of wanting to retire in Curwensville that most convinced Mother to will the property to Kay. After having heard Kay's compelling argument for the past decade—that if the other girls all had homes and Kay needed a place to live, then she should have the Thompson Street homestead—Mother agreed.

Kay's wanting to return to Curwensville reminded Mother of her own need for a place to live a quarter century earlier and of the willingness of her own sisters to sign over their interests in the property to her. "Who would have thought," she said a few years later when she disclosed the contents of her Will to the other three of us, "that you girls would be faced with the same kind of situation as my sisters were? It would have been upsetting to me if you had quarreled over this. I hated to choose one daughter over the other and I am glad everyone understood that Kay seemed to be the only one who was interested in moving back." All of us were fine with Mother's decision.

In early November 1984 Mother traveled to California on what turned out to be an extended visit to Kay when she found her daughter "on edge," declaring that she was unable to go to work. On the day following her arrival, Mother suggested that she go to the office with Kay, concerned that it might be the long drive on the freeway that was bothering her daughter. The journey to the TWA office building was uneventful until Kay approached the turn to enter the parking lot. She began crying and said to her mother, "I can't go in." Because there was no other place to park and traffic was beginning to back up behind them, Mother suggested that they enter the lot, park the car, and just remain in the car.

As they sat there, Kay began telling her mother of the nervousness she had been experiencing, of her crying episodes that sometimes lasted for more than an hour, and of her persistent headaches. Mother suggested calling Bob at work, but since his job was an hour the opposite direction from their home, she thought it better to remain in the parking lot for awhile, knowing she herself could not navigate the Los Angeles Freeway. Once Kay had composed herself, mother and daughter returned home.

While Mother was aware of Kay's history of debilitating

headaches, she assumed they were hereditary, as other family members also suffered migraines, although without the emotional distress that periodically seemed to accompany those Kay suffered. Concerned for her daughter's seeming unstable condition, Mother remained in California for several weeks until Kay located a physician who was able to provide some relief for her through a combination of treatments. Mother later said she had listened with a heavy heart at her daughter's account of her various medical treatments, ranging from medication and bio-feedback to hypnosis and mental therapy.

In the spring of 1985 Mother returned to California because Kay's letters throughout the winter implied she wasn't well. Shortly after her mother's arrival, Kay told her that after Christmas she had suffered a nervous breakdown and had been on medical leave during much of the winter. (Mother later told Nan and me that she wondered why Kay had not written or called, then dismissed her concerns, rationalizing that Kay probably did not want to worry her.) Kay told her mother that she was dreading returning to work full time, but that if she didn't soon return to her job she would be forced to take early retirement. Mother's worries increased at the bleak picture her daughter was painting.

With increased concern Mother was wrestling with the possible cause of Kay's illness, wondering if it was rooted in Kay's perception of financial insecurity, as she could discern no medical reason in what her daughter was telling her. Kay had often voiced worry about having enough money to live comfortably and to have a dependable retirement income. She appeared to see everything in terms of money and at times to become obsessed with the cost of things, from grocery items and medications to the price of gasoline—whatever she was buying at the time. Even in describing gifts Kay would persistently make comments such as, "It cost a lot" or "I got a bargain."

Only much later did Mother begin to suspect that she might have been misled by her daughter. When she tried to reconstruct the chain of events leading to the incidents that later destroyed the family, she began to wonder if this nervous breakdown of Kay's had been only a ruse, a piece of a much broader scheme, or even the beginning of a carefully designed plot.

In looking back Mother said she began to suspect that the first step in Kay's larger plan had been to establish that she (Kay) was frail and needed support. Thus, when Kay would later turn to her mother for help to carry out her plans, Mother would be primed to not risk upsetting Kay's possibly unstable condition. Mother later berated herself that she had fallen for a seeming devious trick and that her concern had led her to appease Kay, leading to a consequence none of us could have imagined.

At the time, the thought that her daughter would betray her was inconceivable to Mother. Later, however, she said she believed that Kay had been further emboldened in her plans, thinking that Mother would take her side in the event any of us sisters questioned any steps of her plan. Thus bolstered, Kay began reminding us how close a relationship she had with Mother.

In the summer of 1986 a curious incident occurred when Kay made a two-day visit to Hummelstown where Mother was spending the summer. Following an afternoon of reminiscing and laughter in the cottage, I returned to the main house to begin dinner preparations. A short time later, Kay entered the house and began lamenting what would happen to her if Bob should die. This conversation was a total change from the laughter we had shared only a few minutes earlier. Kay began speaking of the limited joint income she and Bob would have upon retirement, and that by herself, without Bob's retirement income, she probably would not have enough for her living expenses. Without warning, she began to cry. I was at a loss. We were not a family to readily express emotions and I remember later thinking that I never before had seen any of my sisters cry.

Through Kay's tears came an odd request, "If something happens to Bob, can I come live with you? With Bob gone, I won't have any place to go." Hearing both sadness and desperation in her voice, I answered without hesitation, "Of course." I never questioned the cause of her outburst, believing it had been caused by stress or just an aberration. While I remained uncomfortable, I did not share this unnerving incident with anyone until some years later.

Kay continued to pressure Jo Ellen, Nan, and me to convince Mother to relocate permanently in Hummelstown, and we continued in our reluctance to initiate such a discussion with our mother. We preferred not to influence any decision she might make. Mother was in good health, both physically and mentally; in fact, among ourselves we would laugh and say that she was in better shape than we were. We quietly listened any time Mother wanted to talk about "some day," but none of us would influence her choice as to where she preferred to spend her later years.

In early December (1986) Mother drove to Hummelstown for what had become an annual three-to-four month visit. An invitation had been extended to Jessie that someone from the family would make a trip to Curwensville to bring her down for the holiday or arrange for her to come by bus as she sometimes preferred. On the 17th Kate wrote to her sister,

Dear Jana J.[5]

...It is quiet around here, too. You didn't mention coming down, so I gather you won't be. Judith did say she'd send her car up [to pick you up] if the bus idea turns you off.

...The girls made fudge and deep-fried peanuts last night [and] unless you come down, I'll send yours. Your See's candy should be arriving soon.

Love, Latoya Leah

The two remaining Pifer sisters continued their communication, regardless of whether one or both were in Curwensville, a point worth noting in light of what Kay later claimed.

For some years Kay and Bob had been exploring retirement sites for their second home, with their primary residence planned for Curwensville. They earlier had invested in land in northern California that was to be developed and upon which they had hoped to install a mobile home that would serve as one of the two homes they planned to maintain. They also had invested in a restaurant in Laguna Beach. Both ventures failed.

As a result Kay and Bob despaired as to how to recoup their losses, and, of course, to find a location in which they could afford to retire. The high cost of living in southern California prohibited their remaining there even if its lifestyle had not left both of them jaded. They also considered the high desert where Nan and Joel had lived, but it was a bit too remote for Kay, even though Bob found it ideal. Palm Springs area was another of their favorite sites, but, again, priced out of their reach. They looked at Florida as well, but didn't like its retirement community atmosphere and its "touristy" flavor. As could be noted in Kay's letters and conversations with her family, her anxiety increased with each disappointment.

After several trips to Alabama, Kay and Bob decided that the area along the Gulf Coast would be ideal as it was close enough to Florida to enjoy the attractions there. The Alabama community they selected was near water in a gated community within their price range and boasted a lower cost of living than Florida offered. "Alabama, Here I Come" became Kay's theme song as she and Bob finalized the purchase of a mobile home in the summer of 1987. At that point their plan was to live six months in Alabama and six months in Curwensville. From all indications, Kay had led her mother to believe that she and Bob would be making their headquarters at 410 Thompson Street.

While the Storm Clouds Gathered

Appearing somewhat lighter in heart once their decision was finalized, Kay and Bob concentrated on selling their California home as well as most of its contents. In addition, they made many trips to Alabama, closing on their lot purchase and overseeing the installation of their new mobile home and selecting new furnishings. Kay particularly relished creating a new look in the Alabama mobile. She regaled Mother with tales of her acquisitions, supported by photographs. "We can buy all new for Alabama," she told her mother, "because I won't need to buy much for Curwensville. I'll be using most of the furniture you already have." This comment was typical of Kay who excused her insensitivity by saying, "Well, at least I'm honest in saying what I believe." There was no disputing that point.

We three did not like our sister's comments concerning Mother's possessions and we advised her to tell Kay what items she wanted taken to Hummelstown. Worse than the proprietary attitude about the house and furnishings, however, were Kay's derogatory comments to us about the age of the items in Mother's home as well as the house itself. More than once I wanted to say, "If it is so bad in Curwensville, why are you moving back?" However, what I did tell Kay is that it was inappropriate to disparage Mother's property and that it was hurtful and insensitive to make derisive comments about anyone's home, especially that of an older person who might not have the resources to purchase new items or who, in our mother's case, had made comfortable, attractive living quarters with a limited income.

What was not clear in 1987 is just when Kay and Bob would move to Curwensville permanently. According to Mother, "It was my understanding that Kay and Bob would keep most of their belongings in Alabama and would visit Curwensville on a limited basis until I decided if and when I would make a permanent move to Hummelstown. I was not yet ready to make a final move just because they had decided to come back to town."[6]

The entire situation of Kay's early retirement and return to Curwensville had prompted more frequent conversations among all the sisters as to our mother's options. Kay's persistence in trying to influence her to move to Hummelstown was the major topic of our discussion. Subsequently, when family talks did not lead to the quick result she wanted, Kay began an intensive campaign to convince us sisters that the move would be best for everyone. Every conversation Kay held with us was geared toward the persistent theme: "Get Mother to move."

Kay used various tactics to persuade us, including arguing, crying, and badgering, always presenting herself as needing Mother's house. "It isn't right for Bob and me to be so unsettled after all we've been through. Your fighting against me is upsetting me. I am trying not to have another nervous breakdown, but this is driving me toward the edge." Nan and I began to closely observe Mother to see if Kay's expressed anxiety was affecting Mother's own well-being.

The other consideration regarding Mother's move to Hummelstown was Aunt Jessie. Nan and I were particularly concerned about uprooting Mother from her sister. While we could not fully understand the intricacies of the eighty-year relationship between the two remaining Pifer sisters, we did hold a sense of discomfort at the thought of our mother and aunt being separated after so many years of living next door to each other, each alone yet in many ways interdependent. Even though Nan didn't think Mother would miss Jessie as much as Jessie would miss her younger sister, both of us worried that Mother would miss her own home. I also understood—perhaps even more that Mother did—that a move from one's home and hometown is often traumatic for older people.

When Mother did not leave her home as quickly as Kay expected her to, Kay said to her, "You have another house you can go to in Hummelstown. Why do you think we all helped pay for it?"

Mother later told Nan she felt her face redden at these words, as none of the other girls had ever spoken of the assistance they had provided and, in fact, Kay had contributed very little financial assistance toward the cottage. Mother continued to struggle with the decision to leave her home, knowing there would be no returning.

Kay's next move was to convince us that this unresolved situation was affecting not only her own health but Mother's as well. Kay approached us, each in turn, championing her case and refuting any points of resistance specific to the concerns of each sister. As a result, we three together agreed to broach the subject with Mother. We wanted to do what she wished for herself, but at the same time we were wondering if the uncertainty of making the decision was harder on her than simply making the break.

"We should let Mother decide what *she* wants to do," Jo Ellen said at the time. "It seemed so interfering," Nan would later say. And my constant refrain was, "This has been Mother's home for most of her life and we cannot dictate this choice for her." On the other hand, we couldn't imagine that she would want to share her home in Curwensville with Kay and Bob and we could only hope that Kay would respect Mother's wishes and not intrude upon her to vacate her home until she was ready.

When Kay and Bob arrived in Curwensville in the fall of 1987, Bob went to live temporarily with his Aunt Ruth in Clearfield. Kay hunkered down at 410 Thompson Street, from which she spent a good deal of the time on the telephone with her husband, repeating nearly every word of the conversation she had with various vendors in Alabama. The crash on Wall Street in October added to Kay's fretfulness as she lamented, "Everything we invest in crashes!" This situation likely added to her sense of desperation to cover her losses by any means.

In addition, she had taken on the task of planning her high school reunion for the following spring. All of this was handled by telephone, entailing many loud and extended conversations that led to Mother's impatience. At the same time, Kay's irritation at her mother's constant presence in the house was becoming more evident to everyone, particularly after the day Kay shouted at her mother to turn off the television. This incident led to sharper exchanges between mother and daughter, along with hurt feelings on both sides.

Throughout the next several weeks, Kay moved into the next phase of what later would be viewed as a deliberate plan. Whenever she could create the opportunity, she would suggest to her mother, "You know, it might be a good idea for you to sell this property to me now for a dollar since I'm going to inherit it anyway. It would be easy to do." Offended by Kay's bluntness and indirect reference to her demise, Mother initially resisted.

When Kay repeated the suggestion the following day, Mother asked, "Why should I do that? You sound like you can't wait until I die." Kay replied, "It just would make better sense to have the house in my name. That way there would be no question of my ownership. Besides, it would save inheritance taxes later." Mother said she would have to think about that because it made everything so *final.*

Kay persisted. "You're going to Hummelstown to live anyhow, so why not sign the house over? That way I'll pay the property taxes and all the expenses and you won't have to worry about it." Mother couldn't argue that point, but said, "It just doesn't feel right to sign it over with Jessie living next door. If I give you the house she might think I am abandoning her."

"Well, you will be!" said Kay. "But so what? If you are going to move, what difference does it make? Besides, I'll be right here if Jessie needs anything."

Mother deliberated as to whether or not she should discuss this state of affairs with Jessie, but she simply didn't have the courage. She lived to regret this decision, for what she didn't know is that her daughter was also laying groundwork on the other side of the double house, telling Jessie that Kate would soon be moving to Hummelstown, leaving Jessie to fend for herself.

Despite telling her mother that she and Bob would probably *later* purchase their own home in Curwensville, in reality Kay was making immediate plans to buy a mobile home near Irvin Park on the south side of Curwensville. When she told Mother that she had found a house she liked along the Susquehanna River, Mother was upset.

"What do you mean, you found a place at the Park? It was my understanding that you and Bob were going to live here until you were *sure* you wanted to make Curwensville your permanent home. You have hardly been in town two months; you are buying a house in Alabama, and now you tell me you are buying another house here?" Her voice revealed her disbelief and anger as she added, "You are putting me out of my own house so that you can buy a new one?"

This evidently was not the response Kay had hoped for. "I wish you wouldn't say it that way," she said to her mother. "What difference does it make if it is now or later? You certainly wouldn't expect that Bob and I would want to live in *this* house? All I need is the deed so I can sell the house. I can't sell it without the deed. I don't want to live here. I want the money to buy something Bob and I like."

That being said, Kay continued, "It's for your own good. Why would you want to stay here and end up having to take care of Jessie? I'll take care of whatever needs Jessie has and I will bring her down for visits with you." Unable to control her sarcasm, she added, "Or, if you are so worried about Jessie, maybe you want her to move into the cottage in Hummelstown with you."

The next few weeks were fraught with apprehension and anxiety. As Mother later related, "I tried to be helpful because

Kay was so stressed." Kay, however, did not seem to view her mother's efforts as being helpful. Rather, she seemed to regard her very presence as a hindrance. Thus, Kay's interactions with Mother became brusque, clearly indicating her annoyance that Mother would not acquiesce to her demands.

The displeasure soon turned into signs of resentment of her mother's very presence in the house. Simply put, Mother was not ready to give up her home for any other reason than for Kay and Bob to live there, while at the same time Kay was not about to have her plans thwarted, not then and not later.

Kay's persistence won out as she continued to pressure her sisters who, concerned for their mother's health in this hostile impasse, agreed they would try to persuade their mother to leave her home in Curwensville. Within two weeks Mother reluctantly agreed to deed the house to Kay and remove herself to Hummelstown as soon as it could be arranged.

Holding the unsigned deed in her hand apparently was still not enough for Kay. Once her mother consented to leave, Kay (unknown to us) increased her demands for items of furniture and accessories from the house to move to her new place at the Park. Adding to the injury, each time Mother balked at the demands for these items, Kay lashed out, "Why not? You don't need them." Finally defeated, Mother arrived in Hummelstown the day before Thanksgiving, leaving her remaining possessions to be brought down (or not) at some indefinite later date.

In early December Kay purchased property along the Susquehanna River. She took the furniture she wanted from her mother's home, along with many accessories, including items Mother specifically had told her she could *not* have because they were gifts her other daughters had given her. Disregarding her mother's wishes, Kay took these articles and placed them in her new mobile home on Trail's End, a prophetic name fitting for its newest residents.

Kay next began her move on Jessie, making comments to the effect that Kate had left Jessie to fend for herself. The remarks were at first subtle, just hints dropped now and then, to raise questions and plant doubts in Jessie's mind, such as "before long Mother's furniture, including the piano, will be moved to Hummelstown." She mentioned the piano in particular because in early December Kay had told Jessie, "I don't think that Mother will take the piano since there isn't space in the cottage for it. Would you like to have it?" While this offer was made without Mother's knowledge, Jessie took it as genuine because of Kay's recent visit to Hummelstown.[7]

At the same time, Mother was reminding me that the piano was to be moved to Hummelstown because it had originally been bought for me and I was the only one in the family who was a pianist. Unaware of Kay's promise of the piano to Jessie, I agreed at Mother's insistence to retain the piano while noting to Nan that, while I didn't need another piano, it seemed very important to Mother that I have it because it had been purchased for me when I was five years old. Unfortunately, and to Mother's complete surprise, once the piano was moved to Hummelstown it became an issue between Jessie and her. Later Jessie told her sister what Kay had said to her about Kate's leaving her and taking the piano.

By mid-December, a strained relationship had developed between Kay and Mother over Mother's possessions and her hurt feelings of being pushed out of her own house. After hearing more details, Nan and I were convinced that Kay indeed had forced Mother out of her own home and had bullied her into allowing Kay to take her choice of the contents of that house.

In late December Kay and Bob came to Hummelstown for a post-Christmas visit during which several heated discussions occurred. Several times Kay seemed to be hysterical, making wild accusations against Mother. At first, Kay insisted that her mother had told her she could have items she wanted from Mother's house. She then said that the items belonged to her in the first place and that she had only left them in the care of her mother when she first left for California in 1959 when in actuality Mother had paid Kay for the items left behind because Kay needed the money. Lastly, she said she took the items because her mother didn't need them.

Recriminations continued throughout the visit, near the end of which Kay and Mother had words in private. Kay left the cottage in anger and by the time she had made the short walk to my house, she was crying. As I tried to calm her, Kay began crying anew, saying Mother had been mean to her. "After all I've done for her," she said. "Mother should not question my decisions. Why is everyone ganging up on me over something as stupid as old furniture? I hate her."

For the next several months, we three sisters attempted to serve as peacemakers between Kay and Mother, but to no avail. However, because the return of the items Kay had taken from the house had by then become so important to Mother, we continued to ask Kay to return them.

Unfortunately, these requests only added to Kay's wrath. In a last futile attempt to assure that the items would eventually be retrieved from Kay, Mother added a codicil to her Will, asking that Kay return the two items that were most important to her, a chair that had been a gift from her daughters and a cedar chest that had been an engagement gift from her late, albeit divorced, husband and that she had promised to Shayne.[8] Even this last request was ignored by Kay, both at that time and later at the occasion of her mother's death.

As the date for Kate's 80th birthday anniversary approached, an invitation was extended to Kay and Bob to join the family in the celebration during the weekend of February 14-15. A partial truce prevailed on Saturday. Sunday afternoon, however, the arguments resumed. Until that troubled time arguments had been unheard of in the family, and none of us were comfortable in this mode. Jo Ellen, Nan, and I had hoped to avoid any confrontation on this special occasion, but our optimism soon diminished.

As Kay continued to vent her anger and to rationalize her own position in the quarrel with Mother, the atmosphere of discomfort increased during what should have been a celebratory week-end. Finally, she said to us, "It is really too bad you can't see things the way they are. If you can't see the truth of what has happened, then you are all fools." Bob, enraged, then began shouting at us for the harm he said we were causing our sister. Shortly thereafter Kay and Bob left in anger. His parting words were "You don't know what you are doing. I never want to see any of you again."

In March 1988 Mother's remaining possessions were transported to Hummelstown. Among these few belongings were the piano and Aunt Josephine's prized mahogany bedroom suite Kate earlier had acquired at the sale of her sister's estate. This suite would find its home in the guest bedroom of the cottage. Later, Nan said, "If I had known what was going to happen to Jessie we would have packed her up and brought her back with us as well."

The strain continued without communication between Kay and the other members of the family. In May Mother underwent an emergency appendectomy and was hospitalized for five days. All of our attention was focused on her recovery. A chance comment provided much needed levity to the gloomy circumstance when a nurse said to the eighty-year-old Kate, "It's too bad you're not over sixty-five [Medicare eligible] because then you could have free television in your room."

In early June Kay telephoned her mother asking what she had decided about the deed to the Thompson Street property. Mother told her to mail it to her and she would sign it and have her signature notarized.[9] This was accomplished quickly and ownership of the house was transferred. Unknown to the family, however, was the fact that Kay already had begun persuading Jessie to buy the house from her once it came into her possession. Later, Kay bragged that she had convinced her aunt to purchase the house. "I told her that it would be in her best interests to own both sides of the house so that she could control who would rent the side Mother had vacated."

Later evidence also shows that Kay had told her aunt that Mother left without any thought as to Jessie's well-being. She further told Jessie that it was to her aunt's advantage to buy the property Kay now owned and that she was offering it to her at a very fair price because they were family. Kay admitted, "I told her if someone else buys it, who knows what kind of people they might be or if someone buys it to rent, she could have some undesirable neighbors—loud and with a bunch of kids. I told Jessie I would help her find suitable tenants. I made it very clear to her, 'I need the money from the house and if you won't buy it, then I'll just sell it to anyone who meets my price.' That took care of any argument."

Thus, on July 9, 1988, Jessie's eighty-third birthday and exactly one month and a day from the time Kate had sold the property to Kay for $1, Kay, in turn, sold the house to Jessie.

A week later, Kay's husband had a new Ford Bronco.

Over the next few months, Kay began again to communicate with her mother, and the reports concerning Jessie's welfare were generally positive. The arrangement for Kay to "look after" Jessie became more palatable and we were inclined to relax our stance a bit since Mother believed all was well. For a period of time it was as though Kay's injury to Mother had never happened.

In her letters and telephone calls Kay relayed how she was helping Jessie by running errands and taking her an occasional meal. She also mentioned in passing that she was helping Jessie straighten out her taxes. At the time this seemed reasonable, as Kay had once worked part time for a tax preparer, so helping Jessie with taxes was viewed only as routine.

Soon after, Kay told Mother that Jessie's tax records were not in good order, although she used less kind terms in describing Jessie's financial affairs. "Her bank statements are a mess. She doesn't always fill in the amount in the check register, and I don't know how she keeps track of anything. She tells me she checks her statement every month, but I doubt it. And she hasn't paid her taxes for years." This was not so. Jessie, at best, was careless about details and in 1985, for example, she had sent payments on her taxes but had not returned the form with the payment. She then had written to the Internal Revenue Service in June 1986 inquiring about her tax payments; they responded, and the matter was settled.[10] However, Kay offered to take care of Jessie's financial affairs and during 1988 gained full access to her checkbook, bank statements, savings account information, and bank stock.

Throughout the next year Kay painted for her mother a picture of devotion to Jessie in providing the help her aunt needed. She also noted that when she was not available, cousin Don Bloom was. Kay enumerated the errands she ran for Jessie, making sure to add how grateful their aunt was for the assistance, and added comments such as, "None of you down there need to pretend to worry about Jessie. I'm taking care of everything." Ignoring the personal barb, we were glad for the assurance that Jessie was being helped.

Despite hearing Kay's account of the care she was providing Jessie, we became increasingly uncomfortable with the stories she took such delight in telling of our aunt's eccentricities. Kay appeared to enjoy making fun of Jessie, her clothes, and her living habits. "She seems to think that anything she wears is fine, just because she is Jessie. You should see some of the get-ups she wears. And she doesn't clean out her refrigerator. It is ready to walk. She puts coffee on in the morning and leaves the pot on all day. And she is always insisting that people sit on the porch with her. People cross the street so they can avoid her." At every opportunity Kay criticized Jessie's housekeeping and lack of organization. "Her house is a mess, with clothes in piles all over the bedrooms, and she often misses her hair appointment."

Kate would have described her sister as "clatty," a term used by their own mother to describe someone who was not a good housekeeper—and surely Jessie had never been known for her skill in housekeeping, but Kay began slipping such terms as "incompetent" in descriptions of her aunt. Kay's complaints about having to "take care of" Jessie increased over the next year, without acknowledgement that it was she herself who had created the situation.

Kay's grumbling about Jessie's growing dependence upon her led to further conversations among Jo Ellen, Nan, and me on how to determine the best course of action. Kay's only offered solution was to "get rid of the problem" and "put Jessie away." When asked what she meant by "putting Jessie away," Kay's reply was, "There are places for old people. Put her in a home." When her sisters did not agree with her, Kay's retort was always the same, "Well, maybe you'd like to have her live with you!"

Not getting the kind of agreement she was seeking from us, Kay took matters into her own hands regarding a Will for Jessie. None of us knew if Jessie had a Will and, in retrospect, perhaps we were short-sighted in not directly asking Jessie. On the other hand, neither Mother nor any of us except Kay believed that it was any of our business. We had been brought up to respect others' privacy and to not ask questions regarding other people's finances. Only Kay believed she had the right to ask her aunt directly as to her Will, and had been doing that very thing for at least fifteen years.

While the Storm Clouds Gathered

The first time Kay had asked Jessie about a Will was during one of her annual October pilgrimages East to see the leaves changing. As Kay told it, she and Bob were sitting on the front porch when Kay steered the conversation to the future and asked what would become of the house where Jessie and all her sisters had spent their girlhood. Kay asked Jessie if she had her affairs in order and if she had ever had a Will drawn up. Initially Jessie ignored her niece's probing questions. However, Kay persisted, much to Jessie's annoyance. When Kay asked again what was to happen when Jessie was no longer living, Jessie's answer ended the discussion, "I don't want to think about that."

Later when Kay and Bob visited Nan and her family in the high desert of California, Kay pointedly asked her sister, "Does Jessie have a Will?" Nan did not want to be drawn into such a discussion and she responded very simply to her sister, "I don't know. Why are you asking me? Why don't you just ask Aunt Jessie herself?" "I have asked her," Kay replied, "and she always says she doesn't want to talk about it." "Well, then, just leave it alone," Nan said.

But Kay would not be deterred. "You know she must have a checking or a savings account; and she owns bank stock, her half of the double house, and her car. She probably has some kind of life insurance from NARCO when Jack died. She has her teacher's pension and Social Security to live on with hardly any expenses. She doesn't buy anything but groceries. I'll bet she has a fairly substantial amount. You know the state will step right in and take everything if she doesn't have a Will. Why should we let that happen? Why shouldn't we get some of her money?" Kay continued, including the two husbands in her next question, "Can't you just see something happening to Jessie and no one knowing if she had written a Will? Without a Will, the state will take over. We can't let that happen. Is that what you want?"

Nan never forgot the response she made to her sister's question, "It really isn't any of your business." Kay's reply was seared in Nan's soul, "Then I'll make it my business. I will make sure she has a Will if I have to write it myself."

This earlier promise haunted Nan as she listened to her sister in 1990. Triumphant, Kay shared with her sisters the cleverness that she had employed the year before to convince Jessie to sign a Will making her the sole beneficiary:

> "Jessie asked me to make an appointment for her with Cortez Bell[11] to have a Will drawn up. I called the morning of December 26 (1989) and Mr. Bell was free to see her that afternoon. I picked Jessie up, but on the way to the appointment, she changed her mind. She said she didn't need to talk to a lawyer, and wanted to go home. I turned the car around and took her back. When we got there Jessie said she wanted me to write the Will for her, that she would tell me what to say. It was lucky I had my tape recorder with me."

In the eyes of many, December 26 seemed to be a very odd date for an attorney's appointment, or, for that matter, to draw a Will. While only speculation, it is likely that Kay had visited Jessie Christmas Day and again preyed on her susceptibility, making a point of telling her that of all her nieces and nephews only she came to visit on Christmas Day.[12]

A summary of this taped Will transcript follows:

Kay: *I want the house to go ... to my sister.*

Jessie (repeating): *to my sister, Katherine.*

Kay: *Pifer Thompson; yeah, Pifer Thompson or if she predeceases me, to my niece. You can just put 'Matilda Kay. They'll know who that is. I guess we have to put the whole thing down. My mother's namesake. Well, you don't have to put that down if you don't want to.*

Jessie: *Well, I think so.*

Kay: *Yeah, I think that sounds nice, because I am.*

Jessie: *... and my mother's namesake. Is that right?*

Kay: *Namesake. Correct.*

Kay: *I also want...I'd put "Kay" there, too.*

Kay: *And now I want my car ... put that down... to go to ... ah, you can put Shayne Edmunds.*

Kay: *Now, nothing, zero, next, that's the part I like, is to go to my nephew, Noel Hamilton.*

Jessie: *Yes, me, too.*

Kay: *All money left...after taxes ...You always have to say taxes, you know and expenses, like final bills and something... are paid.*

Kay: *I want ... I don't know what to tell you here. I don't know what you want to do with it.*

Jessie: *I don't know either.*

Kay: *Just say (indistinguishable). You can always change it. ... Let's see. Let me read this over. The house located at 408 Thompson Street and all contents I want to go to my sister Katherine Pifer Thompson or if she predeceases me to my niece, Kay Thompson Walker. I also want my niece, Kay Thompson Walker, to have my diamond rings. I want the car to go to Shayne Edmunds. Nothing. ... zero to go to my nephew, Noel Hamilton. All other relatives not mentioned (Laughter by both) ... are omitted intentionally. All money left after taxes and expenses are paid I want ... You're gonna have to put something down. Now, what do you think?*

Jessie: *I don't know.*

Kay: *Do you want this to be divided among?*

Jessie: *I don't know. I haven't made up my mind yet.*

Kay: *Well, you have to do it. Oh, now, (indistinguishable) executor, Jess. Do you want me to do this, be the executor?*

Jessie: *Yes.*

Kay: *O.K. (indistinguishable) Kay Thompson Walker.*

Jessie: *Yes. Of my last will and testament.*

Kay: *(Indistinguishable) That's all you have to do. I think that's good. I don't know what to tell you here.*

Jessie: *I don't know. Why don't you just say I want all money left after taxes…*

Kay: *and expenses are paid. O.K. If you have any money left over, I want, ah, Kay Thompson Walker.*

Jessie: *Kay Thompson Walker.*

Kay: *O.K.*

Kay: *If that's what you want, that's all you have to say.*

Jessie: *I hope so. I don't feel much like doing it.*

Kay: *Well, it's just good to do. You know.*

Jessie: *I know it is.*

Kay: *You'll feel better about it.*

Jessie: *Yes.*

Kay: *No one likes to think of themselves as mortal, but, well, everybody has to put something down, or the state will take everything, Jess. You don't want that.*

Jessie: *No - - -*

Kay: *Oh, no, of course you don't.*

Jessie: *I sure don't.*

<u>Postscript added by Kay</u>

Jessie's wishes for her Will were relayed to me on December 26, 1989. I wrote down what she wanted, and dictated it back to her as she wrote it. I would like to point out that she did not want to leave her one remaining sister, Katherine, anything, for various reasons unknown to me, but I stated to her at the time I thought that Grandma Pifer would want her to at least leave the house and its contents to her. She agreed to this. I also asked her if she wanted to leave her diamonds to Shayne or Jesse Joel, but she said, No, that they would just give it to some girl. She definitely did not want Noel Hamilton to have anything of hers and did not want to leave anything to anyone else that she could think of, except she wanted Shayne to have the car. I tried to go along with what she wanted and not influence her in any way. That is why I tape-recorded it. Jessie and I went down to the Curwensville Bank. Gary Jewett read the Will and he witnessed the Will, also Marie witnessed it in the presence of Jessie signing it and the notary.

Two days later, Jessie's Curwensville State Bank checking account was changed from a single owner (Jessie) to joint ownership of Jessie and Kay. The amount in the checking account was $28,624.51. In addition, Jessie's 360 shares of bank stock were changed from single ownership to joint ownership.

And this was only the beginning....

408 - 410 Thompson Street

Chapter 12

"Here's That Rainy Day They Told Me About"

Those who do not understand what is happening to them ... are the truest victims, for they do not even know they are being abused.

Cathleen Wilber and Sandra Reynolds[1]

Although the 1990s are still too close to us to have a definitive descriptive designation, some have called this period the Decade of Policing the World, others have named it the Merger Decade, and others will remember it as the decade that ushered in school violence. The 1990s may even be remembered as the capstone of the century-of-world-peace-that-failed or the end-of-the-millennium-of-frontal warfare. But above all, both the decade of American business and Jessie's fate may best be referred to as the "Age of Greed."

In general, the country was enjoying a booming economy and the stock market reached an all-time high as individuals learned to buy and trade via the Internet. The minimum wage increased to $5.15 an hour and there was record low unemployment. Overall, times were good. Work styles began to change with technology, and early in the decade it was clear that working knowledge of a computer would very soon be a necessity in nearly all jobs.

Socially the informality of computer protocol and the possibilities technology offered for persons to interface with others without meeting face-to-face played a large role in the trend toward casualness and informality among business colleagues and between business and the public. Telemarketers and sales clerks could be heard more frequently addressing customers by their first names, thus establishing a familiarity that left those reared in an earlier time feeling uncomfortable and intruded upon.

This relaxed attitude created confusion—and even some discomfort—between and among generations. Companies were at a loss as to how much control they had regarding how their employees dressed for work, and dress codes all but disappeared in many businesses. Numerous churches, trying to attract members who had expressed their dislike of formality, began offering a Contemporary Service and invited worshippers to dress casually, leaving their established congregation in a state of perplexity. It no longer was necessary to be well-dressed for any event and "Wear your Sunday best" lost all meaning.

In this last decade of the 20th Century and the ninth decade of life for Jessie and her younger sister Katherine, in what should have been a decade of dignity, instead became one of confusion, turmoil, and despair—and all of it unwarranted. Early in 1990 Jessie remained at 408 Thompson Street with renters living on the other side of the duplex. Kay left Curwensville to winter in Alabama, but not before crafting a scenario for key people in the Curwensville community as to her devotion to her Aunt Jessie. She made it her business to tell everyone that Kate had moved to Hummelstown, essentially abandoning her sister Jessie.

As we were learning, Kay apparently was a master at ingratiating herself, especially to those who might be of use to her. Joe Errigo, in particular, was one of her targets. Joe, who had been a good friend of both Jessie and Kate from the time they all were school children, lived across the street from Jessie and often would stop and chat with her on his way to and from the post office or on other errands after his retirement. He later told Kate he initially wondered why she had left Jessie there alone (even though he himself, the same age, lived alone as did 24 percent of Americans[2]), but upon further consideration he realized that it was a logical move for Kate to be closer to her other daughters once Kay had returned to Curwensville and would be there to look after Jessie.

Kay, in her letters to her mother, had mentioned Joe as one of those "who understand what I am going through with Jessie." However, what Kate herself didn't and couldn't possibly understand is the extent to which Kay must have talked to numerous people, gathering allies for her final coup and telling tales about how difficult her aunt was and how all other family members had washed their hands of the situation. Because of what later happened, it can be surmised that she courted people at the bank, the utilities offices, the drug store, and the grocery store, as well as Jessie's friends at the Presbyterian Church and the DAR, relating to anyone who would listen that her aunt was becoming troublesome and that she alone was left to care for her.

Kay even went to Bellefonte (an hour's distance) to carry her story to our paternal Aunt Mary Alice. We had no inkling that she was burdening our aunt with exaggerated details of Jessie's behavior, embellished for the purpose of ridiculing Jessie. Mary Alice was in frail health herself and should not have been weighed down with the sad account of her school chum. None of the rest of us in our visits to Mary Alice mentioned this family impasse.[3]

Don Bloom had agreed to check on Jessie occasionally (as had been his habit for years) to make sure she was getting along by herself and to provide any assistance she might need while Kay wintered in Alabama. Kay also had arranged for Bob's cousin to clean the house periodically. Don and the cousin were asked to report details concerning any signs of unusual behavior by Jessie, information that Kay later tried to use as evidence of dementia.

It was during this winter of 1990 when Jessie first mentioned to her nephew Don that she believed Kay had been taking her money. Because Kay had been telling Don that Jessie was becoming confused, he dismissed these accusations as only imaginings on Jessie's part. He did not want to believe that Kay would steal from her aunt and, thus, he ignored Jessie's complaints. When he asked Kay about these accusations she brushed them off with, "Jessie must be even worse than I had thought. She is sounding like a crazy person."

All of the family members were under stress that spring, particularly Kate who harbored fear that her family was splintering and she was powerless to stop it. Wanting to see her sister, Mother accompanied me to Curwensville where I was meeting to help plan my class reunion. We first went to Kay's home for Mother to visit with Kay. Returning from my meeting, I found our mother visibly upset. Uncomfortable because of the unresolved questions regarding Mother's furnishings that were blatantly displayed in Kay's home, I quickly escorted her to the car. She said to me, "It was hard seeing my things in that house."

Once in the car, I began driving in the direction of Jessie's house when Mother said, "Kay doesn't think I should see Jessie. She told me that I wouldn't want to see her as it would upset me." I asked, "Are you sure you don't want to go?" "Yes," she replied. "Kay was so insistent that I shouldn't go that I'm too upset right now. Let's just go home." Concerned at Mother's evident stress, I turned around and we returned to Hummelstown without stopping to see Jessie.

Kay used this incident against Mother when a week later she telephoned to report that a neighbor of Jessie's had said that it was rumored that "Jessie's sister was in town and didn't even stop to visit her." We couldn't imagine who would have known this and who would have made such a comment. To our knowledge Kay was the only person who knew that Mother was in Curwensville that day.

At this time Kay began to keep a journal consisting of negative comments about Jessie as well as a running account of her own visits to Jessie, including details of making a trip to the cemetery "to check if Jessie had a burial lot." An entry for June 10 expressly states that "Mother and Judi were here. Didn't stop to see Jessie." Evidently Kay wanted a record of that event on that date, but did not want to record that she herself had convinced Mother not to visit Jessie. She also mentions on July 3 that she had talked to Sharon Welker at the Curwensville State Bank regarding Jessie's Certificates of Deposit.

Mother and I later realized how naïve we had been and how we likely had been duped. As Mother said, "We just weren't accustomed to devious ploys. It didn't occur to any of us that it must have been Kay herself who had told the neighbor of my visit to Curwensville. She wanted to make it seem that no one except she herself cared about Jessie."

Later that month, Kay made a trip to Hummelstown to again discuss what to do with Jessie. Kay's solution was to, as she termed it, "get rid of the problem" by placing Jessie in a nursing home. She made fun of Jessie, imitating her actions, and mimicking the conversations between them. We were uncomfortable with Kay's demonstrations because the mimicry was unkind and the Jessie we had last seen was not the silly, incompetent person that Kay was caricaturizing.

At Kay's insistence, more extended conversations took place among the five of us concerning care that might be available for Jessie. We did agree that perhaps "the rainy day" Jessie had so prudently planned for was soon arriving. We discussed the possibilities of assisted living homes in the Hummelstown or Curwensville area, arrangements for Jessie to remain in her own home with assistance, or installing a mobile home for Jessie next to Mother's cottage. We further discussed the advantages of Jessie's living close to her sister compared to the advantages of remaining close to her friends in Curwensville. All except Kay agreed to do everything possible to keep Jessie in her own home. Becoming increasingly wary of Kay's resistance, I said to Nan, "I think we should notify Attorney Cortez Bell." That I did not call him came back to haunt me.

Kay was not pleased with our intense expression of support for keeping Jessie in her own home; however, she did not argue with us as much as usual. At that time, Jo Ellen, Nan, and I knew nothing of Jessie's Will.

Seemingly resigned, Kay agreed to make arrangements for assistance for Jessie. However, she first met with her attorney to name herself as power of attorney (POA) for Jessie. Kay's attorney never met Jessie nor did ever he speak with her by telephone. All communication regarding Jessie was through Kay alone. Kay took the document to Jessie to sign on July 6, 1990,[4] three days before her 85th birthday, explaining in her journal, "Jessie signed POA after I explained what I could do for her." However, the POA document was not filed at the Clearfield County court house until four months later while Kay was in Alabama.

On July 9 Kay wrote in her journal that on Jessie's birthday she took her a cake, a meal, presents, and a card; she also added, "No cards received from family." (This is not true in fact, but is what Kay recorded.)

On July 10 Kay presented the POA order, which had not yet been filed with the court, to Sharon Welker at the Curwensville State Bank in preparation for transferring Jessie's assets. On July 27 Kay wrote that she had criticized Jessie for falling asleep in her chair in front of the television. On the following day Kay noted that Jessie told her she had applied as a substitute teacher, but what Kay didn't record is that there was a media announcement concerning the shortage of substitute teachers and that likely Jessie thought it her duty to offer to help (or perhaps it was Kay who made the comment to Jessie that she should apply).

Kay also arranged for Jessie's mail to be forwarded to her, after convincing the Curwensville postmaster that she was taking care of paying Jessie's bills.[5] Thus, the cards and packages that other family members sent to Jessie went to Kay who did not give them to Jessie. As an indicator of how little she understood human nature, Kay made a comment in her journal that Jessie was "very unappreciative of my help and continues to snap at me for no reason."[6] While it is impossible to know what Kay thought she was getting into when she encouraged her mother to leave Curwensville and promised to take care of Jessie, it is likely that she thought the process would be much easier than the daily care and responsibility turned out to be.

Between July and September of that year, Kay transferred virtually all of Jessie's assets to herself. Notable was the transaction of July 16 at which time Kay cashed in a Curwensville State Bank Certificate of Deposit in Jessie's name for $100,000 and subsequently purchased another one at Keystone National Bank in her own name only. Incurring a penalty did not seem to be a concern to her as she acquired further penalties in September when she cashed in two additional Certificates totaling more than $113,000. This money she also placed in accounts in her name only. Following these transactions, Jessie's remaining assets included (1) a joint checking account with a balance of $25,625.62 on August 30, 1990 and a balance of only $59.88 by April 1991[7]; (2) an irrevocable Burial Fund; (3) 360 shares of Penn Laurel stock in the joint names of Kay and Jessie[8]; (4) a gift of $6,000 to Bob Walker on August 23, 1990, allegedly used to purchase a camp site at Glendale; and (5) a gift of $10,000 to Kay herself on September 5, 1990.

A scrap of paper later found in Jessie's desk drawer provides evidence that on the day after Kay transferred $100,000 from Jessie's CD account to her own, Jessie was adding a column of figures, which she had clearly written in her own distinctive handwriting, "as of July 19, 1990." It is possible she was trying to account for some of her funds and was beginning to conclude that her earlier suspicions were well founded.

Kay then began suggesting to others that Jessie had Alzheimer's disease and that she herself would be making all arrangements for Jessie's care. On August 27 she took Jessie to a doctor's appointment where she also suggested that her aunt was suffering from Alzheimer's. Kay noted in her journal that she requested the doctor to sign to put Jessie in a nursing home, but that he declined.

In late September Kay invited cousin Don Bloom to her home, telling him what plans she had made regarding Jessie's care and requesting him to keep an eye on Jessie while she wintered again in Alabama.[9] Kay further told Don that her mother and sisters were in agreement with all the arrangements Kay was making. In truth, we were not. Kay then handed Don an obituary notice she had written for Jessie with all the pertinent information except the date of death and date of funeral services, "just in case you need it."

In October Kay asked her attorney to prepare a deed for the Thompson Street property to be transferred from Jessie to Kate. The immediate net gain for Kay was the money Jessie had paid her for the house on the first sale and the assurance that it would again be hers upon the death of her mother. Kay also drew up a lease making Jessie responsible for all taxes on the property. Later, Kay's attorney admitted upon deposition that there was essentially an "*intent by his own client to defraud*" regarding the inheritance tax.[10]

Also in October Jessie told her nephew Don that Kay was

stealing from her. Don told Jessie he didn't believe that to be so, but if it were, then Jessie's bank statements would reflect those transactions. Jessie then went to the Curwensville State Bank to review her accounts and asked the head teller—incidentally Kay's best friend—to cancel Kay's purchase of the Glendale property. Jessie also told several other people that Kay had stolen $6,000 from her to buy this property.

Kay had already talked to those persons she thought Jessie might turn to, telling them that Jessie might come to them with outlandish stories and accusations against her and that they should pay no attention. In addition, on October 25 Kay talked to Attorney Bell, noting that if Jessie did find someone to take her to his office, Mr. Bell should not meet with her as she (Kay) had power of attorney.[11]

Nan and I asked Jo Ellen, to whom Kay was still speaking, to relay our concerns to our sister. This she did, returning with the response that Kay made it very clear that she alone was going to make the decisions regarding their aunt. More alarming, however, was the question Kay had asked Jo Ellen, "Are you going to the hearing?"—a hearing regarding Jessie which at that point no one except Kay knew had been scheduled.

By mid-October Jessie herself began in earnest to seek help and asked several townspeople to take her to her lawyer, but the groundwork Kay had laid now thwarted that attempt. As Kay noted, "I talked to Joe Errigo who told me Jessie asked him, Chet, Loretta, and Peg Hamilton to take her to see Cortez Bell. All of them refused as they know her condition."[12] Kay also had taken the keys to Jessie's car so Jessie could not drive herself to the attorney. By late October Kay, assured she had Jessie's life totally in her control, departed for Alabama.

On the first of November Jessie called her good friend, Jean Boyce, "Jean, will you take me to see Cort Bell? Kay tricked me. She told me she needed me to sign some papers having to do with my taxes and that she needed to be able to write checks to pay my bills. But Kay took my money, at least $6,000 that I am sure of."[13] Jean wondered why her friend was whispering, discovering later that Mrs. Hamilton (the neighbor who apparently reported Jessie's activities to Kay) was in Jessie's house in an adjoining room. Jean agreed to help her, and after further discussion, they went to the bank and asked for Jessie's bank statements.[14]

Jean then drove Jessie to Mr. Bell's office where Jessie told him that she wanted to name her nephew Don Bloom as her power of attorney; Jessie also told Mr. Bell that as far as she knew she had not given power of attorney to anyone else. He suggested to both ladies that Jessie first ask Mr. Bloom if he would be willing to serve in this capacity. Jean and Jessie then went directly to Don's house and discussed the matter with him, telling him they did not believe that Kay was "doing right by Jessie."[15]

Prior to this visit Don had thought Jessie's charges against Kay were exaggerated, but he listened carefully to his aunt sitting in his living room as she unfolded her tale and her fears that Kay had taken advantage of her. Jean told Don that they had scheduled an appointment for November 7 at which time Mr. Bell would meet with the three of them: Jessie, Jean, and Don.

The day after this unexpected visit from his Aunt Jessie and Jean Boyce, Don telephoned Kay to ask her opinion on sharing a joint power of attorney for Jessie.[16] According to Don, Kay's reaction was one of anger and she warned Don to not agree to help Jessie. She added that she would be in contact with her own lawyer if Don tried to interfere.

By the end of the phone conversation Don resolved he would keep his promise to Jessie. He called Mr. Bell, confirming the appointment for November 7. Mr. Bell then shared with Don that he had received several calls from Kay advising him that Jessie had Alzheimer's and had been making untrue accusations against her.

The following day Kay wrote in her journal, "I had a restraining order placed against Jean Boyce."[17] Thus, Jessie's ally was not going to be permitted to see her. On this same date Kay wrote to Jo Ellen, casting herself as the victim of Jessie's accusations. Excerpts from a letter Kay wrote to Jo Ellen include, "Seems Jessie is asking everyone to take her to Clearfield to the lawyers, including Chet. So far no one will take her."

On November 5 Jean Boyce (evidently not knowing she was to be served with a restraining order) called Jessie to arrange to pick her up to go to the bank and get copies of her bank statements. While this conversation was in progress, Peg Hamilton, the neighbor who seemed to report to Kay, appeared and took the telephone out of Jessie's hands. Mrs. Hamilton then spoke to Jean, suggesting that she stay out of this family matter. (Jean later described an earlier incident when she had called to offer to take Jessie to the bank and Mrs. Hamilton was listening in on the conversation.)[18]

By the time Jean Boyce arrived to pick Jessie up the house was locked and appeared to be empty. Jean hurried to the bank in case Jessie had gone there without waiting for her. Jessie was not there, so Jean returned to the house and then next door to Mrs. Hamilton's house. Mrs. Hamilton told Jean that she had no idea where Jessie might be. Jean then began a systematic search of any places Jessie might have gone and finally found her at the beauty shop where, it was later shown, Mrs. Hamilton herself had taken her.

Jean and Jessie then went to the bank and requested an accounting of Jessie's bank statements. The head teller (Kay's best friend, it will be recalled) suggested that the two women return later in the day and that she would have the documents ready for them. (Shortly after they left the bank, Kay had word from the bank that the two women had been there.) Upon their return trip to the bank they were given the materials which they then took to Don Bloom who quickly realized there was very little money in Jessie's account.

According to her own journal, that same day Kay called her attorney and asked him to start proceedings for legal guardianship of Jessie. She then called her mother to tell her that Jessie and Jean Boyce had an appointment scheduled with Cortez Bell. Kay, however, did not reveal that Don Bloom was also included in this meeting. Rather, Kay told her mother that she was calling to warn her that Jean was using undue influence on Jessie and that Jean previously had tried to bilk another elderly person in town. Kay then added that this information came from her (Kay's) own attorney.[19]

"Jessie needs to be rescued from the clutches of Jean before it is too late," Kay told her mother. Mother, alarmed, not aware of Don's involvement, and believing yet another plausible story from Kay, asked her daughter, "Should we go get Jessie and bring her here?"

Continuing with instructions to her mother, Kay emphasized that it was imperative for Jessie to keep a doctor's appointment in Clearfield before leaving for Hummelstown. Mother called Nan, asking her to take her to Curwensville the following day to rescue Jessie from Jean Boyce. By then, Kay was on the phone talking to Jessie's doctor, not only to change Jessie's appointment to November 6 from its previously scheduled date of November 19 but also to try to convince him of the urgency to diagnose her aunt incompetent.

Nan arranged to take time from work and left early in the morning with Mother and headed for Curwensville. Neither of them had any idea that Kay had talked to Don or that Don was expecting to accompany his aunt to her attorney.

Jessie was surprised to see her sister Kate when she arrived but told her she could not go to Hummelstown with her as she had an appointment with Mr. Bell the following day. This revelation only confirmed in Kate's mind what Kay had told her about Jean Boyce. Jessie didn't protest further when her sister began to help her pack for a visit to Hummelstown. They left Curwensville without further notice to anyone except Peg Hamilton, who waved them off with a smile.

In Clearfield Kate accompanied her sister into the doctor's examining room, a not unusual practice given that Mother had accompanied her to medical appointments numerous times throughout the years. In the examining room Kate did not discuss her sister's situation nor did the doctor share with her his previous day's conversation with Kay. Mother later told Nan that the doctor hesitated to diagnose Jessie as possibly incompetent.

In the end, however, the doctor signed the papers, likely because of Kay's earlier painting such a bleak picture of Jessie's condition both by phone and in person on other visits. It is also probable that seeing both Jessie's sister and a second niece with her confirmed Kay's remarks to him that the family was working together in the best interest of Jessie. (There is evidence that prior to this appointment of November 6 that this same doctor had declined requests to find Jessie incompetent.[20])

One final action Kay took this day was to instruct her attorney to file both the Power of Attorney she had earlier drawn up and to record the deed to the Thompson Street property, transferring it from Jessie to Kate.

The following day, Jean Boyce, unaware of the events of the previous day, arrived at Jessie's home to take her to the office of Cortez Bell, as previously arranged. The house was locked. Jean rapped at both the front and back doors, calling out Jessie's name. Alarmed, she got back in her car and headed straight for Don Bloom's home. They spent the next several hours searching for Jessie. Don had a key to Jessie's house so they were able to search the house, but could find no trace of Jessie or any clue as to where she might be. Don then called his friend Attorney David Ammerman who called Peg Hamilton. It was she who revealed that Jessie was "with her sister in Hummelstown."[21]

Results might have been different if Don had called Mother, but he didn't and she knew nothing of Jessie's plea to Don to help her. If she had known, she would not have interfered. Likewise, once Don heard that Jessie was with her sister he assumed all was well and that Jessie would be in good hands.[22]

Also on this same long day Mr. Bell received a telephone call from Larry Seaman, Kay's attorney, who told him that Jessie was with her sister and would not be keeping her appointment with Mr. Bell. In turn, Mr. Bell called Mother to try to find out what had happened to his client and to ask how she was doing. Much to her later regret, Mother, still thinking Jean Boyce was a threat, told Mr. Bell that the visit of Jessie to her sister in Hummelstown had been pre-arranged.

In any event, Jessie was in Hummelstown where she remained for three weeks during which time she gained the weight she earlier had lost. Her thoughts wandered occasionally, enough for Mother, Nan, and me to accept that some help for Jessie needed to be arranged; however, all in all, we found her improved condition encouraging. Recalling that Jessie always was a bit careless in her housekeeping, the fact that Kay described her home as "messy" was not particularly worrisome. The main concern of the family was that help be arranged for Jessie on a daily basis.

During the three weeks of Jessie's visit, conversation periodically focused on her return to Curwensville and assistance with her housekeeping, grocery shopping, and meals. These discussions were held to help Jessie become accustomed to the fact that someone would be there in her home every day. Jessie was to return to her home as soon as Kay finalized the arrangements for Patty Walker to come in daily to tend to Jessie's needs.

Here's That Rainy Day They Told Me About

Further discussion of nursing homes also continued, but neither Nan nor I believed a nursing home was at this time the best option for Jessie. On the other hand, Kay, still in Alabama, never missed an opportunity to try to persuade us that a nursing home would be the easiest solution. We asked, "Easiest for whom?"

I remained adamant that Jessie remain in her own home, arguing, "That is what Jessie wants and has the means for. When the time comes that she can no longer be maintained in her own home, then we can talk about nursing homes." This resistance angered Kay who consistently came back with her readied response, "Then maybe you would like to take care of her."[23]

What Nan and I did not know was that the position we held was meaningless because Kay had been making plans to deposit Jessie into a nursing home without telling us. On November 12 she wrote to Mother,

> *Talked to DuBois Nursing Home today. They have room now. They said it was a good time to get in as people usually kept them over the holidays and January got busy....*
>
> *I'll be glad to get this behind me and get on with my retirement. Will leave for Calif. when this is over. My legal address is Pennsylvania for the power of attorney....*
>
> *Shall I go ahead and plan on DuBois or do you want her down there? She cannot stay alone and she won't have anyone stay with her....*
>
> *I didn't want to put her away either, but there is no choice now....*

Even years later, the letter stands on its coldness, and at the time Mother received this letter she stuck it in a drawer. She didn't know what to do. It was all too much for her to absorb or sort out in the midst of this turmoil in her family.

Kate wanted what was best for her sister, but found herself in a quandary based on her mistrust of Kay's judgment and a lingering apprehension she retained from an earlier conversation with Kay. At that time she had asked her daughter, "Well, what would you do with me if I were the one in Jessie's situation? I don't have the kind of savings and retirement that Jessie does." Kay's reply froze Kate's heart as she heard her oldest daughter's response, "That's what County Homes are for."

On Saturday, November 17 Kay tried one last time to convince me that a nursing home would be the best choice for Jessie. Shortly into the telephone conversation I stopped her, "Kay, you just can't do this. You promised Jessie, and we all agreed that she could remain at home with help."

"What you don't understand," said Kay, "is that I'm tired of arranging help for her and the sooner we get her placed, the sooner the state will start paying after 30 months. If I spend the money for someone to come to the house, then I'll still have to pay the 30 months in the nursing home before the state takes over."

"But, Kay, that is why Jessie saved her money. You know she always referred to 'a rainy day.' Well, that rainy day has come and she has the money for her own care in her home for now, and then later in a nursing home if that is needed. She *planned* for her own care. We need to honor that."

"Don't be a fool," Kay replied. "That's what the government is for. Why should we spend all of her money for home assistance? There won't be any left."

I could hardly speak without my voice breaking, "But it is Jessie's own money and should be spent for the best care whatever the situation. It is up to us to honor her wishes. The state should not bear the burden of those able to pay. It simply is wrong. Jessie intended her savings to be spent for her care. And, as you well know, private payers are treated with more respect." Kay noted this conversation in her journal, "Judi doesn't think it right to hide money from the state."[24]

Kay was laughing at me but the laughter soon turned to anger, as she responded with her favorite phrase, "Then you can take care of her." She added, "I have had enough."

It was also during this extended visit in Hummelstown that Jessie told Mother that Kay had taken $6,000 from her, but had promised to pay it back. Jessie further said that she had earlier given Kay several thousand dollars "to help with Bob's medical expenses." When Mother questioned Kay during a later telephone conversation, she admitted that she had convinced Jessie that she couldn't afford the expense of Bob's surgery, not revealing to Jessie that she had already persuaded Bob's doctor to accept what Bob's insurance covered as payment in full.

In one final telephone conversation with our older sister, Nan and I reiterated that we all had been in agreement that Jessie would return to her home and that Kay was to arrange for someone to take care of Jessie's needs on a daily basis. As we were to discover later, that reminder, like all the others, was ignored.

In the meantime on November 20 Kay had received guardianship papers for Jessie, signed them, and returned them to her attorney by Federal Express so that a hearing could be held as soon as possible. Copies had been sent to Jessie as well. When we discovered this, we protested. Kay then canceled the hearing and took a flight north, not pleased to have to return to Curwensville in mid-November. Unknown to us until much later, her first stop was the DuBois Medical Center.

On November 26 Kay called Mother to make arrangements for Jessie to be returned from Hummelstown to her home in Curwensville, emphasizing that the date of return "must be the 28th because it is the only date that works for Aunt Ruth whose car I am using. Let's meet in Lewistown. Ruth will be nice company for Jessie on the way back."

On the morning of November 28 Jessie left under the care of my husband Wally to meet Kay and Bob's Aunt Ruth. As Wally had not previously met Aunt Ruth, he did not know that the person accompanying Kay was not Ruth, but Mrs. Hamilton, the next-door neighbor who, it seemed, had been reporting any visitors to Jessie's home. Wally placed Jessie in Kay's care, fully trusting that Jessie was being taken home.

Kay did not take Jessie to her home as promised. Rather, she drove her directly to the Psychiatric Unit of the DuBois Regional Medical Center. Jessie was admitted on a Section 302 (involuntary) commitment and an evaluation began that very day. Jessie, eighty-five years old, had just traveled four hours, thinking she was going home, and instead, was *committed* without any notice to either Jessie herself or to those who had been caring for her. Without any rest or explanation, she was subjected to a battery of tests. There was no adjudication; rather, Kay used her recently filed power of attorney and signed the permission for these tests to be done on her aunt, using Mrs. Hamilton as a witness to the condition of Jessie's life at 408 Thompson Street.

At the Medical Center Jessie's blood pressure was recorded as 170/90. (On November 6 it had been 120/68). Kay later described Jessie that day as "...just like a caged animal," a description none of us could ever forget, for we saw this as Kay's heartless attitude of disregard for Jessie as a human being.

On November 30, the attending physician recorded Jessie's involuntary admittance, "Initial evaluation revealed a well-nourished, pleasant and cooperative lady who minimized any need for inpatient treatment, expressing only minor household concerns. Upon further evaluation, however, it became apparent that Jessie is disoriented especially with regard to time/date. She suffers from impairment of her recent memory while her remote memory appears for the most part intact ... it is apparent that she can no longer be expected to manage her own affairs and *could easily be taken advantage of by designing people.* In conclusion it is my recommendation that guardianship be considered to manage her affairs."

The physical examination of Jessie revealed a remarkably healthy woman. When asked why she was being examined, Jessie replied, "My niece brought me up here and I am not sure why." The medical history the physician had in hand of Jessie's family included that she had a sister who predeceased her and a younger sister who was in apparently good health. On the report in Kay's handwriting is the erroneous information that two additional sisters had died of senile dementia. Further evaluations by a psychologist recommended for Jessie a more structured environment with increased supervision as "it is recommended that she no longer be expected to manage her daily affairs independent of assistance from others." It does *not* recommend a nursing home or any other closed facility.

It was later discovered that while Jessie was in Hummelstown Mrs. Hamilton had filed the 302 commitment and admitted the county mental health workers to Jessie's home. In addition, the inspectors were given a *report written by Kay* describing the *alleged* "terrible condition" of the home. Friends and family who had visited Jessie declared later that they never saw the condition of the house the way Kay reported. In particular, Jean Boyce testified that whenever she visited Jessie the house reflected nothing out of the ordinary.

Nonetheless, a hearing officer/public defender was called upon to determine Jessie's fate when Kay asked for a hearing to hold Jessie in the DuBois facility for an additional 20 days. No one told any other members of Jessie's family of this hearing or even that Jessie was in DuBois. Instead, Kay spoke on behalf of Jessie's family saying she would notify all of them. However, she did not. She simply returned to Curwensville, telling everyone that Jessie had been deemed incompetent. This was a complete untruth. There was no adjudication of incompetence, despite Kay's efforts to get that term included in the findings.

Near the end of the additional 20-day confinement, Jessie was given her choice of residences, Curwensville Nursing Home or Mt. Laurel. In what must have been a plaintive, lonely voice, Jessie responded, "I want to go to my sister's." This plea was ignored. Two days later Jessie was again given two choices, even more frightening to her: Curwensville Nursing Home or *Warren*, the dreaded Warren which, along with *Ridgway*, resonated to Jessie's frame of reference as "state mental ward."

On December 7, Kay admitted Jessie to the Curwensville Nursing Home, taking her directly there from the hospital, with no stopping at her home. Kay's journal notes, "Signed Jess in at 9:00 a.m. and went downtown to inform people," in essence taking a victory lap.

As Kay had left me with harsh words the previous time we spoke, I did not think it odd not to hear from her regarding Aunt Jessie. Presumably Kay talked to Mother during early December but as far as we knew Jessie was in her own home and Kay had found someone to assist her.

What Nan and I could not have known, however, was the fate that had befallen Jessie, and we continued with our plans to visit her at her home. I called Kay to tell her that Mother, Nan, and I would be coming to see Jessie. "She isn't home," Kay informed me.

"What do you mean, she isn't home?" I asked, feeling sick in the pit of my stomach. I will never forget that moment as I sat on a red stool in the kitchen, holding the receiver of the red wall phone in my left hand.

"She was committed to DuBois Mental Hospital."

"When? Why didn't you call? How did this happen? Is she OK?"

"She's fine," Kay said, ignoring the other questions.

"Why was she admitted?"

"Well, they ruled that she is incompetent."

"How could they do that, just like that? People aren't just picked up and taken to …."

"I took her; someone had to do it. She isn't competent to take care of herself. Besides, what value is her life? She's no good to anyone."

"How can you say that? It is morally wrong to say a person has no value. She should be treated with respect for having lived her life, for being a person, for being your aunt and Mother's sister. You have no right to judge her. We should be looking out for her best interests. I can't believe you did this. How could you just take her like that?"

"Because she can't take care of herself. You had a chance to find a nursing home for her and didn't, so I did what needed to be done."

"We were coming to see her this week-end. Where is this hospital anyhow? Is it in DuBois? How do we get there?"

"She isn't there now. There was a hearing and she was sent to Curwensville Nursing Home."

"Just like that?"

"Just like that."

"I didn't think it was allowed against someone's will."

"I can do anything I want with her because I have power of attorney. And in case you didn't know this either, we can stop worrying. Jessie does have a Will. I made sure of that. For the record, she is in the nursing home on my order and will stay there unless I decide otherwise."

I could not believe that my sister would have taken these steps.

My heart sank. "Kay, "this is wrong. You can't do this."

"Well, I did. It was either send her to a nursing home or commit her to Warren."

I was sickened that Jessie—and all of us—had been deceived in a matter of such consequence. I found it unconscionable that one person could make decisions for another so abruptly, especially for a person like Jessie who had trusted her family.

After hearing the stomach-turning news about Aunt Jessie, Nan called Kay to get more information. Following the call she turned to me, "Kay took Jessie to DuBois the same day she picked her up in Lewistown. I can't believe this. She lied to us. She promised us she would take Jessie home and, instead, had her committed to a mental hospital. Oh, Judi, poor Jessie. Poor, poor soul. She thought she was going home and she was whisked off to be committed. I wonder what the poor soul thought. This was all a set-up. Kay had to have planned this, don't you think? So that is why she insisted that Wally meet her on the 28th. He is really going to be upset."

And he was. A person of his word, Wally had told Jessie she would be going home with Kay after they met in Lewistown that Wednesday morning. It bothered him greatly that he had been used and had, unwittingly, delivered Jessie to her ultimate fate. All felt duped and, worse, betrayed.

Several days later Kay told her Uncle Chet (Don Bloom's father) that Jessie was in the Curwensville Nursing Home. Chet, not well himself, accepted the news with some resignation. He likely assumed that all of Kate's daughters had decided together what would be best for Jessie and did not press Kay for details.

However, he dutifully visited his late wife's sister the next day, December 9, and Don went to see her the following day. Don, along with Lorraine, visited again on the 16th at which time Jessie told him, "Kay put me here." Jessie wanted to leave the facility and asked Don and Lorraine to take her home which, of course, they could not do. On the 19th when an old school friend, Virginia Murray Bloom visited Jessie, Jessie told her the same thing she had said to Don, "Kay put me here."

On that same day of Don's visit Kay called him to make sure that his father had told him where Jessie was and to provide more details. She explained that things were so bad with Jessie that she had had to come from Alabama to take her to the DuBois Mental Health Center.

She did not tell Don that her sisters knew nothing about this. Rather, she said nothing, allowing Don to make the assumption that "Kate and the girls" were all in agreement with this plan. She further explained that Jessie had spent approximately a week at DuBois being evaluated, that she had been adjudicated as incompetent,[25] and that the Mental Health Center had committed her to the Curwensville Nursing Home.

She then told him that she held power of attorney for her aunt and that Jessie had a Will. Kay further explained to Don that because both the power of attorney and the Will had been written before the declaration of incompetence, neither could be revoked. She assured him that the money was all accounted for, but that no one could get Jessie out of the nursing home. What Kay did *not* tell him, however, is that in mid-December she had transferred Penn Laurel stock to her name alone from the joint ownership in which she had placed Jessie's stock a few months earlier.

Don was surprised both at Kay's actions and her self-congratulatory tone. He was uneasy at what sounded to him like bragging about what she had done that could not be undone. While he didn't want to interfere he did begin to keep notes, as he sensed that something wasn't quite right. He did not believe that Jessie was incompetent.

Don next called his sister Janet Lynn as he wasn't comfortable enough with the situation to call Kate. He wasn't sure at this point who was deciding what. Janet Lynn told her brother that she felt sure that Nan and I were not involved in any wrongdoing against Jessie. Nonetheless, Don did tell Attorney David Ammerman that he had the impression that Kay had her mother under her thumb.

Later, in a telephone conversation Don told me, "Jessie is not contented in the nursing home. She is not really making it her home." He then related that he had been told by Rick Mattern, the hearing officer, that Attorney Larry Seaman and Kay had tried very hard to get the attending physician at DuBois to certify that Jessie was "incompetent," but that Mr. Mattern had held to his choice of "incapable." Mr. Mattern also told Don that Jessie was capable of remaining in her *own* home if someone could be there or check on her regularly.[26]

It was decided that Wally and I would make the first visit to Jessie on Christmas Eve and that Nan and I would go a few days later. Steeling myself as I entered the nursing home, I intuitively disliked the entire set-up, for that is what it was, a set-up. On the way home, my emotions ranged from indignation to sadness. "It's more than the fact that she is there against her will," I said through tears I could not contain, "When people in your life die, memories help you to cope; but when someone is placed in a nursing home, you watch them and the memories you have of them change from who they were to who they are in this setting. Jessie has no idea of how her life has changed permanently, unless we can help her get back home."

Three days later Nan and I went to visit our aunt. We found the duty staff with their guard up, watching our every move and reluctant to answer even the most basic questions regarding Jessie's care and condition.

When we were shown to Jessie's room, she seemed very happy

to see us, greeting us by name and asking where Kate was. Two factors were, however, very evident. First, we were struck by the Jessie we found. Rather than the vibrant woman who had spent three weeks with us less than a month before, this person behaved like an inmate. She was somewhat confused, mainly about why she was being held in a hospital, and she was not as physically strong as she had been in November. Jessie was also fully aware that she had been told she must stay in the nursing home until the doctor "signs the papers." While Nan and I were there, she looked, then asked at the desk, for the doctor so he could sign the papers for her to leave, but was told he was not on the premises.

Second, we were disturbed at the extent to which Kay had misrepresented the facility. She had painted a picture of comfort and gentility, describing "a lovely private room with a picture window and some of her own furniture," a far rosier scene that was the reality. Kay had told her sisters of a "smoking area," in actuality a chair outside Jessie's room adjacent to the nurse's station, as well as a lounge and dining hall (one and the same, as it turned out). What we saw was a typical hospital setting. Not that there is anything wrong with a nursing home being what it is, but we felt deceived in Kay's description of it and of her assurances that Jessie was happy there.

Before we left that afternoon Jessie asked me to help her. The plea was not the typical "get me out of here," but rather a mournful cry for help against an almost hopeless situation.

Two days later Nan and I visited Jo Ellen to discuss this latest turn of events. We told her what we knew, what we had seen at the Curwensville Nursing Home, and our discomfort with Kay's actions against Jessie. Jo Ellen confirmed that Kay had told her that she had drawn a gift of $10,000 for herself from Jessie's assets and that while Jo Ellen and Ken said such a gift was legal, it was a bit out of the ordinary. What was of even greater interest to Nan and me is that Jo Ellen had been led to believe that Nan and I, along with Mother, were in agreement as to the decisions made regarding Jessie.

Jo Ellen had known of Kay's plan to take Jessie to DuBois for an evaluation but had not known when it was scheduled and had no knowledge of the duplicity in not telling Nan and me. Kay had been assuring Jo Ellen that all of us approved Kay's plans for Jessie. Jo Ellen agreed to relay to Kay our anger and disappointment at her actions and deception.

On January 18, 1991, Mother, Nan, and I visited Jessie. We also had an opportunity to speak briefly with the house osteopathic physician who explained the steps leading to Jessie's placement. Everything he said to us was spoken in the *exact words* earlier used by Kay. What he parroted were incidents or situations not observed or observable by him, but rather stories Kay had told him. He repeated Kay's earlier words to us that Jessie might not know her upon her return from Alabama, where her legal and primary residence had been established.

Most important, the physician told us that there would be no reason why we could not take Jessie for visits to our home. He was aware that Jessie had no medical ailments and that the only medication she was taking was a single Senequan in the evening for sleeping. He also told us that Jessie would be fine in a less restrictive environment but that the nursing home was the best option in the immediate Curwensville area.

This bleak visit solidified our determination to try to get Jessie moved to a facility with less restrictive care. Again, Jessie became teary and did not want us to leave. Kate comforted her sister, "Judith and Nan will see what they can do about moving you."

The next morning I called Jo Ellen to report my observations regarding Jessie and the nursing home. Jo Ellen replied, "Kay asked me a lot of questions about the first visit Nan and you had made, but she didn't like the answers I gave her as to your assessment of the facility. As for your finding the doctor's answers unsatisfactory, Kay told me that the doctor had more information but didn't want to tell you. Kay insisted that Jessie is doing fine and that the court had placed Jessie in the home, not Kay herself. Finally, she firmly believes that uprooting Jessie at this time would be a mistake."

I asked Jo Ellen, "Why is Kay angry that we went up yesterday?"

Jo Ellen answered, "Kay is convinced that she is not being treated well by her family and she feels betrayed by Mother who, she believes, was supposed to prevent you and Nan from interfering. She is also very angry that you haven't called her yourself." Jo Ellen continued, "I don't think Kay is open to any discussion at this point. She insists she is in charge of things—and as Jessie's guardian I guess she is—and doesn't want anyone questioning her. You are going to have a hard time getting any cooperation."

The next day we discussed matters with Mother. I took notes, feeling the need to record all information on a situation that was escalating toward a family crisis. I was concerned, but not surprised, that Mother seemed to be confused by various conversations she had held with Kay, because there had been so many conflicting accounts of events. I was also puzzled by the fact that Mother had not shared with Nan and me the conversations she had had with Kay. Later, I understood that, of course, Mother had been placed in an impossible position. What was most troubling, however, was the possibility that Kay may have tried to make Mother an accomplice.

Late that same evening, Kay telephoned Mother to question her. "Why did Judi and Nan run up there?" she demanded of her mother. "I thought you had promised me to not visit Jessie until spring." Mother responded by asking Kay how she could admit Jessie to a nursing home without cause. Kay replied, "The hearing gave Jessie the choice of Curwensville Nursing Home or Warren." This information, as was discovered later, simply was not so.

Kay continued, "I did it the way I wanted to. Judi would not have agreed to placing Jessie, and I didn't want to deal with that." Kay ended the conversation with an order to her mother, "If Nan and she are going to do anything about the Jessie situation, I want you to tell me."

A week later, Mother received a letter from Kay in which Kay took her mother to task for choosing not to understand Jessie's situation. "I can see very clearly what all of you think of me. Everyone in Curwensville knows what I've gone through with Jessie. There was no other person to help or care.... Everything I have done regarding Jessie's affairs has been legal. Under no circumstance is Jessie to be removed from Curwensville Nursing Home."

Mother relayed this conversation to me, concluding by saying, "I am not sure I want to know what you are going to do about this. Maybe it is better I don't know so that if Kay asks me if you're doing anything I can say I don't know."

With this, I decided to seek legal advice. My attorney was able to ascertain that Jessie's house had been transferred to Kay in October 1990, that the Register of Wills in Clearfield County had no filing of adjudication of incompetence regarding Jessie, and that at some point Kay would have to give an accounting, even though it might not be until after Jessie's death.[27]

Family members continued to visit Jessie as often as we could despite the distance. I also periodically telephoned Aunt Jessie although conversations were difficult because Jessie did not have a telephone in her room. Her medical progress chart of February 6, 1991 noted, "… the patient still says she wants to go home."

Determined to maintain close family contact with Jessie, we decided to bring Jessie to Hummelstown for a visit on February 9, the week-end of Mother's birthday. That action, of course, infuriated Kay because we had not requested her permission, even though Mother and Nan each had earlier tried to call Kay for permission for Jessie to remain in Hummelstown for the week-end.

Jessie had been in her sister's cottage barely an hour when there was a call at 7:45 p.m. from the nursing home. Police Officer Mc Cullough demanded that Jessie be returned to the nursing home immediately. I asked to speak to the nursing supervisor who said Jessie had been taken from the premises illegally and that Jessie must be returned that night. I spoke again to the officer who said that if Jessie were not returned immediately there would be a charge of kidnapping against Mother. With that edict, of course, Jessie had to return.

My attorney contacted the nursing home, advising them that the determination of incompetence was being contested and would revoke the POA. She also offered to fax a letter indicating Jessie's wishes. This was not acceptable. She then talked to the facility's administrator who also said that Jessie must be returned or he would press charges. No one was able to convince anyone—supervisor, police, or administrator—that driving back in the middle of the night was not a safe decision. Regardless, Jessie had to be returned.

It didn't seem to matter that the nursing home physician had earlier told us, "There is no reason Jessie can't leave for visits to her sister." (This he later confirmed in a conversation with Attorney Beth Ammerman Gerg.) He further stated to Attorney Fred Ammerman that Jessie could be in a less restrictive facility, "...even in her own home with proper care."

According to Jessie's medical chart of February 9, 1991 there was nothing prohibiting visits, and, in fact, the chart noted, "... may have LOA with Family Members." It was not until March 28, 1991 (*after* the charge-of-kidnapping threat) that the order was changed to not allow visits, following a telephone call from Kay to the house physician.[28]

What mattered the evening of February 9 was the simple fact that Jessie had no rights of her own. Her life and all decisions were now controlled by Kay, and Jessie had to return to the nursing home that very evening. Wally and Joel left with Jessie at 9:00 p.m., making the six-hour round trip to Curwensville, returning Jessie in the middle of the night to the bleak facility. Jessie's fate appeared to have been sealed.

Chapter 13

In My End Is My Beginning

The cry for dignity is a cry for justice as much as an affirmation of meaning. That is why dignity in old age matters.

Harry H. Moody[1]

The tragedy of human life is that in old age a process occurs that is the opposite of that experienced by a growing child. Whereas over time the child acquires more and more autonomy, both physical and psychological, the elderly person over time exhibits less and less. In caring for a child, adults rejoice in each new adventure, in each new task learned. In contrast, aging adults frequently disremember tasks that at one time were routine and often feel embarrassed that they are unable to recall what once was almost automatic.

Many who knew Jessie before she entered the nursing home saw in her the friend they had known since childhood, the teacher they had loved, a deacon in the Presbyterian Church acknowledged by the congregation, or, perhaps, as the pleasant eccentric who invited friends to join her on the porch during the long days of summer. All showed her respect.

Once she became a resident at the Curwensville Nursing Home, however, Jessie, as all other residents, was viewed through a different lens. Staff called residents by their first names and referred to them in the same manner so that any visitors also soon used the familiar, rather than the more formal and respectful

"Mrs. Mohney" or even "Miss Pifer." This artificial friendliness is a diminution of personhood and reduces the nursing home residents to the status of children. In addition, using the residents' first names establishes a hierarchy in which the attendants carry the status and the residents lose their identity. Other than the notoriety that Mrs. Mohney/Miss Pifer initially held among the staff, residents, and visitors for the intrigue that seemed to be swirling around her, she, too, soon became just "Jessie" to friends and strangers, staff and residents alike.

While Jessie's forced return to the nursing home resulted in disappointment and discouragement, Kay's stance made it evident to what lengths she would go to prevent Jessie's reversing her power of attorney or the Will Kay had led her into signing. In fact, to prevent any possible action her sisters might take, Kay immediately made plans to return to Curwensville despite the fact that her husband was hospitalized. While she would later blame her family for her own choice in leaving Bob, her resolve to arrange for a hearing to declare Jessie incompetent overrode all else.

A week following the midnight return of Jessie to the Curwensville Nursing Home, Nan and I again went to visit our aunt to assure her of our continued efforts on her behalf. During that visit Jessie extracted a promise from me to help her (1) leave the Curwensville Nursing Home and (2) get out from under Kay's financial control and presumed control of her life. Such a promise was difficult for me to make under circumstances over which Jessie appeared to have little or no say, but looking at my aunt, I had to say, "Yes, I promise I will do everything in my power to get you out of here."

Shortly after this visit, Jo Ellen told me that she earlier had suggested to Kay to give Mother fair market price for the property at 410 Thompson Street rather than deed the house itself, but Kay had rejected the suggestion. Jo Ellen also remarked that she found it puzzling that Mother was acting natural towards Kay, despite the family impasse. What most bothered Jo Ellen, however, was a remark Kay had made earlier during a family discussion when we three younger sisters were discussing what arrangements we would make among ourselves should Mother ever require home care. None of us was surprised when we all, in turn, indicated that we already had made provisions in our own homes for Mother. However, when we asked Kay what she thought would be best, Kay's response stunned us all. Looking us straight in the eye, she said, "There are places for that. Let the state take care of her."[2] "This remark," Jo Ellen told her two sisters, "has led me to question the stories Kay has told me about helping Jessie."

Despite the family turmoil, Don and Lorraine Bloom remained very faithful in their visits to Jessie. On March 6 Lorraine, an R.N., wrote, "We saw her last evening and I was somewhat concerned about her condition. First, she seemed vague in her conversation and had very little energy. Second, her feet and ankles were quite swollen. I wanted to go to the desk and inquire of the nurses in regard to the swelling and whether the doctor visits her on a regular basis, but I hesitated to do that because I do not want to overstep my bounds on this matter...."[3]

Several days later, I telephoned Jessie who said to me, "I hope you're working on getting me out of here." Indeed, I was working on a solution to the dilemma and my attorney had already written to Kay's attorney to request permission for the family to have Jessie for week-end visits.[4]

On March 7 Kay's attorney responded, "Kay does not feel that it would be in the best interest of Jessie to have any visits off-premises.... It may be possible for such visitations at some future date and Kay will continue to do what she feels is in the best interest of Jessie. ... Kay has been providing her mother and sisters regular information on Jessie's medical condition and will continue to do so."[5]

With this response, I contacted my attorney, "Will you please represent my mother? We must get Jessie out of Curwensville and down here before it is too late."

Attorney Jean Seibert advised that an attorney in Clearfield be engaged to handle the case in Clearfield County and suggested contacting a law school classmate of hers, Beth Ammerman Gerg, in practice with and daughter of David Ammerman, long-standing friend and classmate of Don Bloom and known and trusted by our entire family. A few days later David Ammerman visited Jessie who assured him that she hadn't known what she was signing when she signed the papers naming Kay as her power of attorney. It was further determined that to have Jessie evaluated at the Hershey Medical Center and her assets returned to her, someone else, such as Nan, Mother, or I, would need to hold the power of attorney.

On March 25, Kay responded to Mother's request for information on Jessie's medical condition, suggesting that she contact the Curwensville Nursing Home directly, yet knowing full well the Nursing Home would give Mother no specific information. She signed her name simply, "Your daughter, Kay."[6]

The Attorneys Ammerman contacted Rick Mattern who confirmed that while the attending physician had advised keeping Jessie at DuBois Medical Center for 20 days, there had been no legal or medical determination made following her release. Further, Jessie had been found to be "*incapable,*" not "incompetent" as Kay had claimed, and had been released to "her family." It was also confirmed that it was not the DuBois Medical Center who had committed Jessie to a nursing home as Kay had contended, but Kay herself who had made the decision.[7]

I made another visit on April 7 to see Jessie. The air was thick with the unspoken question, "Why can't I leave?" It was becoming more difficult to explain to Jessie why she could not leave the nursing home, as it didn't seem possible that a resident could be held prisoner. The following day, Attorney Gerg suggested that a videotape be made of a general conversation with Jessie to demonstrate her capabilities. I voiced my concern that a videotape seemed so contrived. However, following a conversation later that afternoon with Jean Seibert, I agreed that a taping of Jessie signing a new power of attorney would be acceptable to show that Jessie was not being coerced, but rather wanted a change of her power of attorney.[8]

Close to three weeks after our March conversation, I again spoke to Don Bloom at which time he noted that Jessie is "the only one able to get around independently at the nursing home." What bothered him was the nagging feeling that something simply wasn't right. He commented, "There is no reason for Kay's actions." More important was his forethought when he added, "There'll be a time that another voice will be needed. You can count on me."[9]

On April 11 Attorneys Beth Gerg Ammerman and David Ammerman visited Jessie to review with her the document assigning me as Power of Attorney. While the Ammermans were in her room, one of the staff placed a telephone call to Kay, reporting the presence of the attorneys.[10]

Shortly thereafter Kay's attorney called the nursing home director requesting an immediate evaluation of Jessie regarding her "mental status and level of appropriateness." The house physician did as requested and wrote, "The patient is unable to make appropriate decisions in her [own] best interests."[11] This was just what Kay had ordered. (It should be noted that the physician's comments for this date are very detailed. No such elaboration was found in any other evaluations of Jessie conducted by this physician.)

The following day the Ammermans called me to say that during their visit with Jessie she had read the documents carefully, asked questions, and seemed to know what she was signing. At

2:45 I spoke to the nursing home administrator, who was upset because Jessie was packing her clothes. Upon being questioned, Jessie had said to him, "I need to be ready to leave as soon as my sister comes for me." The administrator added, "We will not recognize the new POA as we already have Kay's on record." I reminded him there had been no independent medical review and no adjudication for Jessie's placement and that the nursing home never should have admitted Jessie on Kay's order, but he still refused.

Two days later I wrote to Kay, "To not allow Jessie to leave the nursing home even for a visit is reprehensible. We are heartsick, Kay, at your disregard for Jessie's own wishes and the callousness of your response to our request to bring her here to her own sister's home for a visit. ...you led many people in Curwensville to believe that you were speaking for all of us in your decisions regarding Jessie and that was wrong.... Have you thought what it must be like to be kept confined in that bleak room and to know that your future has been determined by someone else and that you have no hope of ever leaving?"[12]

A day or two later, Jo Ellen confirmed that Kay knew about the attorneys' visit to the nursing home because one of the nurses had called her. Kay also told Jo Ellen that their aunt was "wired" with a beeper so that an alarm would go off if she left the premises.[13]

On April 16 the lines were drawn with the Curwensville Nursing Home when Beth Gerg wrote to the director, asking for a written refusal to honor the new POA or to provide the medical evidence for not honoring it. I asked Jessie's other nieces and nephews to support my challenge to Kay who "has not acted in the best interests of Aunt Jessie. We are trying to remedy what we consider to be a moral wrong and to make Jessie's last years more pleasant and comfortable."[14]

I learned from the cousins' responses that John Wayne (Johnny, Jessie's favorite nephew) had visited Jessie two years earlier. During that visit, Kay and Bob arrived. John later said he sensed something wasn't quite right, but he let it go. He continued to telephone Jessie periodically, but after about a year she didn't answer; shortly thereafter Jessie's telephone was disconnected. Because he himself had crippling arthritis, John asked his daughter Lisa to write to Jessie. Jessie never received the letter; it had been forwarded to Kay who responded to Lisa, assuring her that all was well with Jessie.

On April 22 the President of the Curwensville State Bank mailed me a letter noting revocation of Kay's POA and acknowledgement of the new POA that I now held. The *same day* the head teller at the bank transferred most of the remaining funds from Jessie's checking account to one in Kay's name only.

April 22 also brought the news that the director of the nursing home had been dismissed. With this came the agreement that the nursing home now would recognize the new POA. The following day, April 23, Nan and I went to Curwensville to sign Jessie out for an extended visit. We found her in a barren room where she was sitting at a utility table, slumped in a straight-back metal institutional chair. Her appearance and demeanor confirmed what I had read, that "it is difficult to hold on to one's own sense of self and to one's own dignity when all around there is no affirmation of oneself as a person."[15] I was chilled as I realized that Jessie was becoming one of the invisibles. We spoke her name, "Aunt Jessie?"

Hope resumed when she looked up and, breaking into a smile of recognition, stood up and walked into our open arms. We quickly packed her suitcase and left for Hummelstown. Later we discovered that on the same day, Kay was notifying the Curwensville State Bank to withdraw the remainder of Jessie's account, having the money wired to her in Alabama. She was taking no chance of losing even the final $400.

Once Jessie was settled in the cottage in Hummelstown, I took her to a geriatrics specialist who was skeptical of Kay's contention that Jessie was suffering from advanced Alzheimer's disease. In his opinion, Jessie could do well with what he called an assisted living environment..

During her extended visit Jessie continued to say that Kay had borrowed money from her and that it was time to start paying back. She specifically said to her sister, "Oh, Kate, I'm sorry I believed Kay. I didn't know what she was having me sign. She tricked me."

Kay, however, was not yet ready to give up. Losing power of attorney only made her more determined to keep Jessie's assets and she filed for guardianship, insisting she had transferred Jessie's money for safe keeping.

During an earlier telephone conversation in mid-April, Don Bloom had told me, "Personally I think Kay is being foolish." He assured me he would be very willing to testify in a hearing. Later he said, "Kay told me some time ago that she took Jessie to Cortez Bell to draw a Will, but that on the way Jessie had changed her mind, so Kay took her home and suggested that her aunt dictate a Will to her." He laughed as he added, "Kay also happened to have a tape recorder with her."

A few weeks later we spoke again, Don saying he preferred I take the guardianship, but that he would take Jessie for any appointments she might have locally. He revealed that Jessie had been telling him for the past year that Kay was stealing from her and that in the fall of 1990 he had asked Attorney David Ammerman to review Jessie's bank statements as he feared the worst in what Jessie had told him about the theft.

Through all of this talk about money and CDs and Wills, my

main concern was that no one lose sight of the reason I had agreed to pursue the matter of Jessie. I wrote to David Ammerman, "No human being should be regarded as an object to be 'put away' once 'usefulness' to society has passed. Jessie's savings, in her own words, are 'for a rainy day'"[16] And the only way to assure an accounting of Kay's handling of the estate was to hold the temporary guardianship hearing.

Now fully realizing that Jean Boyce had been helping Jessie and not, as Kay presented, interfering because of ulterior motives, I wrote Miss Boyce a letter of apology, "Last November we did not realize that Kay was manipulating all of us. I am very sorry for the distress we caused you. We now realize that you were trying to help Jessie and that you, out of friendship and regard for Jessie, were doing only what she had asked of you…."[17]

On May 20 a Court Order directed that Jessie remain a resident of Curwensville Nursing Home with Clearfield Bank and Trust Company as temporary guardian of the estate. Kay was ordered to "transmit all financial records to the Clearfield Trust with copies to be delivered to any party upon request."[18] Both POAs were nullified and Cortez Bell was appointed as Jessie's legal counsel, as I had advocated from the beginning.

Attorney Beth Gerg later told me that earlier Attorney Bell had met with Jessie in the nursing home. While this was to be an attorney-client meeting, the director of nursing monitored their conversation.

On May 23 a letter from Kay's attorney to Mr. Bell indicated Kay's desire that Jessie remain in Curwensville. Her case was based on the falsehoods she had been sowing, including the statement, "My mother has never been close to Jessie and moved out of town three years ago and never went back to visit, and both my mother and Judith were in town last summer and didn't visit Jessie." I found this exasperating because it had been Kay's unrelenting persistance that led to Mother's moving to Hummelstown sooner than she otherwise would have and Kay's strong insistence that Mother not visit Jessie during our day trip to Curwensville.

A letter from Attorney Gerg on this same date indicates that she had spoken to the trust officer at the Clearfield Trust with the concern that Kay had misused Jessie's money. Kay was then ordered by the Trust to produce the financial records of all assets: checking accounts; bank statements; special accounts used for the deposit of interest from CDs; the CDs themselves; medical insurance and medical bills; car title; outstanding bills; income tax; investments; money markets; stocks; and a list of major transfers and statement of assets and income.[19]

More revealing, if not astonishing for its flagrancy, were the lists of transactions, in Kay's handwriting, confirming assets of more than $250,000 plus stock, jewelry, and Jessie's house. Even so, by June 17 Kay had not complied with the Trust's order and Beth Gerg threatened to file a motion with the Court.

Attorney Gerg also advised Kay's attorney that I would be taking Jessie on June 19 and returning her to the nursing home on July 1 with a written guarantee that "the purpose of the visit is not to make a Will or to have a psychiatric evaluation conducted."[20]

During the nearly two-week visit in Hummelstown, several times Jessie broached the subject of a new Will, even writing a simple holographic one completely on her own, not realizing that I had signed a guarantee that no new Will would be written during the time of the visit. There was no point in telling Jessie of the condition upon which she was allowed to visit her sister; rather, Kate just told Jessie that they would save the holographic Will until it was needed.

Near the end of July the Clearfield Trust officer announced that Jessie's assets would be liquidated, the house would remain intact for the time being, and that the household effects would be sold at auction. Such news was distressing to everyone, particularly to Mother who did not want to have Jessie's belongings placed for public auction. The response from the trust officer was not comforting, "It's the cleanest way," he said. Yes, it was, for him.

I then wrote to the trust officer, asking specific questions and concerns about the property, fearing its present condition of neglect was an invitation to vandalism and/or injury to parties trespassing or even passing by. I specified particular concerns regarding the possibility of the electricity being shut off which then would prevent the sump pump from removing rain water. I also asked him to consider changing the locks, removing the car, and checking on the insurance and oil delivery.

He replied promptly, admitting that he did not know the limit of his duties and responsibilities and was going to ask the court for direction.[21] Beth Gerg then wrote to the attorney for the Trust, saying she thought they should be marshalling the assets of Jessie and preparing an inventory to reveal any questionable transactions. She also noted that the bank should be preserving Jessie's assets.[22] It was irritatingly apparent that the bank did not appear to know its parameters as guardian of an estate. I had no choice but to resign myself to a long and difficult struggle, disheartened that the Clearfield Trust was disinclined to make decisions concerning Jessie.

I was, however, determined to make Jessie's life in the nursing home as comfortable as possible in an institutional setting, writing letters to Jessie's friends thanking them for their visits and encouraging those visits to continue. I hoped that people were visiting more frequently than the guest book indicated and I had to accept the home's explanation that the regular visitors didn't sign in.

When Nan and I next visited Jessie in early August, we didn't recognize her. She again was sitting at the metal utility table in the all-purpose room, but this time her clothes were stained and her hair uncombed. When we mentioned this to the staff on duty, we were rebuffed. The staff's dislike of "the people from out of town" was evident by their unwelcoming response at each visit. As a result, we worried even more at the kind of care Jessie might be receiving, since the staff didn't make sure she was presentable even when the visits were known in advance.

I couldn't help noticing how the staff failed to see the real person in Jessie, a once young, vibrant, professional woman with great style. It was heartbreaking to think of all the sad souls, Jessie as well as the others, under the care of this staff.

Concerns for the condition of the property on Thompson Street also continued, as upon each visit it was increasingly obvious that the Clearfield Trust—and the trust officer in particular—had not seen to its care. The property invited vandalism, and inside it was discovered that some antique pieces of furniture were missing. Seeing this home, in which our mother and her sisters had grown up, now in its present state of disrepair and neglect, evoked both sadness and an even stronger determination to urge the Trust to fulfill its obligations.

We were dismayed that this trust officer gave the matter of Jessie barely passing attention. He did nothing without being prompted, did not respond to calls, and was not prepared for appointments, making us wait past the scheduled appointment time and then wait again while we sat in his office as he searched for the files he had not reviewed prior to the meeting—this following a nearly three-hour drive for us. Disheartenment turned to distress, as the situation regarding the house became a metaphor for Jessie herself.

On September 3 I again wrote to my cousins: "Five months have passed since last I wrote, and, unfortunately, the situation with Aunt Jessie has not yet been resolved. ...Any real improvement in Jessie's care is negligible and we were dismayed at the apparent lack of attention being paid to her personal condition. What began last winter as a personal concern has now become a complicated matter of litigation. … It appears that the only way I can get Jessie the care she needs is to be named as her legal guardian. While I do not relish the time and work this will entail, I am willing to see this through for Jessie's sake."[23]

Replies of support arrived quickly:

> From Don and Lorraine: "We want you to understand we are in total support of the actions you have taken."[24]
>
> From Janet Lynn: "I'm so glad you're not giving up. I went to see Aunt Jessie three times the week I was home in June. She cried every time I left. It broke my heart. I wanted to take her out for a drive. The mountain laurel were so exceptional this year—but was told I'd have to have Kay's permission. I pray you can get her out of Kay's clutches. God bless you for trying."[25]
>
> From Eugene: "Just a note to let you know that I appreciate and support what you're trying to do for Jessie."[26]

Kay continued to send mixed messages regarding her feelings toward and relationship with Mother. She would speak to us sisters against our mother, then call Mother and hold a conversation as if no breach between the two of them had occurred. Other times she would call Mother very late at night, crying and telling her she had a gun by her bed, and making remarks such as, "I have nothing to live for." She then would follow those midnight calls by sending Mother a small gift, such as a box of candy and a note with messages such as "I never thought my family would betray me."[27]

To the latter, Mother responded, "If you really want to make amends, let the healing begin with you. We will listen."[28] There was no response.

By November, seven months after the Clearfield Trust had assumed guardianship of Jessie, a court ruling finally outlined its duties as temporary guardian of her estate. The trust was to continue to pay the taxes and insurance, the heat was turned on in both sides of the double house, and a plumber checked the heating and water lines. The Trust also engaged an auctioneer to inventory all of Jessie's belongings.[29]

More importantly, this court order gave the Clearfield Trust authority to pay the bills it approved, but hold no responsibility for damage to the property. Nor would it hold any responsibility to investigate any transactions carried out by Kay, including the transference of Jessie's assets to Kay herself. For these limited duties, it would be compensated at the rate of 5% of the estate.[30]

I had difficulty reconciling this ruling. It appeared to me that because Jessie was elderly the court disregarded what had happened to her. She had been incarcerated without consent and without being adjudicated as incompetent, yet she remained a prisoner without recourse. Was it because she was old and, therefore, in their view, dispensable? Of course, there were no satisfactory answers. In fact, there were no answers at all.

I further wrestled with how Jessie had been treated from the moment Kay had entered her life with her plan to control it. It was unfathomable to me that Kay—and, it appeared, the Clearfield Trust and the courts as well—could overlook the fact that Jessie was a person who had had significance in a family, in a neighborhood, and in a community. For that alone she should have been attended to. And Jessie Pifer was even more. Many members of that community had been her pupils, she had served her church as a deacon, she had extended family of note, and her life was legendary in her small town. Nearly everyone in Curwensville knew her. But even if they had not, she was one of them and was at a destination where many others would some day find themselves. If for no other reason than she was a fellow citizen, did they not want to protect her?

It has been said that how we measure any society is a function of how we treat the sick, the needy, or those who are vulnerable, whether they be very young or very old.[31] Why was Jessie not being respected—if not for what she was in her eighties, then for what she once was? Why was there not the courtesy of value for her personhood? Again, there was no explanation.

As Jessie's second Christmas in the Curwensville Nursing Home approached, it was becoming more difficult to be optimistic on visits with her. Topics of conversation were limited, as the unasked question silently loomed in the background of every spoken word, "When will Jessie be free?"

Early in December Nan, Mother, and I again made the long journey to Curwensville. When Jessie saw us she cried and kissed my hand. Such a symbolic gesture sent chills through me for everything it implied, confirming my distress at my aunt's diminishing autonomy. I did not want obeisance from Jessie. I wanted independence *for* Jessie and I longed for that former self-assured personage of "Jebbie." It was not the aging of my aunt that struck me so strongly but her decline of spirit, and for that I had no solution.

Again, even though the staff knew that Jessie would be receiving visitors, her hair still had not been trimmed or styled but rather was hanging limply, nearly touching her shoulders. When Mother later asked Kay about this lack of care of her aunt, she replied, "So? She's no good to anyone anyhow." We later suspected that Kay had directed that no special attention be given Jessie, such as matching and ironed clothes, no appointments for a hair styling, and no spiritual or mental stimulation. In this way, Jessie would look "worse" to all local visitors leading them to concur with Kay that "Jessie is incompetent, Jessie is failing." It was a sorry sight.

Fred Ammerman, then serving as the county district attorney, suggested that everything possible be done to help Jessie draw another Will. However, that was not possible without holding guardianship. This dilemma began to wear on everyone, particularly Mother.

On December 23 we visited Jessie again, this time with the promise to her of a visit to Hummelstown the following week preceding the guardianship hearing scheduled for January 10. The pending hearing raised additional anxiety, adding to the caution from our attorneys that a full-blown court case could be expensive and that it would be best to keep things narrowly focused and ask only for guardianship of Jessie's person and not to delve into Kay's mishandling of funds.

On January 6, 1992 Nan and I went to Curwensville to bring Aunt Jessie back to Hummelstown prior to the guardianship hearing. Because none of us could anticipate the outcome of the hearing, much of the visit in Hummelstown was spent with Jessie and Mother simply reminiscing.

On the morning of January 10 the courtroom in Clearfield was filled with Jessie's friends, including Joe Errigo and Jean Boyce. It had been decided that Jessie would not attend the hearing which turned out to be mainly discussions among the judge and the attorneys, not unusual in such situations. On one side of the bench were Mother and her three daughters and on the opposite side sat Kay. None of the principals were required to testify. A highlight of the brief testimony was that of the nursing home physician who confirmed what I had contended the entire time, that *Jessie could have been and could be in a less restrictive environment*.

The finding of the court was to declare Jessie an incompetent[32] with my being appointed guardian of the person. Kay immediately filed with the court for Jessie's assets to pay her legal fees accrued after she had turned her records over to the

Clearfield Trust. She already had been paying her own attorney's fees from Jessie's account while she had control of it.

Following the hearing, it was decided that Fred Ammerman would officially request the Trust to do a full review of Jessie's assets. He also encouraged pressing criminal charges against Kay. He told Kay's attorney that an arrest was a possibility and he likely also told this to Cortez Bell because Jean Boyce later reported that she had spoken to Mr. Bell the day of the court hearing and he had told her, "Someone could go to jail today."[33]

The next day Joe Errigo called Mother to say, "I will make this right, Kate, and will tell people in Curwensville the truth of what happened. What Kay did was wrong. Poor Jess."

When Joe next told Kate that the Ammermans had said criminal charges should be pressed against Kay, Mother answered, "I think we have had enough."[34]

I wrote to Jessie's friends who had attended the hearing, the new director of the Curwensville Nursing Home, and to Joe Errigo, thanking them for supporting Jessie.[35]

Lorraine then wrote to me, confirming that Fred Ammerman had mentioned to Don the possibility of filing criminal charges against Kay. ...[and] "I'm glad that Joe Errigo called your mother to tell her he would set the record straight."[36]

With my now being legal guardian of Jessie, Beth Ammerman wrote a letter to the trust officer, calling his attention to the various financial transactions of Kay Walker in breach of her fiduciary duty. Beth further requested that he investigate all financial records and transactions, particularly those written to Kay's attorney, the IRS, penalties for transfers of assets from Jessie to Kay, and payments to Kay herself.[37]

I next arranged for Jessie to undergo evaluation tests in the Geriatrics Center of the Hershey Medical Center. Dr. Robert Brennan's notes of April 1992 include these comments:

> Mrs. Mohney is a previously healthy 85-year-old who developed typical organic mental symptoms about one year ago leading to her involuntary commitment to a local chronic care facility. Her family history is negative for stroke or premature dementia.... She is independent in the activities of daily living. However, she is prone to intermittent confusion. Her only other medical problem at this moment is intermittent hypertension. She is generally accurate in her recollections, and does not appear to be delusional, agitated, or hallucinatory. Further, she is fully alert and oriented.
>
> ...Her fund of current events was originally good and she knew the names of the President and Vice President. She was able to do change problems of some complexity. She could do some serial subtractions accurately. Today she was oriented to place and how she had arrived here.[38]

While we had hoped for a better prognosis, admittedly we were not surprised at Jessie's decline after spending more than a year in the nursing home. However, we were encouraged as the facility of choice in Hershey could accommodate the level of care Jessie would likely require, one step down from independent living, but with a large private room and bath.

On March 17 Jessie was seen by a neurologist at the Hershey Medical Center. Her responses were very similar to the evaluation she had had from Dr. Brennan. The doctors said she was very articulate and that it was obvious she was intelligent and educated. The specialist told Nan and me that from his initial impression our aunt had mild dementia. "Not even," he said, "first stage Alzheimer's."

In addition to informing Don and Lorraine of this promising diagnosis, I expressed my discomfort with the Clearfield Trust's inattention to duty in that "...copies of notices from the Trust Company are being copied to Kay and her attorney but *not* to my attorney." [39]

Because Kay had petitioned to have all of her attorney fees paid, in late March the county judge asked the Clearfield Trust to put in writing what information they needed from the attorney to show that his fees were for the benefit of Jessie. The judge ordered Kim Kesner, attorney for the Trust, to depose Laurence Seaman as to his services rendered in handling Jessie's estate.

This deposition confirmed that Mr. Seaman had not had any contact with Jessie in preparing the Power of Attorney. Mr. Seaman also admitted that the document had not been executed in his office, but rather some place outside of the law office and notarized by Sharon Davis whose identity and position were unknown to Mr. Seaman. Thus, Mr. Seaman had prepared the POA document but did not handle its signing nor had he spoken to Jessie concerning its purpose. He did, however, send the invoice to Jessie.

Mr. Seaman also admitted that he had not met with Jessie in preparing a deed, but rather all was arranged with Kay Walker under her power of attorney. He confirmed, "…I never spoke with Jessie." He added that the lease for the house was not to be recorded so it later would not cause a problem for Kay for inheritance tax purposes.

When Mr. Kesner asked him about "…numerous conferences with Kay Walker, numerous telephone conferences with Kay Walker, and then telephone conferences with Dr. Schickling, Attorney Bell, and Attorney Mattern," he said his information regarding Jessie had come only from Kay Walker. When asked why he sent (to Jessie's family doctor) forms for an opinion as to competency, Mr. Seaman explained that "… Kay was concerned and expressed to me that if somebody else came in and placed influence on Jessie that she might revoke the power of attorney given to Kay and substitute somebody else."

Mr. Kesner's next question was, "Again, prior to December 4, did you have any contact with Mrs. Mohney herself?" and Mr.

Seaman's answer again was, "No." When asked if he knew when Jessie was admitted to the Curwensville Nursing Home, Mr. Seaman replied that he did not know.

After reading this deposition Mother said to Nan, "What a mess Kay has made of everything." The distress would continue.

Jessie remained in the Curwensville Nursing Home for the next three months waiting for the wheels of the courts to turn. It is not so much that the care at Curwensville Nursing Home bothered me; rather, like many nursing homes, Curwensville was designed more for physical and medical services, and was viewed as the last resort for those who needed but could not afford private assisted living facilities. The nature of Jessie's condition did not warrant her being there.

On April 9, 1992 Dr. Robert Brennan, who had examined Jessie at Hershey Medical Center, faxed a summary of his medical findings to Judge Reilly in the Clearfield County Court,

> "I would support the family's view that she does not require the extensive medical and supervisory services she is now getting at the Curwensville Nursing Home and could receive perfectly adequate and possibly more appropriate care at a local nursing facility in the area where patients are encouraged to be more independent within their capability limitations. My overall impression is that she is simply too well preserved and too normally functional despite her diagnosis, at this time, to require commitment in an environment such as the Curwensville Nursing Home."[40]

In a letter to Don and Lorraine, I wrote, "I am eager to get this settled and, if a move to an assisted care facility in Hershey can be approved, I would like to arrange for the move during the summer when Jessie could spend more of the time "on the porch" at our place. That would help to make the adjustment easier. Also, the bank wishes to dispose of the house and contents and I just can't see doing that while Jessie is still in Curwensville. We will bring her down here on May 26 and again in late June or early July and then, unless things work to move her permanently, again in September."[41]

Jessie's five-day visit with Mother occurred without incident, just a visit of two sisters. She was returned to Curwensville on Memorial Day, arriving shortly after the annual Memorial Day parade which, like Jessie herself, had been reduced to displaying only a token of its former celebratory character.

The following day, I wrote to Joe Errigo ". . . on Friday we will be moving Jessie to Country Meadows of Hershey. The special geriatric-neurological team of Hershey Medical Center recommends that such a facility as Country Meadows can meet Jessie's needs in a less restrictive environment. I sincerely hope that you and Jessie's other friends can believe that this choice is not a vote against the Curwensville Nursing Home, but rather a choice we made for other reasons. If things do not work out for Jessie down here and/or if she is unhappy and wishes to return to CNH I'll comply with her wishes. Thank you again for your many kindnesses."[42]

On June 6, 1992, Jessie became a resident of Country Meadows of Hershey in the assisted living section where she had a room with traditional, rather then institutional, furnishings and a television set, along with a closet and a private bathroom. This move should have led to a happy ending for Jessie and, for a short time, it held that promise.

With good care and visits from the family the outlook for Jessie was brighter than it had been for some time. However, the stress of the family turmoil took its toll on Mother. She developed what was diagnosed as a mild case of clinical depression. With treatment the depression lasted only a few weeks, but it did give the family reason to reflect on the effects the Jessie situation was having on the family.

Matters with Kay remained unresolved while Jo Ellen, Nan, and I continued to discuss the ramifications of what had happened. Jo Ellen believed that Kay should not be made to return Jessie's assets that had been expended and that the Trust be told that "we are trying to negotiate a reconciliation among the family members because of Kay's possible unstable mental health and Mother's age." Jo Ellen also suggested that the Trust shouldn't be concerned about getting the money back because there remained assets enough to cover all of Jessie's needs. Following a family meeting on Sunday August 16, I composed a letter to Judge Reilly:

> *... While I cannot condone the fiduciary mishandling of Aunt Jessie's assets by my sister Kay, I request that the court not exact restitution of the monies spent prior to January of 1992. The past several years have taken their toll on us as a family; and the dispute over Jessie's care, both personally and financially, has been particularly difficult for my mother, Jessie's sister. Because of Mother's health and the emotional frailty of both my mother, Katherine Pifer Thompson, and my sister, Kay Walker, I am convinced that any judgment against Kay in this pending matter could be fatal to both of them.*
>
> *We are all in agreement that Kay did not always execute her duties as (then) power-of-attorney in an ethical manner; however, we wish to spare our family further grief. In addition, we are aiming for reconciliation between my mother and my sister..., and we believe that not holding Kay liable for restitution of monies spent is essential for this to occur. Further, because there are assets enough to meet all of Jessie's needs for the remainder of her life, restitution would not add to Jessie's comfort.*[43]

The evening the letter was composed, Jo Ellen telephoned Kay's daughter Kim and told her what we had decided. Kim agreed with Jo Ellen that the three younger sisters and their mother were doing the right thing and that Kay should meet them halfway. Kim held concern for her mother but said to Jo Ellen, "My mother is wrong in this situation."[44]

The day following, my daughter told me that she had observed in her Aunt Kay "no signs of depression and certainly no signs of being suicidal," despite what Kay had been telling Jo Ellen. "In fact," Jeanie remarked, "Kay seems like her old self and is thinking about going to California in December or to Jo Ellen's for Christmas. I haven't noticed any difference in her behavior. I have never heard her say anything about 'having nothing to live for,'" which is what Kay had been telling Jo Ellen.[45]

The next day, Jo Ellen called me to share parts of the conversation she had had with Kay the previous evening, particularly whether or not the Clearfield Trust would pay Kay's legal fees and whether or not they would call for her return of Jessie's assets. Jo Ellen had told Kay, "The best thing would be for you to sign that you will not challenge Jessie's new Will in exchange for our asking the bank and judge not to ask for restitution of the funds you spent."

Jo Ellen also suggested that it would be best if Kay backed off any threatened action against their mother. To this Kay responded with an expletive. As a result, Jo Ellen concluded, "Maybe Kay isn't so depressed after all."[46]

Jo Ellen and I continued our conversation the following day at which time Jo Ellen told me that she had spoken to Joanne, Kay's good friend from high school, asking her if she thought Kay was depressed or suicidal. "I have gone to bat for Kay twice now in defending her to Judi and Nan," Jo Ellen told Joanne." I don't know how else I can convince Kay that she needs to bend a little on this or she and Mother will never reconcile."

Joanne responded, "If Kay agrees to go along with what you are proposing as a compromise, she believes she would be admitting she was wrong. And Kay says she hasn't done anything wrong. Furthermore, she isn't even going to discuss this with her attorney because she has made up her mind to not back down."[47]

Attorney Beth Gerg then confirmed that the Clearfield Trust was not taking any position regarding a return of Jessie's assets that were used to pay Kay's attorney and that she had alerted the Trust's attorney that her law firm most likely would pursue an investigation regarding the funds taken by Kay.

After many delays, the trust officer finally responded regarding items Kay previously had taken from Jessie's home. He confirmed that Kay had taken these items but claimed that Jessie had given them to her before being adjudicated incompetent. The letter continued, "I think it would be best for us to proceed with a sale of the balance of what is left in the house."[48]

Reluctantly, Nan and I made a final visit to Jessie's home to select items that might be of interest to her in her room at Country Meadows, items that were personal family mementoes such as photographs and letters, and a few things we thought that Mother would want for their sentimental value. These included Jessie's small writing desk to be taken for her use at Country Meadows; the trunk Jessie had used to transport her belongings to Clarion College that first exciting summer as a co-ed; Ruby's high school diploma; a small corner shelf and a piece of china, hand-painted by our grandmother at the turn of the century, for Janet Lynn who had asked for something by which to remember her grandmother; the Bible that had

belonged to Josephine; Jessie's typewriter upon which she had created worksheets for her students; and a well-worn, artificial bouquet of violets that Jessie had frequently pinned to a belt at her waist.

The only other item I picked up was a valentine, found in the driveway the day after the auctioneer had collected Jessie's furniture and hauled it away for a sale. "So this is what it has come to," I commented to Nan. "Years of living, a household of family belongings, a lifetime of memories, and all that is left are violets and valentines." I shook my head as I spoke to one who could not hear me, "Jessie, it should not have ended like this."

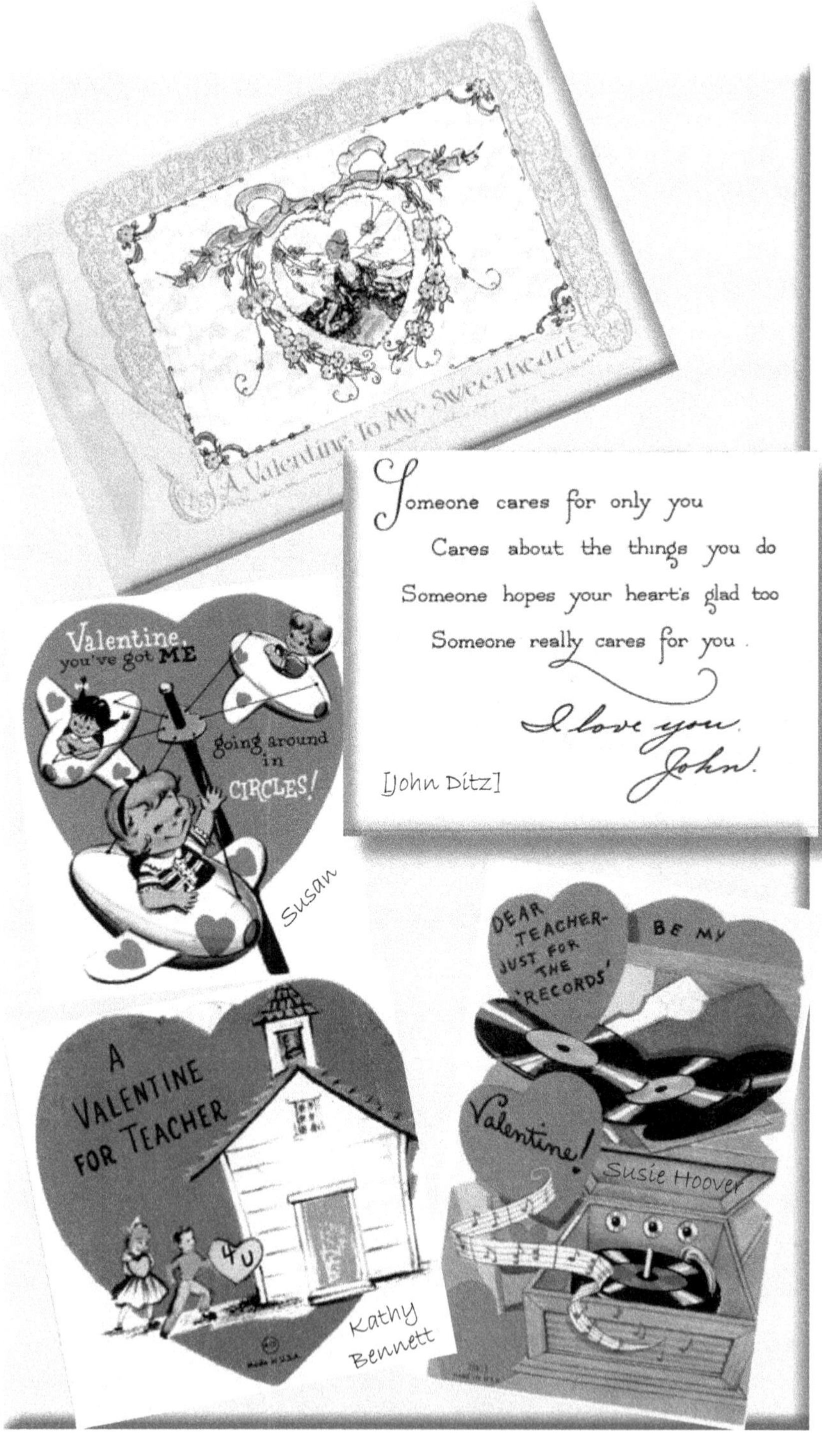
A Valentine To My Sweetheart
Someone cares for only you
Cares about the things you do
Someone hopes your heart's glad too
Someone really cares for you.
I love you
John
[John Ditz]
Valentine, you've got ME going around in CIRCLES!
Susan
DEAR TEACHER- JUST FOR THE 'RECORDS'
BE MY Valentine!
Susie Hoover
A VALENTINE FOR TEACHER
4U
Kathy Bennett

Chapter 14

Violets and Valentines

Faded violets, still wrapped in tissue, preserved with care,
Left as if she had planned to return to wear them one day.
A tattered valentine in the driveway, found by chance,
Left by the auctioneer in his haste.
The violets, a symbol of her flair for style
and her spirit and joy in life,
Remembered by those who knew the youthful Jessie,
With the soprano voice unmatched.
The valentine, one of hundreds she had kept from her schoolchildren,
The many who loved her and grieve for her.[1]

Quiet visits with Jessie gave me time to reflect on how completely she had fallen victim to Kay. When the trouble had first begun, Jessie lived by herself as she had for many years, yet she was not entirely alone in Curwensville. She had other family in the area, notably her nephew Don. Her sister Katherine initially was as close as a rap on the wall that connected their houses and later was available by telephone, as were Jessie's nephews and nieces. Joe Errigo, classmate, neighbor, and lifelong trusted friend, would have responded immediately to any concern. Jessie lived half a block from the center of town and nearly everyone knew her. She did her banking and grocery shopping in the neighborhood; she patronized a local beautician and local pharmacy; she bought her cars around the corner from where she lived. She was a deacon in her church, a member of the DAR, and a retired elementary teacher. She had been a town beauty, full of fun, clever, stylish—a real head-turner with many suitors, and once had been known for her beautiful, crystal clear soprano voice. She was a presence and was known by almost everyone in Curwensville, and anyone could have offered her support. How, then, could it be that no one suspected she was being taken advantage of?

Looking at the indicators of possible elder abuse, Jessie certainly fit the profile; she was elderly, had comfortable assets, owned her home, and lived alone. What doesn't fit the typical scenario is that no one ever would have thought that a family member would take advantage of Jessie, especially with a scheme that was so duplicitous with each part planned and every detail considered. Kay fit the profile of a possible predator, but through scheming she avoided suspicion by those in Curwensville who likely would have blown the whistle had they known what was happening.

Kay did, however, have additional assistance that bordered on complicity. If she had not likely had the help of the bank clerks, taking so many assets from Jessie's accounts might have not been as easily accomplished. Kay's lawyer who, while not legally culpable, was unethical in that he had never met Jessie, yet he helped Kay gain Power of Attorney and file for guardianship. Kay sowed seeds of doubt in the thoughts of Jessie's friends, warning them falsely that Jessie's sister had abandoned her and that Jessie herself was not to be believed. And Kay brought her own mother into the plot only enough to have a confidante whom she then turned against. She told each of the people involved in the situation only as little as she thought they needed to know, and she gained the trust of each one in turn, providing her the additional self-assurance of being invincible. This continued until the one thing she hadn't counted on occurred—a sister's discomfort and subsequent action.

Violets and Valentines

Kay used many people in her plan, a scheme that began from the simple fact that Jessie did not have a Will:

1. ***Her husband, Robert Walker,*** would do anything for his wife. She apparently had him convinced that if they didn't get Jessie's money, it would go to the state or be divided among all Jessie's heirs.
2. ***Her mother, Katherine Thompson,*** suffered as much as Jessie, as she fretted over what she knew, what she didn't know, and in the end, by an acute sense of being betrayed by her own daughter
3. ***Her father, Howard Thompson, Jr.,*** who had deeply disappointed Kay by changing his Will on his deathbed.
4. ***Her sister Judith,*** who could not stand by and watch Jessie be treated merely as the means to Kay's end.
5. ***Her sister Jo Ellen,*** who attempted to remain neutral until she saw the disregard her oldest sister showed for their mother and the firm evidence of Kay's wrong-doing.
6. ***Her sister Nan,*** who for years had been uncomfortable with Kay's obsession concerning the Wills of their father, their mother, and their aunt.
7. ***Her best friend Marie,*** head teller at the Curwensville State Bank without whose action it is possible that a red flag would have been raised at the bank concerning the diminishing of Jessie's funds.
8. ***Family friend Joseph (Joe) Errigo,*** classmate of Jessie who had held an abiding fondness for both Jessie and Kate from the time they all were school chums. Kay believed that if she could convince Joe with her tales, she would have the trust of the town.

10. ***Cousin Don Bloom,*** who, like most of the other members of this Pifer clan, believed in respecting others, their privacy, and their property. Don had looked out for and assisted Jessie the last twenty years of her life.

11. ***Jean Boyce,*** Jessie's friend, a person Kay needed to discredit, as Jean early on suspected something wasn't right when Jessie asked for her help.

12. ***Peg Hamilton,*** Jessie's next door neighbor in later years, who believed Kay's stories and also betrayed Jessie.

The common denominator among all of the above was their trusting natures. Kay's skill was her ability to weave a story, telling each of the characters only what she wanted them to know and knowing them all well enough to expect they would not betray her confidence by comparing notes and seeing through her plot.

The five Pifer sisters, and the four Thompson sisters in turn, kept their own counsel and did not share much with one another as to their conversations—whether in person, by telephone or by letter—with the other sisters. Likewise, they did not carry tales between the households. It also was very unlikely that any of the Thompson sisters would be in close contact with individuals in Curwensville, particularly when they had no idea that Kay was manipulating these persons for her own gain.

This segregation gave Kay the framework she needed. She counted on its being highly unlikely that any two of those involved would share information. She relied on her ability to convince each of them that what she was doing was for Jessie's benefit. Even more, Kay was very skilled at dropping little tidbits of information that later turned out to be significant, or, worse, she would leave out essential details so that the listener would come to the conclusion Kay wanted. She preyed on the sympathy of each sister in turn, each in a different way, and had Jo Ellen believing her oldest sister was suicidal and that the other two were in a plot against her.

The unusual factor in all of this is that the young, exuberant Jebbie of youth was not the Aunt Jessie we Thompson sisters knew. Our Aunt Jessie was a character; she was interesting, and she was kind, although not the loving aunt of novels. So why risk family ties and spend money on litigation, as well as untold hours, days, and years fighting the battle for Jessie? Why sacrifice so much for this cause? Simply because it was the right thing to do. A person who could not defend herself, Jessie was being taken advantage of, was being made a fool, and was being "put away" without cause. There was something reprehensible here. Nan and I—and later Jo Ellen—could not sit back and let Kay take over Jessie's life and then throw her away like something of no worth.

Had Kay shown more regard for Jessie as a person, more kindness, more willingness to see to her real needs and to arrange for her to live out her days in her own home, then likely Nan and I would not have stepped in. Had Kay not lied to all of us, had Kay not spoken cruel words to our own mother and made disparaging remarks such as telling Mother that the County Home would be the place for her if she needed a place to go in her old age, Kay's three sisters could have forgiven her. And if she had had any regard for the moral law[2] of treating each person as an end in himself, never as a mere means—for Kay treated everyone as a means by which to reach her goal of Jessie's money—they might have understood. And Kay made her biggest mistake in turning on her own mother, for none of her three sisters could excuse or forgive her for that.

Regret, remorse, and recriminations nearly overwhelmed the family. Only our resolve for justice remained, but that too was ebbing.

> *Jessie Beverly Pifer Mohney died on June 1, 1993, a little more than a month shy of her 88th birthday.*
>
> *She died alone, in a nursing facility, far from home.*

Coming home as she would have wished, Jessie Beverly Pifer Mohney was laid to rest in a powder blue casket, the color of the dress she had worn for her wedding and her 40th Class Reunion. Surviving classmates and teaching colleagues, as well as students from long ago, paid their respects, their sorrow compounded by the circumstance of her passing. Following the brief service, the funeral cortege took a circuitous route to Oak Hill to avoid driving past the Pifer homestead, its door draped with black crepe, in memory of and in tribute to Miss Jessie Beverly Pifer and a gentler time.

The Aftermath:

A month following Jessie's Memorial Service, on July 13, 1993, Kay engaged an attorney in Dauphin County and told him she had been contacted by a family member with regard to possibly settling the contest of Wills.

To the contrary, two weeks earlier when Kay had suggested to Jo Ellen the possibility of a settlement of the Will, Jo Ellen had told her to "halt any more action,"[1] that enough sorrow had occurred in the family.

Kay chose to pay no heed to her sister's admonition, instead ordering her attorney to tell Mother's attorney that she would not contest Jessie's standing Will *if* she were to receive 60% of Jessie's total estate *before* expenses.

Mother, still heartbroken over her sister's death and Kay's continuing attack, asked her attorney to make it clear that she would bring charges of mishandling of Jessie's funds, false imprisonment, and elder abuse if Kay did not desist in her demands.[2] This threat of criminal action did not stop Kay and she pressed forward with a lawsuit against her own mother.

[Parallel to this action by Kay, in early January 1994 and seven months after Jessie's death, the Clearfield Trust Company finally agreed to do what they had been asked to do for more than a year, to "take such measures necessary, including legal action, to title the 360 shares of Penn Laurel Financial Corporation to Katherine P. Thompson as Executrix."[3] To note just how outlandish this situation was, a few months later it was discovered that the Clearfield Trust officer had been in regular contact with Kay, providing information to her about Jessie's account, while keeping information from Judith, Jessie's court-appointed guardian.[4]]

Mother continued to try to resolve the dispute with Kay, but she could not reason with her. This strained situation and Kay's persistence in the quarrel was very difficult for Mother who wrote, ". . . You must stop this aggression against me. If you don't, you will have to live with the fact that you made my few remaining years sad and painful."[5] But Kay did not stop.

On March 11, 1994 Kay filed a petition for Jessie's holographic Will (the one Kay herself had dictated to Jessie in 1989) to prevail over the standing Will. There would be yet another battle to fight.

On May 5, 1994 the Clearfield Bank and Trust Company finally filed against Kay saying that the Penn Laurel stock belonged to Jessie's estate and not to Kay and that the burden of proof would be on Kay to prove otherwise. Three weeks later, Mother's attorney wrote to Kay's attorney asking that Kay's persistent and distressing telephone calls to her mother be stopped.[6]

Disturbed that Kay was continuing to call Mother, especially late at night, I wrote to Kay, "Why in the world would you ask Mother how she thought you performed when you were on the witness stand testifying against her?"[7] I found it bizarre that Kay would testify against Mother in court and then telephone her asking, in essence, "How do you think I did?"

A full year after Jessie's death, all of this wrangling was becoming tiresome with nothing resolved and with Kay continuing to insist that she be awarded the majority of the remaining assets of Jessie's estate. It was also wearisome that Kay's attorney kept insisting that the late night calls of Kay to her mother were friendly.[8]

Mother did not welcome the calls and Jo Ellen, Nan, and I viewed these late night intrusions as inappropriate and alarming, particularly those that included a harangue as to the choice of burial site for our mother. Kay was insisting to Mother that she "be buried up here (in Curwensville). This is where I want you buried. I'll take care of your grave." Kay even admitted that her attorneys had advised her not to call her mother, but she did anyway, because "I do what I want to do."[9]

Soon after, Jo Ellen shared with her sisters the words Kay had used earlier, threatening their lives, "I didn't want to tell you this before, but Kay did threaten us. She said to me, 'I feel like going up there and shooting them all.' At the time I thought Kay was exaggerating and I didn't give this much thought other than how angry she was, but in light of her strange behavior towards Mother, now I think we need to take this threat more seriously. Mother's telephone number must be changed and not listed."

On August 19, 1994 the Clearfield County Court ordered Kay to return the 360 shares of Penn Laurel stock, as well as the dividends. However, this did not happen, because three weeks later Kay appealed the ruling of the County Judge, John Reilly, to the Superior Court. She also insisted on a court presentation requiring an appearance in person of all parties. We sisters considered this outrageous, both in audacity and cost.

One of the strongest admissible pieces of evidence was the medical report of Dr. Brennan who had examined Jessie on March 17, 1992 that in his "opinion and with reasonable medical certainty, Mrs. Mohney had retained sufficient cognitive abilities during this period to qualify as competent for the specific purpose of testamentary capacity."[10] In other words, Jessie knew what she was doing when she made her own Will in 1992, the one that superseded the one Kay had written.

Following a year of wrangling among attorneys, on September 6, 1995 another court hearing was held with the Judge opening the proceeding with the words, "Will we ever get this case to trial?" While I couldn't agree more, the more overriding feeling was one of great sadness.

In early November word was received that the trial date would be the week of December 18 and that Kay's request for a jury trial had been denied. The waiting game continued.

On the first of December I wrote to our cousin Janet Lynn, enclosing a piano book that had belonged to her in childhood,

"Mother is as well as can be expected for her age. She is very glad that you took the time to visit and still talks about it. If you are inclined, why not give her a call? ... I believe you asked Mother why Jessie's money didn't go to charity. I asked Kay years ago to establish a scholarship at the high school or purchase something appropriate for the school that would honor Jessie at the time and later perpetuate her memory, but she said I was a fool."[11]

At this same time Lisa Wayne, daughter of John Wayne, told us that letters she had sent to her great-aunt during the past five years had been returned, one more indication that Kay had been keeping Jessie's personal mail from her, totally isolating her from as many family members as possible, including her nephew Johnny Wayne for whom Lisa was writing.

On January 3, 1996, following a continuance, and two and a half years after Jessie's death, the trial to settle her estate was about to begin. There was no joy on this morning and there would be no victory for Jessie. Seven long years of trying to right a grievous wrong had led to nothing but heartbreak, first for Jessie and then for Mother.

Before the trial could be formally convened, however, the attorneys met with the judge in his chambers. A short time later they came back into the courtroom. The judge had given them 15 minutes with their clients to work out a settlement. The attorneys told us that the judge was denying all motions with the exception of the motion from Mother's attorney for the burden of proof to be placed on the other party (Kay). This was viewed as a small victory, but by that time, it was all too obvious that there were no victors.

It soon became evident that the attorneys could come to no agreement and that the judge was losing patience. He ordered them to return with agreements from their clients following a lunch break.

The Aftermath

Following the lunch break and the reconvening of court, the three attorneys went to sidebar with the court reporter where a heated discussion occurred. The judge then threw up his hands, said to the attorneys, "Work it out," and left the courtroom without even waiting for the "All rise." Kay's attorney spoke privately to her and returned to speak to the other two attorneys who then sent word to the judge that they had come to a resolution.

The judge returned and adjourned the court, but not until Kay had signed over stock powers, leading to the eventual dispersal of the remaining funds. This was the last action Kay would ever take regarding Jessie, who had not lived to see justice served.

Epilogue:

Four years following Jessie's death, Bill Jackson, our paternal cousin and only child of our Aunt Mary Alice who had been a classmate of Aunt Jessie, approached me after his mother had been moved to an assisted living residence after spending some time in a skilled nursing facility. "I'm so glad you're going up to visit Mother," he said. "Please go as often as you can since I'm not able to visit more than once a month and it helps me to know you are keeping in touch with her. I don't know if you realize that Mother views you and your sisters as the daughters she never had."

Bill then startled me with a question, "Did you know Kay has a key to Mother's house? She told Brad (husband of Mary Alice) it would be a good idea for her to have a key when Rosemary and I were on vacation in August, even though Barbara, the woman who has been cooking and cleaning for Brad (who for a short time was remaining in the home until he joined his wife in the assisted living residence), already has one."

He continued, "While we were away I left a detailed itinerary and list of phone numbers with Barb of where we could be reached day or night. She offered to give the numbers to the nursing home, saving me the trouble. What I later discovered is that rather than giving the telephone numbers directly to the nursing home, Barb instead talked to Kay who said she would relay our contact information to the home when she visited Mother. What happened, however, is that Kay left *her own name and phone number* as the person to be notified in case of any emergency. Worse, while we were gone—and it was only a week, the nursing home tried to reach me, later telling me that they had no contact information for me, only for Kay."

Epilogue

"I also discovered that Kay has Mother's jewelry in her own safety deposit box in Curwensville. She told Mother it was for safe-keeping. I am particularly concerned about the wedding ring my father gave her as it's not in the special place in the house where Mother told me I could find it. There is another problem as well. While we were on vacation Kay got Mother and Brad to designate her as their Power of Attorney."

I had only one question for my cousin,

"Does your mother have a Will?"

Endnotes

Introduction Notes: Identities

1 Tracy Kidder, *Home Town.*

2 Scott, *The History of Jefferson County*, p. 668.

3 John Pifer's business card.

4 *Curwensville in Celebration of 200 Years,* p. 18.

5 *Curwensville in Celebration of 200 Years*, p. 21.

6 Morison, p. 574.

7 Scott, p. 440.

8 *150th Anniversary*, p. 30; *Curwensville 175th Anniversary Celebration*, p. 5.

9 *The Echo,* 1949, p. 96, citing *History of Clearfield County*, 1892.

10 The date given in *150th Anniversary* (p. 78) is 1852 or before; *Curwensville in Celebration of 200 Years* (p. 77) gives the date as 1854. *The Echo,*1949, p. 96, citing *History of Clearfield County*, 1892, dates the school as 1856.

11 *Curwensville in Celebration of 200 Years,* p. 18.

12 Excerpt from *1928 Echo*, reprinted in *Curwensville High School Alumni Association's 100th Anniversary*, a booklet, unpaginated.

13 Program from the 32nd Annual Clearfield County Teachers' Institute, Clearfield, PA, December 16, 17, 18, 19 and 20, 1895.

14 Lavinia Spencer's 1871 *Diary.*

15 Lavinia Spencer's 1871 *Diary.*

16 McCullough, *The Johnstown Flood*, pp. 51-52.

17 The Bulletin, Historical Society (George A. Scott).

18 The Bulletin, Historical Society (George A. Scott).

19 Scott, George A., "Curwensville's Newspapers," *The Progress*, Friday May 5, 1978, p. 4.

20 *Curwensville High School Alumni Association 100th Anniversary, 1887-1987*, unpaginated.

21 *Curwensville in Celebration*, p. 17.

22 McCullough, p. 31.

23 McCullough, p. 32.

24 "The Curwensville Review," June 1889, reported in *150th Anniversary*, p. 127.

25 *150th Anniversary*, p. 147.

26 Black, *The American Girl*, p. 84.

27 Black, *The American Girl*, p. 103.

Chapter 1 Notes: The Young Jessie

1 Morison, p. 813.

2 Bishop and Coblentz, p. 198.

3 *Manual of the Patton Graded Public School*

Endnotes

4 *Manual of the Patton Graded Public School*

5 Wise, *Bridal Greetings.*

6 *The Curwensville Mountaineer/ The Curwensville Herald,* © June 22,1903.

7 Rickard, *Clearfield*, p. 86.

8 "Picture This," *Temple Review*, Winter 2002, p. 48.

9 Morison, pp. 888-889.

10 *1902 Edition of the Sears, Roebuck* Catalogue, Catalogue No. III, p. 169.

11 Potter, "Attack of the 28-Screen Megaplex," *Philadelphia Magazine*, June 1999, p. 58.

12 Lahr, p. 78.

13 Personal letter, in the possession of the author.

14 Pierce, *Medical Advisor*, p. 5.

15 Throughout her lifetime Katherine's name was spelled in various ways, not because of the inconsistencies in spellings that were common in prior centuries, but for reasons mainly of carelessness of others. The Presbyterian Cradle Roll has her name spelled "Katherine;" her first grade teacher spelled it "Kathryn;" her second grade teacher, "Katharyn;" her high school report cards used "Katherine," yet her yearbook identifies her throughout as "Kathryn;" her teaching contract spells her name "Catherine;" and when she married, her husband also used this spelling which she continued to use, although in later years she said, while it didn't really matter, she preferred the original "Katherine."

16 Personal collection of the author.

17 Lahr, p. 77.

18 Letter from Kate to the author, June 2, 1966.

19 Weekly program listing of the Opera House, May 13, 1913.

20 NOAA response to request for information from author, April 17, 2004.

21 Faculty's Farewell Reception to the Class of 1914 program, April 14,1914.

22 Teachers Provisional Certificate, July 1, 1916, Clearfield County.

23 Morison, p. 860.

24 Evans, p. 156.

25 Bailey, p. 349.

26 In 1916, President Woodrow Wilson ordered that Francis Scott Keys' "Star-Spangled Banner" should become the national anthem played by the military and naval services, although officially the song was not so designated by Congress until 1931.

27 George, *Recollections*, p. 22.

28 *Curwensville in Celebration of 200 Years*, p. 55.

29 *CHS Yearbook, 1924,* p. 59.

30 Morison, pp. 873-874.

31 Original deposit record card in the Jessie Pifer Estate.

32 Morison, p. 875.

33 Evans, p. 162.

34 Found among the effects of Jessie Pifer.

Endnotes

Chapter 2 Notes: The Early Not- So- Roaring Twenties

1 *Jazz*, p. 1.
2 Riegel & Long, p. 267.
3 Morison, p. 908.
4. Evans, p. 185.
5 "Senior Class History," *The Echo, 1924.*
6 I came, I saw, I conquered.
7 The melody is from "When the Great Red Dawn is Shining," Copyright, 1917, by J. B. Cramer & Co., Ltd.
8 Later Gertrude Erhard '33 created a very lyrical arrangement of the original musical composition.
9 "Miss Bob White," a playbill, printed by Robison Printing, 1920.
10 *The Echo*, 1922, Sophomore Class History.
11 "Prohibition," *Time Magazine*, Vol. 1, no. 1, March 3, 1923, p. 5.
12 *Clearfield Progress* clipping, circa 1924.
13 *The Girl Graduate.*
14 "Class History," *The Echo,*1924.
15 *Curwensville Sesquicentennial*, p. 150.
16 Evans, p. 182.
17 *The Echo*, 1924, p. 41.
18 *The Echo*, 1924, p. 42.
19 *The Echo*, 1924, p. 72.
20 Loose clipping, n.d.
21 *The Echo*, 1924, p. 73
22 None of them, of course, realized that the deliberate mispronunciation of French probably originated with those serving in France in the Great War. When the soldiers returned they used many French phrases, both Americanized and bastardized.
23 *The Echo*, 1924, p. 72.
24 *The Echo*, 1924, p. 72.
25 Ella M. George, State President, "Pennsylvania's Big Membership Feat," *The Union Signal*, January 24, 1924, p. 6.
26 Elizabeth Putnam Gordon, *Women Torch-Bearers*, The Story of the Woman's Christian Temperance Union. Evanston, IL: National Woman's Christian Temperance Union Publishing House, 1924. pp. 181-182.
27 Program for the Victory Banquet, Matilda Pifer estate.
28 Letter of recommendation from Grant Norris, March 14, 1924.
29 Letter of recommendation from Grant Norris, March 14, 1924.
30 The Tuxedobrook Club no doubt is a take-off on and named for the Tuxedo Club, a private member-owned country club in Tuxedo Park, New York established in 1886 and the Brook Club, founded in 1903 in New York City by wealthy businessmen who were prominent members of other private clubs.
31 Western Union Telegram, 2:39 p.m., April 18, 1924.

32 Graduation announcement, Curwensville High School, Class of 1924.

33 *The Girl Graduate,* designed and illustrated by Louise Perrett and Sarah K. Smith, The Reilly and Lee Co., Chicago.

34 Commencement Exercises program, June 3, 1924.

35 C. H. S. Alumni Reunion program, June 3, 1924.

Chapter 3 Notes: The Co-Ed and the Working Girl

1 Evans, p. 186.

2 Personal collection of the author.

3 Personal collection of the author.

4 An indication that the lessons were delivered orally.

5 Personal collection of the author.

6 Mary George, p. 37.

7 French for "pianist." It might be assumed that this accompanist was simply being pretentious, particularly since Mr. Aaron is not billed as a "violiniste."

8 Personal collection of the author.

9 The modern usage of "dating" as a social engagement was first noted in the 1920's.

10 Teacher's Contract, September 4, 1924.

11 Personal card, collection of the author.

12 Personal collection of the author.

13 Letter of Recommendation, personal collection of the author.

14 Traister, Helen. "Activities," *The Echo 1925*, p. 31.

15 Registration and identification card, June 22, 1925.

16 Even though there were other normal schools in western Pennsylvania, Clarion was often referred to as "the Normal School in Western Pennsylvania."

17 The term "blind date" was first used in the 1920s, originated by college students; according to *Dictionary of American Slang,* 3rd edition, the word "date" was not widely used until 1925.

18 Playbill for the production, author's collection.

Chapter 4 Notes: Marriage and New Families

1 Fass, p. 225.

2 Sacco and Venzetti were two anarchists, convicted (some said unfairly on doubtful and inconclusive evidence) of murder, and whose appeal was denied.

3 Allen, *Only Yesterday*, p. 145.

4 Allen, *Only Yesterday,* p. 145.

5 Estate of Jessie Pifer.

6 It is also said that from their color—and perhaps because the material came from pressed cellulose—came the term "cheesecake" used to describe leggy photography. (See Allen, *The Big Change*, p. 120.)

7 Allen, *The Big Change,* p. 121.

8 Evans, pp. 182-83.

9 Evans, p. 217.

10 Bicentennial Issue, *Life*, 1975, p. 31.

11 Allen, *Only Yesterday*, p. 76.

12 Allen, *The Big Change*, p. 123.

13 Clearfield County Teachers' Institute Program, 1928.

14 Evans, p. 217.

15 Bezilla, 1985, p. 136.

16 Allen, *The Big Change*, p. 126.

17 Another of the many nicknames the Pifer sisters used among themselves.

18 Evans, p. 228.

19 Interview with Evelyn Williams Milligan.

Chapter 5 Notes: Life is Not a Bowl of Cherries

1 Evans, p. 182.

2 Evans, p. 231.

3 Bicentennial Issue*, Life, 1975,* p. 33.

4 Morison, p. 944.

5 Letter from Matilda Pifer's Aunt Agnes, January 31, 1930.

6 *Curwensville 175th Anniversary Celebration*, 1974, p.14. (While the *150th Anniversary of Curwensville* (1949) displays a full page ad from the City Drug Store that has the name of Robert A. McKenzie rather than Mr. Errigo, an article in 1974's *175th Anniversary* book says, "[The City Drug Store] was established by Joseph O. Errigo on April 30, 1930. Mr. Errigo left the store in 1942 to serve in the U.S. Army [he would have been 37 years old]. After World War II, he returned to Curwensville and continued to operate the City Drug Store.)

7 Allen, *Since Yesterday*, p. 107.

8 Allen, *Since Yesterday*, p. 110.

9 Allen, *Since Yesterday,* p. 110.

10 Newspapers throughout the country carried headlines, columns, and editorials about Curwensville's success in reopening of banks. President Herbert Hoover praised the townspeople for setting an example in the campaign against hoarding. (*Curwensville Bicentennial*, p.112.)

11 Allen, *Since Yesterday*, p. 111.

12 The Ritz and Lyric Theatres in Clearfield, Rex in Curwensville, Sherkel in Houtzdale, Dixie in Coalport, Liberty in Madera, State and Plaza Theatres in Bellefonte, and others in Stoneboro, Weedville, Meadville, Sykesville, Reynoldsville, Watsontown, and Montgomery.

13 Bailey, p. 384.

14 Jared McNaul, W. K. Wrigley, Kelly Bloom, Alex Frankhouser, and George D. Ardary, according to the 50th Reunion program of Curwensville High School Class of 1933 held May 28, 1983.

15 Bailey, p. 388.

16 50th Class Reunion program, Class of 1933, May 28, 1983.

17 *Bicentennial Issue*, *Life*, 1975, p. 35.

18 "Mass Meeting Called to Stimulate Drive," *Curwensville Herald,* August 24, 1933, reprinted in *The Bulletin of The Clearfield County Historical Society*, Clearfield, Spring 2002, p. 22.

19 All correspondence above in Jessie's Estate papers.

20 Bressler, "Former Organizations," *Curwensville Sesquicentennial.*

21 "Our History," Clearfield County Fair, PA-Downtown, 06/03/99, http://clearfieldcountyfair.com/history.html.

22 Morgan, ed., *Curwensville in Celebration, 200 Years*, p. 128.

23 "Clubwomen Get Lessons in Cigaret Smoking," *Life 50 Years*, Special Anniversary Issue, Fall 1986, p. 87.

Chapter 6 Notes: For the Duration

1 Evans, p. 284.

2 Lingeman, p. 24.

3 Lingeman, p. 27.

4 Evans, p. 309.

5 Brokaw, p. 11.

6 Matilda Pifer's Bible, p. 103.

7 Joseph A. Lowande, *U.S. Ration Currency & Tokens 1942-1945.*

8 Lingeman, p. 284.

9 Lingeman, p. 284.

10 Lingeman, p. 46.

11 Lingeman, p. 263.

12 1*942 Echo*, p. 3.

13 *1943 Echo*, p. 74.

14 Lingeman, p. 299.

15 Conversations (circa 1996) with Patricia M. Lanshe, who had llived in New York City during these years and experienced the exciting times.

16 Lingeman, p. 262.

17 Riegel and Long, p. 460.

18 Lingeman, p. 81.

19 "Decade of Triumph – The 40s," *Our American Century,* p. 64.

20 Riegel and Long, p. 408.

21 The Lend-Lease Act, passed in 1941, gave President Roosevelt the power to sell to sell, transfer, exchange, lend equipment to any country to help it defend itself against the Axis powers.

22 Lingeman, p. 124.
23 Letter from Kate (her mother) to the author, November 23, 1966.
24 Effects of Jessie Pifer.
25 Morison, p. 1043.

Chapter 7 Notes: Out of a World of Darkness

1 McCullough, 1986, p. 192.
2 Evans, p. 388.
3 Brokaw, p. 152.
4 Breines, p. 2.
5 Goulden, p. 148.
6 Abramson, p. 10.
7 Goulden, p. 21.
8 Brokaw, p. 15.
9 Goulden, p. 71.
10 Goulden, p. 69.
11 Bezilla, 1985, p. 221.
12 Goulden, p. 74.
13 Goulden, p. 75.
14 Riegel and Long, pp. 458-459.
15 Goulden, p. 132.
16 Aldridge, pp. 22-23.
17 Halberstam, p. 591.
18 "Decade of Triumph – The 40s," p. 164.
19 *1946 Echo*, p. 111.
20 Lerner, p. 649.
21 Goulden, p. 166.
22 Goulden, p. 148
23 Berger, n. p.
24 Riegel and Long, p. 462.
25 *The 1947 Echo*, p. 91.
26 Bezilla, 1985, p. 221.
27 Bezilla, 1985, pp. 225-226.
28 "Decade of Triumph – The 40s," p. 178.
29 The first edition had been published by the class of 1922, thus, the 1948 publication would have been the 27th.
30 Bezilla, 2000, p. 8.
31 Bezilla, 1985, p. 224.
32 "Rooms are Needed at Curwensville," *Clearfield Progress,* June 25, 1949, p. 3.
33 "Early Days of Curwensville Will be Marked by Sesqui," *Clearfield Progress,* June 9, 1949, p. 1.

34 "Places Where Women Made History," Park Net, National Park Service, http://www.cr.nps.gov/nr/travel/pwwmh/ny25.htm.

35 Reigel and Long, p. 467.

36 Riegel and Long, p. 461.

Chapter 8 Notes: The Best of Times; The Worst of Times

1 *Time*, March 28, 2005, p. 64.

2 Brienes, p. 2.

3 Breines, p. 2.

4 "Picture This: 1951," *Temple Review*, Fall 2002, p. 48.

5 "Homeward Bound," *Time* Magazine, September 12, 1977, cited in *Time*, November 4, 2002.

6 Halberstam, p. 591.

7 Oakley, p. 292.

8 Sayre, p. 290.

9 "Picture This: 1951," *Temple Review*, Fall 2002, p. 48.

10 Miller & Nowack, p. 245.

11 "'Gentlemen, Be Seated' Acclaimed," *The News*, Curwensville, PA, Thursday, April 26, 1951, p 1.

12 This third- grade child became the top honor student in high school and later earned her PhD.

13 Email letters to the author from Mary Catherine Milligan King, PhD. September 4, 2000 and September 20, 2001.

14 Linda Bordas, conversation with the author, Indiana, PA, November 11, 2008.

15 Sayre, p. 19.

16 Riegel and Long, p. 463.

17 Jessie's tax return for 1955 reflects total wages of $3,566.68.

18 Ellwood, p. 140.

19 "The Rock and Roll Generation," p. 22.

20 Miller & Nowack, p. 145.

21 Miller & Nowack, p. 152.

22 Miller & Nowack, p. 152.

23 From *Modern Woman: The Lost Sex*, by the psychoanalyst Marynia Farnham and the sociologist Ferdinand Lundberg, which was paraphrased in many magazines and in marriage courses, until most of its statements became a part of the conventional, accepted truth of that time.

24 "Picture This: 1951," *Temple Review*, Fall 2002, p. 48.

25 Beines, p. 59.

26 Halberstam, p. 587.

27 *Our American Century, Life*, p. 193.

28 Recommendation by Mr. James Bonsall for Jo Ellen Thompson, 1956.

29 Letter from Morris Silverblatt to Jessie Pifer, October 23, 1956.

30 Letter from Morris Silverblatt to Jessie Pifer, October 26, 1956.
31 Evans, pp. 474-475.
32 Evans, p. 476.
33 Handy, p. 217.
34 Handy, p. 216.
35 *Our American Century,* Time-Life Books, p. 151.

Chapter 9 Notes: Winds of Change

1 Address to the Parliament of South Africa on 3 February 1960 in Cape Town.
2 Brienes, p. 3.
3 Hudnut-Beumler, p. 204.
4 "Picture This," Temple Review, Summer 2000, p. 48.
5 "The Evening Wash." *The Clearfield Progress,* circa 1969.
6 Lerner, p. 664.
7 Letter to the author, May 7, 1965.
8 Lerner, p. 689.
9 Letter to the author, June 27, 1965.
10 Nora Sayre, p. 6.
11 Tina Blue, *SDS: Students for Democratic Society.* http://ma.essortment.com/sdsstudentsfo_rmsx.htm.
12 Letter to the author, March 25, 1965.
13 Fine notice found among Jessie's papers.
14 Letter to the author, January 2, 1964.
15 Letter to the author, March 5, 1964.
16 Letter to the author, March 17, 1964.
17 Letter to the author, May 4, 1964.
18 Letter to the author, March 13, 1964.
19 Letter to the author, March 13, 1964.
20 Letter to the author, April 11, 1964.
21 Letter to the author, May 6, 1964.
22 Letter to the author, November 23, 1964.
23 Letter to the author, Spring 1965.
24 Letter to the author, June 20, 1966.

Chapter 10 Notes: When the Glow Left the Rose

1 "Time of Transition – the 70s," *Our American Century.* Time-Life Books, Alexandria, VA, 1999. Preface by Dick Cavett.
2 Letter to the author, November 22, 1966.
3 Letter to the author, November 22, 1966.
4 Letter to the author, December 31, 1966.

5 Letter to the author, February 6, 1967.
6 Letter to the author, March 18, 1965.
7 Letter to the author, April 4, 1965.
8 Letter from Nan to Jessie, February 25, 1965.
9 Letter to the author, June 27, 1965.
10 Letter to the author, July 18, 1966.
11 Letter to the author, August 9, 1966.
12 Letter to the author, March 27, 1966.
13 Letter to the author, March 27, 1966.
14 Letter to the author, April 9, 1966.
15 Letter to the author, May 9, 1966.
16 Chafe, *The American Woman*.
17 Footnote #22 in Chafe, p. 318.
18 Chafe, p. 239.
19 Letter to the author, late February 1966.
20 The date (October 14) and time were handwritten by Jessie on Jack's newspaper obituary notice and later found in her desk by the author.

Chapter 11 Notes: While the Storm Clouds Gathered

1 Friend, p. 46.
2 Specter, p. 63.
3 Letter from Barry Stopfel to the author, circa 1981.
4 Birthday card sent from Kay to Jessie, July 3, 1982.
5 In typical fashion the sisters used fanciful names for each other, a trend begun when all were still children.
6 Conversation between Kate and Judith.
7 Based on conversations Jessie had with Kate and later repeated to the author.
8 Codicil to Katherine Pifer Thompson's Will, June 8, 1988.
9 The deed is dated June 8, 1988 and recorded July 15.
10 Letter to Jessie Mohney, June 12, 1986, from the Department of Revenue and five cancelled checks as proof of payment.
11 Among Jessie's papers of the mid-to late 1980s was a piece of paper with the name Cortez Bell and his telephone number in Jessie's own distinctive handwriting. She evidently had planned to call him herself. It would be helpful to know if this was for an initial appointment or to make changes in her Will.
12 Kay seemed to have a predilection for conducting such transactions on holidays, a vulnerable time for those, like Jessie, elderly and living alone. She had discussed burial plots with her mother on Christmas Day, the house had been sold to Jessie on her birthday, and the Will decision with Jessie also was made on a Christmas Day.

Endnotes

Chapter 12 Notes: Here's That Rainy Day They Told Me About

1 Wilber and Reynolds, p. 65.

2 Flanagan, p. 34.

3 Mary Alice asked me one day about Jessie's condition and the disagreement we had had with Kay, adding that we really should try not to have a family dispute. That is when I knew Kay had burdened her with this family difficulty.

4 POA legal document, July 6, 1990.

5 Kay's "Journal," July 28, 1990, in her own handwriting. "Had all first class mail sent to me as Jessie hides it from me."

6 Kay's "Journal," comment inserted prior to August 1990.

7 In one transaction on August 30, 1990 Kay wrote a check for $20,000.

8 In December 1990 Kay had the stock reissued in her own name only.

9 Author's notes of a telephone conversation in the spring of 1991 with Don Bloom.

10 Transcript of interview of Attorney Larry Seaman by Attorney Kim Kesner, p. 4.

11 Kay's "Journal," entry in her own handwriting.

12 Kay's "Journal," entry in her own handwriting.

13 Conversations between Jean Boyce and the author.

14 Kay's "Journal," November 2, 1990, "Jean Boyce obtained bank statements."

15 Author's notes on telephone conversation with Don Bloom, March 21, 1991.

16 Kay's Journal, November 2, 1990, "Don Bloom called. Said Jessie asked him to be her POA."

17 Kay's Journal, November 2, 1990.

18 Author's notes on telephone conversation with Don Bloom, January 9, 1991.

19 Information relayed to the author by her mother, Kate.

20 Medical Report, November 6, 1990.

21 Kay's "Journal" entry states, "Mrs. Hamilton called me. Said some attorney called and wanted to know where Jessie was."

22 Conversations between Don Bloom and the author.

23 Entry in Kay's "Journal" on November 17: "Called Judi. (She) was going to talk to Jessie. She needs to go in a home. Judi didn't think it right to hide money from the state." Entry on November 18: "Judi called. Talked to Jessie regarding nursing home. No go."

24 Kay's Journal, November 17, 1990.

25 This is an untruth as Don told the author he had made a point to speak to the hearing officer who told him that despite pressure from Kay to declare her aunt to be incompetent, he would go no further than to use the word "incapable."

26 Author's notes on telephone conversation with Don Bloom, March 21, 1991.

27 Letter from Jean Seibert, January 28, 1991.

28 Chronology of Events, a paper prepared by Attorney Beth Ammerman Gerg.

Endnotes

Chapter 13 Notes: In My End Is My Beginning

1 Moody, p. 37.

2 Notes from a telephone conversation between Jo Ellen and the author, February 1991.

3 Letter from Lorraine Bloom to the author, March 6, 1991.

4 Letter from Jean Seibert to Larry Seaman, February 27, 1991.

5 Letter from Larry Seaman to Jean Seibert, March 7, 1991.

6 Letter from Kay to Katherine, March 25, 1991.

7 Telephone call from Beth Gerg to the author, April 5, 1991.

8 Author's notes from telephone conversations with Beth Gerg and Jean Seibert, April 8, 1991.

9 Author's notes on telephone conversation with Don Bloom, April 9, 1991.

10 Kay's "Journal," April 11, 1991: "Nursing Home called. Cindy Lemms said Dave Ammerman and Beth Gerg were in to see Jessie re changing POA."

11 Physician's Progress Notes, 4/11/91. Dr. Donald Conrad.

12 Letter from the author to Kay, April 14, 1991.

13 Notes taken by the author during a telephone conversation with Jo Ellen, circa April 20, 1991.

14 From letter written to Jessie's nieces and nephews, April 22, 1991.

15 Simmons, cited by Healey, 1986, in Stoller, Gibson, 1994, p. 83.

16 Author's letter to David Ammerman, May 3, 1991.

17 Letter to Jean Boyce from author, May 1991.

18 Court of Common Pleas of Clearfield County, Pennsylvania, Orphan's Court Division, May 20, 1991.

19 Kay's "Journal" entry shows a conversation with Richard Schwab "trying to get half of the 100 stock shares." (Apparently Mr. Schwab **did** have knowledge that Kay had kept the stock, and he **chose not** to pursue its return This is only one of numerous entries regarding this unusual action.)

20 Letter from Attorney Beth Ammerman Gerg to Laurence B. Seaman, Esq., June 17, 1991.

21 Letter from Mr. Schwab to the author, August 26, 1991.

22 Letter from Beth Gerg to Kim Kesner, August 29, 1991.

23 Compilation from letters to the persons mentioned.

24 Letter from Lorraine Bloom to the author, September 8, 1991.

25 Letter from Janet Lynn Bloom to the author, September 9, 1991.

26 Letter from Eugene Bloom to the author, September 11, 1991.

27 Letter from Kay to Kate, circa 1991-1992, undated.

28 Letter from Kate to Kay, circa 1991-1992, undated.

29 Yeager and Associates Auctioneering, price list, November 22, 1991.

30 Letter from Beth Gerg to the author, November 19, 1991.

31 Coles, pp. 11-12.

32 Common Pleas Court order.

33 Notes made by the author following a conversation with attorneys regarding Jean Boyce's being deposed.

34 Notes made by the author following a conversation with Kate regarding her telephone conversation with Joe Errigo, January 11, 1992.

35 Letters from the author to Joe Errigo, Laura Wright, Louise Muir, and Jean Boyce, January 12, 1992.

36 Letter from Lorraine Bloom to the author, January 14, 1992.

37 Letter from Beth Gerg to Richard Schwab, January 30, 1992.

38 Physician's notes regarding medical examination of Jessie, April 1992.

39 Letter from the author to Lorraine Bloom, March 22, 1992.

40 Fax from Dr. Robert Brennan to Judge John Reilly, April 9, 1992.

41 Letter from the author to Lorraine and Don Bloom, May 22, 1992.

42 Letter from the author to Joe Errigo, June 1, 1992.

43 Letter composed to Judge John Reilly from Judith, Jo Ellen, and Nan, August 16, 1992.

44 Author's notes following a telephone conversation with Jo Ellen, August 17, 1992, concerning a conversation between Jo Ellen and Kay, August 16, 1992.

45 Author's notes made following a telephone conversation with Jean Jacobs, August 17, 1992.

46 Author's notes made following a telephone conversation with Jo Ellen, August 18, 1992.

47 Author's notes made following a telephone conversation with Jo Ellen, August 19, 1992.

48 Letter from Mr. Schwab to the author, August 28, 1992.

Chapter 14 Notes: Violets and Valentines

1 Written by the author, Jessie's niece, for Jessie's memorial service.

2 As defined by the philosopher Immanuel Kant.

Aftermath

1 Conversation between Jo Ellen and the author.

2 Letter from Attorney Beth Gerg to Attorney Larry Seaman, September 15,1993.

3 Letter to Attorney Jean Seibert from John McGrail, Clearfield Trust Company.

4 Deposition of Mr. Richard Schwab by Attorney Kim Kesner, March 16, 1994.

5 Letter from Kate to Kay, January 12, 1994.

6 Draft of letter from Attorney Frank Zulli to Attorney Frank Clark, May 28, 1994.

7 Letter from the author to Kay, May 31, 1994.

8 Letter from Attorney Clark to Attorney Zulli, July 5, 1994.

9 Conversations between Kay and Kate as Kate relayed to Frank Zulli, July 12, 1994.

10 Dr. Brennan's medical opinion, June 20, 1995.

11 Letter from the author to Janet Lynn Bloom Carter, December 1, 1995.

References

Books and Periodicals

1949-The Year in Review (*Time* Magazine special, 1950).

Abramson, Rudy. *Spanning the Century: The Life of Averrel Harriman, 1891-1986.* NY: Morrow, 1992.

Aldrich, Lewis Cass. *The History of Clearfield County.* Syracuse, NY: D. Mason & Co., 1887.

Aldridge, John W. *In the Country of the Young*, Harper's Magazine Press Book. NY: Harper & Row, 1969.

Allen, Frederick Lewis. *The Big Change.* NY: Bantam Books, 1952.

Allen, Frederick Lewis. *Only Yesterday.* NY: John Wiley, reprinted 1997.

Allen, Frederick Lewis. *Since Yesterday.* NY: Bantam Books, 1952.

Anderson, Karen. *Wartime Women: Sex Roles, Family Relations, and the Status of Women During World War II.* Westport, CT: Greenwood Press, 1981.

Anderson, Sherwood, *Poor White.* NY: Modern Library, Random House, 1920.

Bailey, Beth L. *From Front Porch to Back Seat: Courtship in Twentieth-Century America.* Baltimore: Johns Hopkins University Press, 1988.

Bailey, Thomas A. *Voices of America.* NY: Free Press, 1976.

Bayley, John. "Elegy for Iris," *The New Yorker*, July 27, 1998, pp. 45-61.

Begley, Sharon. "One Pill Makes You Larger, and One Pill Makes You Smaller," *Newsweek*, February 7, 1994, pp. 37-40.

Bishop, Robert and Patricia Coblentz. *The World of Antiques, Art, and Architecture in Victorian America.* NY: E.P. Dutton, 1979.

Bezilla, Michael, *Penn State, An Illustrated History.* University Park, PA: Penn State University Press, 1985.

Bezilla, Michael. *The Penn Stater* Alumni Magazine, November/December 2000.

Blue, Tina. *SDS: Students for Democratic Society*, http://ma.essortment.com/sdsstudentsfo_rmsx.htm.

Boorstin, Daniel J. "The Luxury of Retrospect," *The 80s, Life* Special Issue, Fall 1989, p. 37.

Boyer, Peter J. "Miracle Man," *The New Yorker*, April 12, 1999, pp. 64-83.

Black, Alexander. *Miss America, Pen and Camera Sketches of the American Girl.* NY: Charles Scribner's, 1898.

Breines, Wini. "Postwar White Girls' Dark Others," in Foreman, Joel. *The Other Fifties: Interrogating Midcentury American Icons.* Urbana, IL: University of Illinois Press, 1997.

Breines, Wini. *Young, White, and Miserable: Growing Up Miserable in the Fifties.* Boston: Beacon Press, 1992.

References

Bressler, Samuel. "Former Organizations," *Curwensville Sesquicentennial*, 1949.

Brokaw, Tom. *The Greatest Generation.* NY: Random House, 1998.

Cavett, Dick. Preface, *Time of Transition – the 70s (Our American Century).* Time-Life Books, Alexandria, VA, 1999.

Chafe, William Henry. *The American Woman: Her Changing Social, Economic, and Political Roles, 1920-1970.* NY: Oxford University Press, 1972.

"Changing Roles in Modern Marriage," *Life*, December 1956. www.inform.umd.edu/EdRes/Colleges.HONR/HONR269J/.WWW/projects/hchunt/quotes.htm.

Clarion State Normal School Catalogue 1923-1924, Vol. XIII, no. 1, June 1923.

Clarke, Gerald. "The Silent Generation Revisited," *Time*, June 29, 1970, pp.38-39.

"Class History," *The 1924 Echo*, Yearbook, Curwensville, PA.

"Clubwomen Get Lessons in Cigaret (sic) Smoking," *Life: 50 Years,* Special Anniversary Issue, Fall 1986.

Coles, Robert. "Dignity Over the Life Course," *Journal of Gerontological Social Work,* Vol. 29, no. 2/3, 1998, pp. 1 - 12.

Cowley, Geoffrey. "The Culture of Prozac," *Newsweek*, February 7, 1994, pp. 41-42.

Decade of Triumph, The 40s (*Our American Century).* Alexandria, VA: Time-Life Books, 1999.

Douglas, Susan J. *Where the Girls Are: Growing Up Female with the Mass Media.* NY: Random House, 1994.

Downs, Sandra. "The Golden Age of Pittsburgh Television," *Tribune-Review*, November 3, 1996.

"Electronic Games Take Firm Hold," *Pride and Prosperity: The 80s* (*Our American Century*). Alexandria, VA: Time-Life Books, 1999.

Ellwood, Robert S. *The Fifties Spiritual Marketplace: American Religion in a Decade of Conflict.* New Brunswick, NJ: Rutgers University Press, 1997.

Evans, Harold. *The American Century.* NY: Alfred A. Knopf, 1998.

Fass, Paula S. *The Damned and the Beautiful.* NY: Oxford University Press, 1977.

Flanagan, Barbara. "Our Elders, Ourselves: Toward a New Community Vision," *Metropolitan Home*, January 1991.

Foreman, Joel. *The Other Fifties: Interrogating Midcentury American Icons.* Urbana, IL: University of Illinois Press, 1997.

Friend, Tad. 'Television is to the culture as the seventies was to the sixties—not the locomotive of change but the caboose,' "You Can't Say That," *The New Yorker*, November 19, 2001.

George, Ella M., State President. "Pennsylvania's Big Membership Fear," *The Union Signal*, January 24, 1924.

References

George, Mary T. *A Long Time Ago, Recollections.* Privately published by Ms. George, 1997.

Gordon, Elizabeth Putnam. *Women Torch Bearers, The Story of the Woman's Christian Temperance Union*. Union Publishing House, 1924.

Goulden, Joseph C. *The Best Years:1945-1950.* NY: Atheneum Press, 1976.

Hajdu, David. *The Ten Cent Plague.* NY: Farrar, Straus and Giroux, 2008.

Halberstam, David. *The Fifties.* NY: Fawcett Columbine, 1993.

Handy, Bruce. "Glamour with Altitude," *Vanity Fair*, October 2002, pp. 214-227.

Henry, Jules. *Culture Against Man.* NY: Random House, 1963.

"Homeward Bound," *Time* Magazine, September 12, 1977, cited in *Time*, November 4, 2002.

Hudnut-Beumler, James. *Looking for God in the Suburbs (The Religion of the American Dream and Its Critics, 1945-1965).* New Brunswick, NJ: Rutgers University Press, 1994.

"Immigration," *Time* Magazine, Vol. 1, no. 1, March 3, 1923.

Kidder, Tracy. *Home Town.* NY: Random House, 1999.

Lahr, John. "Revolutionary Rag," *The New Yorker*, March 8, 1999, pp. 77-82.

Lerner, Max. *America As a Civilization: Volume Two, Culture and Personality.* NY: Simon and Schuster, 1957.

Life, Special Bicentennial Issue, 1975.

Life at 50 Years, Special Anniversary Issue, Fall 1986.

Lingeman, Richard R. *Don't You Know There's a War On? (The American Home Front, 1941-1945)*. NY: G. P. Putnam's Sons, 1970.

Lowande, Joseph A. *U.S. Ration Currency & Tokens 1942-1945.*

Lundberg, Ferdinand and Marynia Farnham. *Modern Woman: The Lost Sex.* NY: Harper and Brothers, 1947.

Manual of the Patton Graded Public Schools of Curwensville, Pa. Curwensville, PA: Press of Will F. Brainard, 1902.

McCarran Act, http://www.english.upenn.edu/~afilreis/50s/mccarran-act-intro.html

McCullough, David. "Extraordinary Times: Living in an Era of Breakneck Change," *Life, Fifty Years*, Special Anniversary Issue, Fall 1986.

McCullough, David. *The Johnstown Flood.* NY: Touchstone (Simon and Schuster), 1968.

Medovoi, Leerom. "Democracy, Capitalism, and American Literature: The Cold War Construction of J. D. Salinger's Paperback Hero," in Joel Foreman. *The Other Fifties: Interrogating Midcentury American Icons*. Urbana, IL: University of Illinois Press, 1997.

Miller, Douglas T. and Marion Nowak. *The Fifties: The Way We Really Were.* Garden City, NY: Doubleday, 1775.

References

Modell, John. *Into One's Own: From Youth to Adulthood in the United States, 1920-1975.* Los Angeles: University of California Press, 1989.

Moody, Harry H. "Why Dignity Over the Life Course Matters," *Journal of Gerontological Social Work*, Vol. 29, nos. 2/3, 1998, pp. 13-38.

Moody, Harry H. "The Cost of Autonomy, the Price of Paternalism," *Journal of Gerontological Social Work,* Vol. 29, nos. 2/3, 1998, pp. 111 - 127.

Morison, Samuel Eliot. *The Oxford History of the American People.* NY: Oxford University Press, 1965.

Morris, M. Robin. "Elder Abuse: What the Law Requires," *RN*, August 1998, Vol. 61, no. 8.

Niebuhr, Reinhold. "Coronation Afterthoughts," *Christian Century*, July 1, 1953.

Oakley, J. Ronald. *God's Country: America in the Fifties.* NY: Barricade Books, 1990.

"Our History," Clearfield County Fair, PA-Downtown, 06/03/99, http://clearfieldcountyfair.com/history.html.

Pennsylvania Department of Conservation and Natural Resources, "History," *Cook Forest State Park*, http://dcnr.state.pa.us/stateparks/parks/cookforest.html.

The Pennsylvania State College *Woman's Handbook*, 1924. Section reprinted on page 45 of *The Penn Stater*, July/August 2001.

Pentz, William, C., *History of the City of DuBois*, 1931. Privately printed and limited to an edition of 300 copies, of which this is no. 274. DuBois: Press of Gray Printing Co., 1932.

Perrett, Louise and Sarah K. Smith, Designers and Illustrators. *The Girl Graduate.* Chicago, IL: The Reilly and Lee Co, circa late 19th or early 20th Century.

"Picture This," *Temple Review*, Winter 2002.

Pierce, R. V., MD. *The People's Common Sense Medical Adviser*, Buffalo, NY: World's Dispensary Printing Office, 1895.

"Places Where Women Made History," Park Net, National Park Service, http://www.cr.nps.gov/nr/travel/pwwmh/ny25.htm.

Potter, Maximillian, "Attack of the 28-Screen Megaplex," *Philadelphia Magazine*, June 1999, 57-59+.

Pride and Prosperity: The 80s (Our American Century). Alexandria, VA: Time-Life Books, 1998.

"Prohibition," *Time* Magazine, Vol. I, no. 1, March 3, 1923.

Ramsey, L. G., Editor. *The Complete Encyclopedia of Antiques*, NY: Hawthorn Books, 1962.

Rickard, Julie Rae. *Clearfield County.* Charleston, SC: Arcadia, 2003.

Riegel, Robert E. and David F. Long. *The American Story, Volume Two: Maturity.* NY: McGraw-Hill, 1955.

References

Rock & Roll Generation: Teen Life in the 50s (Our American Century). Alexandria, VA: Time- Life Books, 1998.

Rule, Ann. *If You Really Love Me*. NY: Simon and Schuster, 1991.

Ruoff, Henry W. *The Universal Manual of Ready Reference*. Springfield, MA: King-Richardson, 1904.

Sayre, Nora. *Previous Convictions: a Journey Through the 1950s*. New Brunswick, NJ: Rutgers University Press, 1995.

Sayre, Nora. *Sixties Going on Seventies*, revised edition. New Brunswick, NJ: Rutgers University Press, 1996.

Scott, George A. *Clearfield: Today and Tomorrow, Railroads of the Area.* Clearfield, PA: Progressive Publishing Company. April 1968, republished 2002.

Scott, Kate M., Editor. *The History of Jefferson County, PA.* Syracuse, NY: D. Mason & Co, 1888. (A Reproduction by Unigraphics, Inc., Evansville, Indiana, 1977)

Siddons, Anne Rivers. *Heartbreak Hotel.* NY: Simon and Schuster, 1976.

Simmons, Henry C. "Spirituality and Community in the Last Stage of Life," *Journal of Gerontological Social Work*, Vol. 29, nos. 2/3, 1998, pp. 73-91.

Simmons, Henry C. "Spirituality and Community in the Last Stage of Life," *Journal*, p. 87 (cited by Healey, 1986, in Stoller, Gibson, 1994, p. 83).

Specter, Michael. "Public Nuisance," *The New Yorker*, May 13, 2002, pp. 56-65.

Stropnicky, G., T. Byrn, J. Goode, and J. Matheny. *Letters to the Editor: Two Hundred Years in the Life of an American Town.* NY: Touchstone (Simon and Schuster), 1998.

Terkel, Studs. *Hard Times.* NY: Pantheon, 1970.

"The Curwensville Review," June 1889, in *150th Anniversary of Curwensville, PA,* 1949.

"The Press," *Time* Magazine, Vol. 1, no. 1, March 3, 1923.---- *Time* Magazine, March 28, 2005, p. 64.

Time of Transition – The 70s (Our American Century). Alexandria, VA: Time-Life Books, 1999.

Traister, Helen. "Activities," *The 1925 Echo*, Yearbook, Curwensville, PA.

Trezise, Lillian N. "Clearfield County," *History of the Pennsylvania Woman's Christian Temperance Union,* 1937.

Trostle, W. P., County School Superintendent, "Rules for Pupils' Reading Course," presented at the Clearfield County Teachers Institute, 1926.

"The Fifties, Re-living It Up," *Life*, August 1985.

"The New Youth," *Life*, Fall 1977.

"The Silent Generation," *Saturday Review*, April 15, 1972.

The Turbulent Years, The 1960s (Our American Century), Alexandria, VA: Time-Life Books, 1998.

'Vonnegut's Gospel,' "American Notes, The Nation," *Time* Magazine, June 29, 1970.

"Wall Street's Big Party," *Pride and Prosperity: The 80s (Our American Century)*. Alexandria, VA: Time-Life Books, 1999.

Wilber, Cathleen H. and Sandra L. Reynolds, "Introducing a Framework for Defining Financial Abuse of the Elderly," *Journal of Elder Abuse & Neglect*, Vol. 8, No. 2, 1996.

Wise, Daniel, D.D. *Bridal Greetings*. NY: Eaton & Mains, 1894.

Booklets and Pamphlets

"Caregiving," *Health Smart*, Holy Spirit Hospital, Camp Hill, June 1993, unpaginated.

County of San Bernardino, CA. Brochure, n.d.

National Committee for the Prevention of Elder Abuse. Brochure, n.d.

Commemorative Publications

32nd Annual Clearfield County Teachers' Institute, Clearfield, PA, December 16, 17, 18, 19, and 20, 1895.

1902 Edition of the Sears, Roebuck Catalogue, Catalogue no. III. NY: Bounty Books, 1969.

Clearfield County Teachers' Institute, 1926.

Clearfield County Teachers' Institute, 1928.

Curwensville 150th Anniversary Celebration, 1949.

Curwensville 175th Anniversary Celebration, 1974.

Curwensville High School Alumni Association 100th Anniversary, 1887-1987.

Morgan, Ed., Editor. *Curwensville in Celebration of 200 Years*, Bicentennial Committee, May 1999.

The 1903 Echo, four-page newsletter, April 24, 1903, reproduced in *The 1953 Echo*, Curwensville Joint High School, Curwensville, PA.

The 1922 Echo, Yearbook, Curwensville High School, Curwensville, PA.

The 1923 Echo, Yearbook, Curwensville High School, Curwensville, PA.

The 1924 Echo, Yearbook, Curwensville High School, Curwensville, PA.

The 1925 Echo, Yearbook, Curwensville High School, Curwensville, PA.

The 1928 Echo, excerpt reprinted in *Curwensville High School Alumni Association's 100th Anniversary*, a booklet, unpaginated.

The 1946 Echo, Yearbook, Curwensville High School, Curwensville, PA.

The 1947 Echo, Yearbook, Curwensville High School, Curwensville, PA.

The 1949 Echo, Yearbook, Curwensville High School, Curwensville, PA.

The 1953 Echo. Yearbook, Curwensville High School, Curwensville, PA.

References

Diaries and Journals

Pifer, Matilda. Journal, 1950. Curwensville, PA

Spencer, Lavinia. *1871 Diary*. Bridgeport, PA.

Thompson, Howard V. *Diary 1920.* Bellefonte, PA.

Walker, Kay Thompson, Journal. Entries cited:
July 28, 1990
Early October, 1990
Late October, 1990
November 2, 1990
November 7, 1990
April 11, 1991
May 30, 1991

Interviews and Conversations

Bordas, Linda. Conversation with the author, Indiana, PA, November 11, 2008.

Boyce, Jean. Conversations with the author throughout the 1990s.

Bloom, Donald. Oral history.

Bloom, Donald. Conversations with the author, 1990-1991.

Lanshe, Patricia M. Interview, circa 1995.

Milligan, Alvin and Evelyn Williams Milligan, Interview with the author, 1990s.

Stopfel, Barry. Conversation with the author, circa 1981.

Thompson, Katherine and Kay Thompson Walker. Conversations as relayed to Frank Zulli, July 12, 1994.

Witmer, Judith Thompson and Jo Ellen Thompson Lorenz. Conversation, July 1993.

Young, William, Interview, December 1, 1999.

Legal and Related Documents

Clark, Frank. Letter to Frank Zulli, July 5, 1994.

Court Order, Court of Common Pleas of Clearfield County, Pennsylvania, Orphan's Court Division, May 20, 1991.

Department of Revenue. Letter to Jessie Pifer Mohney.

Gerg, Beth. Letter to Laurence B. Seaman, June 17, 1991.

Gerg, Beth. Letter to Kim Kesner, August 29, 1991.

Gerg, Beth. Letter to Laurence Seaman, September 16, 1991.

Gerg, Beth. Letter to the author, November 19, 1991.

Gerg, Beth. Letter to Richard Schwab, January 30, 1992.

Gerg, Beth and Laurence Seaman, exchange of letters, July 1993.

References

Gerg, Beth. Chronology of Events, circa 1991.

Kesner, Kim. Deposition of Richard Schwab, March 16, 1994.

McGrail, John. Clearfield Trust Company. Letter to Jean Seibert.

Power of Attorney, Kay Thompson Walker for Jessie Pifer Mohney, July 6, 1990.

Schwab, Richard. Letter to the author, August 26, 1991.

Schwab, Richard. Letter to the author, August 28, 1992.

Seaman, Laurence. Letter to Jean Seibert, March 7, 1991.

Seibert, Jean. Letter to the author, January 28, 1991.

Seibert, Jean. Letter to Laurence Seaman, February 27, 1991.

Silverblatt, Morris, Letters to Jessie Pifer, October 1956.

Silverblatt, Morris. Letter to Jessie Pifer, November 2, 1964.

Thompson, Katherine. Deed, June 8, 1988.

Thompson, Katherine. Will codicil, June 8, 1988.

U.S. Individual Income and Victory Tax Return, 1943, for Jessie Pifer.

Witmer, Judith Thompson, with Jo Ellen and Nan. Letter to Judge John Reilly, Aug.16, 1992.

Zulli, Frank. Letter to Frank Clark, May 28, 1994 (draft).

Letters

Bloom, Eugene. Letter to the author, September 11, 1991.

Bloom, Lorraine. Letter to the author, March 6, 1991.

Bloom, Lorraine. Letter to the author, September 8, 1991.

Bloom, Lorraine. Letter to the author, January 14, 1992.

Carter, Janet Lynn Bloom. Letter to the author, September 9, 1991.

Carter, Janet Lynn Bloom, Christmas card (December 1992) and letter to Katherine Thompson, January 30, 1993.

Clark, Agnes. Letter to her niece, Matilda Pifer, January 31, 1930.

Deitz, John. Letter to Jessie Pifer, February 1925.

Edmunds, E. Nan. Letter to Jessie Pifer, February 25, 1965.

Hamilton, Elizabeth. Letter to Josephine Pifer, January 1920.

King, Mary Catherine Milligan. Email letters to the author, September 4, 2000 and September 20, 2001.

Lorenz, Jo Ellen. Letter to the author, October 13, 1964.

NOAA, Response to a request for information, April 17, 2004.

Pifer, John. Collection of letters to Matilda.

Pifer, Matilda. Letter to her niece, circa 1927.

References

Thompson, Katherine. Letter to the author, December 12, 1963.
Thompson, Katherine. Letter to the author, January 2, 1964.
Thompson, Katherine. Letter to the author, February 7, 1964.
Thompson, Katherine. Letter to the author, March 13, 1964.
Thompson, Katherine. Letter to the author, April 11, 1964.
Thompson, Katherine. Letter to the author, May 6, 1964.
Thompson, Katherine. Letter to the author, October 10, 1964.
Thompson, Katherine. Letter to the author, November 23, 1964.
Thompson, Katherine. Letter to the author, December 30, 1964.
Thompson, Katherine. Letter to the author, March 18, 1965.
Thompson, Katherine. Letter to the author, March 25, 1965.
Thompson, Katherine. Letter to the author, April 4, 1965.
Thompson, Katherine. Letter to the author, September 22, 1965.
Thompson, Katherine. Christmas card the author, December 1965.
Thompson, Katherine. Letter to the author, late February 1966.
Thompson, Katherine. Letter to the author, March 27, 1966.
Thompson, Katherine. Letter to the author, April 9, 1966.
Thompson, Katherine. Letter to the author, May 9, 1966.
Thompson, Katherine. Letter to the author, November 22-23, 1966.
Thompson, Katherine. Letter to the author, December 31, 1966.
Thompson, Katherine. Letter to the author, February 6, 1967.
Thompson, Katherine. Letter to Kay Thompson Walker, January 12, 1994.
Thompson, Katherine. Letter to Kay Thompson Walker, February 19, 1994.
Walker, Kay Thompson. Letter to the author, March 5, 1964.
Walker, Kay Thompson. Letter to the author, March 7, 1964
Walker, Kay Thompson. Letter to Katherine Thompson, early February 1964.
Walker, Kay Thompson. Letter to the author, March 17, 1964.
Walker, Kay Thompson. Letter to the author, May 4, 1964.
Walker, Kay Thompson. Letter to the author, August 2, 1964.
Walker, Kay Thompson. Letter to the author, August 22, 1964.
Walker, Kay Thompson. Letter to the author, October 22, 1964.
Walker, Kay Thompson. Letter to the author, October 27, 1964.
Walker, Kay Thompson. Letter to the author, Spring 1965.
Walker, Kay Thompson. Letter to the author, May 7, 1965
Walker, Kay Thompson. Letter to the author, June 27, 1965.

Walker, Kay Thompson. Letter to the author, February 21, 1966.

Walker, Kay Thompson. Letter to the author, June 20, 1966.

Walker, Kay Thompson. Letter to the author, July 18, 1966.

Walker, Kay Thompson. Letter to the author, August 9, 1966.

Walker, Kay Thompson. Birthday card to Jessie, July 3, 1982.

Walker, Kay Thompson. Letter to Katherine Thompson, March 25, 1991.

Walker, Kay Thompson. Letter to Katherine Thompson, undated, circa 1991-1992.

Witmer, Judith Thompson. Letter to a number of cousins, April 22, 1991.

Witmer, Judith Thompson. Letter to David Ammerman, May 3, 1991.

Witmer, Judith Thompson. Letter to Beth Gerg, September 12, 1991.

Witmer, Judith Thompson. Letters to John Wayne, Gene Bloom, and Janet Bloom Carter, late September 1991.

Witmer, Judith Thompson. Letter to Joseph Errigo, January 12, 1992.

Witmer, Judith Thompson. Letter to Laura Wright, January 12, 1992.

Witmer, Judith Thompson. Letter to Louise Muir, January 13, 1992.

Witmer, Judith Thompson. Letter to Jean Boyce, January 13, 1992.

Witmer, Judith Thompson. Letter to Lorraine Bloom, March 22, 1992.

Witmer, Judith Thompson. Letter to Lorraine Bloom, May 22, 1992.

Witmer, Judith Thompson. Letter to Joseph Errigo, June 1, 1992.

Witmer, Judith Thompson. Letter to Lorraine Bloom, December 5, 1992.

Witmer, Judith Thompson. Letter to Kay Thompson Walker, January 13, 1994.

Witmer, Judith Thompson. Letter to Kay Thompson Walker, May 31, 1994.

Witmer, Judith Thompson. Letter to Janet Lynn Bloom Carter, December 1, 1995.

Medical Documents

Brennan, Robert, MD. Medical Report sent as a fax to Judge John Reilly, April 9, 1992.

Brennan, Robert, MD. Medical opinion regarding Jessie Pifer Mohney, June 20, 1995.

Conrad, Donald, MD. Physician's Progress Notes, April 11, 1991.

Schickling, Leonard, MD. Medical Report for Jessie Pifer, November 6, 1990.

Miscellaneous Materials

Arnold, John C. Political handout stating his platform as a candidate for Clearfield County Judge, 1934.

Clarion State Normal School, Registration and Identification Card, Jessie Pifer, June 22, 1925.

References

Class of 1913, Commencement Announcement, Curwensville High School.

Class of 1924, Graduation Announcement, Curwensville High School.

Clearfield County Bicentennial Calendar, January 16, 2004.

Edmunds, E. Nan. "Jessie's Plight," a record of events.

Liberty Bond, receipt written to John Pifer, circa 1917. Estate of Jessie Pifer.

Norris, Grant. Letter of Recommendation for Jessie Pifer, March 14, 1924.

Norris, Grant. Letter of Recommendation for Katherine Pifer, March 6, 1925.

Pifer, Jessie. Senior Report Card, Curwensville High School, September 10, 1923 – June 1924 and most of the other report cards during her time in school.

Pifer, Jessie. Traffic citation, August 10, 1965.

Pifer, John. Letter of Purchase Agreement with I. A. Black Drilling Company, 1925.

Pifer, Matilda. Personal Bible with notations.

Provisional Teaching Certificate issued to Jessie Pifer, Pennsylvania Department of Public Instruction, August 1924, signed by J. George Becht, Superintendent of Public Instruction, Commonwealth of Pennsylvania.

Receipt for payment to Lowe's on the purchase of a piano, January 6, 1912.

Teacher's Provisional Certificate, Clearfield County, July 1, 1916.

Teaching Contract for Jessie Pifer, September 4, 1924.

"Things That Aren't There Anymore," videotape.

Thompson, Howard V. Valentine sent to Katherine Pifer, 1925.

Western Union Telegram, April 18, 1924.

Witmer, Judith Thompson. *In Memoriam, Jessie Pifer Mohney*, Jessie's Memorial Service, June 3, 1993.

Witmer, Judith Thompson, Notes regarding Jean Boyce, January 1992.

Yeager and Associates Auctioneering, Price list, November 22, 1991.

Newspapers and Newsletters

"Americans Walk on Moon," *The Patriot*, Harrisburg, Monday, July 21, 1969, p. 1.

Berger, David. "Two Guitarists to Be Honored," *Pittsburgh Post-Gazette*, Thursday, July 29, 1999.

"Clearfield County Sesquicentennial," *The Progress* Sesqui Edition, No. 1 (Religion, Professions, Business).

"Clearfield County Sesquicentennial," *The Progress* Sesqui Edition, No. 3 (Education), May 1954.

"Clearfield County Sesquicentennial," *The Progress* Sesqui Edition, No. 4 (Patriotic Edition), June 1954.

"Clearfield County Sesquicentennial," *The Progress* Sesqui Edition, No. 5 (History of Clearfield County), June 1954.

References

The Clearfield Progress, circa 1924.

"Curwensville Bicentennial, History, Pride, Promise, 1799 – 1999, *The Progress* Supplement, July 9, 1999.

The Curwensville Mountaineer / The Curwensville Herald, © June 22, 1903.

"Early Days of Curwensville Will be Marked by Sesqui," *Clearfield Progress*, June 9, 1949.

"The Evening Wash," *The Clearfield Progress,* circa 1969.

Foote, Jennifer. 'Dementia Patients Often Neglected,' "Living," *The Evening News,* Harrisburg PA, May 16, 1996.

Foote, Jennifer. 'Inadequate Care All Too Common,' "Living," *The Evening News*, Harrisburg, PA, Tuesday, May 16, 1996.

"'Gentlemen, Be Seated' Acclaimed," *The News*, Curwensville, PA, Thursday, April 26, 1951.

"In Living Color," Business Section, *The Patriot-News*, Thursday, March 25, 2004.

Kennedy, Ray. Untitled Editorial, *The Falcon Flash*, November 1973, p. 2.

"Man Walks on Moon," *The Philadelphia Inquirer*, Final City Edition, Monday Morning, July 21, 1969, p. 1+

The Marble, Boston University College of Basic Studies, December 8, 1965, Vol. XI, no. 3.

"Mass Meeting Called to Stimulate Drive," *Curwensville Herald*, August 24, 1933, reprinted in *The Bulletin of the Clearfield County Historical Society*, Clearfield, Spring 2002.

"Rooms are Needed at Curwensville," *Clearfield Progress*, June 25, 1949.

Scott, George A. "Curwensville's Newspapers," *The Progress*, Friday, May 5, 1978.

Scott, George A. *The Bulletin*, Clearfield County Historical Society. Date not identified.

Vilbig, Peter. "Hope on the Horizon for Dementia Patients," Health Care, *The Patriot-News*, Harrisburg, PA, May 18, 1995.

Programs

Chestnut Street Opera House, Philadelphia, Playbill, November 1925.

CHS Alumni Reunion, June 3, 1924, Program.

CHS Alumni Reunion, June 3, 1927, Program.

Class of 1924, Commencement Exercises, Program, June 3, 1924.

Class of 1925, Commencement Exercises, Program, May 28, 1925.

Class of 1927, Commencement Exercises (single sheet, order of the program)

Class of 1928, Commencement Exercises, Program, May 31, 1928.

Class of 1933, 59th Reunion Program, May 28, 1982.

Curwensville High School Alumni Reunion, Program, 1924.

References

Curwensville High School Alumni Reunion, Program, June 3, 1927.

Entertainment Guide to Philadelphia, 1925.

Faculty's Farewell Reception to the Class of 1914, Program, April 14, 1914.

Fifth District Education Re-Union Program, Curwensville, PA, January 15 and 16, 1897.

"Have Your Girl Meet My Girl," Program, Chestnut Street Opera House, Philadelphia, 1925.

"Kathleen, The Romantic Musical Program," Advertisement and Program, December 14, 1922 (Town Musical).

"Lost – A Chaperon," Junior Class Play Program, performed on Tuesday, May 13, 1913.

"Miss Bob White," Playbill, December 15 and 17, 1920 (Town Musical).

"Miss Somebody Else," Program, March 21, 1924 (Senior Class Play).

"Oh! Oh! Cindy," Program, November 23 and 25, 1921 (Town Musical)

"Sky High," Chestnut Street Opera House, 1925.

"Spanish Moon," reprint of the program, November 12-13, 1929.

"They Knew What They Wanted," Philadelphia, 1925.

Victory Banquet, Program, WCTU, Matilda Pifer Estate.

Telephone Conversations

Gerg, Beth. Telephone call to the author, April 5, 1991.

Gerg, Beth. Telephone call to the author, August 29, 1991.

Lorenz, Jo Ellen Thompson. Telephone conversation with the author, circa April 20, 1991.

Lorenz, Jo Ellen Thompson. Telephone conversation with Kay Thompson Walker, October/November 1993.

Witmer, Judith Thompson. Telephone conversation with Donald Bloom, spring 1990.

Witmer, Judith Thompson. Telephone conversation with Donald Bloom, January 9, 1991.

Witmer, Judith Thompson. Telephone conversation with Jo Ellen Thompson Lorenz, February 1991.

Witmer, Judith Thompson. Telephone conversation with Donald Bloom, March 21, 1991.

Witmer , Judith Thompson. Telephone conversation with Donald Bloom, April 9, 1991.

Witmer, Judith Thompson. Telephone conversations with Beth Gerg and Jean Seibert, April 5, 1991.

Witmer, Judith Thompson. Telephone conversation with Jo Ellen Thompson Lorenz, August 16, 1992.

www.ingramcontent.com/pod-product-compliance
Lightning Source LLC
Chambersburg PA
CBHW060747100426
42813CB00032B/3423/J
* 9 7 8 0 9 8 3 7 7 6 8 0 2 *